D0961192

FRAMING
THE
SIXTIES

FRAMING THE SIXTIES

The Use and Abuse
of a Decade
from
Ronald Reagan
to George W. Bush

BERNARD von BOTHMER

University of Massachusetts Press
Amherst & Boston

Copyright © 2010 by University of Massachusetts Press
All rights reserved
Printed in the United States of America
LC 2009042881
ISBN 978-1-55849-732-0 (paper); 731-3 (library cloth)

Designed by Jack Harrison
Set in Trump Medieval
Printed and bound by Thomson-Shore, Inc.

Library of Congress Cataloging-in-Publication Data
Bothmer, Bernard von, 1967–
Framing the sixties : the use and abuse of a decade from Ronald Reagan
to George W. Bush / Bernard von Bothmer.
p. cm.
Includes bibliographical references and index.
ISBN 978-1-55849-732-0 (pbk. : alk. paper) —
ISBN 978-1-55849-731-3 (library cloth : alk. paper)
1. United States—History—1961–1969.
2. United States—Social conditions—1960–1980.
3. United States—Politics and government—1981–1989.
4. United States—Politics and government—1989–
5. Presidents—United States—History—20th century.
6. Presidents—United States—History—21st century.
7. Political culture—United States—History—20th century.
8. Political culture—United States—History—21st century.
9. Liberalism—United States. 10. Conservatism—United States.
I. Title.
E841.B68 2009
2009042881

British Library Cataloguing in Publication data are available.

To my parents

Contents

Acknowledgments

I am indebted to a great many people for the completion of this book.

The project began under the thoughtful guidance of Michael McGerr at Indiana University, a mentor of the very highest order. His invaluable advice always steered me in the right direction. I also benefited from my work at Indiana with Nick Cullather and John Bodnar and from their early commentary on the manuscript.

Throughout my research I profited from the assistance of numerous librarians and archivists during my stays at the Ronald Reagan and George H. W. Bush presidential libraries.

I would like to give special thanks to the 122 individuals who were interviewed for this project. Their generosity of spirit took my work in delightfully unexpected directions. Their interviews produced the most rewarding research I have ever done.

During the formative stages of this project in Bloomington, I was fortunate to share much friendship, conversation, and laughter with John Baesler, Dan Gregory, John Beggs, and Dan FitzSimmons.

The manuscript was improved in numerous ways by the skilled work of several first-rate editors. Dennis Briskin read an early version of the manuscript, and much of the book's organization and style stem directly from his indefatigable help. It would never have been ready for publication without the assistance and editorial guidance of my friend and former colleague Charles Hanson, whose tremendous humor, uncanny insight, and ever-critical eye make him as responsible as anyone for the choices that in the end made this book what it is.

The challenges of finding the time and energy to balance teaching with research were more than offset by the pleasure I have taken working with such outstanding educators as my colleagues Tony Fels, Uldis Kruze, Mike Stanfield, Cheryl Czekala, and Kim Connor at the University of San Francisco, and Patty Dougherty and Martin Anderson at Dominican University of California.

I wish every author could have even a taste of the experience I have had working with the University of Massachusetts Press. My sponsoring editor, Clark Dougan, believed in this project from the very start. He showed faith in my work when few others did and was enormously helpful in pushing it forward toward publication. I am forever indebted to him for his encouragement and creative vision. My initial reviewer at the Press, Allan Winkler, offered invaluable advice as to how to improve the book. I would also like to thank the other, anonymous reviewer for the Press. The Press's managing editor, Carol Betsch, majestically orchestrated the journey from manuscript to book. And I frankly remain in awe of my copyeditors, Amanda Heller and Mary Bellino.

My greatest acknowledgment goes to my loving family. My aunt Jane Blaffer Owen and my cousin Sarah Blaffer Hrdy both offered steadfast good cheer throughout this effort. My father Dietrich's lifelong commitment to research, teaching, and the life of the mind has been a tremendous source of inspiration. And my mother, Joyce, has always cheerfully encouraged and supported all of my educational and teaching pursuits. My dear parents have been with me every step of the way, and for that I am truly thankful. This book is dedicated to them.

Finally, I will be forever grateful for the extraordinary patience, flexibility, support, and understanding of my wife, Jane, during the six years it took to research and write the book, and especially for her devotion to our two most precious gifts, Athena and Tatiana.

B. v. B.

FRAMING THE SIXTIES

Introduction
FRAMING THE FRAME

If you look back on the sixties and, on balance, you think there was more good than harm in it, you're probably a Democrat, and if you think there was more harm than good, you're probably a Republican.

Bill Clinton (2004)

"IN CASE YOU MISSED IT, a few days ago Senator Clinton tried to spend one million dollars on the Woodstock concert museum," said Senator John McCain, referring to Hillary Clinton at a 2007 Republican presidential debate. "Now, my friends, I wasn't there," McCain said. "I'm sure it was a cultural and pharmaceutical event. I was tied up at the time." McCain's next words were drowned out by loud cheers and a sustained standing ovation from the partisan audience. McCain was alluding to the fact that, as a navy pilot, he was captured after being shot down by the North Vietnamese in 1967, leading to more than five years' captivity as a prisoner of war. His line about being "tied up" became the centerpiece of a campaign ad a few days later that juxtaposed shots of hippies at Woodstock with an image of McCain strapped to a prison bed in Hanoi.[1]

Nor did McCain stop there. Another campaign ad mocked Barack Obama's campaign theme of "hope" by painting the Illinois senator, who was only six years old in 1967, as having been in sync with the values of the counterculture. "It was a time of uncertainty, hope, and change, the Summer of Love," the voiceover narrates. "Half a world away, another kind of love, of country: John McCain, shot down, bayoneted, tortured. Offered early release, he said, 'No.' He'd sworn an oath." McCain's credo as a public servant, it continued, was "Before party, polls, and self: America." In the background were images of student protesters and embracing hippies followed by scenes from Vietnam, including McCain photographed as a P.O.W. then and saluting from his crutches on returning to the United States.[2]

1

Right before the 2008 Democratic National Convention a conservative group co-founded by a former McCain aide ran nearly $3 million worth of ads seeking to link Obama to a former 1960s radical, William Ayers. The spots compared the antiwar activities of Ayers's Weather Underground with the attack on the Pentagon on September 11, 2001, and argued that Obama's "political career was launched" at the home of this "friend" of the senator.[3] In an Obama response ad a narrator asks, "With all of our problems, why is John McCain talking about the 1960s, trying to link Barack Obama to radical Bill Ayers?"[4]

Because it works, that's why. Republicans have been campaigning against "the sixties" ever since the 1960s themselves. McCain was following a time-tested strategy, employing a tactic used by every Republican presidential candidate since Ronald Reagan. Reagan invented "the sixties" during the 1960s and was against "the sixties" even before the decade ended. His political career also marked the start of the Right's active construction of a mythical alternative, a past that supposedly existed before "the sixties."

This book examines the ways in which four presidents—that is, political winners—used their own selective versions of the 1960s for political gain in the years from 1980 to 2004. It focuses on their conscious manipulation of five topics: John F. Kennedy, Lyndon Johnson's Great Society, the Vietnam War, the civil rights movement, and the era of "the sixties" in general. Each president during this twenty-four-year period offered his own conception of the decade and how Americans should remember it.

Between 1980 and 2004 liberals and conservatives alike used selective memories of "the sixties," a period I define as stretching from 1960 to 1974, to win votes.[5] Liberals evoked the positive associations of the "good sixties" (1960–1963), while conservatives called up the specter of the "bad sixties" (1964–1974). The "good sixties" refers to the era of President Kennedy and conjures a time of strong national defense, a tough stance against communist expansion, peaceful civil rights protests, and the persistence of "traditional" standards of dress, expression, and family life. The "bad sixties," conversely, refers to the presidencies of Lyndon Johnson and Richard Nixon, a time of urban riots, antiwar protests, difficulties in fighting the Vietnam War, increased incivility, crime, drug abuse, and social unrest. The "good sixties" and the "bad sixties" serve as convenient shorthand for the residual emotional attitudes that Republicans and Democrats—conservatives and liberals—elicited, played to, and often deliberately inflamed in the process of constructing their respective narratives of the 1960s.

Republicans wielded painful memories of the 1960s as a political weapon to attack Johnson's Great Society, the antiwar movement, and the era's loosening of social restraints on family structure and personal responsibility. While inveighing against the expensive mistakes of that time, the Right also sought to limit the political power of competing memories of the 1960s. These included Kennedy nostalgia, a longing for the era's idealism, the moral authority of the civil rights movement, and fear of "another Vietnam" through reckless foreign interventions. To avoid these pitfalls, conservatives quite cannily refurbished these inconvenient and even threatening memories. Liberal Democrats, by contrast, largely failed to defend themselves against the political uses of the 1960s.

Republicans won seven of the ten presidential elections from 1968 to 2004. Only once during that time did a Democrat—Bill Clinton in 1996—win a majority of the fifty states. No Democrat in that span of time won a majority of the white vote. Only Jimmy Carter won a majority (50.1 percent) of the popular vote, and he owed his victory primarily to the aberration of Watergate. The Right's backlash against "the sixties" was a huge success.

In explaining in this book how the 1960s have been publicly framed, I am describing a discourse that is essential reading for anyone who wants to know what American politicians are really talking about when they talk about "the sixties." In short, my topic is the polemical cartoonization of the era.

When discussing the 1960s, most textbooks focus on liberalism, the civil rights movement, the progressive legislation of the period, and the conflict over the Vietnam War. They usually give little attention, however, to the Right during that turbulent decade, especially at the grassroots level. It is nevertheless important to acknowledge how crucial the 1960s were to the rise of the Right. Since then the Right has relied extensively on social issues, especially by formulating and exploiting hostility to the perceived excesses of "the sixties." The key to the Right's aggressive counterrevolution was its deliberate manipulation of language in the political arena. In turn, the key to understanding the rise of the Right since 1980 is to trace its success in framing the debate over the meaning of the decade in the minds of voters; hence the title of this book.

When presidents talk, we tend to listen. We sift and weigh the words a president uses because they reveal the worldview of a powerful player. According to Curt Smith, a speechwriter for President George H. W. Bush, "the finished product" of every presidential speech "is the president's work and reflects his philosophy, his verbiage, and his vision."[6] As Republican consultant Craig Shirley explained, "The president gives you an ideological and political and governmental framework in which to operate."[7] While "there's no way the president can get deeply involved in every single piece of rhetoric," in the case of a policy speech it is common for the president to become "involved quite early," said Republican speechwriter Ken Askew.[8]

My research for this study therefore took as its starting point more than twenty years' worth of presidential communications: official speeches, radio and television addresses, announcements, proclamations, statements, interviews, exchanges with reporters, comments, remarks, and memoirs. To put these into context, I also consulted numerous works of other historians, along with presidential and political memoirs dating from the early 1960s to 2004. In addition, I analyzed the speechwriting archives of the Ronald Reagan and George H. W. Bush presidential libraries, which hold speech drafts, speechwriters' comments, and White House memoranda, as well as personal correspondence (much of it handwritten) among speechwriters, presidential aides, cabinet members, colleagues, friends, and the presidents themselves. Finally, and most significantly, in 2004 and early 2005 I interviewed more than 120 political figures, politicians, cabinet members, speechwriters, advisers, strategists, historians, journalists, and activists from across the political spectrum. They spoke candidly, in detail, completely on the record, and often at length on the political and social legacies of the 1960s and how the presidents since 1980 had perceived recent history and modified it for public consumption to suit their partisan purposes.

Some of what I heard surprised me. First, while out-of-power liberals quite predictably recalled the 1960s with nostalgia and passion, conservatives expressed a similar passion for discussing the 1960s. Those on the Right showed even more enthusiasm for this work than did liberals, although conservatives retain great bitterness and anger about that period.

Second, the evocative power of the 1960s endures, as evidenced by how many people—equally divided between the Left and the Right—so eagerly assented to the interviews. Indeed, the majority did not want to stop talking. Both Democratic presidential candidate Bill Bradley[9] and the late Caspar Weinberger, Reagan's secretary of defense,[10] warned me that they had only ten or fifteen minutes to speak, then spent nearly an hour giving their views on the meaning and legacies of the 1960s. Similarly, after the conservative legal scholar Robert H. Bork said that he would not need even the twenty minutes I requested, he then talked for almost an hour.[11]

Things that happened in the 1960s, as well as things that did not happen, still give people an excuse to fight. Those who experienced the era firsthand are still concerned that the public will remember it the wrong way. Unlike the battles over previous contentious decades—the 1860s, the 1890s, and the 1930s—the tensions of the 1960s have not cooled. Each side still wants to get its story out. Liberals believe that they did the right thing in the 1960s and paid the price, whereas conservatives believe that the Left sinned and was rightfully punished. If you are a liberal, your problem with the 1960s is that things did not change enough. If you are a conservative, your problem is that things changed too much.

People recall the 1960s with surprising passion because the fight over "the sixties" has not stopped. The decade is still contested terrain, as the nation has not yet fully come to terms with its impact. The memory of the Vietnam War, the Kennedy presidency, the Great Society, and the changing social norms of the 1960s will not remain hot-button topics forever (who still argues about Calvin Coolidge?), but they still are today. Each of these subjects lends itself to historical interpretation and reinterpretation, and each president since 1980 has attempted to fashion a useful historical memory of these issues in voters' minds.

Reading Framing the Sixties will be uncomfortable for those expecting a different type of book, for a number of reasons. First, this is not a history of the events of the 1960s. I presume the reader's familiarity with the decade. I of course refer to those events, but I do not attempt to narrate them as a whole, much less account for them in an explanatory way. Instead this book is about what use the Right has made of the 1960s. I explain how the most toxic elements of that time have entered the political bloodstream and continue to circulate there.

Second, I was able to interview only ten women and two African Americans. I certainly wish that others I approached had not declined my request for interviews or failed to respond at all. But also, if more women and people of color had been presidential advisers and speechwriters and thus in a position to shape public discourse, this might have been a very different book.

Third, this is an interpretation from a particular viewpoint, primarily a study of political insiders and elites: the view from above. I selected those I interviewed because I am interested in the political and ideological forces that have made only certain things about the 1960s speakable for politicians trying to get elected. I am interested in the discourse that enables and enhances political power. This book is not about evaluating ideas on their merits, least of all their ideological merits. It is about evaluating their political efficacy. It is about ideas that work.

Fourth, in these interviews I felt like a fly on the wall at a reunion of the key players of the 1960s. The blessing and the curse of this method is that I was able to talk to each person no more than once. I was not in a position to demand follow-up interviews; I had only one shot. Nor was I in a position to conduct a hostile or adversarial interview with anyone I disagreed with politically. I could not cross-examine. My intent was merely to record each person's side of the story and then to analyze my data. In a perfect world I would have used a different approach; but readers will still benefit from access to this virtual cocktail party of political insiders talking about Reagan, the two Bushes, Clinton, and the political uses of the 1960s.

Finally, readers will notice the absence of much discussion of the women's movement. That is because it is a moot point for the Right. Neither the women's movement nor, for that matter, the civil rights movement is part of "the sixties" as that has been understood by the public. "The sixties" has come to mean the era's excesses: the antiwar movement, the counterculture, Black Power. Nor has it come to be understood as encompassing gay liberation, disability rights, environmentalism, increased rights for the young and the elderly, birth control, the rise of conservative media, the space program, the American Indian Movement, the United Farm Workers, the Equal Rights Amendment, or consumer safety issues—though all these issues fall within the time period discussed. These are not what "the sixties" are about.

Simply put, it did not serve the Right's interests to demean the women's movement overtly. The four presidents examined here did not address feminism nearly as frequently as they addressed the central issues of this book: JFK, LBJ, the civil rights movement, Vietnam, and "the sixties" as a cultural phenomenon. True, in her speech at the 1992 Republican National Convention, Marilyn Quayle said: "I sometimes think that the liberals are always so angry because they believed the grandiose promises of the liberation movements. They're disappointed because most women do not wish to be liberated from their essential natures as women."[12] But this foray of hers was the exception, not the rule. Others might think these things, but they have not tended to say them in public. The Republican presidents I examined did not by and large resort to such inflammatory antifeminist rhetoric. In my interviews only the Left consistently brought up the women's movement—and almost always to defend the 1960s, often linking gay rights, the environmental movement, and the women's movement together in the same litany. While several prominent liberals mentioned the backlash against feminism, far more prevalent in our discussions was the belief that women's rights have continued to expand since the 1960s.

Even conservatives did not openly contest the gains of the women's and civil rights movements. Among my interviewees there were of course criticisms. Longtime conservative activist Phyllis Schlafly called feminism "a terribly false promise. It's misled a lot of young women. Then they get to be forty and then they can't have a baby. And then they're mad at the world. . . . The feminists created a lot of problems."[13] Lisa Schiffren, who wrote Marilyn Quayle's 1992 address, lamented that although the ERA was defeated, "80 percent of what would have happened had the ERA passed" has taken hold, as "the Left went around the back and legislated it. . . . Women aren't supposed to be in combat, and yet now women are as close to being in combat as you can be."[14]

More common, however, was the Right's acceptance of the gains of the women's movement. Former Republican presidential candidate Gary Bauer—before offering a scathing portrait of the decade—said, "The 1960s were positive to the extent civil rights advanced for American blacks and women."[15] President George W. Bush himself has also openly praised the women's movement. In the 2000 campaign he spoke of "the few wonderful things that came out of the sixties, concern for civil rights and concern for women."[16] He later stressed these sentiments in his acceptance speech at the 2000 Republican National Convention.[17]

Indeed, liberals consistently noted that the gains of the women's movement are no longer contested. "The fundamental changes of the sixties show no signs of being reversed," argued Frank Rich of the *New York Times*. "The status of black people is not going to be reversed. Feminism—that, too, is what we can call a sixties movement, Friedan and Steinem—that's not going to be changed."[18] Former Clinton staffer Jeff Shesol, asked what points about the collective memory of the period he found most interesting, answered, "Many of the fundamental battles of the 1960s—that civil rights needed to be recognized and protected, not just for African Americans but for women as well—that's understood now, and we'll fight over the way it plays out but not over the fundamental content."[19]

The focus of this book is on a quarter century of presidential speeches and the nearly 700,000 words of interviews I conducted. Writing books is partly about making choices, and in the end I decided not to write about the political manipulation of gender sentiments since 1980. It would make a fascinating study, but it is simply not what this one is about.

This book explores first the two notions of the "good" and the "bad" sixties. I look at the ways in which John F. Kennedy is not part of "the sixties" but Richard Nixon is, and also at how part and parcel of the animosity toward the 1960s reflects a nostalgia for the 1950s. I also discuss how "the sixties"—especially Vietnam and Watergate—helped pave the way for the triumph of the conservative movement. Watergate hurt the Republicans in the short term. But in the long run it helped them by discrediting the prestige of government in general. The combination of Watergate and Vietnam moved America away from liberalism and toward conservatism by fueling mistrust in government at both ends of the political spectrum. For the Left, Vietnam revealed the government pursuing an immoral war. For the Right, it demonstrated a government too incompetent to fight a war and win it. By seeming to prove that the United States itself was in decline, Vietnam and Watergate led to a decline in public support for a strong, activist government. Nowhere is this use of "the sixties" more evident than in the story of Ronald Reagan's political career.

So our story begins with the rise of Reagan during the 1960s, when he was elected governor of California, and continues through his two campaigns for the presidency in 1976 and 1980. Once he became president, Reagan vowed to "renew America" after the trauma of the 1960s. Expressing nostalgia for JFK and the "good sixties," Reagan spoke of Kennedy more than he mentioned any other president but harshly attacked Lyndon Johnson's "bad sixties." I discuss the role that race played in Reagan's tactics, his reinterpretation of the Vietnam War, and his desire to overcome the "Vietnam syndrome," broadly defined as reluctance by the United States to intervene militarily overseas after the debacle in Southeast Asia.

Reagan's vice president and successor also longed for a pre-1960s America. George H. W. Bush grew up in an age of strong faith in the power of government to improve people's lives. But that belief did not survive the 1960s. The generation of Reagan (born 1911) and Bush (born 1924) turned against the activist government of the 1960s and the interventionist programs it spawned. This book is also, therefore, about generations.[20]

Like Reagan, Bush staked his political success on demonizing the 1960s. Also like Reagan, he claimed to have "kicked the Vietnam syndrome," in his case by waging the 1991 Persian Gulf War. Bush continued and even accelerated the critique of the 1960s that Reagan had begun through his response to the 1992 riots in Los Angeles occasioned by the police beating of Rodney King, through his vice president Dan Quayle's attacks on the television character Murphy Brown, and through his utter distaste for the candidacy of Bill Clinton.

As the first baby boomer to run for president, Clinton renewed and reintensified the national debate over the meaning of the 1960s. I examine how Clinton constructed the 1960s, and specifically how he recast them to suit the 1990s, a conservative era at odds with everything 1960s liberalism stood for. Clinton used the liberal 1960s icons he so dearly loved—John and Robert Kennedy and Martin Luther King—to promote his own centrist political agenda, his "Third Way." Clinton's pronouncements, especially regarding the Vietnam War and what he considered the true meaning of the 1960s, demonstrate how the constant attacks on "the sixties" during the twelve-year period of the Reagan and Bush presidencies had put the Democrats on the defensive on all matters regarding the era.

Clinton's succession by his fellow baby boomer George W. Bush only prolonged the national debate over the 1960s. Few public officials exemplify anger toward "the sixties" more than Bush, whose political ethos was based primarily on a desire to overturn what he saw as the harm done by that era. And there is a reason he felt this way: by 1968, when he graduated from college, Bush knew that he had lost his cultural inheritance. The East Coast establishment had been challenged by the decade's changes, and the world Bush once expected to inherit had vanished. The times were changing indeed, and too fast for some. To this day George W. Bush remains aggrieved by what did *not* happen in the 1960s: he feels he was cheated out of the legacy that he had coming to him.[21]

Bush's hostility to the 1960s led him all the way to the White House in 2000 and to reelection in 2004. Aping Reagan, he explicitly campaigned on a platform of restoring what the country had supposedly lost under the regrettable influence of liberals. John Kerry was the perfect opponent against whom to test the appeal of an anti-1960s message; the memory of "the sixties," especially of the Vietnam War and the antiwar movement, heavily influenced the 2004 presidential campaign. In four campaigns between 1994 and 2004, two for the governorship of Texas and two for the presidency, Bush thought it expedient to invoke a restoration of the pre-1960s America he had experienced during his childhood in Texas in the 1950s. And he was proved right.

Nostalgia, therefore, plays an integral part in contemporary American political culture. For the Right, the 1960s replaced an earlier version of America in which the country was moral and just. The 1960s elicited anger on the Right by questioning this cherished notion—the mythical view of Americans as noble, fair, honest, and righteous—and arguing that the nation needed to change. The 1960s rejection of traditional values challenged the established view of American exceptionalism, and in doing so eventually destroyed liberalism and propelled the modern Right to power.

The Republican presidents from 1980 on—Reagan and the two Bushes—all vigorously tapped into a national longing for pre-1960s America. Each expressed a desire to return the nation to a past recalled as calmer, rosier, and more certain, an America imagined as free of racial, generational, and ideological conflict. While Reagan and George H. W. Bush came of age well before the 1960s, the younger Bush shared this nostalgia as a kind of cultural legacy. All three promised to restore to public life the virtues supposedly lost through the misguided policies of the "bad sixties."

While a young George W. Bush bridled at the changes taking place in the late 1960s, Bill Clinton was a rising star just beginning to shine. Those changes opened up opportunities to the young man from Arkansas that would not have been available ten years earlier. The country was breaking Clinton's way in 1968, not Bush's way. These perceptions would linger in each man's mind and help define today's political climate.

What drives the differences between liberals and conservatives? This book offers the memory of the 1960s as the answer. When future historians seek to explain the dynamics of U.S. politics in the last quarter of the twentieth century and the first decade of the twenty-first, they will find a helpful tool in the use, and misuse, of the memory of that era. Over three decades later, the 1960s still cast a long shadow over American politics.

"The 1960s serve as a hinge of history," said political author Bob Woodward. One's view of the era answers the question, "Which side were you on?"[22] Former left-wing radical Tom Hayden remarked in 2004 that we were still fighting over the 1960s "because people shaped by the sixties will dominate our institutions for another decade, and also because the issues raised by the sixties have continued."[23] Like the Civil War, "the sixties" divided America, and for a generation or more after the struggles and conflicts of the 1960s ended, the nation has continued to argue over the decade's impact.

Eventually we will get over the 1960s, just as we got over the 1860s, the 1890s, and the 1930s. When every voice heard here has fallen silent, we will be done talking about the 1960s—but only then.

I

"The Sixties"
DEFINING AN ERA

Despite a forty-year remove, the tumult of the sixties and the subsequent backlash continues to drive our political discourse.
                                                        Barack Obama (2006)

AMERICAN POLITICIANS frequently speak of two 1960s—an earlier part, which they view favorably, and a later part, which they do not. Also, when they say "the sixties," they tend to mean 1964–1974, not 1960–1969: "the sixties" thus exclude President Kennedy but include President Nixon. Eager as they are to demonize what they dislike about "the sixties," conservatives owe much to that era. "The sixties" were a gift to the Right, as the decade—along with the Watergate scandal and the loss of the war in Vietnam in the early 1970s—spawned a counterrevolution that subsequently blamed the era for a host of problems. "The sixties" revived the moribund conservative movement and, by 1980, installed it firmly in power.

"The Good" versus "the Bad" Sixties

"There were two sixties for the liberals. You can call them the 'good sixties' and the 'bad sixties,'" noted Democratic speechwriter David Kusnet. "And it remains that way in American memory." Kusnet pointed to a string of people and events to differentiate the two concepts. "The 'good sixties' were John F. Kennedy, Robert Kennedy, the Peace Corps, Martin Luther King, the integrationists, the civil rights movement, the March on Washington in 1963, the Civil Rights Act, the Voting Rights Act, the figures like Congressman John Lewis," he said. "Most Americans to this day think well of that portion of the 1960s." The defining events of the other 1960s began later in that fateful decade. "The 'bad sixties' start with the escalation of the Vietnam War and the escalation of protest at home. The 'bad sixties' are violent protests in the streets, burning the American flag—Americans not just opposing the Vietnam War but rooting for the Viet Cong."[1]

11

Contemporary American politics, according to Kusnet, has become a game of claiming the "good sixties" for one's own side and pinning the "bad sixties" on the opposition. "What conservatives try to do is identify liberals with the 'bad sixties.' And what liberals try to do is identify themselves with the 'good sixties.' To be identified with John F. Kennedy is a good thing. To be identified with Martin Luther King is a good thing. To be identified with the later SDS [Students for a Democratic Society] is a bad thing."[2] In 1992 the Clinton campaign epitomized this technique by repeatedly showing the famous photograph of the candidate shaking hands with John Kennedy twenty-nine years earlier.

When speaking of the 1960s, explained former Democratic National Committee chair Paul Kirk, one needs to differentiate between the two parts of the era. The decade was marked by government dishonesty, an ill-considered war abroad, civil unrest, and political assassinations. But the early 1960s were an inspirational time that "people are still trying to emulate, if not to bring back, in some way."[3]

The Right described a strikingly similar calendar. According to Edwin Feulner, president of the Heritage Foundation: "For at least half of the sixties, the whole thing hadn't erupted yet. It was the latter sixties and early seventies that were bad."[4] Phyllis Schlafly agreed that the worst of the 1960s came in the latter half of the decade. "The biggest thing was the Vietnam War," she recalled. "Although it got started in the mid-sixties . . . it got really messy and bad for our country later on."[5]

When Were "the Sixties"?

"Decades don't begin on time," observed Peter Collier, a former sixties leftist radical who is now a conservative. For him, "'63 is the obvious moment to start the sixties. It's all fifties up till then, fifties aftermath." To Collier the 1960s "is a swatch of history that has a beginning, middle, and end. It begins in the paranoia and culture shock of JFK's assassination. And that Euripidean sixties has its high point in '68, which is the pivotal moment, when revolution was as much a possibility in this country as it ever has been."[6] Reagan speechwriter C. Landon Parvin agreed. "The 'sixties' most people talk about is mid-sixties and beyond. The early parts of the sixties are the orphan years of the fifties."[7]

Republican speechwriter Peter Robinson defined the period even more precisely: "The 1960s run from the assassination of John Kennedy in '63 to the fall of Saigon in '75. Most of it takes place in the sixties, but it's a very loose and rough shorthand for a time of troubles, political unrest, the sexual revolution, protest against Vietnam."[8] In political journalist

David Broder's view: "The Kennedy era is surrounded by all of the myths of Camelot and the romanticism of a bright, attractive young person cut down in the prime of life. . . . The sixties, in terms of the liberal phenomenon, are the Great Society, Lyndon Johnson, Vietnam, and the urban riots."[9] To Robert Bork, "the sixties were the last part of the 1960s and the first part of the seventies."[10] For liberal activist Daniel Ellsberg, "the sixties extended into the seventies."[11]

The Left and Right agree that the Kennedy administration is not what people mean when they refer to "the sixties," in that JFK is not associated with the "bad sixties." And it is the "bad sixties" that have come to define the decade as a whole.

For most Americans the 1960 election did not represent a dramatic break with the past, despite the many differences between Dwight D. Eisenhower and Kennedy: party, age, background, region, religion, experience, and, most glaringly, their belief in the role the federal government should play in the life of the citizenry. To Thomas C. Reed, a special assistant to President Reagan, Kennedy's election represented "a blossoming" of the 1950s. "The Kennedy years were not 'the sixties.' . . . 'The sixties' are a short form for Lyndon Johnson and Robert McNamara bringing to a crashing end all the hopes and dreams that were based on the Eisenhower years and then blossomed with the Kennedy election."[12] The *Washington Post*'s Benjamin C. Bradlee summed it up this way: "Ike for eight years, Kennedy for three years—eleven years of vaguely the same direction."[13]

"The Kennedy era was the ushering in of a new era, but not quite 'the sixties' in the way we often think of it today," agreed journalist David Maraniss. "Kennedy himself was a fairly economically conservative president, and the classic liberal was Hubert Humphrey."[14] Many prominent historians argue as well that Kennedy was a "pre-1960s" figure, and that the later 1960s—for Godfrey Hodgson "an age of turmoil . . . almost national hysteria"—marked a dramatic break from the Kennedy years.[15]

Such definitions of decades are after all quite subjective: much of this type of memory of the 1960s is constructed in such a way as to speak badly of the era. The construction of Kennedy as emblematic of the 1950s reinforces conservatives' negative interpretation of "the sixties." But the Right's successful definition of "the sixties" as a terrible period that does not begin until after Kennedy's death requires an aggressive reinterpretation of Kennedy's actual presidency, for the Kennedy years were themselves filled with conflict and tension. At the time, they *were* the "bad sixties."

"The sixties were scary," declared Rick Perlstein, author of books on Barry Goldwater and Richard Nixon. "Bad things happened in the sixties.

But the early sixties were scary, too, and that's something that's been re-pressed. People don't say: 'Oh, that great Kennedy era. We almost had a nuclear war over Berlin. Oh, that great Kennedy era, when an armed mob took over the University of Mississippi.'" Much of the nostalgia for the early 1960s, Perlstein noted, "has to do with the Camelot industry," which "travestied history" by romanticizing the early 1960s as the calm before the storm. But "the late sixties are a hard time for Democrats to claim because it was traumatic," Perlstein emphasized. "The late 1960s were great if you were young and were having a lot of fun, but for the ma-jority it was the scariest time ever. America seemed to be falling apart."[16] Liberal author and journalist Thomas Frank agreed. "People remember the early 1960s as happy times," whereas "the late sixties were a horrible time. Nobody thinks of 1968 and 1969 as being fun."[17]

In looking nostalgically to the Kennedy presidency, the public endorses the distinction between the years 1960–1963 and the chaos of the latter 1960s. JFK "has never been connected with the 'bad sixties,' as the Right uses [the term]," said historian Alan Brinkley. "Kennedy is still this icon-ic figure of a better time in the history of liberalism. . . . Identifying with Kennedy . . . is a way of skipping over all the bad stuff and going back to the happy time. So that part of the sixties is still very much something that people would like to identify themselves with. It's the late sixties that people want to stay away from."[18] To both the Left and the Right, this desire to disassociate oneself from the "bad sixties" has long defined American politics.

If Kennedy has not been tarred with the brush of the "bad sixties," it is because of his ambiguous political ideology. "I would not categorize Kennedy as a conservative, but maybe the label is a 'realistic liberal,'" said former Republican presidential candidate Pierre S. du Pont IV. "He thought that liberalism was important, but so was growing opportunity and a sound economy."[19] Other Republicans concurred. Kennedy "was a very moderate president, of course," said Curt Smith. "He had to be pushed and kicked, screaming, into doing anything regarding civil rights."[20]

As David Broder noted, Kennedy "was opposed for the nomination by most of the liberals in the Democratic Party. . . . He ran to the right of Nixon in 1960 on national security issues. He put Republicans in to run the Treasury and Defense departments."[21] In 1960, recalled David Kusnet, those on the Left "were either for Hubert Humphrey or Adlai Stevenson, and were not that fond of [JFK] when he was president."[22] Alan Brinkley stressed that while Kennedy "was not particularly liberal, [he] . . . certain-ly wanted to be perceived as liberal because everyone in the Democratic

Party, at least, thought it was of critical importance." In 1963 "the term 'liberal' was still, except on the Right, a widely admired idea. . . . In most parts of the country, being the liberal candidate was a real asset." Kennedy tried to present himself as a liberal, and in fact "became increasingly liberal in every sense of the term at the time during his presidency."[23]

Much of the debate about the meaning of the 1960s in American politics revolves—for both the Right and the Left—around defining the Kennedy years. This debate over whether Kennedy was or was not representative of liberalism in the 1960s would color the rhetoric of Presidents Reagan, George H. W. Bush, Clinton, and George W. Bush.

But just as "the sixties" do not begin until the end of the Kennedy era in 1963, they extend into the 1970s because many across the political spectrum saw the Nixon administration not as a truly conservative one but as an extension of 1960s liberalism. To be sure, many Republicans admired Richard Nixon personally. "Culturally, without question," Nixon was a true conservative, stated Curt Smith, who wrote the speech George H. W. Bush gave at Nixon's funeral and who knew Nixon well. "He hated the national media[,] . . . [coined] the term 'silent majority[,]' . . . opposed busing," Smith recollected. "Nixon was never afraid to attack on behalf of Middle America. He showed great courage."[24]

Yet at the same time Nixon engendered great animosity from the Right. "Nixon was espousing policies that were anathema to conservatives," said Edwin Feulner, who viewed Nixon as a carryover from 1960s liberalism. "Nixon was funding the Great Society to try to buy off the Left."[25] According to conservative activist Morton Blackwell, "Nixon was never beloved by movement conservatives."[26] Asked about an assertion often repeated by conservatives, that "Johnson enacted the Great Society but Nixon funded it," Lisa Schiffren answered: "I would agree 100 percent. Nixon was personally conservative [in] his dress and his manner. But he's the one who said, 'We're all Keynesians now.'" Schiffren went so far as to claim, without elaborating further, "He and his secretaries certainly stated their beliefs that history was on the side of the Soviet Union." Nixon "funded the welfare state. He set affirmative action in motion. He was in favor of D.C. statehood." Nixon "was coming at the tail end of a very liberal moment in American politics." His policies "wouldn't fly now," she noted in 2005.[27]

"He wasn't [a true conservative] in many ways," agreed Robert Bork. "He did do some strange things like impose price controls, and his policy of détente with the Soviets was probably a mistake." Nevertheless, "a lot of conservatives did strange things," said Bork. "[Senator Daniel Patrick]

Moynihan entranced Nixon by talking about liberal policies enacted and pursued by conservative men. The parallel he was suggesting was Disraeli. That phrasing seemed to entrance Nixon."[28]

According to Reagan adviser Stuart K. Spencer, "a counter-conservative revolution" began immediately after the 1960 election. Those on the Right "didn't think Nixon met the criteria of what they called a 'conservative.'" The biggest single point of agreement between Nixon and Reagan, "and the one that carried [Reagan], was anticommunism."[29] Nixon was hardly soft on communism during the 1950s. But conservatives have reshaped historical memory to make Reagan the true standard-bearer of conservatism and Nixon an imposter.

Conservative spokesman L. Brent Bozell III recalled that Nixon created "more new federal programs, liberal programs, than virtually any [other] president in history."[30] David Keene, chairman of the American Conservative Union, even called Nixon "the most liberal president in American history."[31] The late Paul Weyrich, widely considered to be the godfather of modern conservatism, called Nixon "a traitor" to conservatism; "his first loyalty was to liberalism." Nixon's decades-long hostility to liberals notwithstanding, Weyrich claimed that after the Alger Hiss case, Nixon "spent the rest of his career trying to court the establishment liberals. . . . They wanted surrender in Vietnam, and he wasn't prepared to do that. But eventually he did."[32]

Stephen Moore, founder of the Club for Growth, a conservative economic lobbying organization, thought "there's a historical revisionism going on . . . liberals are starting to look at Nixon and saying, 'He wasn't that bad a president,' and conservatives are looking at him and saying, 'He was just a disaster.'" Milton Friedman once told Moore that from an economic standpoint Nixon was the worst president in his lifetime. "The Great Society began under Johnson, but it flourished under Nixon," Moore pointed out. Nixon's presidency "was a great failure."[33]

Moore's claim about "historical revisionism" is supported by the fact that Nixon, once the bane of American liberals, is looked on today in a much softer light. Many Democratic politicians agree that Nixon did not always act like a conservative. Former Democratic presidential nominee Michael Dukakis pointed to the first Earth Day in 1970 as well as to several of Nixon's progressive measures, such as affirmative action. "We can clearly see the effect of the 1960s on Nixon," he said.[34] During the Nixon administration, when future Democratic Senator Timothy Wirth was "working at the old Department of Health, Education and Welfare," Nixon "had probably the most enlightened welfare reform program, and one of the most enlightened national health insurance programs, of any

American president."[35] Two-time Democratic presidential candidate Gary Hart also took a moderate view of Nixon. "Whatever else you say about him, [he] was not Ronald Reagan or George W. Bush. He was very progressive on environmental matters, by and large." The only time he ever met Nixon was at a funeral, Hart recounted, "and he took the occasion—I sat next to him—to talk to me about what a progressive Republican he was. He always felt he was mischaracterized by liberals as being this dark, reactionary person."[36]

Speaking for the far Left, no less a figure than prominent political activist and critic of U.S. foreign and domestic policy Noam Chomsky agreed that "the last liberal president in the United States was Richard Nixon."[37] For his part, the late historian and Kennedy aide Arthur M. Schlesinger Jr., after reciting a list of liberal legislation under Nixon, recalled that domestic policy did not interest Nixon, "but he wasn't an ideologue—he was a rascal, but not an ideologue. That's why the true blood conservative ideologues distrusted him."[38] Liberal pundit Mark Shields concurred that "Nixon was considerably to the left of any conservative today."[39] Veteran White House correspondent Helen Thomas called Nixon a "centrist."[40] Historian Bruce Schulman and former Harvard president Derek Bok both emphasized that Nixon was more liberal than Clinton.[41]

In assessing Nixon's supposed liberalism, it is important to remember that Nixon could not always afford to show his true political stripes when dealing with a Democratic Congress on the one hand and the Vietnam War on the other. Nevertheless, the fact remains that on both sides of the political aisle Nixon is viewed as fundamentally different ideologically from the current Republican Party. Republicans have moved to the Right since the Nixon era, and much of that shift has come as a reaction against "the sixties," a time that is seen to have included Nixon.

1950s Nostalgia on the Right

While highly critical of the 1960s, the Right simultaneously longed for the 1950s. "The fifties were such a glorious time for America, because we had succeeded in the Second World War," said the late Reagan confidant Michael Deaver. "It had been a tremendous sacrifice, and we had seen that we could do anything. And we believed that—unlike in the sixties, when [younger people] had forgotten that and began questioning whether America could or should do anything."[42]

In the 1960s, said Paul Weyrich, "the elite media convinced the country that the 1950s were a terrible time. As a matter of fact it was the best time that we had in my lifetime," but young people "turned against tradition.

Having lived through the fifties, I can tell you, it was a wonderful time," Weyrich continued. "The family was in good shape. . . . It was a great time to be an entrepreneur. . . . You didn't have any revolutionary activity."[43]

Robert Bork, asked why the 1950s are sometimes demonized, replied: "It's a way of justifying the sixties, if the fifties is said to be an era of conformity and stagnation, which is not true. . . . But I suppose if you're going to justify going off on a revolution [in the 1960s] you have to say terrible things about what went before you." (Bork and others on the Right would in turn say terrible things about the 1960s, as we will see.) Although racial segregation still existed in the 1950s, said Bork, "it was coming to an end. . . . Nobody says that the 1950s cured all things, but after all, the Supreme Court outlawed governmental racial discrimination in 1954, and it was supported by a large part of the population." Asked why admirers of the 1960s feel the need to demean the 1950s, Bork answered, "You wouldn't expect Robespierre to have kind things to say about the king whose head he just cut off."[44]

Criticism of the 1950s "shows you how out to lunch, out of touch these [Leftist] clowns are," claimed Curt Smith. "The fifties was the best decade in the twentieth century. George Gallup has had a poll for many years. He asked two questions: Which decade would you most like to relive? And in which decade would you most like to raise your kids? What decade do you think wins? The fifties wins! And which decade finishes last? The 1960s! So most Americans think as I do. The best decade of the century was followed by the worst decade of the century."[45]

But for many, the 1950s reflect a sanitized America, an era of conformity and restrictions. "You can get yourself elected talking about how terrible the sixties were," said historian Doug Rossinow. But "I don't think too many people are going to get elected actually saying to voters, 'Let's go back to the fifties.' There's a certain problem there."[46] To the Left, the 1950s were an oppressive age. The 1960s represented "a real break from the stultifying culture of the fifties," recalled journalist Frances FitzGerald. Nostalgia for the 1950s, she argued, "is like putting everything back in its place so we know where we are. . . . That's where [the late Reverend Jerry] Falwell's people are—it's a fifties middle class and does not include very many blacks at all."[47] Frank Rich wryly observed, "On Fox News Channel, they're still talking to Pat Boone,"[48] and 1960s radical Jo Freeman mockingly noted that "Pat Robertson's favorite refrain is 'the golden age of the fifties.'"[49] Many academics shared this aversion to the 1950s. To historian Maurice Isserman, 1950s nostalgia is emblematic of a deep cultural longing for "strong fathers and no blacks in advertisements."[50]

"There is nostalgia for the fifties because it was stable and we were trying to get back to normalcy. There is something comforting about it, that it wasn't unsettling in the way that the sixties were," observed Derek Bok. While this sentiment was understandable, "in the 1950s lots of very legitimate problems in the United States were simply ignored: poverty, the environment, women's rights, and civil rights. Nostalgia for the 1950s is an emotional feeling, but it doesn't stand up under analysis."[51]

Indeed, many on the Left expressed outright contempt for the decade. "In the 1950s everybody was quiet, obedient, passive; you didn't ask any questions, you did what you were told, you dressed properly; women didn't work, stayed in the home and didn't ask for any rights; blacks stayed in the home, were beaten up; it was perfect," said Noam Chomsky.[52] In the Eisenhower years, Bill Bradley remarked, "men went to work and wore gray flannel suits and women stayed home and essentially didn't seek to have any career. There was continued segregation in America, and the Cold War dominated everything you thought about in international policy."[53]

Michael Dukakis dismissed the Right's memory of the decade as "hallucinogenic." He recalled the climate of fear and conformity and the stifling of dissent during the decade. He was horrified by Joseph McCarthy's witch-hunts; he remembered visiting Washington in the 1950s and hearing McCarthy and his tactics denounced on the Senate floor. Dukakis recounted his disgust at first seeing segregation at work when he attended college in the capital for a semester, though during the 1950s "Boston didn't have any blacks working behind the counters at its department stores. . . . The 1950s were no 'Golden Age' if you were black."[54]

"We came out of the sixties a very, very altered nation, and in part a lot of the myths that people lived by up to the [mid-1950s] were either shattered or dented," said civil rights pioneer Roger Wilkins. "We went into the sixties floating on the myths that we told ourselves about ourselves during World War II and afterward: a nation of good-hearted, big-hearted people, generous, virtuous, and slow to anger but fierce in battle. We didn't much notice the condition of black Americans, Hispanics, Asians, or women and, God knows, not gays and lesbians." In the 1950s "there was order, and you didn't have to live with uppity blacks, or Hispanics, or uppity women, and if those other people did those 'nasty things,' well, damn it, they should do it in secret in dark closets and not talk to reasonable people about it. And for God's sake, we salute our flag and our president because whatever our president says, wherever we are fighting, we are fighting for freedom and decency, and our boys are good and the other boys are bad."[55]

Conservatives "believed [that] . . . and they want that time back," he continued. "They had their blacks and they used and abused them and didn't let them vote, didn't pay them fair wages. They used the threat of 'the blacks' to keep wages for everybody down, and before the decade [the 1960s] was over, this 'supposed-to-be-southern president' [Johnson] had signed the bill that let the niggers vote. That 'Martin Luther Coon' had marched up and down the streets and made all these complacent and happy darkies uppity." To Wilkins, "conservatives, even if they were women, were really happy with the [1950s] hierarchy that existed, and that is the unchallenged authority of the white male in America, and a society in which most conventional norms were never challenged because they were eternal verities. If you take a society and you shake it, shake it, shake it as much as the activists of the sixties did, and you change the country in such profound ways, well, you damn well are going to have a lot of reverberations."[56]

One of the most powerful—though at the time quite unexpected—"reverberations" from the 1960s was the emergence of the Right.

"The Sixties" and the Rise of the Right

Though conservatives romanticize the 1950s and demonize the 1960s, the 1960s were essential to the success of the Right. One insider emphasized how the decade strengthened conservatives. "I've always objected to the idea that 'the sixties' is a bad name," argued Anthony R. Dolan, President Reagan's chief speechwriter for eight years. "The sixties gave us Ronald Reagan. . . . So there are a lot of nice things to say about the sixties. . . . The whole story of the sixties was Reagan standing up to the rioting students" at Berkeley when he was governor of California. To Dolan, speaking in 2004, "the primary political phenomenon of the last forty years has been the rise of the conservatives and their triumph."[57]

Reagan's central technique, the notion of blaming the 1960s, "actually begins in the sixties," observed political scientist Bruce Miroff. In 1966 "Reagan pioneered the backlash against the student revolt: blaming Berkeley and making Berkeley a scapegoat."[58] The late author and journalist David Halberstam remarked, "The sixties give energy to those who didn't like the sixties, who resented them and thought it was a breakdown of the American norm."[59] According to Arthur Schlesinger, "the sixties for the conservatives is a time of 'uppity blacks,' of 'vociferous women,' feminists, of angry riots and lack of patriotism."[60]

Indeed, the political arena in the wake of the 1960s saw the triumph of the conservative critique of the latter part of the decade. The 1964 election "was only in one sense a debacle for the Right," stated Jeff She-sol. "It seemed like Goldwater and Goldwaterism might be relegated to historical backwaters. But we now understand these guys were getting it together. . . . These guys running the country right now [in 2004] are the political and intellectual heirs of those 1960s counterrevolution-aries."[61] Godfrey Hodgson confessed that in his earlier writings on the years 1945 to 1974 he underestimated the Right's strength. "The biggest mistake in my book *America in Our Time* is that, while I think I did un-derstand that traditional political liberalism was running out of steam, I didn't fully appreciate just how vigorous the rise of a new conservatism was." Goldwater and Reagan "were part of the sixties too," he said. "In-deed there was a considerable dynamism to the new conservatism start-ing in 1964, but it was really roaring away by the end of the decade."[62]

Such a misreading of the 1960s understandably irritated the Right. Rea-gan White House aide Donald J. Devine insisted that the media "don't even know the conservatives were around in the sixties, and the conserva-tive movement started then."[63] Many other conservatives share the same anger. When "PBS did a series a number of years ago on the sixties and asked to interview me about how I became a conservative," said Ron Rob-inson, who runs the nation's largest conservative college outreach pro-gram, "they asked me what I thought of the JFK assassination, the Martin Luther King assassination—where I was, and those types of things—and then they asked me about Bobby Kennedy's." Those were the *only* events they asked him about, he complained. Historians overlook the fact that "there was a whole other movement out there that actually did success-fully elect a self-identified movement leader as president, and that that person came from the conservative side of the spectrum, not the liberal side. The first really national leader that emerged from that time period was conservative," Robinson said.[64]

To the Right, their story is one that still has not been told in full. In the 1960s "conservatives were a four-letter word," noted legendary conserva-tive activist Richard Viguerie. On the rare occasions that the press "even noticed us, we were racists, neo-Nazis, bigots, just crazy people—and cer-tainly not the wave of the future. In hindsight, we *were* the wave of the future," he stated. "Those young people that were coming of age in the sixties and seventies . . . Dave Keene, Bill Kristol, Newt Gingrich, Tom DeLay—we were the young kids then, and we're setting public policy in the country and the world now. And the Tom Haydens of the world are long since disappeared."[65]

"The short-term legacy of the sixties was the election of Nixon in '68," remarked David Keene, but "in the long term it was the election of Reagan in 1980. And none of that probably would have happened that quickly had the Left not tweaked everybody—gotten in their face."[66] To conservative publisher William Rusher, "the decade is identified with the Left, but . . . the conservative movement gained 100,000 votes per riot straight through the sixties. . . . It became a lot easier after the 1960s to point to [liberalism] and have the American people understand that this is the thing we oppose. . . . A great many of the tendencies that got going during the 1960s were negative tendencies, harmful tendencies, and did great damage to the country."[67]

Reagan administration official Frank Atkinson agreed. "The cultural and social conservative movement had its roots in reaction to the more radical movements of the 1960s," he said.[68] As former chairman of the Republican National Committee Frank J. Fahrenkopf Jr. recalled, "I went to Berkeley [law school in 1962] as a moderate Republican, and came out [in 1965] much more conservative."[69] Longtime Reagan adviser Edwin Meese III observed that before the 1960s conservatism was "an intellectual movement," but "with the advent of the Goldwater candidacy it became a political movement." Meese believed that the Right benefited most of all from "these excesses of the sixties on the Left [that] gave rise to causes that rallied many people to the conservative movement."[70]

But conservatism was gaining strength in the early 1960s even before the appearance of any such "excesses." "All of a sudden there was this influx of younger conservative people coming to campaign meetings in '61 and '62 in California," recalled Stuart Spencer. "They were intent; they were going to change the damn world."[71] Viguerie called March 1962 "the birthday of the conservative movement," the date when Young Americans for Freedom "rented Madison Square Garden, put on a rally, eighteen thousand people, sold out, people outside, made the above-the-fold of the front page in the *New York Times*, and we had Goldwater and Tower and Thurmond, just every conservative star. . . . It was just a big, big deal, and all of a sudden we saw ourselves as, 'Hey, we can play with the big boys.'"[72]

While the Right did indeed begin to mobilize at the beginning of the decade, it was the later 1960s that provided the movement with its greatest boost. Don Irvine, chairman of Accuracy in Media (AIM), was asked to describe how the late sixties contributed to the views of his father, Reed Irvine, the organization's founder. "Watching the riots at that [1968] convention, looking at the news reports and seeing the visual images—those visual images are so powerful. One of my father's pet peeves was that famous picture of the Vietnamese [man] being shot in the head. 'There's more to it than that,' he said. That image resonated around the world. It helped turn even more sentiment against the war, because the media highlighted things that were labeled as atrocities, but without going further and explaining a lot of things behind it," Irvine argued. Nineteen sixty-nine was the "pinnacle of where sentiment turned, where [radical Left] activism just blossomed, and he was determined to set the record straight," Irvine recalled. "The Tet Offensive was [an American] victory—but you can't find that [written], and so he fought very hard to educate the public. . . . Watching how much the activism and the violence and the protests had gone to extremes was a large part [of AIM's founding]. He said, 'If we don't do something, we're going to lose the country to these people.'" AIM thus sought to provide counterpropaganda.[73]

Irvine concurred that it was the late—not the early—1960s that were crucial to the political rise of the organized Right. "From '69 to '71 is where you see the real roots of the conservative media. We talk about Buckley and Goldwater in the early 1960s and the Young Americans for Freedom, but after Goldwater lost, [the movement] dissipated." Nevertheless, "in that '69–'71 time period you had Reed Irvine forming Accuracy in Media, Phyllis Schlafly putting together the Eagle Forum, Paul Weyrich and Ed Feulner forming Heritage Foundation and then the Free Congress Foundation, and Dick Viguerie becoming the direct mail guru." These were "the fathers and mothers of the movement[,] . . . the heroes."[74]

Liberals tend to agree that the 1960s helped the Right. According to Gary Hart, the Right arose in reaction "to the perceived cultural liberalism of the sixties." Since the 1960s, he noted, there has been a backlash "against the liberalizing values represented by what were seen—by those people at least, if not the whole culture—to be excesses" of the decade.[75] "There's also a conservative sixties: the Goldwater campaign, Reagan giving the speech for Goldwater in 1964 and getting elected governor of California in 1966, William Buckley and Young Americans for Freedom," noted David Kusnet. "The sixties ended with Nixon as president, Reagan as governor, and in the 1970s James Buckley—William F. Buckley's brother—as senator from New York." Building on these successes, the Right put together a winning political coalition. "The conservative sixties is what has been governing America, not the liberal sixties," Kusnet said. Many future prominent conservatives, including Newt Gingrich and Phil Gramm, were "products of the conservative sixties," and "for a lot of conservative baby boomers, William F. Buckley was almost what, on a lesser scale, John Kennedy was to Democrats: an inspirational figure, a mentor. He showed that conservatives could be cool, in his own way."[76]

Several former Clinton officials agreed. "The sixties gave conservatives a huge political advantage," said Paul Glastris, because absent the decade's turmoil, "conservatives would have had no real chance of getting back into power."[77] According to John Shattuck, in the decades after the 1960s the Right united to try to overturn 1960s progressivism and used the era's many social changes "as a whipping boy."[78] To Peter Edelman, "the combination of all the social policy achievements of the 1960s did provoke a backlash."[79]

Signs of this incipient backlash were evident in a confidential 1971 memorandum from Lewis Powell Jr., a corporate lawyer soon to be nominated by Nixon to the Supreme Court. In his memorandum, circulated nationwide to business leaders, Powell urged corporations to fight back against academia, the media, politicians, and a variety of powerful liberal groups. "The American economic system is under broad attack," he wrote, and while the nation had always had enemies, today "the assault on the enterprise system is broadly based and consistently pursued. It is gaining momentum and converts." What worried Powell was not so much "Communists, New Leftists and other revolutionaries who would destroy the entire system" but rather the numerous criticisms of American life coming "from the college campus, the pulpit, the media, the intellectual and literary journals, the arts and sciences, and from politicians." These groups were advancing revolutionary ideas, Powell stressed, and he was disturbed that business leaders, college administrators, and politicians were not responding to this open assault. He urged them to coordinate their efforts. "Strength lies in organization, in careful long-range planning and implementation, in consistency of action over an indefinite period of years."[80]

The attack on capitalism had increased in recent decades to the point where recent college graduates "despise the American political and economic system," Powell wrote, citing *Time*. He proposed "establishing a staff of highly qualified scholars in the social sciences who do believe in the system," for just as "we have seen the civil rights movement insist on re-writing many of the textbooks in our universities and schools," so too must the Right use publications to express its beliefs. Powell urged conservatives to employ many different forms of media, along with "the neglected political arena," to promote the conservative ideology. He was especially concerned by "the anti-business views" of some unnamed presidential candidates, as "Marxist doctrine" and "Leftist propaganda" had "a wide public following." It was thus crucial for corporate interests to lobby the government, since "the American business executive is truly the 'forgotten man.'" Powell wanted advocates of capitalism "to press vigorously in all political arenas for support of the enterprise system" and to "penalize politically those who oppose it." He concluded, "Business and the enterprise system are in deep trouble, and the hour is late."[81]

Powell's call to arms foreshadowed the powerful assault on liberalism that followed the 1960s. The Right would soon focus its efforts on the very arenas Powell suggested: the media, the churches, the universities, and most especially politics. Their efforts would be enormously assisted by two critical events of "the sixties" that at the time inflamed the Left. Both were debacles for conservatism in the near term, but in the end they had the paradoxical effect of galvanizing the Right.

Vietnam, Watergate, and the Ascent of the Right

To the extent that Vietnam and Watergate lessened Americans' faith in government, "the sixties" helped the Right. Ronald Reagan, for example, was astutely conscious of the growing antigovernment sentiment, and he capitalized on it. He repeatedly charged that the government had executed the Vietnam War poorly, and he spoke of the conflict in ways that implied the government could not be trusted. After Watergate and Vietnam, Reagan's message that "government is not the solution to our problem; government is the problem" was one that resonated with the electorate.[82]

According to historian H. W. Brands, the upheavals of the 1960s discredited liberalism. "The sky didn't finally fall on American liberalism until the sky fell in Vietnam," when Americans "decided that government wasn't getting it right." Furthermore, the publication of the Pentagon Papers in 1971 showed that "the government was lying to the American public about what it had been doing in Vietnam for twenty years." Thus "Vietnam and Watergate—these twin issues, the one arises from the other—caused Americans to turn away from government."[83] And, Brands observed, "once they withdrew their trust from government on foreign affairs, it was quite easy to withdraw their trust from government in domestic affairs." By 1980 "Americans found it very easy to throw up their hands and say, 'You can't trust government to do anything.' And it's that feeling that Reagan rides into office."[84]

The link between Vietnam and Watergate is crucial. "There was a huge disillusion that came out of Vietnam," noted Reagan biographer Lou Cannon. "I don't like to think of it as just 'the sixties' or 'the seventies.' Look at the Vietnam War and Watergate back-to-back. People felt that Lyndon Johnson had deceived the American people; even people who agreed with him started to feel that. That's why he wasn't able to run for another term in '68." Then Nixon "becomes a discredited president who not only doesn't end the war, but who gets involved in this Watergate crime and then is forced to resign."[85]

At first Watergate was very damaging for the Right. "Watergate was a tough time for Republicans," acknowledged James A. Baker III. As the Texas Republican Party's finance chairman, Baker "did fourteen counties for Nixon in '72, and then Watergate hit us. And we all believed Nixon." Baker exclaimed: "Boy, it was a dark day for Republicans. And we took a real bath in '74."[86] Former Republican congressman G. William White-hurst concurred that "[Watergate] sure didn't help us in the [1974 mid-term] elections. Watergate, for the short term, was bad for us."[87]

But in the long run, as Brands noted, Watergate fueled a profound hostil-ity to the federal government that worked to the Republicans' advantage. As Derek Bok put it, although Watergate "set back the Republicans in the 1976 election, certainly the longer-term effect was one of discrediting government, 'big government.'"[88] John Shattuck elaborated, "It's those two crises," Vietnam and Watergate, "that discredited government." Since 1976 candidates had "succeeded in getting into the White House by campaigning against Washington. Nixon and Ford didn't do that. Carter invented the campaign against Washington."[89] Godfrey Hodgson agreed: "Watergate starts this idea that everything inside the Beltway is bad. It's what I call the 'Beltway Babylon.' You get this ludicrous thing whereby figures like Bob Dole or Al Gore—people who have been inside the Belt-way, beavering away for years—suddenly denounce it as if they were an-cient Hebrew prophets denouncing the wickedness of Babylon."[90]

Vietnam and Watergate—both part of "the sixties"—thus paved the way for Reagan's election. "If Nixon had not been toppled by Watergate, [there] might have been a realignment that was less conservative," said veteran Republican speechwriter Aram Bakshian. "Watergate creates a re-action against state authority and also knocks Nixon out, so that there is an artificial boom for the Democrats." The 1974 midterm elections and Carter's presidency "were the aberration, the blip on the chart because of Watergate." Without Watergate, "the realignment would have been along a more Nixonian, more big-government line." Social conservatism would have increased, but not with the force that Reagan wanted. "Nixon would never have been capable of taking it the next step further." Watergate "made possible the emergence of Reagan."[91]

Liberalism may have dominated the 1960s, but "the sixties"—constructed as including Vietnam and Watergate—ultimately invigorated the Right. As the nation turned more conservative, an opportunity arose to blame the 1960s for a wide variety of economic, political, and social problems. In the 1968 and 1972 elections the voters twice rejected liberalism. With the liberal tradition in steep decline, the 1960s—which symbolized the triumph of liberalism—became an image the Right could manipulate with ease. It was Reagan who first capitalized on this opportunity. As early as 1964 he had invented and was beginning to use "the sixties" as a political weapon, one he was to deploy again and again throughout his presidency, and to considerable effect.

2

Blaming "the Sixties"
THE RISE OF RONALD REAGAN

Reagan came to power in California in opposition to the riots that were going on. . . . It was a very, very rowdy period in American history. . . . He first ran for president—people don't focus on this—in 1968.

James A. Baker III (2004)

BY CHARACTERIZING his political rise as an antidote to the 1960s, Ronald Reagan successfully propelled debate about the decade to the center of American politics. But long before the phrase "the sixties" entered the national vocabulary, before the backlash against the Great Society had begun, and even before Reagan had won his first election in 1966 as governor of California, he expressed his hostility to the liberal ideas associated with the era. The notion of "the sixties" began to take shape during the 1960s themselves, well before the end of the decade, when conservatives such as Reagan started to rail against Johnson's Great Society and those who did not support the U.S. effort in Vietnam.

In the 1960s and 1970s Reagan strongly and repeatedly criticized big government, liberals, and the era's permissive social ethos. His rhetoric as president was quite consistent with his previous public statements. Throughout his political life he argued for a return to a pre-1960s America. Once elected president in 1980, Reagan continued his assault on "the sixties." He called for an "American renewal" and vowed to do all he could to overturn what he viewed as the sins of the decade, which, he said, had damaged American education, morality, and the economy and had promoted crime and drug abuse.

Turning against "the Sixties"

Michael Deaver, asked if Reagan felt that the 1960s had been harmful to Americans, replied without hesitation: "Oh, I think so. He couldn't go on

28

a campus or they'd blow it up," he said. "The only way to go on campus was to go under armed guard."[1]

Both Reagan and Deaver were especially fond of telling one story.[2] "Back in those riotous days of the sixties," Reagan claimed in 1984, students from the assorted campuses of the University of California "demanded a meeting with me. And they kind of had a chip on their shoulder, but I was pleased to meet with them, because in those days if I went near a campus I could start a riot." (Reagan used this or a similar phrase over ten times during his presidency, especially in his 1984 reelection campaign.) "When they came in, they slouched in the usual uniform of that day, and their spokesman, resplendent in T-shirt and barefoot, opened by telling me . . . 'Your generation doesn't understand its own sons and daughters,'" Reagan recounted. "I tried to pass it off. I said, 'Well, we know more about being young than we do about being old.' And he said, 'No, I'm serious.' He said, 'You didn't grow up in a world of instant electronics, of computers figuring out problems that once took months and even years. You didn't have nuclear power and jet travel and journeys out into space'—and so forth." When the student paused to take a breath, Reagan replied: "'You're right. Our generation didn't have those things when we were your age. We invented them.' It sure did change the tone of the discussion."[3]

Reagan was in full adversarial mode during the 1960s. By the 1964 presidential campaign, he recalled in his 1990 memoir, "Lyndon Johnson had begun to make most of the tax-and-spend Democrats of the past seem miserly by comparison. I thought we sorely needed Goldwater to reverse the trend," he wrote. "I said I'd do anything to help get him elected."[4]

On October 27, 1964, Reagan gave an address—officially titled "A Time for Choosing" but more commonly referred to as "The Speech"—as part of a nationally televised broadcast on behalf of Goldwater, who sponsored the program. Reagan, still an actor at the time, began by declaring that he had switched parties. He then introduced themes that would mark the rise of the Right from the 1960s on. After charging the government with excessive taxation and spending, he turned to the subject of Vietnam. "We are at war with the most dangerous enemy that has ever faced mankind in his long climb from the swamp to the stars," he insisted. Retelling the story of a Cuban refugee who had told two of Reagan's friends how lucky they were to live in America, Reagan said: "If we lose freedom here, there is no place to escape to. This is the last stand on Earth." Striking a theme that would become a hallmark of his presidency, Reagan attacked the federal government and its abuses of power. He railed against Washington's "little intellectual elite" who wanted to run everyone's lives, and he took exception to the Democrats' use of "terms like the 'Great Society'" at election time. He asserted that conservatives rejected both the welfare state and democratic socialism.

Foreshadowing the backlash against the Great Society that would come in the 1966 midterm elections, when Democrats lost forty-seven seats in the House and four in the Senate, and Johnson's popularity sank to 44 percent, Reagan charged that liberalism and nearly three decades of "government planning" had only worsened existing problems.[5] Ridiculing the Democrats' claims of "seventeen million people [who] went to bed hungry each night," he joked that they "were all on a diet." He stated that if the total amount of money being spent on welfare (which he falsely claimed was ten times higher than during the Great Depression)[6] were divided equally among the poor, every family would get $4,600 a year. But in fact, Reagan said, at the time families received only $600. Reagan then mocked Johnson's efforts, announced a few months earlier, to "declare 'War on Poverty,'" predicting that spending more money would not solve the problem. In a precursor of the attacks on "welfare queens" that would become a staple of his presidency, Reagan claimed that a local judge had told him of a woman pregnant with her seventh child who had sought a divorce just so she could receive government assistance. Reagan complained that those who questioned the wisdom of such policies were attacked as uncaring. As for Social Security, while he accepted the legitimacy of the program, he was against those who "practice deception regarding its fiscal shortcomings." The overarching themes of Reagan's address were attacks on "big government," whose programs "never disappear" and threaten individual freedoms; the Democratic Party's leftward turn; and the need to defeat communism.[7]

Reagan thus laid out the basic arguments that would dominate American politics from the 1960s onward. "What Reagan's saying in '64 describes what become bigger issues later in the sixties," noted C. Landon Parvin. "He did have a certain foresight. It was '64, and even then when he's saying 'War on Poverty,' he's got 'War on Poverty' in quotes. . . . He was very clear: he was against the War on Poverty. He started talking about these things early, and kept talking about them." Repeating his concerns was itself central to Reagan's success. As Parvin recounted: "Reagan later told me that you have to pound an argument year after year after year for it to sink into the public's consciousness. And he did that. That's one reason he was easy to write for, too."[8]

Stuart Spencer explained how Reagan capitalized on the public's increasing anxieties about the changes taking place in the 1960s. "Early in

1965 we were running an exploratory committee and we were going up through the Central Valley of California, and he had this well-prepared speech," Spencer recalled. "Every now and then at the end of it he would deviate a little. About two nights in a row he started hitting on the campus unrest up at Berkeley, and I remember one night when we talked about the schedule for the next day, I said, 'Ron, campus unrest isn't even a blip in our polls.' And he looked at me and said, 'It will be when I get through.' He made it an issue." Spencer continued, "The seeds were there and he made it an issue; it started showing up."[9]

Reagan's skill in this regard is readily acknowledged by his opponents. The legendary civil rights activist Julian Bond, asked if Reagan capitalized on anti-sixties sentiments, replied: "Oh, absolutely, absolutely. And it fit naturally into the politics that he had adopted by then. . . . He famously said 'the [Democratic] party left him, he didn't leave it,' but of course, he left the party."[10]

Although it was the early 1960s when Reagan left the Democratic Party for the conservative movement, in the Right's recollection he switched parties because of "the sixties." As Morton Blackwell recalled, "the 'limited government, free enterprise, strong national defense, traditional values' folks were made very uncomfortable in the Democratic Party, and that's why you wound up having Ronald Reagan become a Republican."[11] According to Michael Deaver—whom Lou Cannon called "as important as anybody" in assisting Reagan's political ascent—"Reagan certainly viewed what was going on in the country [in the 1960s] as revolutionary, and counter to what he thought America was about and what Americans wanted."[12] In the 1960s, said conservative legal activist and Federalist Society director Eugene B. Meyer, Reagan felt that protesters "were not just expressing a view, but were attacking the country itself, and that bothered him a lot because, for Reagan—for most people of Reagan's generation—the country did offer the American dream." Reagan interpreted the protesters as saying, "No, we don't want that country."[13] To Frank Fahrenkopf, "what happened in the sixties so upset most Americans—this lack of order, this lack of discipline, this lack of certainty—that it led the American people to look for that constancy" which Reagan promised to provide when elected president in 1980. Reagan offered "discipline and certainty, and the American people were looking for that."[14]

"A lot has been written about college students and other young people who rebelled against society in the 1960s," Reagan wrote in his 1990 memoir. "But there was another, quieter revolution sweeping across the land during the same decade."[15]

Governor Reagan and the "Creative Society"

In his 1966 race for governor Reagan vigorously campaigned against Johnson's Great Society, which by then was well under way in a torrent of new
federal legislation. He even coined a phrase—the "Creative Society"—in
opposition to LBJ's slogan, and complained that "the Great Society grows
greater every day—greater in cost, greater in inefficiency, and greater in
waste." Instead Reagan proposed "a constructive alternative to the Great
Society, which I have chosen to call 'A Creative Society.'" In place of
Johnson's bureaucracy and his tax and welfare increases, Reagan's Creative
Society pledged to reduce the scope and reach of a government which had
grown larger and more intrusive in people's lives. Instead of providing tax
revenue for ineffective welfare programs, the Creative Society sought to
increase volunteerism. Since the nation had traditionally fought poverty
"without federal interference," the Creative Society marked "a return to
the people of the privilege of self-government."[16]

In his 1967 gubernatorial inaugural address, after beating incumbent
governor Pat Brown by more than 1 million votes, Reagan proclaimed the
need to limit government power. "Along this path government will lead
but not rule, listen but not lecture," he said. "It is the path of a Creative
Society." In his remarks Reagan attacked the changes of "the sixties." He
railed against crime and had harsh words for demonstrators: "Lawlessness
by the mob, as with the individual, will not be tolerated." He criticized
welfare and praised a program enacted after the 1965 Los Angeles Watts
riots that used private industry—not federal intervention—to reduce unemployment, a plan he frequently touted. He said that the state's public higher education system should, besides teaching academic subjects,
"build character on accepted moral and ethical standards." He vowed to
lower income and property taxes, the state budget deficit, and the cost of
government, and ended by strongly endorsing U.S. efforts in Vietnam.[17]

In the years that followed Reagan would return frequently to the issues
that had facilitated his 1966 victory, vowing to fight the federal government's intrusions and touting the benefits of his Creative Society. His first
years as governor, he wrote in his memoir, had shown him the damage
caused by "the 'permanent government'—the people in the bureaucracies
who were forever trying to enlarge their power and budgets and prolong
programs after their need had expired."[18]

He also consistently lambasted anyone engaged in street protests, especially against the Vietnam War. "The demonstrations are prolonging the
war in that they're giving the enemy . . . encouragement to continue," he
charged in a May 1967 televised debate with Senator Robert Kennedy. The

demonstrations would be illegal, he said, were there an actual declaration of war. To Reagan, forms of protest "such as avoiding the draft, refusing service, blocking troop trains and shipments of munitions . . . [go] beyond the dissent that is provided [for] in our present governmental system." He also criticized domestic aspects of "the sixties" by subtly questioning the necessity of Johnson's civil rights legislation. "With all of the disorders we've lost sight of some of the progress that has been made," he said, defending the state of U.S. race relations. Though prejudice—"probably the worst of all man's ills and the hardest to correct"—remained, federal legislation was not the answer. Reagan spoke at length of the 1947 decision by the Brooklyn Dodgers to defy baseball's ban on African Americans by signing Jackie Robinson, implying that a better cure than government action was simply for prominent people to speak out against racism.[19]

In 1968 Reagan made his first run for president, though not in an active campaign. "Running for president was the last thing on my mind," he wrote in his memoir, concerning the request that he throw his hat into the ring. At the Republican National Convention, where he announced his "favorite son" candidacy, a last-minute "Draft Reagan" campaign failed. Nixon won the nomination on the first ballot, with 692 votes. Nelson Rockefeller received 277 and Reagan 182. "I was the most relieved person in the world," Reagan recalled. "I knew I wasn't ready to be president."[20]

In his second inaugural address after easily winning reelection as governor in 1970, Reagan again called for a "Creative Society" of smaller government and greater local control, and heightened his criticism of welfare, which he called "a tragic failure" for the poor.[21] He also criticized Washington. In his view, "states and communities . . . [had become] so dependent on [federal] money that, like junkies, they found it all but impossible to break the habit."[22] His basic message as governor of the nation's most populous state never deviated from the positions he had first staked out in the early 1960s. By the end of his second term, however, he was eager to express his political ideas on an even larger stage.

Creating a Conservative Majority

Within weeks of leaving the governorship in 1974, Reagan announced that he would run for president in 1976. In announcing his candidacy, he returned to his familiar anti-sixties themes: the nobility of the country's efforts in Vietnam, the insufficient effort on the part of Washington to win the war, the increasing intrusiveness of the federal government, problems with the Great Society, the progress America had made in race relations, and the many benefits of the American free enterprise system. He also stressed that American society was under attack from ideas left over from the 1960s and lamented the current anti-military climate as well as educators' efforts to convince students "that there is little to admire in America."[23]

With Nixon's resignation in 1974, Reagan found himself in 1976 not simply running for president but challenging a sitting—though unelected—Republican president, Gerald Ford, for the nomination. Reagan chiefly opposed Ford's policy of détente with the Soviets and his failure to reduce the size of the federal government. "The Washington Establishment is not the answer. It's the problem," Reagan proclaimed after criticizing economic conditions. Above all, Reagan said, he sought the presidency "to see this country become once again a country where a little six-year-old girl can grow up knowing the same freedom that I knew when I was six years old, growing up in America."[24]

Reagan nearly defeated Ford in the 1976 primaries—a remarkable achievement, considering that no incumbent president has ever lost the primaries, before or since. At the Republican National Convention, Ford defeated Reagan by a mere 117 votes on the first ballot. Immediately following Carter's slender victory in the election that November, Reagan began campaigning for the 1980 nomination.

He had good reason to continue his quest for the presidency. Support for conservatism had increased throughout the 1970s, a tide Reagan both rode and helped push. In 1977 he told a conservative group that he wanted to see the Right merge the social conservatism of "blue-collar, ethnic and religious" Democrats with Republicans' traditional economic conservatism, as "the old lines that once clearly divided these two kinds of conservatism are disappearing." He argued in favor of free markets and against deficits, and urged Republicans to move beyond "the country club–big business image" and appeal to factory workers, farmers, policemen, and the millions "who may never have thought of joining our party before," because, as he put it, "the Democratic Party turned its back on the majority of social conservatives during the 1960s."[25]

Reagan spoke of "the great conservative majority party we know is waiting to be created," and noted that in the mid-1960s, when most voters trusted government to solve a myriad of problems, conservatives had sounded the alarm over government expansion. Such fears had come true, he said, and now the vast majority opposed the federal government's intrusiveness. "The Great Society is great only in power, in size and in cost," Reagan proclaimed.[26]

When he left the governorship in 1974, it was his harsh memories of the 1960s that fueled his desire to stay politically active. Government expansion had long concerned him, "but the problems increased dramatically during the years I was governor with the start of Lyndon Johnson's 'Great Society' and 'War on Poverty,'" he wrote in his 1990 memoir. Hardly any of the new federal programs helped the poor, he argued, as money was wasted on "giveaway programs that sapped the human spirit, diminished the incentive of people to work, destroyed families, and produced an increase in female and child poverty, deteriorating schools, and disintegrating neighborhoods." In Reagan's view, "the liberals had had their turn at bat in the 1960s and they had struck out."[27]

President Reagan: An "American Renewal"

At the 1980 Republican National Convention, running against Carter's record and the assorted woes of the 1970s, Reagan emphasized, as he would during his presidency, that the 1960s were at the root of many of the nation's problems. During that era, he charged, America had lost its way: the problems of the 1970s were merely the outgrowth of the previous decade's faulty policies. But these changes were reversible, he insisted, and he would return America to the promise and prosperity of that happier time before the 1960s. Vowing "to renew the American spirit and sense of purpose," he called for "a great national crusade to make America great again." A key part of this restoration involved rebuilding a military demoralized after Vietnam, and restoring an assertive foreign policy.[28]

Reagan would reiterate these very themes in his 1981 inaugural address as president, identifying big government as the nation's primary crisis. "Government is not the solution to our problem." He pledged to heal America and urged, "Let us begin an era of national renewal." Once more he ended with a lengthy salute to the military, including those who fought in "a hundred rice paddies and jungles of a place called Vietnam."[29]

As David Broder put it, "Reagan's appeal was his optimism and his belief that America was a special place, that it was God's favorite nation, and that we had the capacity in ourselves to restore that sense of national destiny."[30] Conservative activist Elaine Donnelly, who attended the 1981 inaugural ceremony, fondly recalled the day as "a turning away from the worst of the sixties, and a start of something new."[31]

One month after Reagan's inauguration the cover of *Time* proclaimed an "American Renewal," as two billboard painters on a scaffold were shown repainting an enormous American flag. For the first time in the magazine's sixty-year history, its publisher wrote, all seven Time Inc. magazines were being devoted to this single theme. In a twenty-five-page special section *Time* announced that it too sought to reverse the current "mood of weakness and self-doubt."[32] Several articles referred explicitly to the 1960s in order to draw the same contrast Reagan had invoked. An article on governmental reform noted that the peak of the Great Society had coincided with an "increase in public alienation" and political polarization.[33] Others called for a more muscular foreign policy and increased military spending in the wake of the U.S. defeat in Vietnam. America must "put behind it the self-flagellation of the past 15 years," wrote Strobe Talbott.[34] Some spoke of restoring American patriotism. Lance Morrow claimed that starting in the early 1960s, liberals had led the nation to "a moral inferiority complex of historic proportions." He bemoaned rising crime and decreasing morality, observing that the current rise of the Right "is tending toward the firmer, common-sense moral ground that radicalism and experimental youth abandoned years ago for more fantastic terrain."[35] *Time*'s cover story thrilled Vice President Bush, who wrote Time Inc.'s chairman to congratulate him for standing up to "the liberal establishment."[36]

This same theme of renewal dominated the early 1980s. The administration first used the term "national renewal" after the March 1981 attempt on Reagan's life, an event reminiscent of the horrors of the 1960s. James Baker, in an unpublished speech delivered four weeks after the shooting, quoted an unnamed journalist who wrote after the assassination attempt: "Ronald Reagan has exorcised the national nightmare. . . . We cannot be defeated, at home and abroad, if we refuse to be defeated. Ronald Reagan's conduct . . . may have been a catharsis for the nation—perhaps a turning point that will help mark the return of confidence." History would describe the Reagan years, said Baker, as "an era of national renewal."[37] Two days after Baker's speech, and for the first time since his inauguration, Reagan also used the term, calling older Americans "essential to our effort for national renewal" and referring to the current period as an "era of renewal."[38] In the margin of a draft of the 1982 State of the Union address Reagan wrote, "History will remember this as an era of American renewal," words he asked to have inserted into the speech.[39] He thereafter spoke of national renewal throughout his first term.[40]

The theme of renewal also formed the basis of his 1984 reelection strategy. Reagan favorably contrasted the youth culture of the day with that of the late 1960s and early 1970s. In 1984 he saw "an outpouring of affection and support from college and university students I never expected," he wrote in his memoir. "These students in the eighties seemed so different from those that I'd dealt with as governor."[41] Clearly his unpleasant memories of the 1960s remained vivid. In an early outline of the 1984 State of the Union address a speechwriter suggested that the theme of the introduction should be "Together, we have stopped our long national decline." A handwritten note in the margins reads, "Theme: America is back."[42]

In his address Reagan said, "The cynics were wrong; America never was a sick society," as liberals in the 1960s had claimed. "We're seeing rededication to bedrock values of faith, family, work, neighborhood, peace, and freedom."[43] This notion of a "sick society" had long preoccupied Reagan. In 1970, as governor of California, he gave a speech titled "Ours Is Not a Sick Society."[44] In his second gubernatorial address in 1971 he said, "Those who whine of a sick society aren't talking about us."[45] When he announced his run for the presidency in 1974 he repeated, "We are not a sick society."[46] In his first speech after the failed 1981 assassination attempt, Reagan expressed gratitude for Americans' support during his recovery. Such support debunked the notion that the shooting "was evidence that ours is a sick society. . . . Sick societies don't produce dedicated police officers. . . . Sick societies don't make people like us so proud to be Americans."[47]

Striking a verbal blow against the national decline he attributed to "the sixties," Reagan revisited the renewal theme throughout his 1984 campaign.[48] It also formed the centerpiece of his television ads: "It's morning again in America, and under the leadership of President Reagan, our country is prouder and stronger and better."[49] In his acceptance speech at the Republican National Convention, Reagan declared that the nation had "renewed our faith in the human process" and had renewed the military as well. "America is coming back and is more confident than ever about the future."[50] Near the end of the first presidential debate in 1984 Reagan said, "We've given the American people back their spirit. I think there's an optimism in the land and a patriotism."[51]

After his landslide reelection Reagan's speechwriters prepared his second inaugural address. Among the documents used in preparation was a lengthy memorandum to Ed Meese from three administration members (including John Roberts, future Chief Justice). Under the heading "Purpose," it argued that the speech should answer the question of what Reagan wanted to be remembered for. It then listed "achievements for which history *may* credit 'the Reagan years.'" Among these were an end to national self-doubt, the restoration of "traditional values," a growing economy resulting from decreased government interference, and "the years when Henry Luce's description of this as 'the American century' were—to the surprise of some—fully vindicated at last." The document went on to list seven major themes for the address, one of which was that "the social decay of the '60s and '70s already is beginning to reverse."[52]

At his inauguration Reagan proclaimed, "Americans have restored their confidence and tradition of progress."[53]

The Devastation of "the Sixties"

Reagan believed that a renewal was needed because he also believed that the turmoil of "the sixties" had done enormous damage. Throughout his eight-year presidency he consistently blamed the 1960s for various problems, especially the country's educational, economic, and moral decline and the concomitant rise in drug abuse and crime.

In the sphere of education, to take one example, he argued that the 1960s had brought about lower educational standards and test scores. In 1983 he said that recent high school graduates scored well "below their 1963 counterparts" on the SAT and that it would take years of repeating recent gains "before we achieve the levels of the mid-sixties."[54] He again mentioned the decline of SAT scores since "the early sixties" the following year, noting similar declines despite vastly increased spending.[55] Two weeks later he urged the nation to continue the current progress to earn back "what we lost in the sixties and seventies."[56] In 1986 he charged that "back in the sixties" liberals had severely damaged American education.[57]

Reagan also claimed that the 1960s had eroded school discipline. "Somehow in the sixties and seventies, people decided that discipline was old fashioned and high standards unnecessary," he said in 1984. "It made teaching so difficult."[58] In 1987 he remarked that some schools had been able to avoid declines in SAT scores because they "never accepted the so-called reforms of the sixties and seventies. [They] stuck to basics and kept high academic standards."[59] That same year Reagan castigated those who had neglected "the importance in education of moral and academic standards" in the 1960s and 1970s.[60]

Reagan also consistently pointed to the 1960s as the source of the drug epidemic. "During the sixties and seventies, [drug abuse] spread through the nation like a fever," he said in 1984.[61] In 1986 he noted that the drug problem had worried him and his wife, Nancy, long before he became president, and that "during the late 1960s and into the last decade, a flippant and irresponsible attitude toward drug use permeated too much of our society. The gurus of hedonism and permissiveness were given a respectable hearing back in those days."[62] As first lady, Mrs. Reagan "turn[ed] things around," according to C. Landon Parvin, who said that she deserved credit for being the first public figure to combat drug abuse. "The country was still riding on the sixties mentality toward drugs until she said, 'Just say no.' In her own way, she was rolling back the sixties too."[63]

Reagan blamed the 1960s for the drug problem with particular frequency in 1988, his last year in office. Drug abuse had originated long before his presidency, he said, claiming that many current addicts had "acquired their drug-use habits in the sixties and seventies."[64] Drug abuse had skyrocketed, he said, because "in the 1960s and 1970s, America crossed a deadly line," when drug use was "celebrated by a permissive cultural establishment whose slogan was 'Just Say Yes'" and which sought to limit "restrictions on personal behavior."[65] On one occasion Reagan used especially colorful language to blame the 1960s for the drug problem. Referring to Congress's willingness to pass his anti-drug proposals, the president said, "I hope this means our liberal congressional friends are dropping their nostalgia for the do-your-own-thing-in-your-own-time-baby sixties."[66] According to Meese, "there was no question" that the legacy of the 1960s included the encouragement of drug use. "That was part of the counterculture, the revolt against authority. That was when drug use expanded from the campuses . . . and spread to the adult society."[67]

Reagan believed that the 1960s had sapped the nation's economic strength as well. In 1981 he declared that economic conditions had deteriorated since the early 1960s. As government spending had increased, living standards had decreased, and "the federal government has shown a deficit every year after 1969." Reagan claimed that the 1960s social programs were wasteful and inefficient and entailed excessive regulations.[68] In his 1982 State of the Union address, he blamed the present economic climate on the policies of the previous decades, a charge he often repeated.[69]

Reagan strongly believed that the policies of the 1960s had harmed the economic position of minority groups. In 1981 he held a private meeting with African American supporters. There is no written account of his comments, but his "talking points" offer one interpretation of the 1960s as he presented it. "Government must fully protect our civil rights and aid those who cannot provide for themselves," read his notes, "but the government's social and economic policies have locked many Blacks more firmly behind the bars of ghetto poverty than they were 10 years ago."[70] Reagan observed that increases in the minimum wage during the 1960s coincided with higher unemployment among the young, "especially minorities."[71] In 1983 he said, "Beginning in the late sixties, on the very heels of the breakdown of legal racial barriers, the economy entered a period of contraction." Consequently, as soon as African Americans "achieved the rights to buy a ticket on the [economic] train . . . and got on the train, it started going backward."[72] The president was fond of this metaphor and often returned to it when addressing African Americans.[73]

He consistently argued that poverty had grown worse as a consequence of 1960s social programs.[74] In 1983 he declared that reductions in poverty "began leveling off in the late sixties, reversing almost two decades of dramatic improvement." Reagan blamed the 1960s for a variety of other economic woes as well, and lamented the general decline of the economy since the 1960s.[75] By contrast, he often touted conditions in the 1980s as the best "since the 1960s" and fondly recalled the nation's economy before the upheavals of "the sixties."[76] He frequently called it an economic golden age.[77]

Reagan also linked the 1960s to increasing crime. In 1981 he criticized "the social thinkers of the 1950s and sixties" who emphasized poverty as the root of crime and who urged increased government spending to eliminate society's problems. Such beliefs he found horribly misguided, especially efforts to alter the "material environment" to "permanently change" basic human nature, which only worsened social problems.[78] Reagan often spoke of "a crime epidemic that spread across our country in the sixties and seventies," a plague for which he blamed permissive liberals.[79] Conservatives as a whole maintained that liberal social policies during the 1960s had increased crime. "The Great Society took the ideas of a lot of social engineers, funded them, and put them into federal programs." One of these ideas was to treat lawbreakers as "sick people," argued Meese. "Using the medical model, they essentially said, 'Don't send people to prison unless it was absolutely necessary. Crime increased 300 percent between 1960 and 1980. Violent crime increased about 500 percent."[80]

Reagan's stance on crime was at the center of his 1987 nomination of Judge Robert Bork to the Supreme Court. Bork shared Reagan's views of the 1960s and has criticized the era throughout his career. In all of human history, Bork said in 1996, "individualism and personal freedom of the individual [were] beneficial [to man] so long as there were some limits on what the individual could do. And those limits were set by religion, by a common morality, by law; and they began to break down [with] great rapidity in the 1960s when the student radicals and the so-called establishment proved to be hollow and just rolled over." To Bork, religion and morality "came under heavy attack in the 1960s." Asked whether Reagan was trying to overcome the "1960s values" in the culture, Bork thought "he was, in many ways. He was not in sympathy with sixties values,"[81] although Bork remarked the futility of trying to erase the influence of "the sixties" on the nation's legal system. "Sixties values dominate in the Supreme Court, and I don't care whether they're appointed by Republicans or Democrats."[82] Reagan framed his nomination of Bork for the

Court in terms of reducing crime by reversing legal trends he claimed had begun in the 1960s.[83] "Beyond his scholarship and judicial qualifications, there's nothing more significant for his confirmation than the war on crime," said Reagan, lamenting that for years "we always heard about the rights of criminals, rarely those of their victims."[84] Reagan accused Bork's opponents of being soft on crime and unwilling to "bring criminals to justice."[85]

Reagan's rhetoric reflected the importance of the Bork nomination to conservatives, who viewed it as a key moment of the post-1960s culture wars. In a lengthy personal letter to Reagan, Georgia Republican Newt Gingrich, in discussing various courses of action, urged the president to "save the Supreme Court and Senate from a left-wing lynch mob." Speaking of the nomination in nearly apocalyptic terms, Gingrich wrote that it was urgent to strike a blow against "an arrogant left-wing elite which last won the presidency in 1964."[86]

Nearly four months after the Senate's rejection of Bork's nomination, Reagan returned to this theme of the courts, crime, and the 1960s. To an audience that included many leading conservatives, he expressed disappointment that starting in the 1960s the Supreme Court had emphasized the rights of criminals at the expense of their victims. The 1960s had witnessed the decline of the legal system, Reagan argued. Without offering any evidence for his assertion, he claimed that "the Constitution, as originally intended by the Framers, is itself tough on crime and protective of the victims of crime," adding that "for so long, the liberal message to our national culture was tune in, turn on, let it all hang out."[87]

"Sixties-ism" and the Decline of Moral Values

"For many in the cultural conservative movement," observed Mark Shields, the 1960s have "become a very convenient caricature of promiscuity and drugs, and, worse than youthful rebellion, an insurrection and toppling of what had been by their definition traditional values."[88] Indeed, one unifying theme of the modern Right is to blame "the sixties" for the nation's moral decay. In the 1960s "government began to become an opponent of what large numbers of people thought were American principles," said Morton Blackwell. "Traditional values on social issues were suddenly up for grabs in public policy."[89] For Eugene Meyer, "the sixties had an element that was nihilistic and destructive, and said . . . that hard work was a bourgeois virtue and not a good thing."[90] According to Richard Viguerie, "the war against Christianity began to reach its critical mass in the sixties. . . . Things became looser. . . . Homosexual priests began to come into their own in great numbers in the church."[91] The decade "was a disaster for our core social values," said Gary Bauer. "The growing embrace of moral relativism led to increasing rates of out-of-wedlock births, marital break-up, venereal disease, etc."[92] Peter Collier noted: "The sixties were the archetypal secular era. You can tell somebody who is from the sixties. . . . When somebody fulminates about right-wing Christians, it's almost a litmus test for the degree in which they're infected with 'sixties-ism.'" Another characteristic of "sixties-ism," Collier argued, was a "chaotic libertarianism in the personal realm, an impatience with any notion of deferred gratification."[93] Craig Shirley believed that "so many of the libertine attitudes about abortion, illicit behavior, homosexuality, and drug use find their seeds in the sixties."[94]

In the 1960s "a number of things were permitted that had not been legally permitted before. It's very easy to confuse the toleration of a practice with endorsement of same," said Aram Bakshian. Because of the 1960s, we have had "decades of plummeting standards and morals."[95] According to Pierre du Pont, one legacy of the 1960s was a permissive society that tolerated drug use. "That was part of liberalism: You can do anything you want, with anybody you want. And it's not up to society to tell you how to behave."[96] Don Irvine agreed that the 1960s "tore the fabric of America [with] this drug culture and the free love stuff. . . . We're still fighting a lot of those moral issues today."[97] To William Rusher's mind, in the 1960s "you had the sexual revolution [and] the disintegration of marriage." The forces unleashed by the 1960s remain, he said, "and may in the long run destroy us."[98] Liberal-turned-conservative David Horowitz even claimed that "the sixties are responsible for the AIDS epidemic."[99]

The issue of values has certainly been central to the rise of the Right since the 1960s, and Reagan's main critique of the era involved this very topic. As we have seen, one way Reagan denigrated the 1960s was by remarking how youth culture had changed for the better since then. Given that his first campaign for the California governorship had occurred during "those riotous days of the sixties," Reagan was pleased that in his 1980 campaign "there was a large contingent of teen-age Republicans who were working their hearts out."[100] Reagan often used this device of favorably contrasting the youth of the 1980s with those from the 1960s.[101] "In the rebellious sixties and early seventies," he said in 1981, there had been "a discarding of basic truths."[102] He went so far as to reveal how the era's mores had affected his own family. When his daughter Patti learned that he had been elected governor in 1966, "she started to cry. She was only fourteen, but as a child of the sixties she believed the antiestablishment rhetoric that was popular among members of her generation, and she let me know that she didn't like having a member of the establishment in the family."[103]

Reagan similarly devalued the 1960s by praising the religious revival that had occurred since then. "The abolitionist movement was at heart a moral and religious movement; so was the modern civil rights struggle," Reagan said in 1984, and in these periods there was tolerance of faith-based political activism. "But in the 1960s this began to change" with the rise of secularization. In his view "politics and morality are inseparable. And as morality's foundation is religion, religion and politics are necessarily related."[104] Reagan was pleased to note that whereas in the 1960s college students had rebelled, now they were interested in issues of faith. "Today America is in the midst of a spiritual revival," Reagan said in 1988. "On our campuses the political activism of the sixties has been replaced with the religious commitment of the eighties."[105]

Curt Smith, asked if the rise of secularism was an outgrowth of the 1960s, replied: "Of course, it is. Absolutely." Noting FDR's "enormous religious faith," Smith emphasized that on the founding of the Atlantic Charter, Roosevelt and Churchill "sang 'Onward Christian Soldiers.'" Roosevelt "would be appalled at the party today, which hates religion, particularly Christianity." From the beginning, said Smith, America was "devoutly and avowedly and openly religious. The Democratic Party [has] turned upon the whole tradition of this country."[106] Robert Bork felt that "marriage and the family no longer have the characteristic of something that's regarded as sacred. Religion is certainly not regarded that way anymore, and the Supreme Court is constantly assaulting religion." To Bork, religion and the family are "under attack in the elite culture, which reflects the 1960s' values."[107]

Reagan assailed the values of "the sixties" in a variety of ways. Noting the recent migratory trend toward small towns and rural areas, he recalled that "during the 1960s, there were those who scoffed at small-town values: . . . family and God and neighborhood." But fortunately the nation had outgrown those ideas, and recently "there's been some growing up in this country."[108]

Reagan's speechwriter Peggy Noonan shared his hostility toward "the sixties." Remembering her classmates when she began college in 1970, she wrote, "We were first-in-our-family college students, and we were working a job and studying and partying, and only rich kids wanted to occupy a dean's office, normal kids just wanted to not get called on the carpet there." She had believed then that "America is essentially good, the [Vietnam] war is being fought for serious and valid reasons," government programs were not a cure-all, intrusive government was a threat to individual freedom, "and God is real as a rock." It was on a 1971 bus trip to an antiwar rally, Noonan wrote, that "I knew I wasn't of the Left." She "couldn't get into the spirit, into the swing. There was contempt for America." As her peers spoke of the horrors of a culture that worshipped John Wayne, of a nation founded on violence and imperialism, she thought: *"Get me off this bus! . . .* What am I doing with these intellectuals or whatever they are . . . this contemptuous elite? . . . *And what was the Democratic Party doing on the side of these people?"*[109]

Ronald Reagan invented "the sixties" and throughout his political career defined himself in opposition to a carefully constructed negative image of that decade. Yet Reagan was also inspired by the 1960s, as the era's turmoil gave rise to the very movement that propelled him to the presidency. Fiercely proud of his generation, Reagan often clashed with the dissidents of the 1960s. But his political rise was directly linked with that decade, especially the second half.

As early as 1964 Reagan publicly opposed "the sixties," years before the public even formed an opinion of the tumultuous times they were living through. Critiquing the decade soon became his mantra. When elected president in 1980 he immediately set out to reverse the changes he saw as having been brought on by the 1960s. Throughout his presidency he consistently blamed "the sixties" for a variety of social and economic ills. In so doing he blazed a trail for his successors. Seeing how well the technique worked for Reagan, each succeeding president would seize the opportunity to define his own version of "the sixties."

3

A Tale of Two Sixties

REAGAN'S USE OF JFK AND LBJ

The American people are being left by the first President they could manage to love since John Kennedy a quarter century ago.
Peggy Noonan to Ronald Reagan (1989)

REAGAN MAY HAVE DEMONIZED the 1960s throughout his presidency, but he was always careful to distinguish between the Kennedy and the Johnson years. Reagan must have felt almost as much disdain for the Kennedy administration as he did for Johnson's—he voted for neither candidate and publicly criticized each—but as president he could not openly say so, for the Kennedy myth had grown much too powerful by the 1980s. So Reagan simply co-opted Kennedy and claimed to admire him as much as anyone else. One thing Reagan learned in show business was that there was nothing to be gained by openly attacking another performer, especially a beloved dead one. Reagan astutely—and explicitly—believed that the 1960s could be divided into two parts. When he criticized the 1960s, he meant the post-Kennedy "bad sixties," not the "good" early sixties. Throughout his presidency Reagan presented himself as a political admirer and even descendant of John Kennedy.

It was to promote his own plans that Reagan drew such a sharp distinction between Kennedy's early 1960s and "the sixties." "Where has all the money gone?" he asked in 1985, referring to the exploding federal budget deficit. In the 1950s "and through the Kennedy years, we kept spending in check," he claimed. "During those years there was a tax cut proposed similar to our cut. It was enacted in 1964," resulting in economic growth, he argued. But the government did not go on to cut taxes further; instead it "did the opposite [and] began to take over America. In the name of the Great Society, it began doing things never before felt possible or desirable."[1]

The memory of Kennedy, even the longing for him, represented a political minefield for the Right. Reagan adroitly sidestepped the dangers and used JFK to his political advantage by claiming to agree with his policies. He asserted that Kennedy would not have recognized his own Democratic Party in the late 1960s and beyond. Praising Kennedy paradoxically gave Reagan a crucial political opportunity, allowing him to intensify his critique of the "bad sixties" by contrasting it with the Kennedy years. In attacking the Great Society, he could assert that Democrats had abandoned Kennedy's wise policies after his death.

Reagan used the 1960s as a political weapon against his own opponents in the 1980s with considerable success and even a certain subtlety. While the themes of renewing America and recalling the Kennedy years dominated Reagan's first term, in his second term he focused his attack on Johnson's Great Society and the "bad sixties."

Nostalgia for the "Good Sixties": Reagan on JFK

Reagan's most extensive and personal remarks on Kennedy were delivered at a 1985 fund-raising reception for the John F. Kennedy Library at Senator Ted Kennedy's Virginia home. "Typically generous of Reagan to show up at the competition's blood drive," wrote Peggy Noonan in her memoir. She recalled that Reagan "waved his speech cards at Pat Buchanan as he left [for the event] that night. 'I bet you love my speech, Pat!' he said, and laughed as he bounded out of the West Wing."[2]

Reagan began his remarks by stating that ever since a recent visit to the White House by the late president's children, "I've found myself thinking . . . about the man himself and what his life meant to our country and our times." Speaking of Kennedy's world vision, Reagan implied a bond between them. Both were wary of the Soviets. Kennedy "loved mankind as it was, in spite of itself," he said, "had little patience with those who would perfect what was not really meant to be perfect," and had "a good, hard, unillusioned understanding of man and his political choices." Kennedy realized that the United States had "real adversaries" who could not be managed "by soft reason and good intentions. He tried always to be strong with them and shrewd. He wanted our defense system to be unsurpassed."[3]

Reagan claimed that the members of his administration shared his admiration for Kennedy: "It is a matter of pride to me that so many men and women who were inspired by his bracing vision and moved by his call to 'ask not,' serve now in the White House."[4] (Indeed, crucial members of Reagan's inner circle remembered Kennedy fondly. "We were in love with the Kennedys," recalled Noonan. "They were smart and glamorous with their tuxedos and silk dresses, and they always said the right thing and had a wonderful humor." In the 1960s she had a pair of goldfish named Jack and Jackie and kept a photo of Robert Kennedy on her wall.)[5]

"Which is not to say I supported John Kennedy when he ran for president; I didn't," Reagan continued. "I was for the other fellow. But you know, it's true, when the battle's over and the ground is cooled, well, it's then that you see the opposing general's valor." Noting that Kennedy's image adorned the walls of homes worldwide, he remarked: "When they honored John Kennedy, they honored the nation whose virtues, genius, and contradictions he so fully reflected. Many men are great, but few capture the imagination and the spirit of the times. The ones who do are unforgettable. A life given in service to one's country is a living thing that never dies. . . . [H]istory is, as young John Kennedy demonstrated, as heroic as you want it to be, as heroic as you are."[6]

The next day Reagan recalled that after the speech Jacqueline Kennedy Onassis had told him, "just glowing, 'Mr. President, nobody ever captured him like that. That was Jack.'" Ted Kennedy later wrote to Reagan: "I only wish Jack could have been there too last night. Your presence itself was such a magnificent tribute to my brother."[7] According to Peter Robinson, Ted Kennedy was so moved "that he gave Reagan . . . a paperweight. . . that had been on John Kennedy's desk in the Oval Office, and said, 'I think my brother would want that back on your desk.'"[8]

Before 1981 Reagan's favorite Democrat was Franklin Roosevelt. He spoke often of his admiration for FDR, quoting him in his 1964 address in support of Goldwater, and in his 1980 Republican National Convention speech. But once elected president he quoted Kennedy more than any other predecessor—almost twice as often as he cited Roosevelt and more than any other president had since Johnson.[9] This was ironic, as Reagan had openly supported Nixon in 1960 and Goldwater in 1964. Furthermore, Reagan's memoir makes no mention of Kennedy's assassination, and reflections on the Kennedy family's government service in the 1960s are also nearly entirely absent. (Robert Kennedy is mentioned only once in passing.) As Mark Shields sardonically noted, "Kennedy was attacked by no greater authority than Ronald Reagan as being an ornery Leftist in 1960, as I recall, in his letter to Richard Nixon."[10]

Many of the pillars of the conservative movement that Reagan spearheaded disdain Kennedy. "Tell me what JFK's legacy is," demanded Brent Bozell. "Substance? Camelot? What the hell does Camelot mean? . . . [I]f Jack Kennedy hadn't been assassinated, he would have a legacy like Jimmy Carter's: nothing."[11] Curt Smith called Kennedy "unbelievably shallow and superficial." Kennedy's accomplishments as president "are almost none. . . . Camelot has nothing to do with substance, nothing to do with character."[12] Yet many others on the Right claimed that Reagan's extensive use of Kennedy was completely justifiable. "Reagan very much admired some of Kennedy's policies," claimed the Heritage Foundation's Edwin Feulner. Though Kennedy was a few years younger, "they were more or less contemporaries—if Kennedy had lived he'd be [nearly] as old as Reagan today. Both were World War II [generation], both came of age in the late forties: Reagan was [in the] Screen Actors Guild, Kennedy going into the Senate."[13] Frank Fahrenkopf, chairman of the Republican National Committee (RNC) in the 1980s, also saw similarities between Reagan and Kennedy and had personally often heard Reagan praise Kennedy.[14] To Michael Deaver, "Kennedy was much more a Republican than he was a Democrat."[15] Adam Walinsky, a chief aide to Robert Kennedy, considered Reagan's program "an almost exact duplicate of John Kennedy's platform of 1960."[16]

Most liberals, however, failed to see any ideological similarities between the two. Unlike Reagan, "Kennedy believed in the government," explained Arthur Schlesinger. "He gave a speech at the T.V.A. where he outlined his philosophy of government, and he did not believe government was the problem. He was not a 'Reagan Democrat.'"[17] Mark Shields noted that while "Kennedy was not the most liberal candidate in 1960 by far," he did believe that "an energetic government was an instrument of social justice that could bring about positive change and had a responsibility to those less fortunate [that required] intervening in the market."[18] Asked if Kennedy would have considered himself a liberal, the late Archibald Cox, JFK's solicitor general, thought "he would, yes. He wouldn't perhaps be quite so categorical. A clever politician like he was doesn't adopt any label. But he was on the whole on the liberal side."[19] Indeed, Kennedy proposed a myriad of liberal policies as president: he began the Peace Corps, wanted government to play a larger role in solving domestic problems, and—though he came late to the issue—spoke out in favor of civil rights more than any other president since the Civil War. He also inspired an entire generation of future liberal politicians, and he became more liberal as his presidency evolved. Both his brothers moved leftward as the 1960s progressed.

Democrats argued that Reagan's use of Kennedy was a political strategy designed to take possession of a powerful icon of the opposition. "Conservatives, the smarter ones, try to co-opt 'the good sixties' and make it theirs," noted David Kusnet. "They tried to co-opt John Kennedy."[20]

Indeed, Reagan's use of Kennedy successfully exploited the public's continued admiration for him. In 1983, 30 percent of Americans said they wished Kennedy were president, and in 1985 "Kennedy was rated best among the preceding nine presidents in areas concerning confidence, personality, trust, ability to get things done, domestic affairs, and the setting of high moral standards."[21] Kennedy's 70 percent average approval rating remains the highest of any president.[22] He has the highest retrospective job approval rating, 83 percent.[23] And his ratings have only improved over time.[24]

Mentioning Kennedy was therefore politically advantageous to Reagan. "Since 1963 you get the shadow of JFK: JFK becomes the model for how to conduct the presidency," argued Kennedy biographer Herbert Parmet. "It has passed into mythology. . . . He's emblematic of an American aspiration for greatness."[25] Bruce Schulman observed, "Nobody wants to mess with the Kennedy myth, and everybody wants to try to appropriate it."[26]

Reagan's invocation of Kennedy's legacy was frequent but not random. In the context of domestic affairs he often mentioned Kennedy to promote his plan to cut taxes. Reagan was "proud of quoting Kennedy on the tax cut issue," said Frank Fahrenkopf. "He'd constantly point out that it was John F. Kennedy who says you bring back the economy by cutting taxes, not raising them."[27] Historians challenged this view. Rick Perlstein pointed out that it was Lyndon Johnson—not Kennedy—who actually passed the early 1960s tax cuts. But "no one calls it the Johnson tax cut. It was one more of those things that Kennedy got credit for. At least Johnson got credit for the Civil Rights Act."[28] Schulman echoed this analysis, arguing that Kennedy's tax proposal "wasn't the 'reduce the size of government, de-fund the government' . . . supply-side conservative style of tax cut."[29]

There were indeed significant differences between Reagan's and Kennedy's tax cuts. When Kennedy proposed to cut marginal rates from 91 to 70 percent, most business leaders were opposed. According to a 1962 poll of thirty thousand business leaders, almost 90 percent thought that Kennedy was an enemy of business. Furthermore, Kennedy's goal was a Keynesian demand-side cut: he wanted to create a deficit in order to assist the economy by putting money in the hands of middle- and working-class consumers. Reagan's tax policy, a supply-side cut, aimed to raise revenue and reduce the deficit; he wanted to put more money in the hands of business leaders and the rich in order to spur investment. Finally, Kennedy's ultimate plan was to use government spending to increase purchasing power, the opposite of what Reagan wanted. As Kennedy told his economic adviser, "First we'll get your tax cut, and then we'll get my expenditure program."[30]

Yet many conservatives were quick to identify connections between Reagan and Kennedy. "The idea that you can improve the economy dramatically and also increase tax revenues by cutting top marginal tax rates is a conservative idea," said Morton Blackwell, who served in Reagan's White House.[31] In the words of Stephen Moore, Kennedy campaigned in 1960 as an "anticommunist tax cutter."[32] As Ed Meese recalled, "Reagan admired what Kennedy did on cutting taxes."[33] To Paul Weyrich, Kennedy "was a supply-sider."[34]

Reagan first linked Kennedy to his own desire to enact tax cuts, proposed early in 1981, in September of that year. Asking rhetorically if tax cuts could lower inflation, Reagan quoted Kennedy from 1962, when he proposed broad tax cuts and stated that "restrictive tax rates" harmed the economy. Kennedy was correct, Reagan said, for "the last tax cut, literally, that we've had, actually produced more revenue for government."[35]

Quoting Kennedy became an essential component of Reagan's efforts to sell his tax cuts. Later in 1981 he declared that lowering taxes would boost living standards, claiming, "John Kennedy knew this twenty years ago when he proposed a tax cut based on the same principle."[36] In December, Reagan proclaimed that at the time of Kennedy's cuts "economists by and large opposed him," though the government reaped enormous revenue in their wake.[37] Reagan believed that JFK's tax cuts were responsible for the economic growth of the 1960s. He spoke of "the record of strong, sustained expansion sparked by the Kennedy tax cuts,"[38] and recalled that the nation's highest marginal tax rate had been reduced "when a young man named John Kennedy decided some time back that while it's all right for the federal government to be your partner, it's not quite fair that he be your boss."[39] According to speechwriter Anthony Dolan, Reagan "noted often that it was Kennedy who first came up with" the idea of using tax cuts to improve the economy.[40] In his first term at least, Reagan quoted Kennedy extensively to support his proposals.[41]

Reagan was especially fond of one Kennedy phrase. In 1981, claiming that his economic plan would benefit the nation as a whole, he added, "There's truth to the words spoken by John F. Kennedy that a rising tide lifts all boats."[42] Many conservatives believed that Kennedy's tax cuts had reduced poverty and unemployment in the 1960s, and used the "rising tide" phrase as evidence. The cuts "were pretty important," stated Stephen Moore. "We did see a very robust [economic] expansion, and I believe that a rising tide does lift all boats—that was exactly Kennedy's line. And he said if you want to reduce poverty, we have to put in place policies that make everyone better off." According to Moore, the Kennedy tax cuts "were a very strong antipoverty program."[43]

It is impossible to say what Kennedy would have thought about Reagan's brand of supply-side economics, his desire to reduce social welfare programs, or his aggressive quoting of Kennedy in defense of his economic agenda. Nevertheless, the success of Reagan's use of Kennedy to promote a conservative economic agenda only encouraged him to extend the strategy to the international arena.

Reagan regularly invoked his conception of the "good sixties" to support his foreign policy goals. He claimed that here too he was Kennedy's heir, in that they both believed in a strong national defense and in resisting communism. Conservatives echoed this sentiment. To Peter Collier, "there's not a hell of a lot of daylight between Ronald Reagan and John Kennedy in terms of their foreign policy."[44] Thomas Reed recalled that "Kennedy was a real Cold Warrior,"[45] and Paul Weyrich called Kennedy "a rabid anticommunist."[46] David Horowitz also insisted that Reagan was Kennedy's heir. "Half [Kennedy's] cabinet—and the most important half—were Republicans, hawks on defense, militant anticommunists. . . . Kennedy had the biggest peacetime military buildup in history." For Horowitz, "Kennedy was a Reagan Democrat. His politics were identical to Ronald Reagan's. There's no difference politically between Kennedy and Ronald Reagan. *None.*"[47]

On Veterans Day in 1982 Reagan quoted Kennedy extensively concerning the need for a strong defense. When World War II was fully raging, Reagan said, and the United States was slow to act, "warning us of the impending crisis, a young Harvard student, John Fitzgerald Kennedy, wrote a book titled *Why England Slept*. His thoughtful study holds as true now, forty-two years later." Reagan went on to quote at length from Kennedy's book, urging the need for an aggressive military buildup.[48]

A few weeks later, in a national address on the anniversary of Kennedy's death, Reagan claimed that in 1962 almost half the federal budget went to defense, but the figures had since fallen to only about 25 percent, while the amount for social programs had nearly doubled. As a result, he asserted, the Soviets had gained "a decided advantage" militarily.[49] Reagan later referred in his 1990 memoir to the Kennedy era as a military golden age, for "in the early 1960s, it had been relatively easy to stand up to the Soviets," whereas now the Soviets were "building missiles hand over fist."[50] Reagan spoke often of "John Kennedy's warning that only when our arms are certain beyond doubt can we be certain beyond doubt they will never be used."[51] He frequently charged that the policies of the later 1960s, by contrast, had damaged U.S. defense capabilities. Johnson's budget priorities—"social programs that mushroomed during the Great Society"—he claimed, had made the country vulnerable to attack.[52]

Reagan was similarly fond of emphasizing the way he, like Kennedy, stood up to communism. "We're in the midst of what President John F. Kennedy called 'a long twilight struggle' to defend freedom in the world," declared Reagan in a 1984 national address on Central America. Kennedy "understood . . . the long-term goals of the Soviet Union in this region," and when he spoke out against "the threat of communist penetration in our hemisphere," Congress "overwhelmingly" supported him. "Were John Kennedy alive today, I think he would be appalled by the gullibility of some who invoke his name," said Reagan.[53]

He mentioned Kennedy most frequently by far during the election year 1984—more than twice as often as in 1981 or 1983.[54] Reagan asserted throughout the campaign that the Democrats had changed drastically after 1963 and had become soft on defense since Kennedy's time. At the 1984 Republican National Convention, Senator Paul Laxalt of Nevada alluded to Kennedy several times in his speech nominating Reagan. He spoke of "another great political party . . . of Roosevelt, Truman, and Kennedy. (You remember Jack Kennedy—he cut taxes and called Communism 'an evil system.')" But, said Laxalt, "creeping McGovernism is now McGovernism triumphant. The Democratic Party has become the party of the Left."[55] Laxalt also pointed to 1972 candidate George McGovern to associate the Democrats with the excesses of "the sixties."[56] In his own remarks at the convention Reagan too invoked Kennedy to paint present-day Democrats as weak on defense. Charging that Democrats had "likened" the 1983 Grenada invasion "to the Soviet invasion of Afghanistan, the crushing of human rights in Poland or the genocide in Cambodia," he asked, "Could you imagine Harry Truman, John Kennedy, Hubert Humphrey, or Scoop Jackson making such a shocking comparison?"[57]

Reagan continued to refer to Kennedy throughout the 1984 campaign. "To all those Democrats who have been loyal to the party of FDR, Harry Truman, and JFK," he said on one occasion, "but who believe [Democrats] no longer stand firmly for America's responsibilities in the world, that they no longer protect the working people of this country—we say to them, 'You are not abandoned, our arms are open, join us.'"[58] He often reiterated his wish to reach out to "patriotic Democrats . . . who believed in freedom."[59]

Reagan's most dramatic reference to Kennedy came at a Waterbury, Connecticut, rally. Two nights before the 1960 election, forty thousand people had waited in front of a local hotel to hear Kennedy. The fact that

Reagan was not present in 1960 did not stop him from describing the scene that evening:

> John Kennedy stood there in the darkness. It was almost 3 o'clock in the morning. His campaign was near ending, and he was exhausted. But the night was bright with lights, and they lit the faces of the tens of thousands of people below who had showed up to cheer John Kennedy on. And he looked down at them. He smiled in the glow, and even though it was the fall, it seemed like springtime, those days. I see our country today, and I think it is springtime for America once again—so many new beginnings. And I think John Kennedy would be proud of you.[60]

The next day, mocking Democrats who invoked Truman, Reagan declared, "Truman believed—with FDR before him and John Kennedy after him—in strength abroad and self-reliance at home," as he urged Democrats once again to switch parties.[61] Six days later Reagan invoked the same trio of Democrats, claiming that he spoke to those "who cherish the memories of FDR and Harry Truman and John Kennedy" and who realized that Democrats of the 1980s were "abandoning the decent, patriotic Democrats of the JFK and FDR and Harry Truman tradition."[62] That same day at another rally he quoted Kennedy in claiming that "the primary purpose of our arms is peace, not war. Our preparation against danger is our hope of safety." This was a quotation Reagan repeated throughout the campaign.[63] He urged those "who knew the party of FDR and Harry Truman and JFK" to "walk with us."[64] Reagan declared that whenever he spoke of Kennedy, "my opponents start tearing their hair out. They just can't stand it."[65]

Realizing that Reagan's use of Kennedy was working, Democrats made an aggressive—and much too tardy—attempt to recapture Kennedy for themselves. Early in the first presidential debate with Democratic nominee Walter Mondale, Reagan spoke of how the Democrats had changed in the 1960s. After stating that he had reduced spending and given more power to local and state governments, Reagan noted that those used to be Democratic policies. "I know, because I was a Democrat at that time," he said. Mondale seized on this remark to imply that Reagan was hostile to Kennedy. "The year that [Reagan] decided we had lost our way was the year that John F. Kennedy was running against Richard Nixon," Mondale said. "I was chairman of Minnesotans for Kennedy; President Reagan was chairman of a thing called Democrats for Nixon. Now, maybe we made a wrong turn with Kennedy, but I'll be proud of supporting him all of my life. And I'm very happy that John Kennedy was elected." In response Reagan defensively stated that his switch predated 1960, that he had voted for Eisenhower in 1956 before campaigning for Nixon four years later.

"I hadn't gotten around to reregistering as yet. . . . But I finally did it." Reagan did not mention Kennedy in the debate, but Mondale made sure to emphasize JFK, directly quoting him, with attribution, in his closing remarks.[66]

Reagan continued to argue during the campaign that the Democratic Party had changed since the early 1960s.[67] His speechwriters were committed to dividing the Democrats into pre- and post-Kennedy factions; in the margin of a speech draft one of them wrote: "need to distinguish between two types of Demos."[68] In the campaign's closing days Reagan spoke of Kennedy more than ever. In Boston, Kennedy's hometown, he told a few hecklers "to have the respect to listen to the words that I'm going to say in quoting John F. Kennedy."[69]

As he cheerfully noted, Reagan's rhetoric did anger many Democrats. On October 31 more than one hundred representatives of various academic and professional institutions, including five Nobel Prize winners, ran a quarter-page ad in the *New York Times* headed "Would FDR, Truman, and JFK Vote for Reagan?" These Mondale supporters called Reagan's assertions that he shared positions with previous Democratic presidents "a flagrant distortion of reality to serve his own political purpose," and declared that Mondale was "the true heir to Roosevelt, Kennedy and Truman."[70]

Still, there was no denying the effectiveness of Reagan's tactics. "I ran for the Democratic chairmanship after the '84 election in large part out of anger that Reagan so successfully stole the Democratic heroes," Paul Kirk explained. As Reagan constantly referred to FDR, Truman, Scoop Jackson, JFK, and Hubert Humphrey, Kirk asked himself, "'Wait a second. What party am I in?' This was campaign highway robbery out in the open, and we didn't defend it."[71]

Conservatives, by contrast, found Reagan's use of Kennedy completely appropriate. "I wish [Democrats] would remember Kennedy more," said former RNC communications director Clifford May. "Many Democrats do not represent . . . the belief in human rights and liberty that President Kennedy had."[72] Elaine Donnelly recalled, "Our family used to be Democrats, until the post-Kennedy sixties drove that party hard to the left."[73]

Attacking the "Bad Sixties": Reagan and the Great Society

If Reagan fondly recalled the early 1960s of JFK as a time of tax cuts, strong anticommunism, and military strength, he had nothing but contempt for the post-Kennedy 1960s. Criticizing Lyndon Johnson's "bad sixties" became one of Reagan's major rhetorical strategies as president.

In the first debate of his 1984 reelection campaign, one questioner, after remarking that the War on Poverty did not eliminate poverty "although it may have dented it," asked Walter Mondale what role government should play to help the nation's 35 million poor. Mondale pointed out that poverty had greatly increased under Reagan and that cuts in government aid had harmed the poor. When asked if Americans "have lost interest in the kinds of programs you're discussing to help those less privileged," Mondale said that while he supported civil rights and educational training, he desired "a balanced program that gives us long-term growth so that [the government is] not having to take money [from taxpayers] . . . and give it to someone else."[74] In these remarks and throughout his campaign, Mondale did not call for any programs remotely resembling the War on Poverty, the Great Society, or any other reminder of the "bad" 1960s. By this point Democrats were reacting defensively to Reagan's relentless attacks on "the sixties." Reagan's professed love for the Kennedy era was surpassed in intensity only by the vitriol he directed at the Johnson years.

Hostility to the Great Society was in fact the kernel of the modern conservative movement. "The Great Society spawned a lot of what turned out to be ineffective social programs," Ed Meese stressed. "I don't know of anybody who really thinks they were effective." Meese proceeded to conflate the predominantly middle-class hippies of the era with the disadvantaged who received government assistance in the 1960s. "The Great Society was an assault with federal tax money on local institutions," he said, "and it funded a counterculture to fight against citizens and taxpayers and the law-abiding citizenry during the sixties."[75] Eugene Meyer charged that the Great Society "subsidized illegitimacy and not working," thereby increasing both.[76] Morton Blackwell railed against the "incredible increase in the cost, functions, and intrusiveness of government."[77] In Richard Viguerie's opinion the Great Society "made people dependent on government."[78]

Reagan's criticisms of the Great Society covered a wide range of social, economic, and political issues. He considered it a dramatic departure from the goals of the New Deal, which he had supported. "The press is trying to paint me now trying to undo the New Deal," Reagan wrote in his diary in early 1982. "I remind them I voted for FDR four times. I'm trying to undo the 'Great Society.' It was LBJ's War on Poverty that led us to our present mess."[79]

Government expansion, he said in 1983, had undermined the cohesiveness of the family. In Reagan's view the "Great Society–type programs contributed to family breakups, welfare dependency, and a large increase in births out of wedlock," and the steep post-1960s rise in single-parent families in turn caused a myriad of social problems.[80] Welfare had thus destroyed "the very support system the poor need most to lift themselves up and out of destitution—the family."[81] Poverty programs, he declared, must "sustain and not disrupt families, because intact, self-reliant families are the best antipoverty insurance ever devised."[82]

"Without question," said Michael Deaver, Reagan was already convinced in the 1960s that the Great Society would be destructive to poor families and would create dependency. "Reagan thought that most of the federal government programs were disastrous," Deaver recalled. "His second term [as governor] in California was dedicated to welfare reform. . . . The Clinton welfare reforms were basically the programs that Reagan had suggested." To Deaver, the view that the Great Society had damaged family life "was the basis of most of Reagan's speaking" during the 1960s. His theme was consistent: government programs "took away our individual liberties and promoted dependence."[83]

Reagan found the "bad sixties" a convenient scapegoat for budget problems as well. By 1985 the federal deficit had become a political liability for Reagan. His tax cuts and defense spending increases contributed to rising deficits each year of his presidency. The national debt tripled under Reagan from $914 billion in 1980 to $2.7 trillion in 1989.[84] He nevertheless contended that it was the Great Society that had caused the deficit. "In the years following '65, when the Great Society got underway," he said in 1984, "the deficit increased thirty-eight times."[85] Reagan insisted that he had previously warned about deficits, but "along came the War on Poverty back in the middle sixties," and as a result "the deficit increased to fifty-eight times what it had been in 1965."[86]

The more often Reagan told this story, the greater the deficits became. In 1984 he claimed that the Great Society had caused the deficit to increase by 1980 to thirty-eight times what it had been in 1965. In 1985 the figure changed to fifty times. In January 1988, it was back to thirty-eight times, but by August it was fifty-two times, and by October it was fifty-eight times, a figure he repeated after the election of George H. W. Bush in November. In his 1990 memoir it was fifty-three times.[87] Reagan's rhetoric regarding the federal deficit demonstrates the degree of flexibility "the sixties" had acquired by his second term: Johnson's programs could now be used to explain away almost any problem.

Indeed, Reagan discovered as early as 1964 that preaching against the Great Society and the 1960s was far more politically beneficial than criticizing the New Deal. "The Right hangs 'welfare queens'—Reagan's memorable phrase—around Johnson's neck before they'd hang it around

Roosevelt's neck," noted Jeff Shesol.[88] For a variety of reasons, including the different constituencies they aided, Roosevelt and his policies remained enormously popular in ways that Johnson and his programs did not. Reagan understood this and capitalized on it. He argued that Johnson had strayed from the Roosevelt tradition, conveniently ignoring the fact that FDR was LBJ's hero and the model for his Great Society.

A variety of conservative legal scholars and think tank members echoed Reagan in sharply differentiating the New Deal from the Great Society. "Roosevelt always said the New Deal was temporary," said Ed Meese. "The so-called Great Society, by comparison, attempted to realign the political framework of the country. . . . It was a recipe for disaster. It destroyed the ability of the citizens themselves to run their own government."[89] To Robert Bork "the New Deal emphasized economic equality," but with the Great Society "the emphasis begins to shift from economic to social goals. And that's what we have now."[90] According to Brent Bozell, Johnson's programs, unlike FDR's, were "long term and open-ended. And that's the problem. . . . It's like *Night of the Living Dead* around here." Johnson's programs "didn't die; they just continued."[91]

"I was a New Deal Democrat," Reagan often claimed. But "during the sixties and seventies, the Great Society and other federal programs led to massive increases in social spending," he said in 1984. Problems arose because of "the firm difference between the New Deal and the Great Society." The former "gave cash to the poor, but the Great Society failed to target assistance to the truly needy [and instead] fostered dependence on government" and created huge bureaucracies that made it almost "impossible" to deliver needed funds to the poor.[92]

Others on the Right also strongly differentiated between the programs of FDR and LBJ. "The New Deal did not corrupt the character of the people," Phyllis Schlafly stated (though of course this was precisely what the GOP charged throughout the 1930s and well beyond). "But because of the Great Society, shame went out of our system. It's not shameful to have an illegitimate baby . . . to be dependent on the government . . . to have a divorce . . . to have an abortion. Poverty doesn't cause these problems," Schlafly said. "That happened because of these entitlements of Lyndon Johnson and the sixties."[93] (Schlafly also failed to mention that Reagan was our nation's first divorced president and that Ronald and Nancy Reagan's first child, Patti, was born seven and a half months after their 1952 wedding.) Reagan, too, constantly insisted that the Great Society weakened the moral fiber of the populace. In one of his last presidential speeches he said that because of the War on Poverty, poor people "became dependent on government payments and lost the moral strength that has always given the poor the determination to climb America's ladder of opportunity."[94]

For their part, Reagan's speechwriters diligently emphasized the message that the New Deal differed from the Great Society. Reagan "always made a strict delineation between the New Deal and the Great Society, and it was an accurate one," claimed Reagan speechwriter Aram Bakshian. "Reagan, who actually lived through the New Deal," saw FDR's programs as "emergency measures during an actual emergency—not a conversion into an ever-expanding welfare state, come rain or come shine. So he never turned on the New Deal," Bakshian stated. "The Great Society he saw as an effort—partially idealistic, partially cynical—to create a welfare state where the government was not only confiscating more wealth but also misspending it" on programs that encouraged "behavior that is damaging" to poor families and to society.[95] "Reagan had no intention of attacking the New Deal," according to Peter Robinson, "certainly not the notion that the government had accepted responsibility for the regulation of the economy. The Great Society, on the other hand, had enormous expansion of the government's role as its arm of redistribution. And Reagan did want to take that on."[96]

But Reagan did occasionally attack Roosevelt's program. In 1986 he spoke of "the long, liberal experiment that began in the 1930's, the New Deal, the Great Society, the so-called War on Poverty—which we lost." Reagan saw himself as battling nearly half a century of government expansion, a crusade he was willing to take on because, as he said, "I remember the government of the New Deal, but I remember an earlier America as well, an America in which the essentially private values of the individual, the family, and the community commanded the day."[97] Such pre–New Deal nostalgia calls into question the distinction conservatives drew between the programs of LBJ and FDR, for it envisions the Great Society as merely an extension of principles first set forth by the New Deal in contrast to those of an earlier, idyllic America.

Reagan believed not merely that Johnson's programs had destroyed the family and increased the deficit but that they were *designed* to keep people poor. In 1982 he responded to critics who charged that his budget cuts, in his words, "picked on the helpless, the needy, the poor." Such claims were false, he said, for he was in fact attacking the root of the problem. "The War on Poverty created a great new upper-middle class of bureaucrats," who purposely tried to "keep enough needy people there to justify their existence."[98] Reagan was convinced that his policies assisted the impoverished more than those of the 1960s. He claimed that Senator Daniel Patrick Moynihan had told him that his Fair Share tax plan would "do more for the poor than Lyndon Johnson ever did during the years of the Great Society."[99]

One of Reagan's most far-reaching accusations about the Great Society increasing poverty occurred at a 1983 dinner. "Government has intervened in areas where it is neither competent nor needed nor wanted," he said. Citing the scholar Charles Murray, Reagan charged that "the Great Society coincided with an end to economic progress for America's poor." Between 1949 and 1964, "just before the Great Society got underway," the poverty rate fell from nearly 33 percent to 18 percent. "But by 1980, with the full impact of the Great Society's programs being felt, . . . there was an even higher proportion of people living in poverty than in 1969." The economic expansion before the Great Society helped the poor, said Reagan, whereas Johnson's programs thwarted such growth.[100]

But Reagan's allusion to Murray was problematic. Murray's work "didn't factor in the recession of the early [to mid-] seventies," noted historian Michael Kazin. "His data go from the early sixties into the mid-seventies, and he didn't break down from the early sixties to the late sixties, when the figures would have looked different."[101]

Furthermore, Reagan never explained how there could have been sustained economic expansion *after* the 1964 tax cut but *before* the Great Society. He consistently claimed that "Kennedy's" tax cuts were followed by an economic boom. Yet he also routinely asserted that the Great Society caused economic damage. Distinguishing between "the sixties" and the pre-1963 Kennedy era was a rhetorical device, not a historical one. Reagan asserted, for example, that "back in the sixties, the early sixties[,] we had fewer people living below the poverty line than we had in the later sixties after the great War on Poverty got underway," after which, he said, there was a "steady increase" in poverty.[102] Conservative solutions to poverty, Reagan believed, were more effective than "the so-called social programs that have been a part of the Great Society."[103] The inflation caused by excessive government spending "threw millions of people into poverty . . . for a program the government called the War on Poverty," but as a result of his own tax cuts, he claimed, "poverty dropped faster and farther than it had in over 10 years."[104] Reagan continued until the end of his presidency to claim that the Great Society had increased poverty.[105]

How convinced were Reagan's speechwriters of their assertions that the Great Society increased poverty? A draft of his February 7, 1987, radio address on welfare included a note that read, "Poverty rate fell sharply through 1969 (+ fell until 1973)." The draft read: "Then in the 1960s, in spite of billions spent on programs like the so-called 'War on Poverty,' poverty, as measured by dependency, stopped shrinking and actually began to grow worse. I guess you could say that poverty actually won the war." In the draft "1960s" has been crossed out and replaced with "1970s."[106] Reagan's speechwriters were apparently reluctant to state categorically that poverty worsened during the 1960s, when the Great Society programs were under way. Instead this speech and others like it argued that 1960s programs *led to* economic problems in the 1970s. Reagan was thus able to blame "the sixties" without having to cite definitive economic data from the decade.

"The 1960s" may have been changed to "the 1970s" because one or more of Reagan's speechwriters knew that the facts did not support the president's assertion that poverty increased in the 1960s. Around the time of the February 1987 address, while preparing for a welfare reform briefing, Reagan's speechwriters consulted a table of figures from the Bureau of the Census on poverty rates in the 1960s. The table plainly showed that poverty did not increase as a result of the Great Society and did not decrease under Reagan in the 1980s, as he had been claiming for years. Under the heading "Persons below Poverty Level," the numbers showed that the poverty rate fell between 1960 and 1970 from 22.2 percent to 12.1 percent, and dropped further to 11.7 percent by 1979. By 1985, however, it had risen again to 14 percent.[107] In their eagerness to blame the 1960s, Reagan's speechwriters knowingly misstated the facts.[108]

Arthur Schlesinger asserted: "The Great Society reduced poverty, according to government statistics. It was the worst thing in the world for the very rich. It had an enormous benefit for the American people."[109] Johnson attorney general and undersecretary of state Nicholas Katzenbach also vigorously challenged Reagan's assertions. "I don't think the Great Society programs increased poverty [or] increased anybody's dependence on anybody," he said. "The effort was to free people from the shackles of poverty, to give them an opportunity to get educated."[110] Jeff Shesol, a Johnson biographer, argued that Johnson was always against welfare.[111] The Right, he said, "has worked assiduously to discredit wholesale the Great Society—that it was some utopian statist vision, socialism bordering on totalitarianism. Those of us who actually spent some time reading history, rather than just using it, know that that's just political manipulation of the record. But they've been very effective." Shesol expressed frustration that "Reagan says the line that sums it all up for everybody and it becomes 'the truth': 'We waged War on Poverty, and poverty won.' It's historically false."[112]

Many leading conservative spokesmen and speechwriters, such as Brent Bozell, Stephen Moore, and Clark Judge, continued to support Reagan's claim that Johnson's programs increased poverty.[113] Recent data, however, dispute Reagan's oft-repeated assertions and confirm the accuracy of the table his speechwriters consulted for his 1987 speech on welfare. As the *New York Times* reported in 2005, "poverty levels have changed only modestly in the last three decades, rising in the 1980s and falling in the 1990s, after having dropped sharply in the 1960s. They reached a low of 11.1 percent in 1973, from more than 22 percent in 1960."[114]

Reagan, Race, and the 1960s

Reagan was convinced that the Great Society hurt African Americans. His first attack as president on Johnson's domestic programs came in an address at the 1981 NAACP convention. Blacks' incomes rose in the 1960s, he claimed, but dropped in the 1970s. Reagan argued that this demonstrated the ineffectiveness of federal aid, emphasizing his belief that "a strong economy returns the greatest good to the black population." Reagan again differentiated between the "good" early 1960s and the "bad" late 1960s when he said, "Productivity . . . started downhill after 1965," claiming that these developments especially hurt minorities.[115]

White House documents illuminate the strategy behind the speech. Speechwriter and adviser John McClaughry urged that the speech should "emphasize further that racism rears its ugly head when people are fearful of losing their economic security to blacks, immigrants, etc."[116] McClaughry made sure that Reagan did not promise too much to the African American audience. An earlier draft pledged, "We plan to assemble a comprehensive program for the cities." Concerned with this, McClaughry wrote: "We do????? It's sure not too damn obvious that we do. . . . This paragraph implies $$$$$. And who is this 'we'? Washington? Echhh."[117] An aide made note that Benjamin Hooks, executive director of the NAACP, had said at a March 1980 conference, "The economic decline of the late '70s has all but wiped out the steady economic progress that blacks made in the 1960s."[118] The quote was not used in Reagan's speech, perhaps because it was not essential—or perhaps because Reagan did not wish to acknowledge, after his repeated charges that the 1960s had hurt African Americans, that material progress had in fact been made in that decade.

Reagan even claimed that African Americans were opposed to the War on Poverty. At a 1981 rally he declared that it was a joy to get letters such as one he had recently received from an elderly black woman that read: "'Thanks for destroying the War on Poverty. Maybe now, we at last can get back to growing our own muscles and taking care of ourselves the way we should.'"[119] Some of his most extensive comments on the Great Society came at a 1982 National Black Republican Council dinner, where he again emphasized that Johnson's programs had retarded African American progress. After declaring at the outset that as California governor "I appointed more blacks and other minorities" than all his predecessors combined, Reagan charged that "liberal economic policies" had damaged the economy. Poverty decreased from 1949 to 1964, but then the Great Society undermined "the private enterprise system," and tax-and-spend policies eroded the national character. Because of the Great Society, by 1981 "more people, including more blacks," were poor than in 1969.[120] On a number of other occasions Reagan argued when speaking to African Americans that the Great Society hurt minorities.[121]

Reagan's view that the Great Society was hurtful to African Americans was shared by leading conservative activists. "It was the Lyndon Johnson welfare system that broke up the black family," declared Phyllis Schlafly. "Black families went through the depression of the thirties and stayed intact," but the Great Society "made all the money go through the woman, which made the father irrelevant. And as these guys would say, 'She don't need me; she's got welfare.'"[122] Ed Meese argued that welfare, "which was at crescendo heights during the sixties, was one of the greatest detrimental factors for family life in the United States, particularly in minority communities."[123] According to Morton Blackwell, "many black communities will tell you that welfare was a disaster for blacks and destroyed the family."[124]

Although he habitually criticized the Great Society, Reagan did not feel as free to criticize specifically the struggle for African American freedom and equality. One of his few positive references to the 1960s occurred in 1984, when he was speaking of the civil rights movement. "Prior to the 1960s it was an accepted and sometimes legal practice to discriminate," he observed in something of an understatement, then went on to praise "the historic achievements of great Americans who have managed to overcome such discrimination."[125] Three years later he acknowledged that "in the 1950s and 1960s, great strides were made through political action" as "laws protecting the civil rights of all Americans were put in place, and racism was, in effect, outlawed." This progress he attributed to "the struggle and commitment of generations and the outstanding leadership of individuals like Dr. Martin Luther King," whose movement "enormously strengthened the moral foundation of the United States."[126]

As president, Reagan did not often speak of his feelings on race, but in his memoir he claimed, "I'd grown up in a home where no sin was more grievous than racial bigotry."[127] He also wrote of his irritation with foreign leaders, such as the Soviet Union's Mikhail Gorbachev, who did not appreciate America's progress in overcoming bigotry toward African Americans. "It seemed clear Gorbachev believed propaganda about us that he had probably heard all his life," Reagan lamented. "A lot of the 'facts' he came armed with and cited so authoritatively about America—such as those about the treatment of blacks in the South—were long out of date, and he didn't know, for example, about the vast improvements we'd made in race relations."[128]

Yet King's name does not appear even once in Reagan's memoir. And during Reagan's presidency, many conservatives fiercely opposed the creation of a national holiday for King; Reagan himself at first opposed the idea. When the King Holiday Bill reached Congress in 1983, Republican senator Jesse Helms of North Carolina led attempts to block it.[129] Helms charged that King had had communist associations and sympathies, had gone against the interests of his country when he opposed the Vietnam War, and was not an appropriate "role model" for youth.[130] Democratic senator Daniel Patrick Moynihan of New York "loudly tossed a bound copy of Mr. Helms's charges to the floor and denounced the contents as 'filth' and 'obscenities.'"[131] That same day a judge refused Helms's request to open up King's FBI files, sealed for fifty years by court order in 1977. Helms wanted to see the records—which, as William Safire wrote, included "transcripts of recordings from bugs placed under hotel room beds"—before voting on the bill.[132] The records were sealed to resolve a fight between the FBI and King's family, who believed that the material violated their privacy.[133] On October 19 Helms's motion to send the bill back to committee was defeated, garnering the support of only twelve Republican senators.

After the final bill passed, with only four Democrats and eighteen Republicans voting against it, Helms complained that it was approved "in an atmosphere of intimidation and political harassment. . . . It's a tyranny of the minority." Republican senator Bob Dole, the bill's manager, clearly disagreed. When Coretta Scott King declared, "For those of us who believe in the dream, it is a great day for America and the world," Dole was standing next to her.[134] He remarked: "I'm proud of my party today. We're in the mainstream."[135] Certainly the vote was cast in a tense atmosphere; senators had been deluged with comments opposing the holiday. "If the voting was based on mail and phone calls, I'm not sure there would be any votes for it," recounted Dole.[136] Republican senator Dan Quayle of Indiana, who voted for the bill, said that many of his Senate colleagues were not enthusiastic because they had "real questions about King as an individual."[137]

At a press conference that evening Reagan was asked if he agreed with Helms's remarks. Reagan did not answer directly but said, "We'll know in

about thirty-five years, won't we?" presumably referring to the approxi-
mate time when the FBI files would be opened. "No, I don't fault Senator Helms's sincerity with regard to wanting the records opened up," he
responded to another question. Helms simply felt "we should know everything there is to know about an individual" before naming a holiday
after him. Reagan expressed ambivalence about signing the bill into law.
"I would have preferred a day of recognition for his accomplishments . . .
similar to, say, Lincoln's birthday, which is not technically a national
holiday, but is certainly a day reverenced by a great many people in our
country. . . . [B]ut since they seem bent on making it a national holiday, I
believe the symbolism of that day is important enough that I'll sign that
legislation when it reaches my desk."[138] He signed, and the holiday was
officially recognized in 1986.

Reagan's earlier statement implying that King might have been a communist sympathizer ignited controversy. The next day Walter Mondale,
asked about Helms's statements on King in a public meeting, said they
were false and that "the President ought to be on the phone today and
call Coretta and tell her just that."[139] Mrs. King described Reagan's reluctance to sign the bill as an "insult," adding: "It's hard for me to see that
someone like that really believes in equality. What kind of America does
he want it to be?"[140]

A *New York Times* editorial, describing Reagan's "in about thirty-five
years" remark as "graceless," asked if he really needed that much time "to
decide that Dr. King was a patriot in the best sense of the word? Does he
doubt that Dr. King eloquently expressed his generation's dream for racial
justice and equality and pursued it nonviolently, in the finest American
tradition?"[141] Columnist Anthony Lewis called Reagan's words "a moment of chilling self-revelation." Reagan, he said, failed to mention what
King had achieved, and his "flippant tone" was "grotesquely inappropri-
ate," his comments "utterly insensitive," as was the remark Reagan made
at the time of King's funeral "that his death was 'a great tragedy that began when we began compromising with law and order and people started
choosing which laws they'd break.'"[142]

On October 21, in response to the controversy, Reagan called Coretta
King to apologize for his insinuation that her husband might have had
communist connections. Mrs. King accepted his apology. According to
a White House spokesperson, Reagan called her "to make sure he hadn't
been misunderstood."[143] It remained unclear what exactly Reagan did
mean by his initial comments.

That same day new revelations surfaced regarding Reagan's feelings
about King when Meldrim Thomson Jr., a Republican former governor of

New Hampshire active in the John Birch Society, released a portion of a letter concerning King that Reagan had recently sent him. Thomson had written Reagan to ask that he veto the bill because King was "a man of immoral character" with "well established" ties to communists. Reagan replied that he shared such reservations and argued that the movement to create the King holiday was "based on an image, not reality."[144]

Looking back in 2004, several former aides claimed that Reagan admired King. Peter Robinson, who wrote the speech Reagan delivered when the King holiday was made official in 1986, did not comment on Reagan's reluctance to invoke King. Although, he maintained, Reagan "admired Martin Luther King and civil rights per se, equality of rights under the law," by the 1980s "the civil rights movement had already mutated into an effort to lay claim to the fruits of redistribution. And he didn't like redistribution."[145] Even though Reagan rarely praised King, most conservatives saw the two as philosophical comrades on some level. Regarding his preparation for Reagan's speech recognizing the King holiday Robinson said: "Finding material for the remarks was easy. The dignity of the individual, the equality of all men before God, the promise that America could set an example for the world—I kept finding passage after passage in King's work that Reagan might almost have written himself."[146] To historian and political scientist Kiron Skinner, this showed that Reagan and King "shared an unswerving commitment to democracy, liberty and equality." Reagan signed the King holiday bill because "the values Dr. King championed trumped political differences."[147]

A more nuanced view of Reagan's views on race came from Lou Cannon. "Reagan was really against racism," he stated. "He hated it. Mike Deaver said, 'Reagan never got beyond the Jackie Robinson story.' The Jackie Robinson thing was a big thing to him. He thought it was just wonderful. But Reagan described racial prejudice like it was all in the past," Cannon recounted. "He never got to the next level on that issue. And there was never anybody politically who was trying to get him to the next level on that issue, because Reagan never did well with black voters.[148]

"Now there's another part of the calculus, and it's a complicated one," Cannon continued. "Speaking for Goldwater in 1964 was when Reagan became known to most people, and Goldwater wasn't racist either, but Goldwater was following the Southern Strategy [and] was perceived as such," Cannon said. "Reagan did appoint the first black to a [state] cabinet post in California . . . but it never registered with people. It's striking because he always ran above his poll numbers with almost every other ethnic group, but he was always a tick or two below among African Americans, and I think it goes back to Goldwater."[149]

But for many Democrats, the Right's post-1960s rise cynically exploited white hostility to African Americans. "You've got [the issue of] race coming in almost every election [since the 1960s], but never publicly so," said Nicholas Katzenbach. "That's certainly a reflection on the sixties. . . . George Wallace taught [Republicans] how to [use race] in '68. Wallace was racist, but Wallace then knew that he couldn't run for president on a racist ticket, so he found a way to be racist without saying so. And that's been copied by Republicans ever since."[150]

Great Society bashing arises "from a lot of ignorance," said Bill Bradley. "There was a decrease in poverty and an increase in health care [under the Great Society]. . . . It took a lot of courage from Lyndon Johnson to make it happen," recalled Bradley. "I don't think that the Civil Rights Act of 1964 that allowed blacks to drink at the same water fountain as whites and not be discriminated against in hotels and restaurants is a bad thing. That's what [conservatives are] talking about—that's the code." Reagan's opposition to the Great Society—and thus the political agenda of the United States in the mid-1960s—was not based on the era's fiscal and defense policies, as "defense spending was pretty high during the Great Society. One of the biggest tax cuts in history was offered in the Kennedy administration." To Bradley, the central issue for the Right was that under Kennedy and Johnson "there were significant strides in racial equality."[151]

Historians also tend to interpret Reagan's criticisms of the Great Society as evidence of animosity toward African Americans. "The New Deal was designed and perceived as benefiting the middle class," explained Maurice Isserman. "The Great Society was perceived as something that was designed for and worked for the benefit of minorities, the poor, and other despised marginal groups. And that's, of course, part of the mythology, because actually the most expensive component of the Great Society and the social welfare spending in the 1960s was the introduction of Medicare, universal benefits," he noted. "But it was all those 'ungrateful blacks' who responded to the 'generosity' of middle-class taxpayers by rioting in Watts, and Newark, and Detroit, and hence sealing the historical reputation of the Great Society as a wasteful expenditure."[152] According to Isserman's co-author, Michael Kazin, "the political rhetoric [of the Right] was that Democrats, liberals, were taking money away from the middle class and giving it to the undeserving poor, and a lot of those undeserving poor were seen as black welfare mothers."[153]

Racial unrest in the 1960s unquestionably hurt liberalism. "The benefits of the New Deal were intended, and turned out to be, very broadly based in the society," said Al From, founder of the centrist Democratic

Leadership Council. "The Great Society was much more [narrowly] targeted, and that of course means that some people aren't going to be as supportive. But there was a great consensus in this country for civil rights legislation, for voting rights legislation." While in some regions "race caused a lot of problems, and there was resentment, civil rights legislation per se was probably pretty popular in this country. But when the Great Society became much less popular was through the riots," From noted. "The riots after the King assassination polarized the country more on race than any of the Great Society programs."[154] David Broder agreed: "Urban riots became the single most destructive symbol of the fruits of liberalism in the '68 campaign and thereafter, and that obviously had a strong racial component to it."[155]

Clinton adviser Harold Ickes noted that "Democrats were on the right side of the race issue—although they came to it somewhat slowly and haltingly—but Republicans have used it for decades to help define the Democrats for their own electoral purposes." He explained: "On the issue of segregation and integration, the national Republican leadership decided in the 1950s and into the sixties that they were going to use race to try to take away the white South from the Democrats, and they were successful in that." He didn't think that the Democrats should have done anything differently though. "They did the honorable thing, the moral thing, that made the country a stronger country by siding with the forces of integration."[156]

Former members of the Johnson administration emphasized that LBJ enacted civil rights legislation although he knew that doing so would damage his party. Johnson "was aware that the civil rights advances would contribute to turmoil in two ways," noted Harry J. Middleton, a speechwriter for the president. "One, the South would go Republican, and two, the advances [of Johnson's legislation] would throw a harsh light on the problems still to be addressed."[157] Another Democratic insider agreed that the post-1960s political realignment which fueled Reagan's rise was based on race. "The first time Republicans started using [liberal] as a tattoo was after Lyndon Johnson did the right thing on the Voting Rights Act," said Paul Kirk. "While the Democrats have paid some price for it, the country is a lot better off." To Kirk "it was clearly the race issue" that caused the Democrats to lose southern support. "Johnson was a guy from the South himself, dealing with guys like Richard Russell and others in the Senate, and he knew exactly what the ramifications would be."[158] Nicholas Katzenbach made the same point, adding, "Johnson feared it, and Johnson was sure of it."[159] To David Maraniss, "the conservative rise was politically and statistically dependent upon racism. That's not to say that all conservatives are racists, but the reaction to the changes brought about by, particularly, Johnson and the civil rights movement really pushed a lot of white males, particularly in the South, over to the Republican Party."[160]

Republicans "would deny it vehemently, but if you say you want to overthrow the changes of the sixties, you're saying something that's borderline racist," emphasized Clinton speechwriter Ted Widmer, as it is implicit that one opposes the legal changes that helped African Americans in that decade. "Fifties nostalgia is a half step from racism. It's unconscious. It's deep below the surface. But it's in there. [Republicans] remember lily-white neighborhoods."[161] Nicholas Katzenbach concurred: "I don't think the Republican candidates for the most part try to do anything for [African Americans]." Reagan, "it seemed to me, was very anti-black."[162]

Roger Wilkins offered a personal account of Reagan's views on race. "If Reagan wasn't a racist, he surely could convey sympathy for racists in the most congenial ways when he went [in 1980] to Philadelphia, Mississippi," he recalled. "It was a signal: 'I am for states' rights,' 'I am going to help you put things aright,' a promise that he was going to try to restore white male supremacy. He said at Stone Mountain, Georgia, that 'Jefferson Davis was one of my heroes.' Now on the other hand, he was personally very congenial and convivial with black people." Wilkins remembered writing in 1981 that Reagan's "'Constructive Engagement' policy with South Africa was conceived in ignorance and bigotry. He called me up, talked to me for twenty-five minutes trying to convince me that he was not a racist, and then I said, 'Can I talk to you about something else?' and he said, 'Sure.' I talked about his tax cut policies and how bad they were. He talked to me for forty-five minutes at least," Wilkins said, noting he was extremely surprised that Reagan had time to "talk to a lowly journalist" for so long. "He was convivial, he was cordial—and he really didn't believe that he was a racist, and he didn't believe that his policies were racist.[163]

"I find this with other real conservatives," Wilkins noted. "I am now looking at a photograph of my wife and my baby daughter when she must have been only about eighteen months old, and she is sitting on her mother's lap. It is my favorite picture of my wife and my daughter. It was taken at Ben Bradlee's house at a birthday party. Barry Goldwater took the photograph," Wilkins said. "And as a result of meeting at these parties, Goldwater and I became—not friends, but very friendly. Even though he had run quite a racist campaign in '64, he did everything he could to tell me that he was just not a racist. He just didn't have a racist bone in his body, as he would say over and over again." In Wilkins's view, Reagan and Goldwater "deeply believed that the strength of the country was in white male entrepreneurs, and so let the white guys do what they need to do to be entrepreneurs, and sure, they get wealthy, but they use their wealth to create things and that creates jobs and the country is strong and healthy. That is not racist in their view."[164]

Reagan's successful use of the 1960s as a political weapon was premised on a distinction between Kennedy's "good sixties" and Johnson's "bad sixties" and on an insistence that his own fiscal and defense policies in the 1980s were of a piece with Kennedy's. While claiming to long for the early 1960s, he gained enormous political advantage by preaching repeatedly about the evils of the later years of the decade. But in order to make best use of the distinction—and neutralize the political threat of one potentially inconvenient lesson of the 1960s—Reagan had to respond to the memory of the most volatile aspect of the period: the Vietnam War. For just as Kennedy nostalgia posed enormous political dangers to Reagan and therefore needed to be co-opted, so too did the memory of Vietnam.

4

Reagan and the Memory of the Vietnam War

The veterans of Vietnam were never welcomed home with speeches and bands, but were never defeated in battle and were heroes as surely as any who have ever fought in a noble cause.

Ronald Reagan (1984)

WHILE PRESIDENT RONALD REAGAN blamed the 1960s for many problems, he saw as its greatest sin the shattering of the nation's morale. The country had ceased to believe in itself, he said in 1980. Reagan vowed to renew America by curing the Vietnam syndrome, broadly defined as a reluctance to project military force abroad after the defeat in Vietnam. Nine years later, in his farewell address, he confidently claimed that he had lifted the lingering malaise of "the sixties" and Vietnam. Yet however deftly he tried to exorcise it, the pain of the Vietnam misadventure restricted Reagan's ability and even his desire to pursue the kind of aggressive foreign policy Americans associated with memories of the "good sixties."

Reagan's Foreign Policy and the Legacy of Vietnam

In 1986, midway through his second term, Reagan described the American prisoners of war and those still missing in action in Vietnam as "part of a noble cause and history's heroes."[1] The first time Reagan referred to Vietnam as "a noble cause" was in 1979. Why did he use that phrase? "Those exact words were Reagan's—and unique to him," Michael Deaver recalled. "He didn't have a speechwriter in those days," according to Deaver.[2] What did Reagan mean by "noble cause"? According to Thomas Reed, Reagan viewed the Vietnamese communists as "terrorists, just like the guys that are killing people in the streets of Baghdad today," who had invaded South Vietnam after the French left in 1954. "He thought that the war was standing up to communist terrorists who were coming in and executing village chiefs."[3]

70

Reagan's choice of words infuriated liberals. "Both Reagan and [George H. W.] Bush tried in every way to revise history," argued Helen Thomas. "They couldn't stand the fact that we may be in a syndrome where we think some wars are not to be fought. So they kept referring to Vietnam as a 'noble cause.' Baloney. The American people woke up and finally we pulled out of Saigon by our fingertips," she said. "Reagan and the Republican Party wanted to change the mentality."[4] And indeed as president, Reagan moved quickly to do just that.

Caspar Weinberger, Reagan's secretary of defense, stated at the time of his confirmation hearings in 1981 that faith in the army's volunteer recruitment system had reached an all-time low. Members of Congress repeatedly asked him when the draft would resume. At the time, the military had a growing problem of personnel leaving before the end of their tours of duty. Looking back more than twenty years later, Weinberger observed with satisfaction that Reagan had restored pride in the military after Vietnam. Thanks, he said, to the clear criteria for overseas military intervention Weinberger laid out early in his tenure at the Pentagon, "people started volunteering again in great numbers, and very soon— amazingly soon—we were having more people than we had the funds for lining up at the recruitment depots all over the country. This was a very welcome change and certainly marked the end of any kind of Vietnam syndrome."[5]

Why did Reagan speak so much about Vietnam during his presidency? In part, conservatives saw the war as a defining experience of the 1960s. While most war protesters came from the Left, the conflict also angered conservatives, whose memories lingered well into the 1980s. "The sentiment that Reagan expressed was not quite 'We could have won the war if we'd tried'; it was more a negative expression of the idea 'We can't win a war with our hands tied behind our backs,'" explained Lou Cannon. "[Today] we're not quite as aware how much the Right was disillusioned [because of Vietnam]," he emphasized.[6] "Reagan's picture of a golden, patriotic past was filtered through the dark, distorting lens of Vietnam," wrote Cannon in a biography of Reagan. The domestic political turmoil over the war indelibly marked Reagan's experience as California governor during the 1960s. As protests against the war increased during the decade, "Reagan became a spokesman for those who believed the United States was losing the war in Vietnam because it lacked the will to win it. This view fit with his all-purpose contention that the federal government was responsible for most of what was wrong with America."[7] Presidents Nixon, Ford, and even Carter never admitted "defeat" in Vietnam—but Reagan did.

Asked if Reagan had tried to counteract the effect of the 1960s, Frances FitzGerald, whose 1972 book on the war won a Pulitzer Prize and the National Book Award, answered, "Yes, in all kinds of ways," especially with the military. "The American army was destroyed by [Vietnam,] . . . shattered in terms of morale more than anything else." To FitzGerald "the echoes of the Vietnam War were still going on in 1980, and Reagan was reasserting this old-fashioned 1950s anticommunism which had bypassed and gone over the sixties, and that appealed to a lot of people." By invading Afghanistan in 1979, FitzGerald added, the Soviets "were bringing up the echoes of this defeat in Vietnam. So Reagan was reassuring people that America was not on the decline."[8]

For Reagan, maintaining America's position as the strong moral leader of the freedom-loving Western world required the ability to act vigorously. "Most importantly, he realized that the Vietnam legacy had deprived American presidents of the option of deploying U.S. troops in protracted wars designed to stop the spread of Communism," wrote Cannon. While he firmly believed that it was crucial to arm those who were fighting against communists—whether in Afghanistan or in Nicaragua—"Reagan had mastered the most valuable lesson of Vietnam. He knew that it was realistically impossible for any president to commit U.S. troops to a protracted war that lacked the support of the American people."[9] Reagan spent much of his presidency reestablishing public support for decisive—but also small-scale—executive action in response to threats to national security.

As Weinberger recalled, Reagan "had a very clear policy that we were going to use the military carefully and only in situations where we had to win, and that combat would be in effect the last resort. All of this I put into a talk that I gave at the National Press Club in 1984—the six categories."[10] By this he meant the so-called Weinberger doctrine, a direct response to the loss in Vietnam, which prescribed six conditions for American military intervention overseas. In the 1984 address introducing this doctrine, Weinberger argued that a war should be fought only when it involved a vital national interest; that it must be fought with the intention of winning (Weinberger did not say when he thought the United States had ever fought with any other goal in mind); that political and military objectives needed to be clearly defined; that the military forces and objectives must be consistently reassessed; that there must be "reasonable assurance" of public support; and that military force must be used only as a last resort.[11]

In Cannon's view, the reluctance to use military force in the early 1980s "was primarily the application of lessons learned in Vietnam. . . . Beyond its toll in casualties, the Vietnam War had cost the professional military the public standing and much of the high morale it had won in World War II and retained throughout the Korean conflict. . . . Vietnam encouraged leaders of the services . . . to resist combat operations that lacked popular support." (Korea, of course, was a deeply unpopular war, but Cannon shared the view of the 1950s as a golden age.) Weinberger's attitude to the U.S. military—like Reagan's—was permanently altered by what he had witnessed in "the sixties." "Weinberger had been appalled at the backlash against the military after Vietnam and what he saw as shabby treatment accorded veterans of that conflict," Cannon wrote, without providing any evidence of such mistreatment. Weinberger was especially wary of getting the nation "drawn gradually into conflict by political commitments." He once said, "You can't fight Congress and public opinion and an enemy at the same time. That's why Vietnam was the crime of the century." In Cannon's view, Weinberger "was even more cautious than the Joint Chiefs of Staff" and "even more averse than Reagan to military risks."[12]

Weinberger's criteria for action caused divisions among Reagan's top advisers, as some felt that to read the lessons of Vietnam so strictly would unduly constrain the nation. Secretary of State George Shultz repeatedly clashed with Weinberger over his limits on the use of military force. Believing Weinberger's criteria too restrictive, Shultz asked, "How would prior 'reasonable assurance' of support from the American people be obtained?" Would the public have to agree on intervention ahead of time, "and even then, only if we were assured of winning swiftly and at minimal cost?" Was a vote of Congress needed to intervene immediately even to save Americans? To Shultz "this was the Vietnam syndrome in spades, carried to an absurd level, and a complete abdication of the duties of leadership."[13]

This disagreement between Weinberger and Shultz laid bare the essential paradox Vietnam had created: to restore American prestige, Reagan would have to demonstrate that the nation would oppose communism with military force. But any such action ran the risk of stimulating public opposition if it was seen as "leading to another Vietnam." Thus the legacy of Vietnam and "the sixties" forced him to adopt a delicate balancing act as he pursued his foreign policy objectives.

Reagan believed that the constraints on presidential action imposed by the Vietnam syndrome could be seen around the globe. "Before we commit our troops to combat," he wrote in his memoir, referring to the 1984 withdrawal of U.S. Marines stationed in Lebanon to quell a civil war, "there must be reasonable assurance that the cause we are fighting for and the actions we take will have the support of the American people and Congress. (We all felt that the Vietnam War had turned into such a tragedy because military action had been undertaken without sufficient assurances that the American people were behind it.)"[14] In recounting his own version of the crisis in Lebanon, Shultz confirmed that Reagan "was worried by what he called 'the Vietnam problem,' the reluctance of the United States to use its troops again in tough spots and the perception that we would not."[15]

Shultz saw the memory of Vietnam as a powerful force. "Throughout the 1980s, every time the United States tried to deal with a regional conflict anywhere, the cries of 'another Vietnam' were immediately heard," he wrote.[16] "The lesson of Vietnam was continuously being cited to reject any use of military force unless in exceptional circumstances and with near total public support in advance," he lamented. On April 3, 1984, addressing the Tri-Lateral Commission, Shultz said, "The need to avoid no-win situations cannot mean that we turn automatically away from hard-to-win situations that call for prudent involvement."[17]

This frustration was most apparent in Reagan's Central American policies. In Nicaragua the United States supported a rebel group, the contras, who sought to overthrow the Sandinista regime, which had come to power in a 1979 revolution. The U.S. government also supported a right-wing dictatorship in neighboring El Salvador. "The situation in Central America was a problem of immense importance to the United States," Shultz wrote, "and I knew we had to confront it. This was our neighborhood." The Soviets were expanding in the area, and they understood that it was a place "where the American press and American public opinion were the most sensitive to the possibility of 'another Vietnam.' Trying to forge policy was like walking through a swamp."[18]

Reagan shared Shultz's concerns about the harm done by the lingering impact of Vietnam. He claimed in his memoir that he could "never understand" why his congressional critics—who "were in effect furthering Moscow's agenda in Latin America"—would not support his Central American policies, and he expressed deep frustration at the public's indifference to "Communist penetration of the Americas." Answering his own question, he wrote: "Part of this reluctance, I'm sure, was a result of the post-Vietnam syndrome. There was a depth of isolationism in the country that I hadn't seen since the Great Depression." Reagan also blamed popular resistance to intervention in Latin America on press manipulation by the Sandinistas, which succeeded because, "perhaps after Vietnam, when many reporters cast Uncle Sam in the role of villain, they didn't want to put white hats on the contra freedom fighters because the U.S. government was supporting them."[19]

Shultz concurred. "The Vietnam War had left one indisputable legacy: massive press, public, and congressional anxiety that the United States—at all costs—avoid getting mired in 'another Vietnam,'" he wrote. "News items datelined from Central America or the Caribbean raised the alarm that this or that country of the region was about to become our next quagmire. We knew that any covert action by the CIA would be severely scrutinized [and] probably disallowed by the Congress." Referring to the 1973 War Powers Resolution, limiting the president's ability to wage war without congressional approval, Shultz wrote, "The American agonies subsumed under the terms 'Vietnam' and 'Watergate' had us tied in knots."[20]

Though he projected confidence, Reagan was quite conscious of the Vietnam syndrome's impact on his Central American policy. In 1983 he told a joint session of Congress: "To those who invoke the memory of Vietnam, there is no thought of sending American combat troops to Central America. They are not needed," a promise that drew applause. "They have not been requested there. All our neighbors ask of us is assistance in training and arms to protect themselves while they build a better, freer life."[21] Reagan intended his reference to Vietnam to stifle any comparisons between that war and the current conflict in Central America, a reference he added in longhand to the draft of the speech following a section requesting generous funding for the contras. At the end a speechwriter added, "Vietnam—great nation can't forever let [illegible] from the past paralyze us," as well as a note to "check parallel w/ Gulf of Tonkin—make sure this doesn't parallel LBJ's speech."[22]

Referring in his memoir to his efforts to stop the spread of communism in the region, Reagan wrote, "After Vietnam, I knew that Americans would be just as reluctant to send their sons to fight in Central America, and I had no intention of doing that." He later reiterated this point: "I *never* considered sending U.S. troops to fight in Latin America."[23]

Reagan's supporters, especially those who favored a more aggressive American presence in Central America, also sought to erase the Vietnam syndrome—and heartily welcomed Reagan's aggressive stance toward the region. Al Keller, the head of the American Legion, the nation's largest veterans' organization, sent the president a lengthy letter in 1983 praising his Central American policy. "As another expression of concern for the vital importance of Central America to U.S. national security," Keller wrote, he had devoted his upcoming editorial, "The Lessons of Vietnam," in the Legion's magazine to "debunking the 'Vietnam syndrome.'" He urged the president: "We cannot allow incorrect lessons drawn from the Vietnam War to restrict American policy. Carried to its logical conclusion, the 'Vietnam syndrome' would tie America's hands and lead inexorably to withdrawal into Fortress America with a concomitant diminishment of freedom and prosperity throughout the world."[24]

One way Reagan addressed the Vietnam syndrome was through an invasion of the tiny Caribbean island of Grenada in October 1983 after a coup by the People's Revolutionary Government, which Reagan saw as a Marxist threat to American interests and security. The first major U.S. military deployment since the end of the Vietnam War in 1975, the invasion came only two days after 241 U.S. servicemen were killed in a terrorist bomb attack in Lebanon. According to Gary Hart, Reagan was quite explicit about using this incident to reverse the Vietnam syndrome. "There wasn't any subtlety about it. It was 'Democrats are weak, and we are strong, and we're not going to let the communists, or anyone else, push us around.' It was central to Reagan's appeal to the country."[25] Asked if Reagan felt hampered by the Vietnam syndrome, Ed Meese replied, "He decided to eclipse that [with] the rescue mission to Grenada."[26]

Reagan revealed that at the time of the Grenada invasion he was acutely aware of how the memory of the earlier war might influence public opinion. One reason he wanted complete secrecy surrounding the mission was, he wrote, "what I call the 'post-Vietnam syndrome,' the resistance of many in Congress to the use of military force abroad for any reason, because of our nation's experience in Vietnam." Reagan feared that if Congress knew in advance of the invasion, "even under terms of strictest confidentiality, there would be some who would leak it to the press together with the prediction that Grenada was going to become 'another Vietnam.' We were already running into this phenomenon in our efforts to halt the spread of Communism in Central America, and some congressmen were raising the issue of 'another Vietnam' in Lebanon." If Congress knew of his plans, Reagan recalled, they would tell him, "'Sure, it's starting small, but once you make that first commitment, Grenada's going to become another Vietnam.' Well, that wasn't true," Reagan wrote. "And that's one reason why the rescue operation on Grenada was conducted in total secrecy. We didn't ask anybody, we just did it."[27]

One congressman's recollections supported this view. "The Vietnam War put handcuffs on the presidents," G. William Whitehurst argued. When Reagan invaded Grenada, people "immediately brought up the War Powers Act: it hadn't gone to Congress. Well, the damn thing only lasted a little less than a week, but there were people crabbing about it: 'We can't do this. We can't get involved.'"[28]

James Baker, Reagan's chief of staff, vividly recalled how Vietnam had influenced the decision to invade the Caribbean island: "We were so conscious of [the Vietnam syndrome] that we didn't let anybody know what we were doing, including the congressional leadership. We called them up to the residence one evening to brief them on the operation that was going to go down the next morning, and gave them a full briefing, and Tip O'Neill said to the president, 'Mr. President, this is not a consultation, it's a notification! Good luck!' And he stood up and walked out." Margaret Thatcher was also angry at not being told of the invasion, said Baker, "but the idea of taking even one casualty as a consequence of a leak was more than we were willing to risk, and so we held it very, very closely."[29]

Caspar Weinberger, asked if Reagan felt that the Vietnam syndrome had restricted his efforts in Central America, responded: "In all ways, yes. He thought that people had been so badly burned during Vietnam [that they] didn't want any part of any kind of aggressive war, assertive foreign policy."[30] To Reagan, the Grenada invasion, rather than creating "another Vietnam," as opponents claimed, was "a necessary step to foil Communist penetration of our hemisphere."[31] ("The press is trying to give this the Vietnam treatment but I don't think the people will buy it," he wrote in his diary on October 30, 1983.)[32] Reagan also contrasted the invasion's aftermath with the late 1960s. When the American medical students airlifted from Grenada "came to the White House and embraced the soldiers who had rescued them, it was quite a sight for a former governor who had once seen college students spit on anyone wearing a military uniform," he wrote, repeating an often told though never verified anecdote of the era.[33] Reagan was convinced that the Grenada invasion had begun to liberate the nation from the Vietnam syndrome. Fully 63 percent of the public supported the invasion, and Reagan's personal popularity also increased.[34]

By April 1985, George Shultz wrote in his memoir, a "debate was raging within the administration, unnoticed by the media, over how the United States should approach" the tenth anniversary of the fall of Saigon. Although "the overwhelming weight of opinion, expressed with increasing vehemence, was, 'Don't open old wounds,'" Shultz decided to give a speech. His decision caused consternation among Reagan's staff—but not for Reagan, who saw it as an opportunity to justify the war. "I took my speech over to the president to read. He liked it and gave it his vote of approval: thumbs up." Shultz's account attests to the lingering power of the war to shape the public debate about U.S. foreign policy. In his address, delivered to a standing-room-only audience in the diplomatic lobby of the State Department, Shultz emphasized that while America had made moral, military, and political mistakes, the "true horror" was the communist takeover of Vietnam, and "the worst horror of all" was the coming to power of the Khmer Rouge in Cambodia. Critics of America's effort in Vietnam had long argued that the rise of the Khmer Rouge had resulted from the chaos that ensued in that nation following the 1970 U.S. bombings, but in his remarks Shultz blamed the genocide on the 1975 withdrawal of American forces from Vietnam. Regardless of the execution of the war or our reasons for becoming involved, Shultz declared, "the *morality* of our effort must now be clear. . . . Our sacrifice was in the service of noble ideals—to save innocent people from brutal tyranny." When asked if his secretary of state was speaking for the administration, Reagan said, "Damn right he was."[35]

Reagan's speechwriters agreed with Shultz's interpretation. Vietnam was "the formative political experience of my life," Peggy Noonan wrote in her memoir, "because it involved one of the most painful political injustices of our time." The effort to "resist a Communist takeover was not proof of America's cynicism but an illustration of that peculiar American mix, one part idealism and one part strategic calculation, which may have been wrong but at least had a point." To Noonan it was the antiwar protesters and the politicians who facilitated the U.S. retreat from Vietnam who had "helped produce the boat people, the Cambodian holocaust, a gulag called Vietnam, and an untold increase in horror for the people of that part of the planet."[36]

Shultz's remarks were as much about Central America as about Vietnam. He argued that aid to the contras was needed to save Nicaragua "from the fate of the people of Cuba, of South Vietnam, Cambodia and Laos." Shultz warned of the repercussions of U.S. withdrawal from the region, given "the special ruthlessness of Communist rule." The United States only wanted to promote "freedom and democracy" and was "tired of setbacks, especially those that result from restraints we impose on ourselves," a reference to what he considered the regrettable decision of Congress not to fund the contras. Communist rule in Vietnam "was precisely what we were trying to prevent. Broken promises. Communist dictatorship. Refugees. Widened Soviet influence, this time near our very borders. Here is your parallel between Vietnam and Central America." Communism had devastated Indochina, he said, and as in Vietnam, "the Nicaraguan Communists employ slogans of social reform, nationalism, and democracy to obscure their totalitarian goals."[37]

Whereas Reagan's critics often referred to Nicaragua as "another Vietnam," in these remarks Shultz instead used the Vietnam analogy to rally support for the contras. On the same day Shultz delivered his speech, the Reagan administration pressed Congress again to approve aid for the contras and expressed frustration over the defeat of several recent requests for aid. "We will be back and back and back until America does the right thing," promised Vice President Bush.[38]

Purging the Ghosts of Vietnam

Reagan used Vietnam specifically—as he used "the sixties" in general—to his political advantage. Exploiting a president's ability to shape public debate, he worked to define the war in ways that stressed the nobility of the cause, the bravery of the soldiers, and especially the culpability of his political predecessors. His first mention of Vietnam as president occurred as he was presenting the Congressional Medal of Honor to Master Sergeant Roy P. Benavidez in February 1981. Prior to the ceremony Benavidez and members of his family met with Reagan in the Oval Office. In presenting the award "for conspicuous gallantry and intrepidity in action at the risk of his life above and beyond the call of duty" on May 2, 1968, Reagan began, "Several years ago, we brought home a group of American fighting men who had obeyed their country's call and who had fought as bravely and as well as any Americans in our history." He continued, "They came home without a victory not because they'd been defeated, but because they'd been denied permission to win."[39] (An earlier draft of his remarks used even harsher language, claiming that "our Government had not permitted them to win.")[40] He recalled: "They were greeted by no parades, no bands, no waving of the flag they had so nobly served. There's been no 'Thank you' for their sacrifice. There's been no effort to honor [them]." Reagan then listed many acts of heroism, bravery, humanitarianism, and personal generosity of servicemen in Vietnam, including building schools, hospitals, orphanages, churches, and temples. "It's time to show our pride in them and to thank them."[41]

Reagan's most frequent references to Vietnam came during his 1984 reelection campaign. By praising both the war's purpose and its participants, Reagan hoped to paint his opponents as weak on defense. He was also attempting to dissuade Democrats from trying to use Vietnam to their own political advantage, fearing that by reminding voters of America's lost war, they might draw attention to his own recent actions in Central America. This election year marked the twentieth anniversary of the Tonkin Gulf resolution authorizing the use of force in Vietnam. He could ill afford a full-fledged national debate about the merits of U.S. involvement in the nation's least popular war.

Reagan spoke extensively about the war's meaning at a Memorial Day ceremony at Arlington National Cemetery honoring a Vietnam Unknown Serviceman. Using the term "noble" nearly half a dozen times, he argued for the need to restore pride in the military, show respect to Vietnam veterans, and bring home the remains of all servicemen from Vietnam. The events surrounding the 1982 dedication of the Vietnam Veterans Memorial, such as the three-day candlelight ceremony at the National Cathedral where the names of the dead and the missing were read aloud, demonstrated, he said, "how our nation could learn and grow and transcend the tragedies of the past." Vietnam veterans who staged a parade on Constitution Avenue were soldiers "never welcomed home with speeches and bands," he claimed. But as America watched the proud veterans, a unified nation could feel "that we had, at long last, welcomed the boys home." Because of the war, "Americans have learned to listen to each other and to trust each other again." But Vietnam had also proved another of Reagan's favorite themes: that government cannot be trusted. "We've learned that government owes the people an explanation and needs their support for its actions at home and abroad," Reagan said. The Unknown Soldier had confronted the horrors of war, "certain his own cause and his country's cause was a noble one." The troops in Vietnam, he repeated, were "offered no parades, no flags, and so little thanks," but now "a grateful nation opens her heart today in gratitude for their sacrifice, for their courage, and for their noble service."[42]

In the summer of 1984, in handwritten (later typed) responses to people who had written him supportive letters following that Memorial Day speech, Reagan reiterated that the loss in Vietnam was the government's fault and not that of the troops. To Mr. and Mrs. George Brooks of New Windsor, New York, whose son's remains were returned from Laos in 1982, he wrote: "Your son and those who fought beside him were serving a noble cause and they fought nobly. They were betrayed by indecision and strategic blunders in high government echelons." He thanked a Vietnam veteran, B. T. Collins of Sacramento, for writing. "I don't know when I have been so moved, unless it was at the ceremony itself where I had trouble getting the words past the lump in my throat. If I have done anything to help bring a proper focus on the noble purpose you all served so well, I'll be more than proud," read the president's letter. "You fought as bravely and as well as any American in our history, and literally with one arm tied behind you. Sometimes two. The tragedy—indeed, the immorality—of those years was that for the first time in our history, our country and its government failed to match your heroic sacrifices."[43] His frequent assertion that the nation had not treated Vietnam veterans with the respect they deserved was the subject of many letters to Reagan after the Memorial Day speech. Another Vietnam veteran, Robert Eastburn of Stanton, Delaware, wrote: "We returned to the United States to be called baby-killers and butchers, people spat on us. We were ostracized by the society that fostered us."[44]

Reagan used Vietnam strategically throughout his 1984 reelection campaign, attacking Walter Mondale as soft on defense on the grounds that Mondale did not believe Vietnam was a noble cause. Among the Reagan campaign strategy tips listed in a lengthy memorandum was a note that read: "RR's 'greatest strength' is the perception 'He will keep our defenses strong.' . . . Mondale's record on defense issues is appalling, a problem he is trying to correct." Quoting from a Republican research pamphlet, the memorandum emphasized that Mondale is "eager to admit that supporting the Kennedy-Johnson Vietnam policy was 'the worst mistake of my political life,' and has no obvious complaint with anything that's occurred in Southeast Asia since 1975."[45]

Reagan was so eager to invoke Vietnam in a positive light that he even invoked a rock star who sang about it. "There's a new feeling of patriotism in our land, a recognition that by any standard America is a decent and generous place, a force for good in the world," he proclaimed at a New Jersey rally in September. "And I don't know about you, but I'm a little tired of hearing people run her down." Reagan referred to "the message of hope in songs of a man so many young Americans admire—New Jersey's own, Bruce Springsteen." Chants of "USA, USA" soon erupted.[46]

Reagan's reference to Springsteen carries true irony. Springsteen's 1984 hit song and album *Born in the U.S.A.* describes a disillusioned Vietnam veteran, "born down in a dead man's town," who fought in the war not because it was a noble cause but because he "got in a little hometown jam / So they put a rifle in my hands / Sent me off to a foreign land / To go and kill the yellow man." Back home and unable to return to his old job, he asks his "V.A. man" for assistance, but to no avail. While in Vietnam, "I had a brother at Khe Sahn, fighting off the Viet Cong / They're still there, he's all gone."[47] What's the veteran's future? "Down in the shadow of the penitentiary / Out by the gas fires of the refinery / I'm ten years burning down the road / Nowhere to run, ain't got nowhere to go."[48] Amid the patriotic fervor of 1984 the lyrics did not matter; the chorus—"Born in the U.S.A."—was enough to make the song an unintended staple of Reagan rallies.[49]

Indeed, Reagan had wanted Springsteen to appear with him at the New Jersey rally. George Will, after attending a Springsteen concert a few days earlier, made the same mistake. Despite the downbeat portrayals of American life in many of Springsteen's songs, he wrote, these "problems always seem punctuated by a grand, cheerful affirmation: 'Born in the USA!'" and abundant flag waving. Although Reagan's bid to meet Springsteen was unsuccessful, his broader efforts made political sense, as Springsteen's and Reagan's popular support alike derived from the allegiance of the white ethnic working class. "The attempt to appropriate Springsteen's appeal was more than routine political window dressing; it reflected a broader strategy that had precipitated a major political realignment," wrote historian Jim Cullen. "Among other tactics, this strategy involved stoking the resentments of working-class whites uneasy about black gains since the Civil Rights movement, and capitalized on the ill will generated by white liberals who had regarded the working class with suspicion, if not outright hostility, since the sixties."[50]

After handily winning reelection in 1984, Reagan continued to reiterate an interpretation of Vietnam that stressed the war's essential nobility. At the dedication of the Vietnam Veterans Memorial Statue on the National Mall (Frederick Hart's *Three Fighting Men*), held shortly after election day, Reagan spoke of "the loyalty and the valor of those who served us in Vietnam." The three figures depicted in the statue "answered the call of their country. . . . They died uncomplaining." The troops in Vietnam had "performed with a steadfastness and valor that veterans of other wars salute." For the first time President Reagan also spoke of the war protesters in the 1960s. "Vietnam threatened to tear our society apart," he said, "and the political and philosophical disagreements that animated each side continue to some extent." But the nation desired to heal these wounds, and "since Vietnam, the healing has begun." Many returning veterans, most notably John Kerry, had protested against the Vietnam War, but Reagan rhetorically separated veterans from protesters. He also reminded veterans that when they came home, "little solace was given to you," but the country could now say, "Thank you for your courage."[51] In his diary later that day Reagan wrote, "It was quite an event & I hope it finally makes up for the way the Vietnam Returnees were treated when they came home."[52]

Reagan still remembered the clashes over Vietnam that took place while he was California's governor. In 1986 he contrasted the character of the troops in Vietnam with those who did not serve, concluding that the former had superior morals. The "unpampered boys of the working class" waged war "without enough support from home[,] . . . dodging bullets while we debated the efficacy of the battle." The government and civilians had let the troops down, he said, while those who fought "chose to reject the fashionable skepticism of their time." The troops, in contrast to protesters at home, "stood for something."[53]

In his final speech on Vietnam Reagan called the troops "champions of a noble cause" and said the war's lesson was that "Americans must never

again be sent to fight and die unless we are prepared to let them win"—
implying that the Vietnam War could have been won if not for failure
of nerve in Washington. For too long, he claimed, Vietnam veterans had
been ignored, but as he prepared to leave the presidency, "I see Vietnam
veterans take their rightful place among America's heroes. . . . What can I
say to our Vietnam veterans but: Welcome home."[54]

Key conservatives shared Reagan's view that the government had not
allowed the troops to win. "Johnson did not have any effective strategy
for winning the war," said longtime conservative activist William Rusher.
"He just kept on feeding American soldiers in there while he tried to think
of something."[55] To Caspar Weinberger "the worst thing was sending some
565,000 troops into a war that we didn't intend to win and not supporting
the troops in the way that would have enabled them to win."[56]

Reagan, like many conservatives, engaged in some strategic reshaping
of the memory of Vietnam. "Veterans actually weren't spat on; that's an
urban legend," said historian Rick Perlstein. "The Nixon administration
created some of this mythology for political purposes. Returning veterans
in every war are kind of taboo figures. A lot of the same things we think
about only in terms of Vietnam also happened after World War II."[57] In
The Spitting Image, Vietnam veteran Jerry Lembcke argued, "The myth
of the spat-upon veteran . . . says, in effect, that we were not beaten by
the Vietnamese but were defeated on the home front by fifth columnists."
There is a political purpose to this myth, for if Vietnam is "remembered
as a war that was lost because of betrayal at home, [it] becomes a modern-
day Alamo that must be avenged, a pretext for more war and generations
of more veterans."[58]

Reagan misrepresented history in other ways as well when he spoke
of Vietnam. "The 'noble cause' thing was unfortunately never effectively
attacked in this country," Daniel Ellsberg, the former military analyst
who in 1971 released the Pentagon Papers to the *New York Times*, said,
"in part because to understand that it was not a 'noble cause' you had to
know the history of Vietnam. The Pentagon Papers did do that, but very
few people read that part of the Pentagon Papers." But Ellsberg had. Those
sections demonstrated "how close our war came to an illegal aggressive
war; otherwise it looked like this justified war in support of a sovereign
nation [whose] government was resisting aggression in South Vietnam."
Ellsberg called this notion "totally illusory, because [the South Vietnamese regime] was essentially a puppet government."[59] Chroniclers of the
Vietnam War echoed his views. "There was no way we could have won"
in Vietnam, Frances FitzGerald stated.[60] Author and journalist Stanley
Karnow, who reported on the war for its duration, declared: "I don't think

Reagan had a clue to what the hell was going on in Vietnam. I don't think he had any idea what Vietnam was all about."[61]

After Vietnam many Americans "were jarred by the fact that we 'didn't win,'" remarked David Halberstam, who won a Pulitzer Prize for his Vietnam War reporting. "They asked, 'What went wrong?' and the idea [arose] that maybe we were betrayed. There had to be some kind of explanation."[62] Reagan fed this belief as he stressed that the war had been poorly executed by Washington's "elites"—those who also implemented the Great Society and many other liberal programs of the 1960s. "The notion that we could win [in Vietnam] was very unpopular, and realistically so, in the late sixties and seventies," noted Ellsberg. "What was required to restore the notion that Vietnam was winnable was loss of memory. Enough time had to elapse that a new generation came along who were easily persuaded of what is, after all, compellingly plausible: that a country of our strength and power, relative to theirs, could not fail to win; that if we had enough will, we obviously could win."[63]

Curing the Vietnam Syndrome

Reagan was the first presidential candidate, and the first president, to use the term "Vietnam syndrome." His predecessor, Jimmy Carter, according to the Carter Presidential Library, never used the phrase in any speeches or public statements in his campaigns or during his presidency.[64] Its origins are unclear. "Vietnam syndrome" and "*the* Vietnam syndrome" began as two different terms: "Vietnam syndrome" was originally used in the early 1970s to describe the difficulties returning veterans experienced in adjusting to civilian life. It was also called "returnee's syndrome,"[65] later "post-Vietnam syndrome,"[66] and eventually "post-traumatic stress disorder."[67] "Post-Vietnam syndrome" in the late 1970s had a medical meaning,[68] and "Vietnam syndrome" continued to be more commonly used in a purely clinical sense rather than to describe a political sentiment.[69] As late as 1980 "Vietnam syndrome" was still also used to describe a medical condition, one "recognized as an emotional illness by the American Psychiatric Association and the Veterans Administration."[70]

But soon after the end of the Vietnam War the term began to take on its current meaning, signifying the reluctance of the United States to intervene militarily overseas. In 1975 the term surfaced in discussions of a Senate bill providing that the president could place thousands of military reservists on active duty for three months. Senator Sam Nunn, a conservative Georgia Democrat and member of the Senate Armed Services Committee, was instrumental in writing the bill. The *New York Times* reported that Nunn saw the legislation "as a means of bolstering the readiness of the military Reserve forces and countering what he calls the 'Vietnam syndrome.'"[71] The term was rarely used in the next few years but began to reappear in 1978, when the *Times* described Nunn as believing "that the 'Vietnam syndrome' has led to mistaken emphasis on the need for a national consensus before a move can be made in foreign affairs. He believes that reaction to the Vietnam War has also led to a fear that any foreign involvement . . . could lead to the commitment of American troops."[72] Others have attributed the first use of the phrase to a member of Carter's administration. "I think the term 'syndrome' was invented by [Zbigniew] Brzezinski when he was head of the [National Security Council] under Carter," recalled Stanley Karnow.[73]

In December 1979 government officials from both ends of the political spectrum viewed the Iran hostage crisis—which began on November 4, 1979, when student radicals stormed the U.S. embassy and took sixty-six Americans hostage—"as a pivotal event marking the close of the post-Vietnam era," wrote Hedrick Smith. One official said, "In terms of domestic politics, this has put the end to the Vietnam syndrome." Another argued, "We are moving away from our post-Vietnam reticence." Government leaders and the public were steadily moving in favor of a more interventionist foreign policy.[74] Arthur Schlesinger expressed great concern about this shift in mood. Vietnam, "the most useless and the most shameful war," taught us "the hazards of military intervention in parts of the world remote from our vital interest." He feared that this lesson was being forgotten. "Legislators rejoice that 'the Vietnam syndrome' is dead. At last, it would appear, we are free to be fools again."[75]

The year 1980 saw "the Vietnam syndrome" used quite freely to describe a myriad of foreign policy situations. The Soviet invasion of Afghanistan in 1979 and Carter's failed 1980 attempt to rescue the hostages in Iran contributed to increased support for a more vigorous U.S. foreign policy. "The prospect of another Vietnam War is alarming," warned an editorial on a crisis in Thailand. "How America responded would show whether we had overcome our 'Vietnam syndrome'—an apparent unwillingness to stand up for our allies and global interests."[76]

One month after his acceptance speech at the 1980 Republican National Convention, Reagan began to use the phrase. In August, referring to Vietnam, Reagan told the Veterans of Foreign Wars, "It's time we recognize that ours was, in truth, a noble cause. We dishonor the memory of 50,000 young Americans who died in that cause when we give way to feelings of guilt as if we were doing something shameful." The *New York Times* reported that Reagan "criticized what he called the 'Vietnam syndrome,' which, he said, has made Americans timid and apologetic for their opposition to aggression."[77] This definition of the Vietnam syndrome would play a recurring role in Reagan's rhetoric as president.

For many on the Left, the Vietnam syndrome is a positive constraint, one that is "realistic and encourages us to obey international law when it comes to avoiding unilateral intervention," said Daniel Ellsberg.[78] Others concurred. "I disagreed with the use of that term 'syndrome,' because 'syndrome' is a mental disorder," noted Stanley Karnow. "And for people to say, 'We don't want to get involved in another Vietnam,' which is a position that many very respectable people took—like Caspar Weinberger and Colin Powell and others—it's not a syndrome at all," he said. "It's a very healthy reaction, to be un-involved. Whatever you want to call the term—awareness, fear, whatever, syndrome—nobody wanted to get involved in anything after Vietnam. Vietnam hung over everyone's mind."[79]

But for the Right, the Vietnam syndrome lowered morale and restrained America's ability to conduct necessary military action, and thus needed to be conquered. Carter certainly had not done so, they claimed. "Reagan's building up and restoring the morale of the military, and the patriotic feelings—getting the military back into wearing their uniforms, putting marine guards visibly at the White House—were all part of overcoming the Vietnam syndrome," noted Ed Meese. "It was a conscious effort. Reagan said Vietnam was 'a noble effort,' and while I don't think we ever made a big deal out of it, it was certainly his desire to eliminate the vestiges of the Vietnam War in terms of public perception," in part through frequent visits to military bases. Reagan even "went out in an aircraft carrier in his first summer as president to watch air maneuvers." Overcoming the Vietnam syndrome "was at least implicit if not explicit in our discussions at the time."[80]

During his presidency Reagan mentioned the term "Vietnam syndrome" several times. Asked in February 1981, "Is there any danger that we can become involved in El Salvador to the point that we might not be able to extricate ourselves easily?" Reagan replied: "No, I don't think so. I know that this is a great concern. I think it's part of the Vietnam syndrome, but we have no intention of that kind of involvement."[81] The irony of his remark is that by promising to limit U.S. military involvement, he was succumbing to the Vietnam syndrome rather than repudiating it. Nevertheless, William Safire immediately praised Reagan's El Salvador policy. "We should let it be known that we are determined to see to it that the anti-Communists win," the former Nixon speechwriter wrote. "The anguish of American doves who cry 'another Vietnam!' is helpful—it makes the point that what Mr. Reagan calls 'the Vietnam syndrome' no longer paralyzes U.S. policy."[82]

Reagan next alluded to the Vietnam syndrome in a commencement address at the U.S. Military Academy in May 1981. He complained that in the 1970s "there was a widespread lack of respect for the uniform, born perhaps of what has been called the Vietnam syndrome." The inevitable result was fewer enlistments and, even worse, fewer reenlistments.[83] A memorandum urged Reagan's speechwriters preparing that address: "Above all stress that military service is honorable, indeed noble. Vietnam veterans are just beginning to obtain deserved recognition, a fact that has not been lost on the cadets or the country."[84] On another occasion two years later Reagan remarked, "We're ending the Vietnam syndrome that had broken the will of the American people."[85]

Reagan also invoked the term to criticize Congress for not funding the contras to fight the Sandinistas, "a totalitarian, Communist government." He charged that members of Congress were "suffering from something I call the Vietnam syndrome. Too many of them," with fresh memories of that war, had become overly cautious when it came to protecting our hemisphere's security. But, he went on to say, "we have no intention of military involvement nor do I think it is needed."[86]

Reagan used the term most frequently in 1986, when he began to claim that his policies had successfully reversed the syndrome. He told supporters of the contras that he had increased the defense budget, aided Central American nations, and eliminated legal obstacles to giving aid to those who were resisting communism. "Only a few years ago, to hope for all of this would have seemed to be asking for far too much." But now "what we're seeing is the end of the post-Vietnam syndrome, the return of realism about the Communist danger." Accordingly, Reagan urged Congress to fund Nicaragua's "freedom fighters."[87] On another occasion he said that the spread of democracy around the world showed "that the eighties is a break with the past. . . . The old politics, the post-Vietnam syndrome, the partisans of 'Blame America First,' are fading fast."[88] He equated his own policy in El Salvador with Truman's support of the democratic forces in Greece. While some in the United States had opposed this, "America unflinchingly met its responsibility" in a bipartisan fashion to secure the country. "Some historians believe the trauma of the Vietnam War irreparably destroyed the spirit of cooperation," Reagan said. But he himself disagreed, as "America is leaving the Vietnam syndrome behind."[89]

As he had done with "the sixties," Reagan made skillful use of the "Vietnam syndrome" as a rhetorical device. He employed the phrase to build support for his Central American policies, to argue that Americans were better off as a result of his efforts to overcome the legacy of Vietnam, and to put his political opponents on the defensive.

The conservative establishment defined Reagan as a leader who had renewed America after Vietnam. William Rusher, asked to name Reagan's greatest accomplishment, said, "Reagan managed—this was not long, remember, after the Vietnam War—to reinspire the American people, give them more confidence in themselves, believe that this was a better country than they had been told it was in the sixties. It was a tremendous achievement."[90] To Michael Deaver, "Vietnam for Reagan was part of what had gone wrong" with America, and he was upset with "the way the country had dealt with it. Reagan saw it as a big part of his presidency to restore confidence in America and get Americans to believe again that they could do anything they wanted to do, because he was of that '[Greatest] Generation.'" Reagan made a special effort to emphasize American renewal, "both consciously and unconsciously always thinking of how to restore credibility to the presidency [and] government. Remember, he was the first president in thirty years to have two full terms," Deaver noted. "He restored confidence in the presidency and restored America's belief in itself."[91]

Aram Bakshian explained how such beliefs were expressed in Reagan's speeches. "It was always understood that you were trying to rehabilitate the American attitudes toward defense [and] the armed forces, and the honor of their commitment, and you did it in small ways. It was just a constant thing in the back of your head—it wasn't a matter of 'We've got to fight the Vietnam syndrome by talking about the Vietnam syndrome,'" he explained. "You talked about the positive nature of America's contribution and the importance of American strength."[92]

One lesson learned from the Vietnam syndrome was the danger of "getting involved in wars without winning," said Thomas Reed, Reagan's special assistant for national security policy. "Reagan, while ending the Cold War, said to me, 'There's a war going on and somebody's going to win and somebody's going to lose, and let's decide who it is and set about it. And the objective is not to kill as many people as possible, it's to end it on terms that are satisfactory to American values.' And so the Vietnam syndrome very definitely came into play in the Reagan years, in Reagan's understanding that you just cannot go on endlessly [fighting a war]."[93]

But if the Vietnam syndrome was in retreat, then why did Reagan eschew the use of military force, both in public and in private? His speeches on Vietnam illustrate a striking irony: while the president spoke of restoring American might, he was extremely hesitant to send troops abroad.

"There was one invasion of Grenada, and then we used proxies in El Salvador and Nicaragua," noted David Halberstam. "The Reagan years were very cautious in terms of actual deeds. . . . They did not get themselves impaled."[94] Benjamin Bradlee said: "I hope the Vietnam syndrome is what restrained him. If we didn't learn any lesson out of Vietnam it would be such a waste, even more of a waste than it was. But I don't think of Reagan as a recklessly adventurous president."[95] As historian William Berman explained, "Reagan, ever so astutely, knew that he could not send troops to Nicaragua, and he opposed those people in the administration and elsewhere who advised him to do that."[96]

Reagan "felt hamstrung by the aftermath of the Vietnam War," observed former 1960s radical Todd Gitlin, who co-founded Students for a Democratic Society (SDS) in 1962. The president "got around the so-called 'Vietnam syndrome' by a combination of underhanded covert aid, covert action, and weekend wars—quick in-and-out: first the marines in Lebanon, then Grenada, then covert action in Nicaragua and El Salvador."[97] Even conservatives acknowledged Reagan's caution when it came to sending troops. "Reagan was very careful in his use of military force: Grenada, which is a small nothing of a country, and Lebanon," said Eugene Meyer. "And he removed the troops from Lebanon after a couple of months."[98] And the U.S. Marines in Lebanon were prohibited from firing back, he might have added.

"Without the so-called Vietnam syndrome—a skepticism toward unilateral wars against nationalist opposition, a lack of confidence that we could win those cheaply and quickly, which was very realistic—Reagan would have invaded Nicaragua directly, and not just with the contras," remarked Daniel Ellsberg. "He probably would have intervened in El Salvador directly and not just relied on the right-wing death squads. I'll give Reagan credit for something: he quickly got out of Lebanon when that looked unpromising, instead of escalating, after the marines were blown up."[99]

Michael Dukakis thought that Reagan was "definitely" conscious of the Vietnam syndrome when dealing with Latin America and would have been more aggressive had the syndrome not existed.[100] Other Democrats concurred. Asked if Reagan would have been more assertive but for the Vietnam syndrome, Timothy Wirth, a Democrat elected to the senate in 1986, replied, "I wouldn't be surprised," though he noted that "there was also a populist revulsion against American intervention, going back to United Fruit overthrowing the government in Guatemala [in 1954], and the [1973 coup] in Chile. American adventurism was stopped by liberal America."[101] As Walter Isaacson wrote, "Reagan invaded fewer countries than most modern presidents."[102]

The Vietnam syndrome thus seemingly constrained Reagan in a number of ways. "The reason for covert action was that the Vietnam War made [Reagan and George H. W. Bush] realize if they were to engage in activities that would bring broad opposition, well, they couldn't do it overtly," emphasized veteran liberal activist and political scientist Howard Zinn. "And so where they didn't make wars overtly, they did it against very weak enemies: Grenada, Panama, Iraq [in 1991]. . . . They kept talking about the necessity to do away with the Vietnam syndrome. Well, if they had to keep talking about it, it must be pretty powerful."[103]

Stanley Karnow recalled that the Vietnam syndrome also led directly to the covert arms trade deal that became known as the Iran-contra affair. "Reagan wanted to get involved in helping to overthrow the Sandinistas, and he couldn't do it," Karnow said. "The public was against it. So that's why we got Iran-contra, which was illegal. Guys were convicted on it, such as [National Security Council Staff member] Ollie North. He [Reagan] had to do it illegally, because he couldn't do it openly, and if you want to call that [a result of] the Vietnam syndrome, you can call it that. People just weren't alarmed by the Sandinistas."[104] Thus, despite Reagan's claim that he overturned the Vietnam syndrome, the lingering effects of the conflict and of the 1960s had an enormous impact on his foreign policy.

"My friends: We did it.": Reagan's 1989 Farewell Address

In late 1989 Jerry Falwell proclaimed that in the decade just ending "there's been a witnessing of the bankruptcy of the liberal philosophy and the anti-moral and amoral philosophies that were so prevalent in the 1960s and '70s."[105] Reagan would most certainly have agreed. Throughout his presidency he claimed to have replaced the sense of pessimism that followed the 1960s with a new feeling of confidence. In 1983 he remarked: "My greatest satisfaction is the conviction that a country that was skidding dangerously in the wrong direction . . . has been set on the right course. We've begun to undo the damage that the overtaxing, overspending, over-regulating binge of the sixties and seventies inflicted. . . . We've made America respected in the world again."[106] In 1986 Reagan observed that "the self-doubt, the weakness abroad and at home that marked so much of the sixties and the seventies" had been replaced with "confidence, self-assurance, [and] . . . patriotism."[107]

Reagan also conveyed such sentiments in his correspondence. "Like you, I can remember well the period in the late fifties and early sixties when America's self-confidence and optimism were almost palpable," he wrote presidential aide Dick Darman in 1985. "The years that followed brought pain, national division, and an uncharacteristic pessimism. . . . But I believe that we have made great progress during the past four years in bringing America back to its traditional optimism."[108]

This same restoration of confidence formed the central theme of Reagan's January 1989 farewell address, a speech that identified the 1960s as a terrible time in American history. Reagan put much time into the address. "I went back to my desk to work on my farewell address—Peggy Noonan has sent 1st draft," he wrote in his diary on January 3, 1989. Part of Reagan's entry the next day read, "More homework including some changes in Peggy N.'s draft of the farewell address."[109]

Reagan began his address, televised from the Oval Office, with an anecdote from the early 1980s. A U.S. sailor who, "like most American servicemen, was young, smart, and fiercely observant," was patrolling the South China Sea on the U.S.S. *Midway* when he saw in the distance a tiny vessel full of "refugees from Indochina hoping to get to America." When the boat was rescued by a *Midway* launch, one refugee exclaimed to the sailor, "'Hello, American sailor. Hello, freedom man.' That's what it was to be an American in the 1980s," Reagan said. "We stood, again, for freedom. I know we always have, but in the past few years the world again—and in a way, we ourselves—rediscovered it."[110]

The "two great triumphs" of the 1980s, he declared, were "the economic recovery [and] the recovery of our morale. America is respected again in the world." Reagan then once again blamed the 1960s for changing the course of history. "Back in the 1960s, when I began, it seemed to me that we'd begun reversing the order of things" as government expanded considerably. "I went into politics in part to put up my hand and say, 'Stop.' . . . I think we have stopped a lot of what needed stopping." Toward the end of his speech Reagan referred directly to the damage done by the 1960s. He offered a warning "that's been on my mind for some time. But oddly enough it starts with one of the things I'm proudest of in the past eight years: the resurgence of national pride that I called the new patriotism." While important, "it won't last unless it's grounded in thoughtfulness and knowledge." Reagan desired "an informed patriotism" and questioned the teaching of American values and history. As he had done throughout his political career, the departing president waxed nostalgic for an earlier time. "Those of us who are over thirty-five or so years of age grew up in a different America," he said. "We were taught, very directly, what it means to be an American. And we absorbed, almost in the air, a love of country and an appreciation of its institutions," along with values inculcated by family, neighborhood, and school. Even "movies celebrated democratic values and implicitly reinforced the idea that America was special. TV was like that, too, through the mid-sixties."[111]

But because of the "bad sixties" these traditional values were no longer guaranteed. "Younger parents aren't sure that an unambivalent appreciation of America is the right thing to teach modern children," he lamented, and for the makers of popular culture, "well-grounded patriotism is no longer the style." Though America's "spirit is back," he said, "we've got to do a better job of getting across that America is freedom." Reagan feared "an eradication of the American memory that could result, ultimately, in an erosion of the American spirit," and urged "more attention to American history and a greater emphasis on civic ritual." He finished by asserting that he had kept the promise which had ignited his candidacy nine years earlier: the pledge to renew America. The nation was now "more prosperous, more secure, and happier than it was eight years ago." Under his administration Americans had "brought America back." In short, "My friends: We did it."[112]

Brought America back, that is, from the brink of "the sixties." In his effort to renew America, Reagan used both Vietnam and the 1960s protest movements to best his opponents and advance his own policies. He claimed that Vietnam was a "noble cause," that the country needed finally to honor the war's veterans, and that the troops had been defeated not on the battlefield but by a government at home that was unwilling to do whatever it would take to win. Yet despite his confident rhetoric, ultimately Reagan was unable to reverse one lingering aftershock of the 1960s: the reluctance of Americans to engage in a lengthy ground war to fight communism. Although he claimed that his Central American policies had cured the Vietnam syndrome, Reagan's actions proved the contrary: the memory of the 1960s was fresh enough that any effort to intervene in Central America was hampered by public fear of "another Vietnam." Nevertheless, Reagan gained tremendous political mileage out of blaming "the sixties" and refurbishing the memory of Vietnam. He was able to brand the Democrats as weak on defense, a charge that helped him win the 1980 and 1984 elections. It was a lesson—and a political strategy—that would not be lost on his vice president and successor, George H. W. Bush.

5

Remembering Vietnam and the Civil Rights Movement

GEORGE H. W. BUSH'S 1960s

The Vietnam War was tearing our country apart. The protests were often ugly, violent, and personal.... [T]oo many young people used the war as an excuse to break the law, practice free sex, take drugs, and eschew responsibility of any kind. The personal values I had been taught as a child were threatened and, at least for a time, seemed lost.

George H. W. Bush (1999)

GEORGE H. W. BUSH's positions on the critical issues of the 1960s played a prominent role in his presidency. He referred often to the Vietnam War as well as to the civil rights movement. The 1988 election turned in large part on memories of the 1960s, as Bush used the themes of patriotism, race, and crime to discredit the Democratic nominee, Massachusetts governor Michael Dukakis. Like Reagan, Bush constantly used the "bad sixties" as a stick to beat his opponents, blaming the era for Americans' reluctance to employ military force and a decline in patriotism, among other ills. Bush also echoed Reagan in lavishing praise on Vietnam veterans and arguing that the war had been lost at home rather than on the battlefield. Although Bush would make the rhetorical claim that the 1991 Gulf War banished the Vietnam syndrome, he, like Reagan, failed to overcome it in his own actions as president.

He also made use of the 1960s to assert that since the United States had transcended much of its racist past, no further government activism in race relations was needed. In doing so, he made Martin Luther King Jr. out to be a far less radical figure than he actually was. To bolster the conservative Republican agenda of undoing Johnson's Great Society programs, Bush replaced King the social critic and 1960s radical with his own version of a convenient and unthreatening textbook icon. Such a portrayal

93

suited Bush's oft-stated belief that government attempts to improve social welfare had only made inner-city problems worse.

"The Sixties" and the 1988 Election

In the 1988 campaign Bush skillfully tarred Dukakis with the brush of the "bad sixties." With the eager help of the Republican National Committee (RNC), Bush made the moderate, rather bland Dukakis appear to the voting public as a wild-eyed 1960s radical who was unpatriotic and soft on crime. An internal document from the RNC's communications division in September 1988, "The Hazards of Duke," contained sections titled "Dukakis and the Criminal Justice System: The Coddler of Criminals" and "Compassion to Criminals—Not to Victims." Another focused on Dukakis's opposition to capital punishment.

The document also noted that on August 28, 1988, George Will, on ABC's *This Week with David Brinkley*, had responded to the question "Do we have a patriotism factor working in this election?" by saying, "We do to the extent that the Democratic Party, in the late '60s and '70s, acquired a lot of baggage, a sort of suspicion that there were prominent people in it setting the tone of it, who had a hyper-critical attitude about the United States, blame-America-first Democrats." Without naming any Democrats who had said such things, Will continued: "You had people who said this was a racist, imperialistic, sick society. And it takes some getting over that. And that's why, when they nominated the governor of the state emblematic of McGovernism, the only state, Massachusetts, that McGovern carried, they made themselves vulnerable to this." In pure Orwellian tones Will concluded: "No one has had the courage, and I hope they won't muster the courage, to say that Michael Dukakis is not patriotic. Clearly, he is. But his party acquired this kind of aura."[1]

Bush made similar attacks in his personal correspondence. In June 1988 he described Dukakis as "the consummate traditional McGovern-type liberal" in a letter to the pastor of his church in Maine. Bush was concerned that "people don't see that yet," and even claimed that most of Dukakis's supporters believed their candidate was "more conservative" than Bush. "My job will be to get things in focus," he wrote.[2]

Bush made the 1960s a presidential campaign issue in 1988 the moment he chose as his running mate Senator Dan Quayle of Indiana, the first baby boomer on a national ticket. By choosing a conservative member of the generation that came of age in the 1960s, Bush reminded the nation of the "silent majority" Nixon spoke of at the time. "I am proud to have put my trust in a whole generation of young people," Bush said in support of Quayle, in a direct appeal to conservative baby boomers.[3]

Although Quayle came of age in the 1960s, he took his inspiration from an earlier generation and distanced himself from his own. In his acceptance speech at the 1988 Republican National Convention he contrasted baby boomers with the generation who came of age during World War II. "I don't presume to talk for everyone of my generation," Quayle said, "but I know that a great many will agree with me when I express my thanks to the generation of George Bush for bringing us to an era of peace and freedom and opportunity. My generation has a profound debt to them."[4]

In the fall campaign Quayle invoked "the good sixties" in the hope of turning his relative political inexperience into an asset by repeatedly saying that he had the same amount of experience in Congress that John F. Kennedy had before he became president. In late August, after Dukakis's running mate, Senator Lloyd Bentsen of Texas, had questioned Quayle's gravitas, Quayle countered, "I'm very close to the same age as Jack Kennedy was when he was elected—not Vice President, but President."[5] The issue came to a head in the vice presidential debate between Quayle and Bentsen. After describing his presidential qualifications should Bush be unable to serve, Quayle again said that he had "far more experience than" numerous other vice presidential candidates and "as much experience in the Congress as Jack Kennedy did when he sought the presidency." In rebuttal Bentsen pounced: "Senator, I served with Jack Kennedy. I knew Jack Kennedy. Jack Kennedy was a friend of mine. Senator, you are no Jack Kennedy."[6]

"You are no Jack Kennedy" dogged Quayle throughout the campaign. While this attempt to use the "good sixties" to his benefit had failed, Bush increased his assault on the "bad sixties" as the campaign intensified. He railed against the "permissive philosophy" which in the 1960s had led to increased drug abuse and crime, adding that "people used to talk like those movies of the sixties. They thought drug use was 'cool' and advised you to 'Do your own thing.'" Bush mocked such sentiments and vowed to get tough on street gangs, pursue tougher sentencing laws for gang members, and construct more federal prisons. He also began running television ads attacking Dukakis for a weekend furlough program for prisoners established in Massachusetts, sensationalizing the fact that while on furlough one inmate, a man named Willie Horton, committed armed robbery and rape.[7]

Looking back on the 1988 election, Dukakis said that Bush's focus on matters such as the Pledge of Allegiance, flag burning, and the charge that

Dukakis was a "card-carrying member of the ACLU" was part of a strategy designed precisely "to brand the Democrats as unpatriotic." Dukakis responded with particular outrage to Bush's unsubstantiated charge that his wife, Kitty, had burned an American flag at an antiwar rally in the 1960s. Sixteen years later Dukakis was still angered by the Bush campaign's efforts to paint him as a 1960s radical.[8]

Bush's framing of his opponent as a "sixties" radical was disingenuous; Dukakis came of age in the 1950s, not the 1960s. His personal appearance and public demeanor were thoroughly conventional, and politically he was a moderate, doggedly pushing the use of efficient government to solve problems. He came across in person as earnest, hardworking, sober to the point of being dull, and concerned above all with how government could improve people's lives. "I don't think anyone ever could imagine Michael Dukakis in bell-bottom trousers, long hair, smoking a joint," remarked Dukakis speechwriter David Kusnet. Rather, in 1988 "Dukakis was labeled more as someone who would be soft on the sixties, soft on disruptive behavior."[9]

In the end it did not matter that the northeasterner did not have a liberal record, that he had instituted elements of the "New Democrat" positions of the Democratic Leadership Council (DLC) while governor of Massachusetts, and had passed welfare reform and cut taxes. Dukakis "was not a raging liberal," acknowledged political scientist Darrell West, "but by the end of the campaign, many Americans thought that he was." The percentage of voters who considered Dukakis a liberal rose nearly twenty points during the campaign.[10] Historian William Berman called the 1988 campaign "a good example of using the sixties as a bludgeon."[11] Dukakis became the unwilling but hapless target of the Right's enduring anger toward "the sixties."

John F. Kennedy in his 1960 presidential campaign could say, "I'm proud to be a liberal."[12] But by 1988 "liberal" was a dirty word. "Dukakis shrank from the accusation of being a liberal like Dracula shrinking from the sign of the crucifix," said psychologist David Barash, the author of a treatise in defense of liberalism.[13] Those who worked for Dukakis agreed. "He avoided the L-word, any ideological definition of himself," said Kusnet. "And at the very end [of the campaign], he said, 'Yes, I am a liberal,' on a train trip through California," when he developed "a much more populist approach to his rhetoric." But "if in 1988 you said you were a liberal, it was hard to also define yourself as a populist, because liberalism that year had connotations [of elitism] rather than bread-and-butter liberalism."[14] After Dukakis referred to himself as "a liberal in the tradition of Franklin Roosevelt and Harry Truman and John Kennedy," Bush exclaimed: "Miracle of miracles. Headlines. Read all about it. My opponent finally . . . called himself the big 'L,' called himself a liberal."[15]

Explaining Dukakis's predicament, political scientist Nicol Rae noted that in the early 1960s "Kennedy didn't have to worry about the social connotations, because [saying, 'I am a liberal'] is basically saying, 'I'm a New Dealer.'" But in 1988 "'I'm a liberal' carries a whole lot of other meanings: 'Oh, I'm against the death penalty'; 'Oh, I think crime just comes because people are poor and they don't have a chance.'"[16] Long-time Democratic Party activist and election strategist Donna Brazile, who worked for the Dukakis campaign, charged that "liberals have repeatedly failed to define themselves as patriotic, God-fearing Americans. Rather, the GOP has painted liberals as godless, spineless, and elitist."[17] Republican rhetoric confirmed Brazile's point. "'Liberal' has come to be associated with higher taxes, a weak foreign policy, and radical social policies on issues like abortion—thus its unpopularity," said Gary Bauer.[18]

Following Reagan's example, the Republican candidates praised the early 1960s in order to tarnish Dukakis with the late 1960s by comparison. Bush derided Dukakis's interpretations of Reagan's foreign policy as "a rejection of America's role as a world leader and a repudiation of the Truman Doctrine and the vision of John Kennedy."[19] Bush continued this line of attack throughout the campaign, especially in its closing days. "Mainstream Americans no longer feel represented by the Democratic Party," he said on October 31. "And so my pitch here in the last eight days [before the election] is to those good Democrats, the rank and file, the 'silent majority.'"[20] Ignoring the fact that the nuclear freeze movement did not begin until after the 1960s, Bush said of Dukakis: "He's out there comparing himself to JFK. John Kennedy understood military strength. . . . He never believed, as my opponent did, in this nuclear freeze, and he never backed unilateral disarmament." Former president Gerald Ford, while introducing Bush at a campaign event, called Dukakis's references to Democrats such as Kennedy "an insult."[21] If Lloyd Bentsen had stymied Quayle's attempt to associate himself with Kennedy, Bush did his best to return the favor.

In 1988 Reagan also used glowing memories of Kennedy to endorse Bush. Reagan expressed his views on liberalism only once in 1985 and three times in 1986 but more than sixty times in his successor's 1988 campaign.[22] He said at one rally, "It's time to talk issues; to use the dreaded 'L' word; to say the policies of our opposition and the congressional leadership of his party are liberal, liberal, liberal."[23] An earlier draft read, "The party of Roosevelt, Truman, John Kennedy, and Johnson has become the party of McGovern, Carter, Mondale, Ted Kennedy, and Dukakis."[24]

In 1988 "it was very much a conscious decision to use the word 'liberal,'" remarked Bush speechwriter Josh Gilder, "because if you asked your pollsters, it scored very low." Dukakis's crime policy "was absolutely summed up in the fact that this rapist and murderer [Willie Horton] who was in jail for life without parole was being given vacation time, during which he held a couple hostage and raped a woman. So, we weren't disparaging liberalism," he stressed. "We were simply calling a duck a duck. Liberalism had failed on its own."[25]

The highly charged use of Horton, an African American, also made race central to the attacks on Dukakis. "The roots of [using "liberal" as an insult] are in the fight over de facto segregation in the sixties and seventies, affirmative action, and busing, and the idea that a liberal is a comfortably situated white person who wants the white working class to pay the price of his social engineering," observed Doug Rossinow. Republicans also highlighted the damaging repercussions "of an allegedly more permissive and tolerant attitude toward criminal defendants," which the public blamed on "the sixties' permissiveness." Bush's charge that Dukakis was soft on crime was meant to remind voters of the consequence of "a more generous attitude toward African Americans."[26]

Once elected, Bush distanced himself from this aspect of his campaign's strategy. Asked about his use of Willie Horton, he dismissively said, "That's history."[27] But the past was very much alive, and Bush continued to exploit the political power of many remnants of the 1960s, not least the legacy of the Vietnam War.

Restoring "Lost" Patriotism

Bush biographer Herbert Parmet, asked how Bush would describe his sentiments toward the 1960s, said, "He would probably emphasize the true disdain for the military. It's very important to him." Bush was "very much a supporter of those in the military and manifestations of flag-waving patriotism. There is a sensitivity to the man, and he is swayed by that kind of traditional emotionalism."[28]

Like Reagan, Bush aimed to rekindle the nation's patriotism. At a 1989 press conference, commenting on the Supreme Court's recent decision upholding the right to burn the American flag as symbolic speech protected under the First Amendment, Bush said that although the right to protest needed to be protected, the flag "should never be the object of desecration." Asked if his visits to flag factories in his 1988 campaign were for political gain, Bush responded that he never claimed "Republicans are for the flag and Democrats are not," but that he did "feel viscerally about burning the American flag."[29]

Bush invoked the Vietnam War at the Iwo Jima Memorial when he proposed a constitutional amendment to outlaw flag burning. "The flag represents and reflects the fabric of our nation," he remarked. At the end of his speech he quoted at length the words of a naturalized U.S. citizen who was serving as a marine in Vietnam, including his call "to protect the flag now, as when we were in uniform—if not for us, then for those fallen veterans."[30]

At the start of his presidency, Bush's fight against flag burning was more than just residue from his successful use of patriotic themes in the 1988 campaign. He was firmly aware of the divisions the war in Vietnam had caused, and he identified it as a conflict that continued to harm the nation's morale, for which he primarily blamed those who had opposed the war in "the sixties."

In his inaugural address President Bush pushed for a greater spirit of co-operation in Washington and for transcending the divisions of the 1960s. "Congress, too, has changed in our time. There has grown a certain divisiveness. We have seen the hard looks." Bush bemoaned this rise of partisanship, declaring: "It's been this way since Vietnam. That war cleaves us still. But, friends, that war began in earnest a quarter of a century ago, and surely the statute of limitations has been reached. This is a fact: The final lesson of Vietnam is that no great nation can long afford to be sundered by a memory. A new breeze is blowing, and the old bipartisanship must be made new again."[31]

During the 1960s, Bush later noted in his memoir, he "supported the Administration's Vietnam policy." He had expressed this support in a very public gesture: he was the sole Republican to attend Lyndon Johnson's departure from Washington in 1969. Instead of watching Nixon's inaugural parade, Bush, who had been easily reelected to a second term in Congress, went to Andrews Air Force Base, where members of Johnson's cabinet, as well as a few friends from both houses of Congress, were lined up to say good-bye. "I was the only Republican there," Bush recalled. "Hard as I'd worked against the man over the years—not Johnson personally, but his policies—I couldn't help but feel the poignancy of the moment." After three decades of government service, Johnson had hoped to match the legacy of his hero, FDR. "But because of Vietnam, the cheering had stopped, and he was going back to Texas a defeated man."[32]

Bush's letters and diary entries from the 1960s and early 1970s show the depth of his support for the war. In 1968 he wrote to a friend from whom he had received an antiwar letter, "I just don't buy that this is an immoral war on our part." He was particularly critical of the press coverage. "The biased reporting on [the progress of the war] stinks. . . . The emphasis is on our round that falls short—or the brutality of the South Vietnamese—or the civilians killed by our napalm." Bush called the coverage "grossly unfair." Most of all he was dismissive of the war's critics, especially the behavior of those in the antiwar movement. He railed against their "arrogance and total lack of compassion," noted that "I detest this suggestion that the President doesn't care about human lives," and claimed that the protesters "definitively strengthened Hanoi's will." In 1971, after the *New York Times* began publishing the Pentagon Papers, Bush dictated into his diary: "The press is a very liberal press. People are trying to make a hero out of [Daniel] Ellsberg."[33]

"He stayed pro-war right through to the end," noted David Halberstam, who also recalled Bush's presence at Johnson's 1969 departure. Though Bush "was in no rush to have a son go off to war"—whereas he himself had immediately enlisted for World War II—"he never showed any doubt on the war . . . and has never been a critic of it."[34]

Like Reagan, Bush praised the motives for the Vietnam War. Like Reagan, Bush charged that veterans were treated poorly on their return, saying at the 1989 dedication of a Vietnam veterans' memorial: "Unlike other veterans, the brave boys who went to Vietnam had to endure two wars. The first was that one waged in the swamps and the jungles abroad, and the second was fought for respect and recognition at home. And with the passage of time, they have won the battle for the hearts of their countrymen—and in my view, it's about time."[35] Bush's speechwriters struggled with defining the war on this occasion, deleting wording that implied it had been lost. One draft read, "If ultimate victory was denied them in the first, victory is finally theirs in the second." National security adviser Brent Scowcroft suggested saying instead, "'They won every major battle in which they fought and with the passage of time they have finally won the battle for the hearts of their countrymen.' The rewritten sentence," Scowcroft noted, "better expresses the military accomplishments of Vietnam Veterans."[36]

Bush spoke often of how the war had affected the nation's mores. In 1989 he said, in his peculiar way with words, "We condoned [drug use] in my theory in a kind of a post-Vietnam period, or even in the Vietnam War period."[37] Asked in 1990 about young people's "sense of hopelessness," Bush said that he had "a philosophy of what happened, a theory. We came out of the Vietnam War; it was very divisive." The war, along with Watergate, "increased a certain national cynicism."[38] He expressed similar views in his private correspondence both before and after his presidency. In a 1982 letter to Yale president A. Bartlett Giamatti, he wrote that "in our post–Viet Nam, post-Watergate guilt, we have condoned things we should have condemned." In a 1998 letter to Bob Woodward he complained, "Watergate and the Vietnam war are the two things that moved beltway journalism into this aggressive, intrusive 'take no prisoners' kind of reporting that I can now say I find offensive."[39]

Bush blamed criticism of the war for other social problems as well. Asked about "self-indulgence and immediate gratification" as values of the 1980s, Bush mused that during Vietnam the young "were told that our cause was immoral. . . . I still don't accept that view." Such criticism, he charged, had in turn led to other ills. Academics and politicians taught Americans that "our cause was wrong. And then we condoned as a society certain excesses that we should have condemned," such as drug use and even graffiti.[40]

Between 1989 and 1991 Bush spoke often of the progress he had made toward overcoming a variety of negative social and cultural trends he saw as traceable to Vietnam. As president he demonstrated an eagerness to repair the damage caused by the war. International events soon provided him with an opportunity to eradicate the lingering ghosts of Vietnam.

A Chance to Reverse the Vietnam Syndrome: The Gulf War

The memory of Vietnam played a crucial role in drumming up public support for the 1991 war in the Persian Gulf, and President Reagan's frequent focus on Vietnam veterans influenced his successor's efforts to build that support. "The Gulf War was [seen as] a kind of necessary shock therapy to jolt the American people out of their reluctance to go to war, a reluctance that, allegedly, was a hangover from the defeat in Vietnam," wrote war critic Jerry Lembcke. The war's planners hoped that victory would be so overwhelming that "positive identification with it would be irresistible." Crucial to building popular support was resurrecting certain images from "the sixties." Chief among these was, in Lembcke's words, "the myth of the spat-upon veteran." He quotes one American soldier in the Persian Gulf saying, "If I go back home like the Vietnam vets did and somebody spits on me, I swear to God I'll kill them." According to its promoters, the war was as much about supporting the troops already stationed in Saudi Arabia as about any specific policy goals. The public was told that the Gulf War's opponents were like "those who opposed the Vietnam War and spat on Vietnam veterans," Lembcke asserted. People therefore reasoned that, like the Vietnam vets, "the soldiers being sent to the Gulf must also be good soldiers. We had to support them." The triumphant parades that marked the soldiers' return were also framed as a contrast to the way Vietnam veterans were supposedly treated when they came home.[41]

Vietnam weighed heavily on the minds of Americans during the lead-up to the conflict. When peace activists warned of a loss of life on a scale similar to that in Vietnam, Bush echoed the conservative critique of the Vietnam War: the United States lost because of unnecessary interference by civilian politicians. On February 14, 1991, weeks before ground action began, Bush reviewed the military plan. "I have not second-guessed [,] . . . told them what targets to hit[,] . . . what weapons to use and not to use," read his diary entry. "I have learned from Vietnam." In 1999 Bush added a footnote to this entry clarifying his meaning: "Civilian leaders micromanaged the Vietnam War and second-guessed the military leaders."[42]

Bush hoped that the Gulf War would eclipse one particular legacy of the 1960s and return the nation to the unity he fondly remembered during World War II. In an exchange with reporters on February 17, referring to the war's planning he said: "It is my hope that when this is over we will have kicked, for once and for all, the so-called Vietnam syndrome. And the country's pulling together, unlike any time . . . since World War II. And that's a good thing for our country.[43] Once the ground war ended, Bush set out to convince the public that the war had finally laid to rest the ghosts of Vietnam. "It's a proud day for America," he declared. "And, by God, we've kicked the Vietnam syndrome once and for all."[44] Asked when Bush first used the phrase "Vietnam syndrome" and whether it was in a prepared speech, Bush's longtime speechwriter Curt Smith clarified, "No, that was ad lib."[45]

Three days later, while delivering a speech, Bush did not mention the Vietnam syndrome.[46] In spontaneous remarks at the end, however, he did use the term:

> I made a comment right here at this podium the other day about shedding the divisions that incurred from the Vietnam War. And I want to repeat and say especially to the Vietnam veterans that are here: it is long overdue that we kicked the Vietnam syndrome, because many veterans from that conflict came back and did not receive the proper acclaim that they deserve. When these troops come home, I hope that message goes out to those that served this country in the Vietnam War that we appreciate their service as well.[47]

Bush's speechwriters repeatedly encouraged him to address the Vietnam syndrome. One draft includes this handwritten note: "VA [Veterans Administration] . . . would encourage some additional, spontaneous remarks by the president to this group. The Pres. [Bush] really warms to Veterans, especially when he speaks *informally* & spontaneously to them." A note at the end of another draft reads: "Shedding divisions—long overdue to kick Vietnam syndrome. Nation *was* divided. Didn't get proper homecoming. Hope message gets out to all Viet vets (they did a great job?)."[48] With a certain unintended eloquence, the hesitation attested to by the question mark indicates that his speechwriters were unsure how to praise the losing effort.

Bush continued to emphasize the importance of overcoming the Vietnam syndrome. "Our successes have banished the Vietnam-era phantoms of doubt and distrust," he said in a major 1991 policy address at the University of Michigan that also offered a lengthy attack on the Great Society. The country, he said, now showed "an idealism that we Americans supposedly had lost."[49] But implicit in such statements was the notion that during his own two terms Reagan had not banished the Vietnam syndrome after all. A first draft of the speech used even bolder language: "Our success in the [Gulf] war helped kill Vietnam-era doubts that we could not function in world affairs, that we lacked the certainty or reliability to take a stand in tough times."[50] Another speech draft discussed Vietnam in greater detail: "But the [Gulf] war also revived our belief in ourselves. It seemed to rouse us from a fitful Vietnam-era sleep, a nightmare time in which we doubted our decency, our values, our abilities. The days of doubt and malaise are over." Here a speechwriter wrote in the margin, "What does this imply about the first two years of the Bush administration (to say nothing of the RR years)." The irony was clearly not lost on Bush's speechwriters.[51]

The claim that the Gulf War had finally banished the ghosts of Vietnam was one that Bush used throughout his 1992 reelection campaign. "Don't let the revisionists, don't let these smart alecks that opposed [the Gulf War] from day one come back a year later and try to take it away from you," he told one audience. "It was a clear, solid victory. It reversed the Vietnam syndrome; it gave us pride."[52] At another appearance later that day Bush said that Saddam Hussein assumed we would not attack Iraq because "he thought that the Vietnam syndrome was with us forever." But the Iraqi dictator "mistook a voice of protest and a handful of editorials and a couple of speeches in the Congress for the United States lacking the will. . . . Our country came together with a pride that we hadn't had since the end of World War II."[53]

Until the end of his presidency Bush remained preoccupied with the shadow of Vietnam. Less than a week after his defeat by Bill Clinton in the 1992 election, Bush visited the Vietnam Memorial the day before Veterans Day. "There is not much time left to say what is in my heart, but one thing I care about is Vietnam," he dictated into his diary.[54]

Did Bush Cure the Syndrome?

Politics aside, the memory of Vietnam played a crucial role in the actual prosecution of the Gulf War. During the lead-up to war, members of Bush's inner circle were "very aware" of the Vietnam syndrome, recalled James Baker, Bush's secretary of state.[55] (Bush described Baker as "perhaps my closest confidant during my political days. I trusted him completely.")[56] "This was really the first major war in terms of commitment of troops [since Vietnam]. We had 500,000 Americans in the Gulf," Baker noted. "I went into the Oval Office when we were thinking about escalating from economic sanctions and political sanctions to military action to kick Iraq out of Kuwait, and I said, 'Mr. President, this has all the earmarks of the type of action or crisis that has brought down prior presidencies. You've got $40 oil, you've got body bags, you've got dire predictions about casualties.' That didn't turn out to be true, fortunately," Baker added. "And we were dealing with a House and Senate of Democrats, and they were very much against our doing this, and they didn't stop at demagoguing."[57]

Baker expressed irritation at the way the memory of Vietnam colored the prewar Senate hearings, especially when Democrats tried to use "the sixties" for their own purposes. "Look at the testimony I gave before the Senate, particularly questions" from Democrats, such as, "'Mr. Secretary, how many dead is it worth to go do this?' I mean, those kinds of outrageous questions. We did it right politically and militarily and diplomatically, but we had a Congress who was trying to use it for political purposes, so we had that against us," Baker said.[58]

"By any measure, our Gulf policy was fraught with risk," Baker wrote in his 1995 memoir of his diplomatic service under President Bush. "In yet another refrain of the Vietnam syndrome, members [of Congress] did not wish to be held responsible for sending troops from their states and districts off to what might be a bloody war. So many in Congress preferred the politically safer course of doing nothing at all."[59] Baker never made clear how this was a "refrain" of Vietnam any more than a "refrain" of the years preceding World Wars I and II. But Vietnam was an easier target, and the lingering memory of that war irritated Bush's secretary of state.

Many Republicans do believe that Bush succeeded in overcoming the Vietnam syndrome. Reagan initiated the rehabilitation of the U.S. military, recalled Frank Carlucci, Reagan's secretary of defense during the last year of his presidency, but "the process wasn't completed until Desert Storm. That particular action erased the Vietnam syndrome."[60] To Craig Shirley, "Reagan kicked the Vietnam syndrome, but if there's any doubt, then Bush stomped it into submission."[61] And Baker wrote in 1995, "Ultimately, the Persian Gulf crisis would establish in rather convincing fashion that our country's long and oftentimes debilitating post-Vietnam hangover had at least temporarily run its course."[62]

As for the public's perception of the military, "the status of the military went way up as a result of the Gulf War; in fact, it's one of the higher-rated institutions now, if not the highest-rated institution," said political scientist Gary Jacobson. "And that was a big change from Vietnam, when the military was roundly excoriated." Though Bush's popularity "wasn't very sustained, [the war] did make the point that exercising U.S. military force overseas wasn't always disastrous, which was the Vietnam lesson."[63]

Several observers agreed that the nation experienced a catharsis in reaction to the Gulf War. "It was not only about American victory," recalled author Frances FitzGerald. "Suddenly the soldier is the hero, and everybody had their yellow ribbons out. You should have seen it in Bangor, Maine, when the soldiers came back. The whole town was just out there. It was a certain amount of guilt on the part of older people who had felt that Vietnam-era grunts had not been treated well."[64]

Others, however, did not believe that it was Bush who erased the Vietnam syndrome. Caspar Weinberger felt that the credit belonged to the administration in which he had served. "President Reagan set the stage for success in the Gulf War. We would not have been able to win so quickly there if we had not built up the military and brought it to full strength during the Reagan years." Nevertheless, our rapid victory in the war "certainly made it quite clear that things had changed."[65]

Some denied that the Vietnam syndrome had been erased at all. Asked if Bush had ever spoken to him of it, Curt Smith replied, "He did, and he felt, I think mistakenly so, that the Gulf War in 1991 had in essence put the syndrome to rest." Noting that in his inaugural address Bush referred to Vietnam as "the war that cleaves us still," Smith recalled that in 1991 he said "something to the effect that 'My God, the Vietnam syndrome is dead.' Well, it's not, as we have seen in the 2000 election and regarding Iraq now [in 2004], because the media, the institutions, including the clergy, the entire Democratic Party, were in effect hijacked by 'peace at any price,' 'hate America,' 'hate the military' in the 1960s, and they've never quite recovered their moorings and their bearings." U.S. service members, Smith said, "know that the Democratic Party detests them."[66]

The Vietnam syndrome continued in other ways. Conservatives still declare, "We've kicked the Vietnam syndrome," complained Stanley Karnow. "If they have to keep saying it, then it must not be true."[67] Julian Bond said, "I'm not sure if we kicked it; if we did kick it, it's kicking us back in Iraq."[68] As far as Bob Woodward was concerned, the Gulf War merely affirmed the Powell doctrine. "His [Colin Powell's] solution was to only go into operations where you can guarantee success, and that meant overwhelming force." According to Woodward's research, "[Defense Secretary Dick] Cheney and Bush very much agreed. They asked the military, 'What are you going to need?'" When Powell, as chairman of the Joint Chiefs of Staff, asked for twice as many troops as had been anticipated, Bush immediately said yes.[69] (In his memoir Powell wrote, "When we go to war, we should have a purpose that our people understand and support; we should mobilize the country's resources to fulfill that mission and then go in to win." Powell did not believe the nation did that in the 1960s in Vietnam.)[70]

If anything, thought some, the Gulf War showed that the Vietnam syndrome was alive and well. "I'll give Bush a little credit for having a better memory of Vietnam than Bush II had: he did not invade Iraq," noted Daniel Ellsberg. "Bush bowed to the Vietnam syndrome at the same time that he was describing it as overcome."[71] The 1991 conflict initiated a renewed period of reluctance to use military force. "You didn't see us eager to intervene militarily in the years after the Gulf War," observed Michael Dukakis.[72] As John Shattuck, Clinton's undersecretary of state for democracy, human rights, and labor, noted, Bush "did nothing about Bosnia," and "the Vietnam syndrome kept [Clinton] from going in."[73] To historian Bruce Schulman, the Gulf War was an "itemized bill of how the Vietnam syndrome *continued* to have its effect." Unlike in Vietnam, in the Persian Gulf the military "announced that everyone was going to serve for the duration." The military also made special efforts to control the press.[74]

Bush's decision not to invade Baghdad after expelling Iraqi forces from Kuwait demonstrated the continuing influence of the Vietnam War on foreign policy. While the public opinion of the U.S. military improved and Gulf War veterans were treated as heroes, Bush overstated the case that the country had freed itself of the Vietnam syndrome as a restraint on all foreign military intervention.

Just as Vietnam continued to cast a long shadow during the Bush administration, so too would another pivotal aspect of the 1960s: the civil rights movement. As with Vietnam, in matters of race Bush tried to paint a picture of a nation that had overcome past tensions and moved forward, beyond the crises of the 1960s.

Remembering the Civil Rights Movement:
Bush and African Americans

"I opposed discrimination of any kind and abhorred racism," Bush wrote in his 1999 memoir in discussing his opposition to the Civil Rights Act of 1964. "Changes obviously needed to be made, but I agreed with Barry Goldwater and others who supported the concept of civil rights but felt strongly that this bill was unconstitutional and threatened more rights than it protected. . . . [M]y reasons for not supporting the bill were very different from those who hated the bill for racist reasons."[75]

Bush's personal correspondence of the era made his opposition to the bill clear. In July 1964, during his unsuccessful campaign for the U.S. Senate, Bush wrote Majorie Arsht, a leader in the Jewish community of Houston and a strong Bush supporter, that "Goldwater's position is correct (and parenthetically so is mine)—for Texas and for the USA. We must develop this position reasonably, prudently, sensitively—we must be sure we don't inflame the passions of unthinking men to garner a vote; yet it is essential that the position I believe in be explained."[76] On the campaign trail, however, Bush was firm in his opposition to the Civil Rights Act. He repeatedly told rallies that Congress had enacted "the new civil rights act to protect fourteen percent of the people" but that he was interested in "the other eighty-six percent."[77]

In a letter to Richard Nixon shortly after the election, Bush noted that in his losing campaign he had "received more votes than any other Republican has ever gotten in Texas, polling over 1,100,000[,] but with the Johnson landslide it was not enough. . . . The minority groups, principally the Negroes[,] went to the polls and voted 98.5 percent to 1.5 percent against me. It was not [because of] my position on civil rights," Bush wrote, because African Americans had overwhelmingly supported all of the nineteen Texas Democrats who "voted against the Civil Rights Bill." (Of Texas's twenty-four congressmen in 1964, all but two were Democrats.)[78]

Despite opposing the Civil Rights Act, Bush took pride in his outreach efforts to African Americans. Looking back in 1999 Bush recalled, "One of my goals as county GOP chairman was to reach out to minority voters." He had expressed the same sentiments in 1963, when he told a Houston Republican, "We should make an honorable appeal to the Negro vote, realizing that we are working against very difficult odds."[79] In describing his landslide victory in his 1966 race for Congress, Bush lamented that he had not done better among African American voters. "It was both puzzling and frustrating," he wrote in 1987, recounting in detail the extensive efforts he had made to build bridges with African Americans dating back to "when I headed the UNCF [United Negro College Fund] drive on the Yale campus in 1948."[80] His biggest disappointment as vice president, he claimed, was Reagan's inability to attract African American voters.[81] (This regret runs in the family: in 2005 his son said that he was "disappointed, frankly, in the vote I got in the African-American community" in the 2004 election—11 percent.[82] And James Baker was at a loss to explain the low level of African American support for Republicans, though he insisted that it was not due to a lack of effort.[83])

Bush also made the case for his strong record on race in discussing his unpopular support for the open housing bill that came before Congress in 1968 in the wake of Martin Luther King's assassination. After he voted to support it, he was deluged with hate mail. When he attended a district rally one week later, Bush faced a hostile all-white audience who jeered him when he was introduced. After he had finished speaking, Bush heard a swell of applause that turned into a standing ovation. "More than twenty years later," he wrote, "I can truthfully say that nothing I've experienced in public life, before or since, has measured up to the feeling I had when I went home that night."[84] Unlike in 1964, Bush supported the Civil Rights Act of 1968.

Despite his professed long-standing support of African Americans, when Bush became president he opposed increasing the role of the federal government to achieve social justice. He often referred to the civil rights movement in a way that implied America's improved racial climate had made such activism unnecessary.

At first Bush supported government involvement, and urged using the federal government in partnership with the private sector to correct past injustices. "Government can be an instrument of healing," he told a gathering of the United Negro College Fund in 1989. "There are times when government must step in where others fear to tread. My friends, I share those beliefs, and as president, I will act on them." He later praised Reagan's 1981 Executive Order 12320, "committing the federal government to increase its support of historically black colleges and universities."[85]

One of the goals of that speech was to show that Bush was not as hostile toward African Americans as some believed. In one draft, next to a list of prominent individuals who had been helped by the UNCF, Bush's assistant for special activities and initiatives, Stephen M. Studdert, wrote, "What about Sec. Sullivan?" referring to Bush's African American secretary of health and human services, Dr. Louis W. Sullivan, whose name did not appear in the list. On the next page Studdert wrote again, "What about Dr. Sullivan, *our* Sec of HHS—What about a woman?"[86] The final draft showed the influence of these suggestions, with Bush referring to "my dear friend, Dr. Lou Sullivan, who is here with us tonight," and further noting that the first lady had been a board member when Sullivan was president of the medical school at Morehouse College.[87]

Bush addressed the problem of racism on the twenty-fifth anniversary of the 1964 Civil Rights Act, a bill he had opposed. Quoting King, he spoke of the need for "a society in which individuals are judged 'not by the color of their skin, but by the content of their character,'" and mentioned his support for affirmative action. But he also urged going beyond 1960s-type government programs. When President Kennedy proposed his landmark 1963 civil rights bill, Bush said, he understood that "even the most comprehensive of laws could never meet the challenge of civil rights. The problem, he declared, 'must be solved in the homes of every American in every community across our country.'"[88]

Bush's speechwriters were sensitive to the need to avoid pessimism in portraying the degree of progress made in race relations since the 1960s. An earlier draft of this speech stated that since 1964, "we have seen much that was done and undone." But as a speechwriter wrote in the margins of an earlier draft, the phrase "might imply that we have taken steps backward." In the final draft the last five words were changed to strike a more optimistic note, reading, "We have seen much progress." The draft version also spoke of the need "to move forward into the century's final decade with a civil rights mission that fully embraces every disadvantaged American, whether black, yellow, or brown—whether women, children, or the aged; whether the disabled, the unemployed, or the homeless." In the final draft "disadvantaged American" was changed to "deserving American, regardless of race." And the draft's "whether black, yellow, or brown" was changed to "whether black, or yellow, brown or white." Bush thus diluted the goal and focus of the 1964 act—to help African Americans—by broadening it to include all races and a variety of constituents.[89]

Another phrase was changed as well. The rough draft noted that the 1964 bill had moved toward enactment after "the longest debate in its history and a 74-day filibuster by Southern Senators," but the final draft deleted the phrase "by Southern Senators." Bush wanted to avoid angering the South, so crucial to the Republican political realignment since the 1960s. As one aide suggested, "if it is not being too coy, it seems wise to avoid noting the fact that the senators were mainly Southerners, if only for the reason that a few, not many, but a few of the filibusterers were operating out of principled motives not based on racism. The South has been thoroughly bashed for racism. The larger point is that it is unnecessary, so long as we are not being revisionist, to call attention to the locus of racism in the '60s."[90]

These textual changes were indeed a form of historical revisionism. The speech intentionally ignored the historical reality that opposition to the 1964 Civil Rights Bill came primarily from southern whites. On at least one other occasion Bush again chose to avoid mentioning the South's ugly racial past. "I heard a shocking story that took place right here in America in 1943, in the middle of World War II," Bush said in 1991 in an observance of National Afro-American History Month. "Black soldiers stopped and tried to eat at a restaurant. Inside German prisoners, German prisoners of war, were being served a meal, but the restaurant refused to admit the black soldiers."[91] The original version had placed the story specifically "in the South," not "right here in America" as Bush softened it.[92]

In addressing civil rights issues Bush was often very complimentary toward Martin Luther King. In 1990 he described him as "a crusader and an evangelist [who] bore the weight of a pioneer. He was a force against evil. His life was a metaphor for courage."[93] Introduced by Coretta Scott King at a 1989 ceremony, he again stressed the role of the individual in overcoming racism. Quoting a prizewinning essay on King written by a fifth-grade student, Bush said, "He writes: 'I am only 11 years old, so I cannot really stop the racism. But I can control what happens in my heart and what I do with my life.'" Bush added, "A truly free society is within reach if, in our hearts, we abolish bias and bigotry and discrimination."[94]

The president's speechwriters made sure not to portray King as he was—a radical who had sought to make profound changes in American life. One speechwriter, Jim Pinkerton, suggested changing the line "Dr. King did not seek to break with our system, but to perfect it," arguing: "In this day and age it is not necessary to defend King against the charge that he was some sort of radical bent on overturning the system. Use of the word 'break' sets up the straw man of unreconstructed racism. I'm not arguing that there is no racism any more, but even the civil rights community would agree that it has grown more subtle and more sophisticated. Thus I would simply say that 'Dr. King was a reformer, a crusader. His mission was to move America closer to the ideal—to bring the promise.'" This last phrase replaced in the final draft the phrase to which Pinkerton objected.[95]

Bush's most extensive reconstruction of King came in an article he wrote for the *Washington Times* in 1990 in anticipation of the upcoming King federal holiday. "The civil rights movement is a story about courage, about determined Americans whose belief in Dr. King's words gave them the strength to stand up for what is right," Bush wrote. Most Americans "are judged . . . not by their color, but by their character. Yet, 'most' isn't good enough." He also stressed the relevance of conservative

Republican principles for African Americans. Since the 1960s, he noted, "we have learned that education creates economic empowerment[,] . . . that free markets work[,] . . . [and] the truth of Dr. King's words, 'Injustice anywhere is a threat to justice everywhere.'" He then cited recent global changes in an effort to transform King from a radical critic of American racism to a critic of communism and—by extension—a champion of capitalism and free markets. The civil rights movement had inspired people worldwide, he wrote, and "from Prague to Pretoria, Dr. King's belief in the inherent dignity of the individual is central to the universal dream for mankind." Expanding this connection between eastern European anticommunists and 1960s civil rights marchers, Bush remarked that eastern Europeans had "the same dreams and hopes that energized a generation of Americans who fought in the great struggle for civil rights." King's message "lives on through Lech Walesa and the millions like him marching for freedom," Bush wrote, noting that recently "hundreds of East and West Germans stood on the Berlin Wall and sang the same hopeful words" of the song "We Shall Overcome." Critics of Reagan and Bush charged that more was needed to further the cause of racial justice at home, but Bush suggested that King's work was near completion: "Around the world, we see changes that are making Dr. King's words of 'justice and righteousness' come true."[96]

This use of King to interpret events overseas rather than in the United States was an essential device for Bush's speechwriters. As one wrote, "the [*Washington Times*] piece places the civil rights movement in an international perspective—by comparing the movement to the march toward democracy around the world."[97]

Nor was this the only instance in which Bush linked King to conservative policies. On the King holiday in 1992 he stressed the key role of family structures in helping African Americans, presenting the movement King spearheaded as centered on personal rather than political issues. "At the heart of these values, as Dr. King knew, is the family," Bush declared, as "urban problems stem in large part from the weakening of the family." Instead of urging government intervention to cure problems of poverty, Bush declared that change needed to come from African Americans themselves.[98]

Here again Bush used the memory of the 1960s to champion Republican policies by constructing a less radical and literally revised image of King. An earlier draft was far more biting in portraying life before the civil rights movement. "America is a different country today—a better country, because of the faith Martin Luther King had in the American people," it read. "Dr. King faced a nation disfigured by a kind of homegrown apartheid that twisted the force of law to segregate some Americans from others, depriving them of even the rudiments of common citizenship. Jim Crow was quite simply un-American, an insult to the American creed, and Dr. King knew it." This paragraph was deleted, as were two sentences emphasizing the continued existence of racism, which concluded, "Racism and bigotry, blind hatred and intolerance still exist in our land." Next to this Curt Smith wrote, "Too negative—why raise this."[99] As Bush depicted him, King espoused internal rather than external solutions to the plight of African Americans. Bush argued that 1960s-style legislation was no longer needed, as the global forces of freedom and democracy were doing work no mere act of legislation could accomplish. In the 1960s King had advocated an increase in funding for the Great Society and strongly criticized the government, arguing that the war in Vietnam drained resources from the War on Poverty. But Bush—like Reagan—reinterpreted the 1960s by portraying King as a far less radical figure while minimizing the Great Society's positive impact on African Americans.

Bush planned to address these issues at a 1989 NAACP fund-raiser, an appearance he canceled because of illness. The intended speech, never released, declared that in the 1970s African Americans had suffered economically "even as government was spending more on new social programs." (In the margin an aide wrote, "Note: We did not have statistics to verify these figures.") But the 1980s reversed these trends, the speech argued. "It was in 1965 that Lyndon Johnson declared his war . . . to give people a chance," the speech continued. "It was a noble effort, but . . . the War on Poverty fell short. . . . Poverty cannot be fought with dollars alone."[100]

For George H. W. Bush, the legacy of the Vietnam War continued to damage the nation at the start of his presidency. Bush also argued that the tremendous progress that had been made in race relations since the 1960s made an activist approach by government unnecessary, as he spoke often of the failure of government programs to improve the lives of African Americans. Just as he felt that his Gulf War had erased the Vietnam syndrome, he also wanted to eliminate two other legacies of the 1960s that he believed were detrimental to American life: Johnson's Great Society and the decline in moral values. It was in these two areas that Bush would use the 1960s to greatest effect.

6

George H. W. Bush and the Great Society

*George H. W. Bush would not view [the 1960s] favorably. Why
would he? It was the antithesis of what he embodies as a human
being: duty, honor, country. It was an immoral decade...
promiscuous... lascivious... a decade of decadence and self-
absorption, [all] polar opposites of George Bush. His life had been
founded upon sacrifice and courtesy and good manners and deep
religious faith. Those traits were in effect incinerated and trashed
by the 1960s. I can't imagine that he would look with anything
but contempt upon the entire decade.*

Curt Smith, speechwriter for George H. W. Bush (2004)

FUNDAMENTAL TO George H. W. Bush's sentiments toward the 1960s was
the belief that the government was encouraging bad personal behavior. He
consistently attacked the Great Society, asserting that the ambitious government programs of the 1960s had failed. He argued that his own volunteerism program, "A Thousand Points of Light," would improve society
more than Johnson's government programs had. Bush's response to the
1992 Los Angeles riots and Dan Quayle's 1992 "Murphy Brown" speech
show how the Right continued to blame the 1960s for the nation's ills.
Though Democrats sharply questioned Bush's negative view of the Great
Society's impact, he made a familiar theme out of attacking the influence
of the 1960s on the nation's mores. Right-wing criticism of the 1960s only
intensified in 1992, when Arkansas governor Bill Clinton became the first
baby boomer to be nominated for president. In his reelection campaign
Bush attacked Clinton by blaming the "bad sixties" for increased drug
abuse and crime, the decline of family values and patriotism, and Clinton's personal failure to serve in Vietnam.

Attacking Johnson's Great Society and the War on Poverty

Bush first met Lyndon Johnson in 1953, when Johnson was a senator from Texas and Bush was working in the oil industry. Bush wrote his father, Senator Prescott Bush, a Connecticut Republican, that he had recently introduced himself to Johnson as Prescott Bush's son as the senator was leaving a Texas hotel. Johnson warmly praised Bush's father, even though he was from the other party, saying, "Your father and I don't like to be thought of as Republican or Democrat, rather as good Americans!"[1]

That cordial first encounter notwithstanding, Bush strongly opposed Johnson in the 1964 presidential election. "I like Goldwater," he wrote to his close friend Congressman T. W. L. Ashley, an Ohio Democrat, that June. "I find him far more reasonable than one would believe from reading the newspapers about him." Soon after Johnson's landslide triumph, Bush wrote a long letter to Richard Nixon saying that he had "great respect" for Goldwater and agreed with "most of his positions. . . . Goldwater's philosophy was not rejected. It was the false image that people had about Goldwater and the Johnson presence on the ticket."[2]

After Johnson was elected to a full term of his own as president, he moved to implement his program of social welfare. Bush was a vocal opponent of the Great Society from the start, pledging in his 1966 congressional race to cut Johnson's programs.[3] Johnson's presidency ended in January 1969, two decades before President Bush succeeded to that office. But Bush nevertheless made attacking the Great Society and the War on Poverty the focus of his domestic policy.

His most extensive attack on the Great Society as president came at the University of Michigan's 1991 commencement ceremony, soon after the Gulf War ended. The choice of setting was intentional: in May 1964 Johnson had announced his "Great Society" program before eighty thousand people at a Michigan commencement address in a warmly received twenty-minute speech interrupted by applause at least twenty-seven times. Bush's speechwriters were acutely aware of the significance of LBJ's 1964 speech, as evidenced by an extensively highlighted copy of it in the speech files at the Bush Presidential Library. The extensive preparations for Bush's speech demonstrate that he saw the occasion as a major address, one he hoped would be quoted for years to come, just as Johnson's had been.[4]

Bush's aides were also well attuned to the negative reception his visit might receive on the predominantly liberal campus. The speech files are filled with articles about the university's political environment. One article, from *Michigan Alumnus*, described a 1991 rally protesting the Gulf

War. Whereas "the late sixties antiwar movement involved primarily students and professors," a Michigan professor said, "this time there were church leaders, Vietnam vets, and many more general members of the community."[5] A speechwriting assistant had included supportive letters from a Michigan pro-war group for possible use in Bush's address. One war supporter had written, "I guarantee that soldiers/airmen/sailors/ and marines take antiwar rallies personally."[6] Bush's advisers blamed the anger toward Bush on nostalgia for the late 1960s. "Advance is doing its best to seat any potential protesters behind the camera's line of sight," planners were assured, "but be forewarned. The reasons put forward are the Gulf War, the basic dislike of the President and his Administration. Michigan—like other large universities—has a portion of the student body (including many full-time-student graduate students) who still think it's 1968."[7]

After he and the first lady received honorary law degrees, Bush began his speech by mentioning two Democratic presidents from the 1960s. He noted that he had last been at Michigan to honor John F. Kennedy's Peace Corps, and that it was at Michigan that "Lyndon Johnson introduced the Great Society." Bush then praised Reagan's economic policies, which "exposed forever the failures of socialism"; stated that the Gulf War had erased Americans' lack of confidence after Vietnam; and saluted recent American relief efforts in the Middle East and Asia as "an essential element of our American character." He touted the benefits of capitalism over socialism and remarked that the achievements of Lincoln, Henry Ford, and Martin Luther King "testify to the greatness of our free enterprise system." Thus, as he often did, Bush defined King not as a critic of racism and capitalism but as a Horatio Alger figure. After stressing the merits of free enterprise by way of contrast, Bush likened the Great Society to socialism and proposed market-based solutions rather than government programs to address current problems. He also alluded to recent developments in eastern Europe to argue against the policies of the 1960s.[8] (In the margin of a draft of the speech, an unnamed editor noted "The Great Irony" that as socialism was declining throughout the world, some in the United States advocated "empowering bureaucracy and not the individual." America's "inner city poverty" was similar to eastern European economies, the aide wrote, adding: "Making this analogy takes the first step towards both exposing the Welfare State for what it is and tagging it 'trash.' THE PROMISE OF THE 1960S HAS BEEN FAILED BY INCOMPETENT BUREAUCRACY AND LACK OF FAITH IN HUMAN POTENTIAL.")[9]

Bush then moved on to his final point: a passionate attack on the Great Society. "When government tries to serve as a parent or a teacher or a moral guide, individuals may be tempted to discard their own sense of responsibility, to argue that only government must help people in need. If we've learned anything in the past quarter century, it is that we cannot federalize virtue," he said, referring to the programs of the 1960s. Excessive laws, programs, and rules "actually can weaken people's moral sensitivity."[10] (An earlier draft more urgently assailed such programs, claiming that despite more than double the spending for social programs since 1965, the lives of the poor had failed to improve.)[11]

Bush then criticized Johnson by name, a controversial decision. C. Gregg Petersmeyer, assistant to the president and director of the Office of National Service, wrote in the margin of a preliminary draft: "This comes close to being an *ad hominem* attack on LBJ which I doubt POTUS [President of the United States] would want to make. Can achieve the same result circumstantially."[12] Bush rejected this advice, instead saying, "When Lyndon Johnson—President Johnson—spoke here in 1964, he addressed issues that remain with us." In attempting to build his Great Society, according to Bush, LBJ "believed that cadres of experts really could care for the millions. . . . And gradually, we got to the point of equating dollars with commitment. And when programs failed to produce progress, we demanded more money. And in time, this crusade backfired," worsening the very problems it sought to ameliorate. "We should have learned that while the ideals behind the Great Society were noble—and indeed they were—the programs weren't always up to the task," he said. Bush then attempted to coin a phrase of his own, just as Reagan did in 1966 with the "Creative Society": "We don't need another Great Society with huge and ambitious programs administered by the incumbent few. We need a Good Society built upon the deeds of the many, a society that promotes service, selflessness, action. The Good Society . . . dares you to explore the full promise of citizenship . . . to make our world better. The Good Society . . . requires something within everyone's reach: common decency."[13]

This speech was the opening blow of the 1992 election campaign. Robert Pear wrote in the *New York Times* that by attacking the Great Society, Bush "invigorated a national debate about what type of social welfare programs the nation needs, and how effective other presidents have been in combating poverty and racial bias." To Pear "the debate is political," as Bush aimed to contrast Republican and Democratic ideals. Pear found Bush's attacks ironic, however, since so many Great Society programs have "been accepted and embedded in the nation's social fabric." Also, the speech did not address Great Society measures Bush favored, "like Head Start and a number of environmental laws." Bush's attacks were "sweeping and unqualified," wrote Pear. Joseph A. Califano Jr., a Johnson official from 1965 through 1968, told Pear, "Mr. Bush doesn't know his history," for "the goal of the Great Society was to redistribute opportunity and wealth and to empower poor people."[14] Pear wrote that in the booming economy of the mid-1960s, LBJ vowed to eliminate racial discrimination and poverty but did not anticipate the cost of the Vietnam War. This angered Bush's speechwriters. In the margins of a copy of Pear's article in Bush's speechwriting files someone sarcastically wrote, "Recipe for success: Great Society needed more resources!" Bush's aides also rejected a variety of Pear's other statements that cast the Great Society in a favorable light.[15]

Over a decade later, Bush's inner circle remained hostile to the programs of the mid-1960s, especially those of LBJ. The Great Society "was redistribution, a total mocking of the middle class," observed Curt Smith in 2004. The Democrats' drop from 61 percent of the vote in 1964 to 43 percent in 1968 "was a massive repudiation by largely white middle-class America of the Great Society. Lyndon Johnson was one of the most catastrophic presidents in the history of America," Smith declared. "He left 548,000 troops in Vietnam. He left our cities burning. He left a sexual revolution from which we have yet to recover. He left institutions that were falling off the cliff to the Left. Not much of a record, is it?"[16]

Bush's solution to the problems created by the Great Society, as well as to those it failed even to address, was his "Thousand Points of Light" program. Asked if the program hadn't shifted the burden of caring for the underprivileged away from government and toward the private sector, as if it were an early form of George W. Bush's "compassionate conservatism," Josh Gilder, a Bush speechwriter in the 1988 campaign, answered: "That's a good way of looking at it. I wouldn't say 'shift the burden,' but the idea was that churches and private charities could do a lot of this work better. That's what 'A Thousand Points of Light' stood for."[17]

As early as the 1988 Republican convention Bush presented many of the themes that would characterize his presidency, especially an emphasis on individual acts of assistance instead of federal aid. "This is America," Bush said, reciting a lengthy list of civic and fraternal organizations, "a brilliant diversity spread like stars, like a thousand points of light in a broad and peaceful sky." He then defined his philosophy: "Government is part of the nation of communities—not the whole, just a part. I do not hate government. A government that remembers that the people are its master is a good and needed thing. I respect old-fashioned common sense and have no great love for the imaginings of social planners."[18]

In his inaugural address Bush proclaimed that America's purpose was "to make kinder the face of the nation and gentler the face of the world," thus implying that the Reagan Revolution had left some citizens behind.

"My friends, we have work to do," he said, mentioning a range of social ills such as homelessness, poverty, drug abuse, crime, and single mother-hood. But he made clear that he would not return to the Great Society of the 1960s. "The old solution, . . . that public money alone could end these problems," had failed. Instead of looking to the government to solve these problems, Bush looked to private citizens. "I have spoken of a Thousand Points of Light, of all the community organizations that are spread like stars throughout the nation, doing good."[19]

While he frequently attacked the Great Society as a whole, Bush also celebrated those aspects of it that promoted volunteerism, in the process redefining the intent of Johnson's programs. In 1990 he honored the anniversary of Volunteers in Service to America (VISTA), a Great Society program. Shortly after Johnson created VISTA, Bush said, "the first volunteers started their service. And today 100,000 Americans . . . can proudly say: 'I was a VISTA volunteer.'" Bush praised the more than three thousand current volunteers' hard work. "When I talk of the Thousand Points of Light," he said, "please know that no light is more dazzling, brighter, than the VISTA volunteers."[20] Similarly, at a 1990 celebration for Head Start he proclaimed, "Over 600,000 committed volunteers, each one a Point of Light, are giving their all to make Head Start a national treasure."[21]

Bush consistently stressed the importance of volunteerism and emphasized the federal government's limitations.[22] "We envision national service not as a government program, not even as a White House initiative, but as a grassroots movement," he said in 1993. "People, not programs, solve problems."[23] An undated statement summed up the philosophy behind Bush's program. "Points of light are the only solution to our social problems," it read, declaring that there was "almost universal disillusionment with the incapacity of government to solve social problems."[24]

Rodney King, Murphy Brown, and the Legacy of the 1960s

Bush's attitudes toward the 1960s were vividly displayed in his response to the riots that broke out in Los Angeles in 1992 after an all-white jury acquitted four Los Angeles police officers in the beating of Rodney King, an African American motorist. For many Americans the riots were an unwelcome reminder of 1960s social unrest. Indeed, for conservatives the 1960s equaled urban violence. James Baker gave voice to a typical establishment view of "the sixties," noting that in the period between 1963 and 1974 "you had all the riots in the streets, and then you had Vietnam, and then you had Watergate."[25] Other conservatives echoed this sentiment. "The sixties—that period of revolt—really began in the late sixties, with the campus revolts and protests and the riots in the streets of Detroit and Los Angeles," said Stephen Moore.[26] Journalists commonly voiced similar perceptions. To David Broder the 1960s were "a period of enormous social change" regarding race, gender, and the family, "and on top of that we had Vietnam [and] the urban riots."[27]

Bush's initial response to the 1992 riots made him appear both tough on crime and sensitive to its underlying causes. The unrest "is not about civil rights" or "a message of protest," he said in a televised speech from the Oval Office. "It's been the brutality of a mob, pure and simple." But at the same time, saying, "We must then turn again to the underlying causes of such tragic events," he acknowledged that the riots stemmed from past wrongs.[28] His attempt at evenhandedness did not sit well with some conservatives. Press secretary Marlin Fitzwater recalled that there were those who were angered by Bush's language "on the grounds that it signaled opposition to the verdict."[29]

The riots fell in the midst of Bush's reelection campaign and soon became a political issue. Within days Bush was linking the riots to the liberal policies of the 1960s. "Marlin Fitzwater said that the failure of the Great Society programs undertaken by President Johnson in the 1960s is at the root of these problems," reported the *Los Angeles Times* on May 5. "Calling for 'a conservative agenda that creates jobs and housing and home ownership and involvement in the community,' Fitzwater criticized liberal programs that 'redistribute the wealth or that deal with direct handouts.'" He spoke by contrast of the pride that comes with employment and homeownership and said, "The social welfare programs of the '60s and '70s ignored that and we're now paying a price." Fitzwater said that Bush favored granting tax advantages to companies operating in inner cities (enterprise zones) and selling public housing to tenants. Noting that Reagan and Bush had both "sought to slow the growth of federal programs offering direct aid to the poor," the paper reported that when asked if he blamed the riots on Johnson and Carter, Fitzwater stated that "the liberal programs of the '60s and '70s did not work" and had on the contrary damaged family structure and community leadership. Pressed further, Fitzwater did not mention specific programs that had failed, and even acknowledged the success of Head Start. Democrats responded with anger. "The president is clearly disconnected from reality when he would suggest to you that policies of the Great Society some 25 years ago"—which improved education, fought poverty, and developed businesses—"somehow contributed to and are responsible for these riots," responded California Assembly Speaker Willie Brown. "The president is just flat wrong."[30]

In retrospect, Fitzwater believed that in the wake of the *Los Angeles Times* story, the *Washington Post* had leaped to defend the "liberal legacy" and made his remarks a political issue in order to help Bill Clinton. He also complained that the *Post* "ran a full page of academic responses . . . on the 'Fitzwater Theory.'" His comments were accurate, he wrote in his memoir, but "any attack on the Great Society programs of the 1960s was immediately challenged and ridiculed."[31]

Fitzwater did not mention that blaming the 1960s for the riots soon became the central thesis of the administration. Addressing the role of the federal government in providing relief for urban problems on May 6, Bush argued that the riots had resulted not from too little spending but from too much. "In the past decades spending is up, the number of programs is up, and yet, let's face it, that has not solved many of the fundamental problems that plague our cities," he said. "We need an honest, open national discussion about family, about values, about public policy, and about race." A reporter asked Bush about that day's lead editorial in the *New York Times* asserting that inflation-adjusted spending for cities had decreased since 1981 by over 60 percent. Bush replied that the reverse was true—but problems had only worsened: many urban projects were "hopeless," and additional funds did not provide "work [and] learning incentives."[32] (The data do not confirm Bush's claims. During the Reagan administration, spending for programs for the poor was cut by 54 percent, spending for subsidized housing by 80.7 percent, and support for training and employment services by 68.3 percent. As economist John Miller wrote soon after Reagan's death in 2004, "relative to the size of the economy, one-third of domestic discretionary spending disappeared: it fell from 4.7% of GDP in 1980 to 3.1% in 1988."[33]

In Los Angeles later that day Bush explained his own proposed solutions. (As before, he used liberal icons to serve conservative ends. A memorandum outlining Bush's remarks on this occasion referred to a speech by King on nonviolence as background material.) Bush's speechwriters suggested a phrase that would become Bush's theme that day and after: "Let me state in the clearest possible terms. This violence cannot and will not be tolerated."[34] He then attacked the Great Society and urged reducing government's role in fighting poverty.[35]

To Bush, urban problems were not caused by spending cuts but arose instead from the actions of individuals. An earlier draft noted the sharp rise since 1960 of births to unwed mothers, the increase in violent deaths, the decline of high school graduation rates, and the increase in drug and alcohol abuse among African Americans, all "clearly influenced by the absence of values that come from strong families." In the margin next to this statement was written: "determining fact(or): Not level of fed [Federal] aid."[36] In the conservative view such degenerate behavior had been fostered by the loosening of traditional restraints during the 1960s. The speech did not mention declining aid to cities since then. Bush's team also stressed a "law and order" response. A confidential California National Guard memorandum to speechwriters noted: "Public support has been tremendous. As military convoys converged on the Los Angeles area, they were greeted by honking horns and shouts of encouragement."[37] Bush echoed these conservative themes throughout his remarks of May 1992.[38]

Bush's proposals grew out of research on poverty by several conservative think tanks. Background material for this speech came from a report by the Heritage Foundation's Robert Rector. This scathing eleven-page portrait of the welfare system stressed that the public and the government knew that the "welfare system has harmed rather than helped the poor." Rector distinguished between "material poverty" and "behavioral poverty," declaring that "there is little material poverty in the U.S.," as the poor were better fed, taller, and heavier than forty years ago. Obesity, not hunger, was their main problem. Furthermore, "nearly all" of the poor "live in decent housing. . . . Nearly 40% of the households defined as 'poor' by the U.S. government actually own their own homes." By contrast "behavioral poverty," defined as "a breakdown in the values and conduct which lead to the formation of healthy families, stable personalities, and self-sufficiency," was "abundant and growing." To Rector the "liberal" approach was the cause of this breakdown, as "[increasing] income does not inculcate middle class values and behavior."[39]

Bush officials agreed that the Great Society programs of the 1960s had caused harm. Children's problems "are not the result of simple medical difficulties, but of social and behavioral choices of their parents," said Deputy Secretary of Health and Human Services Constance Horner in a 1991 interview. "It is culture more than money that provides the kind of life-giving, community-supporting behavior that produces healthy children." Tony Snow mined this interview for material to use when composing the speeches Bush gave after the riots.[40]

Some of the most extensive attacks on the 1960s and the Great Society in the Bush years came not from Bush himself but from Vice President Dan Quayle in a May 1992 speech, "Restoring Basic Values: Strengthening the Family," which would become known as the "Murphy Brown" speech. For Quayle the riots were "directly related to the breakdown of the family structure, personal responsibility and social order." Great progress on racial issues had been made since the 1960s, he said. "The evil of

slavery has left a long and ugly legacy. But we have faced racism squarely and we have made progress in the past quarter of a century." Quayle
praised the "landmark civil rights bills of the 1960s," remarking, "The
America of 1992 is more egalitarian, more integrated, and offers more opportunities to black Americans and all other minority members than the
America of 1964." Although that work was not finished, "since 1967, the
median income of black two-parent families has risen by 60 percent in
real terms," and African American education levels and political power
had also increased dramatically.[41]

Yet Quayle too blamed the 1960s for creating the conditions that led
to the Los Angeles riots. Since 1964, he said, "we have also developed a
culture of poverty." Quayle cited statistics demonstrating the decline of
the African American family, noting enormous drops in the percentage
of two-parent households and increases in illegitimacy and youth unemployment since the 1960s. He asserted that homicide was "the leading
cause of death of young black males." While, he acknowledged, it was
"overly simplistic to blame this . . . on the programs of the Great Society"—though Bush had in the previous weeks said exactly that—Quayle
believed that America was nevertheless "reaping the consequences of the
decades of changes in social mores."[42]

One "unfortunate legacy" of his own baby boom generation, Quayle
said, was that "when we were young, it was fashionable to declare war
against traditional values. Indulgence and self-gratification seemed to
have no consequences. Many of our generation glamorized casual sex and
drug use, evaded responsibility and trashed authority." While most of the
middle class "survived the turbulent legacy of the sixties and seventies,"
the same could not be said for many poor people. The current "inter-
generational poverty . . . is predominantly a poverty of values," said the
vice president, arguing that government policies "must be premised on
and must reinforce values such as family, hard work, integrity, and personal responsibility." Quayle then touted Bush's efforts to reduce crime,
empower the poor, increase homeownership, encourage enterprise zones,
and improve education.[43]

Above all, said Quayle, "when family fails, society fails." Parents teach
children values, and "marriage is probably the best anti-poverty program
of all." He suggested a variety of solutions, including reforming welfare.
"Ultimately, however, marriage is a moral issue that requires cultural
consensus and the use of social sanctions," he continued, emphasizing
the need for parents to be responsible and to support their children. Then
came the remark for which the speech would become famous: "It doesn't
help matters when primetime TV has Murphy Brown, a character who

supposedly epitomizes today's intelligent, highly paid professional woman, mocking the importance of fathers by bearing a child alone and calling it just another lifestyle choice," said Quayle, referring to the unwed pregnancy of the popular sitcom character. "I know it's not fashionable to talk about moral values, but we need to do it!"[44]

How closely did this public rhetoric reflect Quayle's personal views of the 1960s? "I have heard him say that he thinks there was great progress, certainly on the race issue," recalled Lisa Schiffren, author of the speech. "I don't think you'll find a politician in America who isn't in favor of equality for blacks. Even people who opposed it at the time, I think in retrospect, believe that was all good and important. But also, clearly, his values were in fact heartland conservative. Clearly there was conflict," she said, implying that many of the changes of the 1960s were anathema to midwestern conservatives. Although "the civil rights legislation of the sixties opened a lot of doors that had been clearly unjustly shut to black Americans," both she and Quayle thought that the Great Society "meddled deep in the mechanisms of family life and cultural life," and this "undermined black family life." To Schiffren there was "no question" that the Great Society had increased illegitimacy. "I don't begin to understand how Peter Edelman [a critic of the 1996 welfare reform bill] looks at the data and doesn't come to the same conclusion." Schiffren added that in the 1960s "people openly had to defend" traditional beliefs "that we, as a civilization, had lived with for a couple of thousand years."[45]

With his rhetorical use of the 1960s Quayle aimed to produce the maximum partisan effect. The speech was "a direct appeal to the Republican conservative base," wrote reporter Andrew Rosenthal. It came shortly before the California primary, where conservative Patrick Buchanan was still campaigning even though Bush had already secured the nomination. Quayle's speech appealed to those who believed that Bush did not speak enough about social issues, and while it did not depart from Bush's urban policies, it used "much stronger and more intensely ideological language" designed to counteract the "confused and sometimes contradictory responses" Bush had given after the L.A. riots.[46]

The vice president's words stirred up considerable anger among the Democratic opposition. "Quayle's speech is another fairly obvious attempt by Republicans to play the old race card," wrote *New York Times* columnist Russell Baker.[47] Diane English, producer of the television show *Murphy Brown*, issued a statement that if Quayle was against an unmarried woman having a child and that if he thought two parents were needed to raise children, "then he'd better make sure abortion remains safe and legal."[48] Bill Clinton said that the problem with TV was not Murphy Brown but rather the "crass commercialism and glorification of selfishness and violence. . . . Family values alone won't feed a hungry child, and material security cannot provide a moral compass. We must have both."[49] The *New York Times* editorialized that Quayle's speech echoed "Reagan's infamous denunciation of black mothers as 'welfare queens.' It reflects the chill, abstract view of conservatives sure the true enemy is not poverty but poor people."[50]

Bush's response to the speech was muddled. The next day Marlin Fitzwater supported Quayle's criticism, stating that Bush was concerned about the negative influence of television as well as "the breakup of the American family." But he was uncomfortable criticizing the show since the Murphy Brown character's decision to bear her child demonstrated "pro-life values, which we think are good, and strong family values."[51] Fitzwater at first condemned "the glorification of the life of an unwed mother" but later corrected himself, saying that the actress who played the character (Candice Bergen) was a "personal favorite" and that he was eager to meet her.[52] At a news conference that day Bush admitted, "I don't know that much about the show" but emphasized that he supported families.[53] Asked if he agreed with Quayle that the riots were caused by "a lack of family values," Bush declared that traditional two-parent households provided "the best environment in which to raise kids."[54]

Conservatives were thrilled with Quayle's remarks. "People out there agree with what he's saying," a Quayle spokesperson said. "The press will make fun of it, but in the meantime, the cards and letters are going to come pouring in."[55] Gary Bauer urged Bush to campaign on "the larger theme of the breakdown of the family." A former Bush adviser recommended that "Bush should give a speech like this. Whether he can do that or not, given where he is coming from ideologically, is another question," he added, echoing the misgivings many conservatives felt toward the president.[56]

Bush and Quayle turned Johnson's Great Society program into a catchall term of abuse. Starting in the late 1960s, said Stephen Moore, there was a "cultural collapse, as seen in the fall in educational achievement and rises in out-of-wedlock births, crime, abortions, and drug use." But "the Great Society was blaming society, not the criminals, for crimes; paying women to have kids out of wedlock; paying adults not to work." Johnson's Great Society programs "created a social nightmare," especially for "the black family."[57]

Historian Rick Perlstein noted the "very powerful mobilization of propaganda by the Right that operates in defiance of the facts [by asserting a] fundamental linkage between hippies, crime, civil rights, race riots, liberal social programs, and taxes." The message was, "If you hate hippies, then you have to hate the Great Society." As Perlstein observed, "the Great Society was filled with middle-class entitlements. But it's seen as . . . handouts to the poor."[58]

Democrat Timothy Wirth also vehemently disagreed with the Right's enduring portrayal of Johnson's programs. Conservatives "want to reduce government to nothing," he said. "They have no sense of obligation, of common responsibilities, or belief in commonwealth. The Great Society programs put a very sharp focus on poverty in America, which was a totally hidden phenomenon in the political discourse until Lyndon Johnson."[59] Unsurprisingly, Johnson administration officials concurred. The Great Society made "major accomplishments," noted Nicholas Katzenbach, citing the civil rights acts, education reform, conservation, "and the social welfare [programs], particularly Medicare." Conservatives hate the Great Society "because they see it as a form of collectivism. They feel that the rich are subsidizing the poor, and then they pay more taxes."[60]

Democrats vigorously challenged the Right's view that the Great Society failed to decrease poverty. Such interpretations "are done proactively, they do not magically happen," noted Perlstein. "It's part of an organized political attempt to construct the sixties that way. Strategically, the Right latched onto a fairy tale about the Great Society; of course poverty went down."[61] The Right's claim concerning poverty is "propaganda," agreed Noam Chomsky, though conservatives were correct to see that the Great Society ran counter to their own material interests. After all, it "did do more harm than good to rich people. . . . If your belief is that the super-rich and the privileged should run the world, and everybody should be their slave, then the Great Society did harm."[62]

But only a tiny elite could honestly claim to have suffered from the redistribution of wealth. "The anti–Great Society sentiment among a [broad] section of Republicans is not justified," said Benjamin Bradlee. And there was far more to the Great Society than higher taxes. The racial legislation of the mid-1960s "was a major legislative achievement comparable to the changes under Roosevelt. Kennedy had plans to [propose civil rights legislation], but he never got there. It took Lyndon Johnson to do it. I'm not sure Kennedy could have brought along those southern senators." The debate over the Great Society, said Bradlee, is "the great American divide between the Right and the Left."[63] Archibald Cox, asked if the Great Society had helped make the country more tolerant, answered: "Oh, yes, very much so. It helped it with civil rights a great deal. And there was improvement in various forms of social security." But, he noted, "the material interests of the top business people are against the things that the Great Society stood for."[64]

"Johnson's achievements were magnificent," said Donna Shalala, President Clinton's secretary of health and human services. "Before Medicare, less than half of Americans over sixty-five had decent health insurance. The Great Society changed what it meant to grow old [and] it made a dramatic difference in the health of poor women and their children."[65] To Tom Hayden, the Great Society's successes included "Medicaid, civil rights, (briefly) the War on Poverty, and, above all, continued recognition of the New Deal insight that government must act where the market fails to address human, social or environmental needs."[66]

But as David Halberstam observed, "the Great Society increased prosperity, but it was underfunded."[67] Johnson's defenders often repeated Halberstam's caveat. Asked why the Right calls the Great Society a failure, Maurice Isserman cited Senator Daniel Patrick Moynihan's refrain that "the War on Poverty was 'oversold and underfinanced to the point that its failure was guaranteed.'" To Isserman, "the great success of the Right has been to manufacture this myth, first enunciated by President Nixon, that the sixties taught us that you can't solve problems by throwing money at them. In fact, with Vietnam, they *were* throwing money, but on the domestic front it was never even tried. Johnson was a New Deal Democrat and would have—if he hadn't gotten distracted by Vietnam—done a lot more."[68]

Many also stressed that the Great Society had only a brief life. "What actually was the Great Society?" asked Rick Perlstein. "In the 1966 midterm elections the Democrats lost forty-seven House seats"—one shy of the number Republicans lost in the 1974 midterm elections shortly after Nixon's resignation—"and by 1967 the Great Society was over. People talk about this mostly in terms of Vietnam, but it has as much to do with the civil rights backlash and the riots in the summer of '66 and 'guns-and-butter.'" By 1967 the Great Society had run out of both financial and political capital. Perlstein discovered, as an example of backlash against the Great Society, a "debate in Congress in 1967 over an appropriation for rodent control in the slums that was defeated by a coalition of conservatives who called it the 'Civil Rats Program.'"[69]

The vigor with which Perlstein and others defended the Great Society is a testament to the lingering damage inflicted on Johnson's programs by conservatives since the 1960s. Blaming "the sixties," which began under President Reagan, reached new heights in the Bush administration. It would also be central to President Bush's reelection effort.

Competing Versions of "the Sixties":
The 1992 Presidential Campaign

Bush made a strong effort in 1992 to court the social conservatives who had been an essential part of the Reagan coalition but were now threatening either to support Patrick Buchanan's insurgent campaign or to sit out the fall election. Bush expressed anger toward the 1960s as a way to win their support. The campaign against Bill Clinton—the first baby boomer presidential candidate—was above all a battle of competing versions of the 1960s.

As they had in 1988, Bush's attacks on the 1960s came to dominate the campaign, especially at the Republican National Convention in August. On opening night Buchanan proclaimed that at the Democrats' recent convention, "20,000 radicals and liberals came dressed up as moderates and centrists—in the greatest single exhibition of cross-dressing in American political history," and that Americans "are not going to buy back into the failed liberalism of the 1960s and seventies, no matter how slick the package in 1992." Comparing the 1960s generation with Bush's, Buchanan stated (incorrectly) that right after Pearl Harbor the seventeen-year-old Bush "left his high school class, walked down to the recruiting office, and signed up to become the youngest fighter pilot in the Pacific war.[70] When Bill Clinton's turn came in Vietnam, he sat up in a dormitory in Oxford, England, and figured out how to dodge the draft. Which of these two men has won the moral authority to call on Americans to put their lives at risk?" Buchanan expressed his disgust at "the raw sewage of pornography that pollutes our popular culture," and declared that the upcoming election would be about "what we stand for as Americans. There is a religious war going on in our country for the soul of America. It is a cultural war, as critical to the kind of nation we will one day be as was the Cold War itself. And in that struggle for the soul of America, [Bill] Clinton and [Hillary] Clinton are on the other side, and George Bush is on our side."[71]

Some observers believed that this speech helped bring about Bush's defeat. "Buchanan behaved as if he were a mole and sapper in the employ of the Democratic National Committee," wrote Lance Morrow, as he "delivered a snarling, bigoted attack on minorities, gays and his other enemies in what he called the 'cultural war' and 'religious war' in America. Buchanan's ugly speech . . . set a tone of right-wing intolerance that drove moderate Republicans and Reagan Democrats away from the president's cause."[72]

But not everyone agreed, least of all the cultural conservatives at whom Buchanan's appeal had been aimed. Curt Smith called the charge that "Buchanan's intolerance" hurt Bush "ridiculous and insipid." As a result of the speech "Bush gained," but he "lost when he gave his own acceptance speech." (As recently as September 2008 Buchanan's sister and spokesperson Bay Buchanan made the same point.)[73] "That tells me that Buchanan was right," he said, "right about virtually every social and cultural issue." Referring to Buchanan's view of "a cultural war," Smith said, "Who in their right mind could argue with that today [in 2004]? The question is, 'Is the Republican Party willing to fight [the cultural wars]?' Buchanan was. Bush was not. The fact is that over the last forty years social and cultural issues win for Republicans. In fact, we *only* win when we talk about issues like multiculturalism, and voluntary prayer, and racial quotas, and the cultural decline of America."[74]

Marilyn Quayle, also a baby boomer, joined the fight against the "bad sixties" two days later. Appearing in a red, white, and blue dress, the vice president's wife spoke of her own experience during that era. She and young people like her "did not believe in destroying America to save it. I came of age in a time of turbulent social change. Some of it was good, such as civil rights. Much of it was questionable." But she remembered the 1960s as a time when "not everyone joined the counterculture, not everyone demonstrated, dropped out, took drugs, joined in the sexual revolution or dodged the draft." (These remarks drew the loudest applause.) "Not everyone concluded that American society was so bad that it had to be radically remade by social revolution." Some now thought "the moment has come for a couple of baby boomers to take the helm of this great and complex nation; that the time has come for generational change."[75] Clearly she did not agree.

David Broder considered this speech an especially significant political use of the 1960s. "You get a very clear sense of the affirmation of the resurgence of conservative values in the face of what had seemed to many the breakdown of social norms in the sixties."[76] Lisa Schiffren, who wrote the words Mrs. Quayle delivered, explained the background. "I had written a longer, in certain ways even tougher, speech, for the vice president that included everything in that speech." But Dan Quayle never gave that speech, and it "was sitting on the shelf." Marilyn Quayle read it and liked it, and asked Schiffren before the convention, "Can you turn this into a speech for me?"[77]

Why did the speech dwell at such length on the 1960s? "The thing that we think of as 'the sixties'—the revolutionary behavior—was very frightening to most people," Schiffren said. "And not just frightening, it was distasteful . . . offensive. . . . That was how people like the Quayles experienced that time." The revolt against the 1960s "was always there," Schiffren said. "The Quayles were from the 'silent majority'—whereas the Clintons were from the noisy, and often quite successful, minority." To Schiffren, appeals to Nixon's "silent majority" naturally helped Republicans, "because that is the majority feeling on these issues. That's what [Marilyn Quayle] explained."[78]

After the convention Bush picked up where he had left off, linking Clinton with the excesses of "the sixties." The forty-six-year-old Clinton kept evoking the forty-two-year-old candidate JFK as an argument for generational change. But as Michael Kelly noted, the generational contrast was most explicit "in the matter of who did what in each generation's war." The Bush campaign kept "reminding voters that [Clinton] is not really of Mr. Kennedy's generation"—that is, those who had fought in World War II. Although Clinton was about the same age Kennedy had been when he was elected president, the Bush campaign was eager to point out that it was Bush who had fought in the same war as Kennedy. Bush instead sought to connect Clinton with "Abbie Hoffman's [generation] and to link the Democrat with a decade remembered unhappily by many as a time when liberalism was turned into radicalism." Republicans worked "to portray the Democrat as a closet hippie." To Democrats, Clinton was JFK, "the young, vigorous candidate poised to lead the country into an exciting (but not radical) era of growth and change, a time of bold experiments in leadership," whereas to the Republicans, Bush was Eisenhower, "the sober, sensible steward, shaped by the ways of the old, good days, and imbued with the half-mythic values of those days." For Republicans, Clinton "does not represent the promise of the early 1960s but the traumas of the decade's later years; he is a secret radical hiding behind the mask of moderatism."[79]

The issue of crime also played a key role in the Bush reelection strategy. As Tom Hayden observed, "the Republicans developed the 'war on crime' in response to the sixties, and found it very effective in winning support away from liberals."[80] And for Bush, the source of the crime epidemic was clear: "We got soft on crime way back in the sixties, and we paid for it. By the time we cracked down again in the eighties, violent crime had gone up 400 percent in twenty years."[81]

Throughout the fall campaign Bush stepped up his attacks, frequently mentioning Clinton's use of marijuana in the late 1960s. As for Clinton's not having served in the military, Bush had said earlier in the campaign that the issue was not Clinton's failure to serve in Vietnam but his dissembling about the reasons why. Now Bush changed course, emphasizing the importance of military service as "a good criterion for being commander-in-chief of the armed forces." At one campaign stop, the *New York Times* reported, he sent onstage ahead of him a decorated Vietnam veteran and a man who had served in ROTC "to accuse Mr. Clinton of having been disloyal to his country by avoiding the Vietnam draft."[82]

"The president we entrust with these [military] decisions must have character, honesty, and integrity," Bush remarked a few days later. "My opponent has written that he once mobilized demonstrations in London against the Vietnam War. I simply for the life of me cannot understand how someone can go to London, another country, and mobilize demonstrations against the United States of America when our kids are dying halfway around the world. The issue here isn't patriotism," he argued rather disingenuously. "You can demonstrate all you want here at home. . . . But I can't understand someone mobilizing demonstrations in a foreign country when poor kids, drafted out of the ghettos, are dying in a faraway land. You can call me old-fashioned, but that just does not make sense to me."[83]

Throughout his long career, whether campaigning or in office, George H. W. Bush advanced his political interests by attacking the pivotal events of the 1960s: the Vietnam War, the civil rights movement, the Great Society, and an associated decline in mores. In many respects he defined his presidency as a crusade to overcome the negative consequences of all these changes. After Bush lost to Clinton in 1992, the political fight over the meaning of the 1960s grew even more intense, for the next group of presidential actors on the national stage had something in common, something they did not share with either the 1960s liberals of the Kennedy and Johnson administrations or with Reagan and Bush. These new figures—the Clintons, Al Gore, George W. Bush, Dick Cheney, and John Kerry—all came of age during the 1960s.

7

Bill Clinton and the Heroes of the 1960s

USING LIBERAL ICONS
FOR CONSERVATIVE ENDS

*There were excesses and self-indulgences in the sixties. And all
that stuff people say that's critical of me, and my generation,
there's some truth in all of it. But it was also a profoundly
idealistic generation of people who loved their country and
believed it could be better.*

Bill Clinton (2004)

*I came of age at the height of the civil rights struggles of the
sixties: the 1963 March on Washington, the passage of the Civil
Rights Act of 1964 and the Voting Rights Act of 1965. I vividly
remember the assassinations of John F. Kennedy, Martin Luther
King and Bobby Kennedy. Like any American who grew up in
that era, my life was shaped by those triumphs and tragedies.*

Bill Clinton (2001)

THE 1960s FIGURED PROMINENTLY in Bill Clinton's presidency. Clinton
and his supporters tried to identify themselves with the idealism of the
early 1960s: John F. Kennedy, the Peace Corps, and Martin Luther King
and the pre-1965 civil rights movement, while Clinton's detractors tried
to link him with the second half of the decade, focusing on his having
avoided the draft, smoked marijuana, and strayed from his marriage. Clinton's presidency was defined by this battle between his supporters, who
valued his origins in the "good sixties," and his opponents, who hated the
hallmarks of the "bad sixties" that they saw in him.

For twelve years, since the election of Ronald Reagan in 1980, the
Republicans had won presidential elections by wielding their version
of the 1960s as an effective weapon against the Democrats. In 1992, to
counter this successful strategy, Clinton sought to resurrect the decade's

131

liberal reputation by stressing its more "conservative" elements. A study of Clinton's words and actions shows him distancing himself from the radical years of the 1960s while finding inspiration in the first half of the decade. But Clinton also presented a more subtle, nuanced version of the 1960s. He attempted to merge its positive and negative aspects into a co-alition of those who admired the period along with those who rejected it as an age of excesses. This blending and integrating of apparent opposites formed the essence of Clinton's "Third Way." Like Reagan and Bush be-fore him, he used the memory of the 1960s to build political support, but this time to serve different ends.

"The Sixties" and the 1992 Election

Bill Clinton was highly attuned to the national nostalgia for Jack Kennedy and made skillful use of his famous encounter with the president. The sixteen-year-old Clinton had been elected Arkansas's delegate to Boys Na-tion in 1963, and while attending the conference in Washington that July, he was photographed shaking hands with Kennedy in the Rose Garden. Asked in 1995 about meeting the president, Clinton said, "It was an in-credible experience" for a boy who had left Arkansas only twice before his White House visit. Clinton had especially wanted to meet Kennedy because he "agreed with what [JFK] was trying to do," especially "trying to finish the work of the Civil War" by attempting "to pass all the civil rights legislation" and "eliminate racial discrimination." Although many southerners were against this policy, Clinton "was for him because of it" and believed that Kennedy "was really looking out for our future." Their handshake was also symbolic. "That's a great thing about this country. [I came] from a modest-sized town, and one day I was shaking hands with the president."[1]

Clinton described this meeting in great detail in a video for the JFK Library, the last item one sees on exiting. "It had a very profound impact on me," he recalled, "something that I carried with me always. . . . [I]t had an even bigger impact in retrospect because he was killed so soon after-ward." To Clinton, Kennedy was a great president because he "[put] items on the national agenda which then had to be resolved. . . . It's very hard for a people and a democracy to change, unless they have confidence in their leaders and confidence in themselves and confidence in their ability to do better."[2]

Clinton brought the 1960s to the forefront according to his own design in the way he orchestrated memories of the decade during the 1992 Dem-ocratic National Convention. The third night of the convention directly evoked the era with a lengthy tribute to the Kennedy family; the 1968 hit song "Abraham, Martin, and John" (with an added verse for Robert Kennedy); and speeches by Ted Kennedy and Representative Joe Kennedy, who praised Clinton and vice presidential nominee Al Gore as sharing John Kennedy's values.[3] At evening's end Clinton made a surprise appearance—"the first candidate to come to the convention before the night of [the] acceptance speech since John Kennedy did it in 1960," as he proudly wrote in his 2004 memoir. Looking back, he admitted that he "wanted to identify with the spirit of John Kennedy's campaign."[4]

Clinton constantly referred to Kennedy and the 1960s in his run for the nomination and in the general election. His campaign introduced him to the convention with a biographical film that devoted an entire section to his 1963 handshake with Kennedy. The film also featured other images from the 1960s, especially the civil rights movement. Viewers saw and heard Clinton's younger brother, Roger, saying, "One of my earliest memories is of my brother reciting the 'I Have a Dream' speech by heart from beginning to end." The film served as a tribute to the idealism of the pre-1963 "good sixties," while at the same time ignoring the "bad sixties" by failing to mention the Great Society, the War on Poverty, or even Lyndon Johnson.[5]

Clinton's acceptance speech that night also focused on the early 1960s while ignoring the turbulent years that followed. "As a teenager, I heard John Kennedy's summons to citizenship," Clinton said. Eleven times he told the crowd that he wanted to create a "New Covenant," a slogan reminiscent of Kennedy's "New Frontier." Clinton defined the New Covenant as "based not simply on what each of us can take but what all of us must give to our nation," evoking Kennedy's challenge, "Ask not what your country can do for you—ask what you can do for your country."[6] Clinton's New Covenant was based on his recognition that the 1960s offered the Democrats opportunities as well as dangers. His program blended 1960s liberalism with post-1960s conservatism, a combination he used to neutralize the backlash from the Right that had followed the 1960s. It proved popular but angered the political extremes: the far Left accused Clinton of abandoning liberalism, while the far Right disdained him as an especially devious exemplar of the excesses of the decade.

In the words of Clinton's deputy chief of staff, Harold Ickes, both he and Bill Clinton "were children of the sixties. Clinton's formative political experiences were in the sixties, culturally, politically, music, the whole deal. Notwithstanding his assertion that 'the era of big government is over,' he profoundly believed and continues to believe that government is an instrument of good." But Clinton also thought Democrats needed "to start talking about helping the less fortunate" by using "different ways, different language, and different programs."[7]

Clinton first formulated his ambiguous use of the 1960s during Reagan's second term. He wrote in his memoir that by late 1986 he had developed the basic ideas of his New Democratic program. In 1988 he allied himself with the Democratic Leadership Council (DLC), a group that arose out of the desire of some Democrats to distance themselves from the "bad sixties." As early as 1988 Clinton considered running for president; because of his centrist record, "I didn't think the Republicans could paint me as an ultra-liberal Democrat." A Democrat could be elected president, he believed, only "if we could escape the 'alien' box the Republicans had put us in since 1968." Clinton knew that the DLC's move to the center was controversial. The Reverend Jesse Jackson called the DLC the "Democratic Leisure Class." But Clinton defended the approach, arguing that the public supported it, and it could be effective in uniting whites and African Americans. He first saw proof it could work in 1992 when he visited Michigan's suburban Macomb County, whose voters, he wrote in his memoir, "had begun voting Republican in the 1960s" but were showing signs of returning to the Democratic fold.[8]

Clinton's election victory brought back all the more vivid memories of the early 1960s. *Time*, in naming Clinton its Man of the Year for 1992, suggested that he might restore the country's pre-1963 optimism. "Americans have been in a kind of vague mourning for something that they sensed they had lost somewhere—what was best in the country," wrote Lance Morrow. "They had squandered it[,] . . . thrown it away in the messy interval between the assassination of John Kennedy and the wan custodial regime of George Bush." Pondering whether Clinton's desire to rekindle this idealism would ultimately prove successful, Morrow predicted that Clinton would manage to blend liberalism and conservatism. Clinton's victory signaled that the children of the 1960s had supplanted the "Greatest Generation" as the public discarded a president shaped by World War II for one formed by "the vastly different historical pageant of the '60s." The election would be seen as a referendum on Clinton's generation, Morrow predicted, as Clinton's future success would carry the baby boomers "to the power and responsibility that they clamored to overthrow in the streets a quarter of a century ago."[9]

Clinton echoed these sentiments in his memoir, writing: "The election represented a generational shift in America, the World War II veterans to the baby boomers, who were alternately derided as spoiled and self-absorbed, and lauded as idealistic and committed to the common good. Whether liberal or conservative, our politics were forged by Vietnam, civil rights, and the tumult of 1968, with its protests, riots, and assassinations."[10]

According to Ed Meese, conservatives labeled Clinton as the embodiment of the 1960s not because of his idealism but "because of his lifestyle. He claimed he didn't inhale, but he smoked marijuana. He was a draft dodger. From a cultural standpoint, he was a creature of the sixties."[11] William Rusher agreed. "We certainly identified [Clinton] as one of the people who in the sixties was against the Vietnam War and demonstrating in front of the American Embassy in London and going off to Moscow to visit the 'workers' paradise.'"[12]

When Clinton was elected, "there was a feeling of real outrage among conservatives," said Godfrey Hodgson. "This wasn't the normal feeling of a party that has lost power and lost office. These were guys who felt that the world had gone wrong; the ungodly were rioting in the seats of the mighty."[13]

But Clinton did not anger all conservatives; far from it, in fact. David Horowitz remarked that Clinton hired "a lot of leftists" but that his policies were "pretty reasonable . . . fairly centrist. And even conservative." Saying, "I like Al From" (founder of the DLC), Horowitz noted that he supported the DLC and had told From: "You're the only person who could cause me to retire from politics. If your faction took over the Democratic Party, the stakes would be so low."[14] The Club for Growth's Stephen Moore admitted that he voted for Clinton in 1992. "I'm not a Clinton basher. Clinton was a decent president."[15]

"I don't think Clinton liked going around saying he was a liberal; I'm not sure he was a liberal," Clinton speechwriter Ted Widmer recalled. "The Right may have seen him as more liberal than he actually was. He liked being in the center, where things happen," Widmer argued.[16] Todd Gitlin felt that "it was actually shrewd of Clinton to walk away from [liberalism] because it was nothing but an albatross."[17] Clinton speechwriter Paul Glastris confirmed that Clinton consciously avoided the term "liberal," saying, "No question about it; it never even occurred to any of us to use the word 'liberal,' because it had been appropriated [by the Right]." In the 1990s "liberal" connoted someone "more concerned about minorities than the majority, . . . about the rights of criminals [more] than crime victims," more interested in raising taxes than in improving the economy, and who had a "knee-jerk dislike of the American military" and was mostly against its use. "That is what liberalism had become. Clinton was all about recapturing the center Left for common sense," which necessitated finding a new language, since "liberals have ruined liberalism. The term that took over was 'progressive.'" To Glastris "the clever thing that Al From did was to call Clinton progressive."[18] Reporters who covered Clinton in the White House consistently recalled him as a pragmatic centrist.[19]

For the most part, however, conservatives believed that Clinton avoided the word "liberal" because he lacked core political convictions. "Clinton goes with whatever the dominant flow seems to be," said Robert Bork. "In the sixties he was over in London protesting outside the American embassy. Clinton is all about Clinton, and if you tell him that he's going to pay a heavy price for being liberal on something, he won't do it."[20] Meese asserted: "Clinton was not really a leftist. Generally his philosophy was liberal and to the left, but he would go wherever the political winds were going."[21]

At the same time, Clinton's centrism angered many Democrats. "You [could] get consensus [to] build a social safety net under the middle class," observed Gary Hart, but "much less consensus—certainly in the last third of the twentieth century—about poverty programs." So Clinton's famous assertion "The era of big government is over" was "code for saying, 'We're not going to do antipoverty activism anymore.'" Hart believed that Reagan's antigovernment rhetoric had inflicted great damage and that "Clinton had a unique opportunity to change it, given his age and what was perceived to be his charisma. And he didn't take advantage of it. . . . He was the victim of his DLC leanings."[22]

Clinton "supposed himself to be in the tradition of activist presidents. He associated himself with FDR and Truman and the Kennedys," recalled Arthur Schlesinger. "He believed in the use of government. But he didn't fight for it, and he swam with the tide. When he said, 'The era of big government is over,' that was a melancholy line." For Schlesinger, Clinton differed markedly from his political hero. "Kennedy represented government activism and public action, and he regarded that as a key," but Clinton did not replicate Kennedy's government activism for fear of not being liked. "The last thing Bill Clinton wanted to do was make enemies, probably as a result of his childhood."[23]

Clinton's unwillingness to fight for liberal causes frustrated many prominent Democrats. "Clinton was a genius because he managed to make himself look a lot better on the issue of race than he really was politically, although personally he was more at ease and liked black people better than probably any president," said Roger Wilkins. "But when it came to actual policies, he was ready to split the loaf or give it away in a minute."[24] As Bill Bradley saw it, "Reagan took the position way over on the right, and held it to the very end of the passage of a law, and then he'd compromise and move to the center." With Clinton, "as soon as somebody said something about 'liberal,' he immediately compromised 50 percent and he ended up getting 25 percent of what he wanted instead of 50 percent, which is what Reagan got."[25]

Clinton's exact ideology remains the subject of much speculation among both supporters and detractors. But he encouraged such speculation, as he longed to remain in the political center and did not want to be easily categorized politically. One clue to his beliefs can be found in the ways Clinton spoke of the leaders of the 1960s.

Clinton and JFK: Idealism and Inspiration

Like Reagan before him, Clinton referred to Kennedy more often than to any other president. But while Reagan alluded to Kennedy to call for tax cuts and a strong defense and decry the Democrats' leftward drift since the 1960s, Clinton used Kennedy to evoke the inspirational power of the late president and to conjure the idealism of the early 1960s, as well as to argue for "conservative" positions such as the need for smaller government. Whereas Reagan depicted Kennedy as essentially a conservative, Clinton used him in support of his own more centrist policies.

Clinton well understood Kennedy's hold on the American psyche, and especially on Democrats. Michael Dukakis spoke glowingly of Kennedy's ability to answer questions from a room of Harvard Law School students in 1958, when Dukakis was a student there, and talked at length about a trip he took with a friend to attend the 1960 Los Angeles convention that nominated Kennedy.[26] Many Americans recall the Kennedy years "as a golden age," acknowledged Gary Hart. "It was the introduction of a new generation of leaders, of people in government who were the best and the brightest, Rhodes scholars, achievers, bright people with high expectations and high standards for themselves and the country. And it *was* a golden era."[27] Former Democratic National Committee chair Paul Kirk praised Kennedy's "idealism mixed with pragmatism," his ability to inspire, and his sense of humor. "Kennedy calls to the inner best instincts of every individual and tells him or her that each of us can make a difference."[28] Archibald Cox, who served in the Kennedy Administration, noted "the ideals that a lot of us around Kennedy had, indeed, that Kennedy inspired in a great many people."[29] John Shattuck, chief executive officer of the John F. Kennedy Library Foundation, praised Kennedy's understanding of "the moral crisis that was created by segregation."[30]

Observers of the scene agreed. "For a long time, for a whole generation of Democrats, Kennedy was it," noted Mark Shields.[31] To Kennedy biographer Robert Dallek, "Kennedy remains the principal inspirational political figure in American life and around the world, the last inspirational figure in politics."[32] As historian H. W. Brands wryly observed, "there are a lot of aging Democrats—aging liberals—who remember their first kiss in politics with John Kennedy."[33]

Clinton paid public homage to Kennedy the day before his inauguration. "Hillary and I started the day with a visit to the graves of John and Robert Kennedy at Arlington National Cemetery," he wrote in his memoir. "Accompanied by John Kennedy, Jr., Ethel Kennedy, several of her children, and Senator Ted Kennedy, I knelt at the eternal flame and said a short prayer, thanking God for their lives and service and asking for wisdom and strength in the great adventures just ahead."[34] Like Kennedy with Robert Frost, Clinton invited a poet, Maya Angelou, to read at his inauguration. The next day, "on my first day as president, I started out by taking Mother down to the Rose Garden, to show her exactly where I stood when I shook hands with President Kennedy almost 30 years ago."[35] One of his first presidential acts was to retrieve Kennedy's desk from storage and place it in the Oval Office. Like Kennedy, Clinton was photographed at the start of his presidency by Yousuf Karsh. "Made three decades later, Mr. Clinton's portrait indicates, perhaps, a kindred spirit," noted a caption in the *New York Times* below facing photographs of Kennedy and Clinton. The images were published days before the thirtieth anniversary of Kennedy's assassination.[36]

During his first two years as president, Clinton's most frequent allusions to Kennedy spoke to the lost idealism of the early 1960s and defined the era as one of great promise unfulfilled. "We have in this country a crisis of belief and hope," Clinton said in 1993. "When President Kennedy took office . . . over 70 percent of the American people fundamentally believed that their leaders would tell them the truth and that their system could succeed." Clinton vowed to "restore the confidence of our people in our democracy."[37] He told House Democrats that when he met Kennedy in 1963, he "had no doubt whatever" that Congress and the president "could meet whatever challenge we were facing." But Kennedy's death had started a painful journey. "Now, people all over America don't believe that anymore," he said. "Thirty years ago when I was here, I didn't have an instant of a doubt," but soon afterward "President Kennedy was assassinated, and the pain of that still lives on in this country, and perhaps was the beginning of the slow undoing of our collective confidence in ourselves and our institutions."[38] Clinton told Boys Nation that when he met Kennedy in 1963 "it was a very different time for America. There was virtually no cynicism. None of us had any doubt that our country could solve its problems."[39]

Like countless others, Clinton credited Kennedy for his own decision to enter public service.[40] In speaking of this inspiration, Clinton again contrasted the idealism of the early 1960s with the widespread cynicism of his own time in office. Soon after the death of Jacqueline Kennedy Onassis in 1994 Clinton remarked, "She and President Kennedy inspired me and an entire generation of Americans to see the nobility of helping others and the good that could come from public service." He lamented that John Kennedy "would be absolutely shocked at the pessimism, the negativism, the division, the destructive tone of public discourse" today.[41] Clinton frequently and at great length spoke of Kennedy's influence on his generation.[42] Closing his remarks at the JFK Library in 1998 he said, "Finally, and most personally, I am here because President Kennedy and Robert Kennedy, their generation, made me admire and believe in public service."[43]

Some of Clinton's most extensive remarks on Kennedy came at a 1993 tribute at the JFK Library. Clinton said that Kennedy had brought hope, "changed the way we think about our country," and "inspired millions" to confront problems at home and abroad. He believed that he was carrying on Kennedy's legacy. Consistent with Kennedy's appeal "for basic civil rights," said Clinton, "we passed the Motor Voter Act, which was the most important piece of civil rights legislation passed in a long time." Furthermore, "from . . . the Peace Corps to [Clinton's] creation of the National Service Corps . . . we see a common thread of challenging our young people to a higher calling." He and Kennedy also shared a similar courage to be innovative, he said, as seen in their commitment to space travel and their health care policies. Clinton even borrowed from Kennedy to bolster his case for globalization, asserting: "This new global economy is our new frontier. Our generation must now decide, just as John Kennedy and his generation had to decide at the end of World War II, whether we will harness the galloping changes of our time in the best tradition of John Kennedy and the post-war generation." He ended with a flourish of Kennedyesque rhetoric, "Let us embrace the future with vigor." The next century would be ours "if we approach it with the vigor, the determination, the wisdom, and the sheer confidence and joy of life that John Kennedy brought to America in 1960."[44]

In Clinton's view, the main inspirational vehicle by which Kennedy brought about change was the Peace Corps, and he tried to emulate Kennedy's service organization with his own ambitious national service program, AmeriCorps. As Reagan used Kennedy to market his tax cuts, Clinton used Kennedy to sell AmeriCorps.

"When President Kennedy created the Peace Corps thirty-five years ago . . . he tapped an overflowing reservoir of energy and idealism," Clinton observed on the program's 1996 anniversary. "The Peace Corps symbolized everything that inspired my generation to service."[45] At the signing ceremony for the 1993 bill creating AmeriCorps, as Clinton proudly recalled in his memoir, Sargent Shriver, the first director of the Peace Corps, let him "use one of the pens President Kennedy had used thirty-two years earlier to sign the Peace Corps legislation." More people joined AmeriCorps in the 1990s, he noted, than "in the entire forty-year history of the Peace Corps."[46]

On numerous occasions Clinton compared his program with Kennedy's.[47] The Peace Corps "defined the character of a whole generation of Americans committed to serving people around the world," he said in his first State of the Union address, pledging that AmeriCorps would provide more than twice the number of people "to be in national service than ever served in the Peace Corps."[48] At the JFK Library in 1998 Clinton called the signing of the first AmeriCorps bill, with Ted Kennedy at his side, "one of my happiest days as president."[49]

While he often spoke of Kennedy's idealism and optimism, Clinton also astutely referred to JFK and the early 1960s to deflect the charge that he was himself a late 1960s liberal. Kennedy was "very pragmatic," said John Shattuck. "Clinton came from a very different background, but politically [JFK] was a role model, particularly the pragmatism."[50] Clinton's pragmatism showed in the Kennedyesque quality he most often displayed: a passion for small government and fiscal responsibility.

When he spoke about the size of the government, Clinton often drew a distinction between the early and later 1960s. This contrast was first mentioned several months before the 1994 midterm elections as pressure from the Right intensified. In April 1994 Clinton claimed that his proposed budget would create "the smallest federal government since the 1960s—the early sixties."[51] Soon "the early sixties" was defined more specifically when, in July 1994, he argued that he had "dramatically" reduced government and that by 2000 it "will be under two million people in size for the first time since . . . Kennedy was president."[52]

After the Republicans regained control of Congress in 1994, the issue became central to Clinton's reelection strategy. "The federal workforce is shrinking to its lowest level since President Kennedy was in office," he said late that year.[53] In 1995 he promised that the federal government would soon be smaller "than at any time since President Kennedy."[54] In

1996 Clinton proclaimed that by year's end the government "will be the smallest it has been since President Kennedy."[55]

At the 1996 Democratic National Convention, unlike in 1992, Clinton did not allude to Kennedy to recall the idealism of the 1960s. Instead he now stressed Kennedy's fiscal responsibility and adherence to small government, thus using Kennedy—as Reagan had—to demonstrate that the liberal icons of the 1960s also had a "conservative" streak. "The federal workforce is the smallest it's been since John Kennedy," Clinton announced.[56] He repeated this throughout the campaign, sometimes adding that his effort to eliminate regulations and programs "exceeds that of my two Republican predecessors."[57]

After the Republican triumph in the 1994 congressional elections, Clinton became a defensive president. The fact that his most frequent mention of Kennedy was to demonstrate he was not a "tax-and-spend liberal" was a testament to Reagan's, Bush's, and Newt Gingrich's successful partisan use of "the sixties." Reflecting the era's conservatism—and to deflect charges that he was a 1960s radical—Clinton continued to mention Kennedy most often in connection with traditional conservative concerns, such as balanced budgets and small government. At bottom, though, Clinton's use of Kennedy reflected a broad-based longing for Kennedy's "good sixties" that crossed party lines. Much more problematic was how to define the post-1963 period of Lyndon Johnson—that is, the "bad sixties."

Clinton and LBJ: A Complicated Relationship

Until well into the twenty-first century Lyndon Johnson consistently polled second only to Richard Nixon as the nation's least popular president, ratings that remained remarkably consistent across ideologies and races. Even though he passed the most civil rights legislation since Lincoln, African Americans have expressed very low approval of Johnson.[58] When the public was asked, in seven separate polls between 1999 and 2007, who was America's greatest president, Johnson was not even among the fourteen or fifteen (when one includes George W. Bush) named—unique among post-1932 presidents. George W. Bush made the list in every year of his presidency, and even Nixon, though he always came in last, had enough supporters to make the list of greatest presidents in six of these years by scoring at least 1 percent, a threshold LBJ never cracked.[59]

During his presidency, Johnson's highest disapproval rating, 52 percent, places him squarely in the middle of the lowest and highest disapproval ratings of the twelve presidents since polling began during World War II,[60] although that figure does not reflect the way his presidency is remembered. But more than anything, Johnson is simply *forgotten*: when members of the public are asked whether they approve or disapprove of past presidents, Johnson always leads in the category "unsure."

With the exception of Jesse Jackson in 1988 and Bill Bradley in 2000, Democratic candidates have long treated LBJ as a pariah. Only once from 1969 to 2004 was as much as a whole sentence devoted to him in any presidential candidate's acceptance speech at the Democratic convention, when Jimmy Carter praised him a single time in his 1976 address; in 1980 Carter mentioned Johnson once, together with Hubert Humphrey, and in his 1988 remarks Dukakis mentioned Johnson once together with Kennedy. Johnson was not mentioned even in passing in the remaining nominating speeches.

Yet Clinton felt an affinity with Johnson. In his memoir he wrote that as a college freshman in 1964 "I was a hard-core Democrat for LBJ."[61] Clinton, who worked in Texas on the 1972 McGovern campaign, noted that as a "pro–civil rights Southerner," he "liked Johnson more than most of [my] McGovern coworkers did."[62] According to Arthur Schlesinger, Clinton "was inspired by Kennedy, but he had more of a fellow feeling for Johnson because Johnson was a southerner and a politician of a familiar sort."[63]

But while Clinton openly admired Kennedy, as president he rarely praised Johnson, and his memoir contains twice as many references to JFK as to LBJ.[64] Given that Johnson and Clinton were southerners with a shared passion for civil rights, among other interests, Clinton's reluctance to speak of Johnson revealed the danger he sensed in speaking positively of the author of the Great Society and the Vietnam escalation. Johnson, as the emblematic and most memorable personality of the later 1960s, was still treated like political poison twenty-four years after he left office.

Unlike Reagan and Bush, however, who continually blamed Johnson for the problems of the 1960s and beyond, Clinton occasionally spoke highly of the nation's thirty-sixth president. At a 1999 Rosa Parks tribute Clinton paid tribute to "the magnificent legislative achievements of President Johnson."[65] He especially praised Johnson for Medicare.[66] In 1994 Clinton said that Johnson heard objections to Medicare from conservative critics "until the very end of the vote" but nevertheless enacted the law "that has helped hundreds of millions of older Americans and their families."[67]

But when Clinton mentioned Johnson in speeches and in writing, it was most often in reference to the mid-1960s civil rights legislation. Clinton spoke of the "triumph" of Johnson's 1965 Voting Rights Act.[68] Johnson's civil rights laws, he said, were "the greatest domestic achievement of my lifetime, and it helped to make possible so many good things."[69] He praised Johnson's governance in an address on the day of the 1995 Million Man March, noting that LBJ "spoke so powerfully for the dignity of man and the destiny of democracy in demanding that Congress guarantee full voting rights to blacks."[70]

Although Clinton praised Johnson's Medicare and civil rights programs, he almost never defended the rest of Johnson's domestic agenda. Conscious of how politically unpopular such programs were, and how vigorously Reagan and Bush had attacked them, Clinton only once uttered the words "War on Poverty."[71] He referred to the Great Society by name only four times in his entire presidency. The first mention did not come until a full year after his 1996 reelection, and even then it was only to link Johnson's program with other twentieth-century reform measures from Wilson onward.[72]

When Clinton next mentioned the Great Society, he simply referred to it as the high-water mark of government spending, which he was pleased to have reduced.[73] His aides proudly contrasted the Great Society expenditures with his administration's fiscal discipline, as when two advisers stated in 1994 that the percentage being devoted to discretionary federal government spending was lower than before the Great Society began.[74]

Clinton's only praise of the Great Society came in three interviews over two weeks in 1999. In June he told *BusinessWeek*: "In the 1960s, there was this great effort, through the Great Society programs, to build up the poor urban and rural areas. And we found that, actually, they did a lot of good," especially regarding education, nutrition, and health care. He then quickly noted the Great Society's limitations, adding, "But government alone could not build a [self-]sustaining economy."[75] In a July interview he portrayed his antipoverty programs as having achieved a middle ground between those of Johnson and Reagan and praised the results of "community development financial institutions"—unlike, he added, "either the Great Society of the sixties or the great neglect of the eighties."[76]

Clinton's greatest praise for Johnson occurred in the election year 2000. In February, contradicting his previous statements about the early 1960s, Clinton said: "I disagree with all these people that date the start of American cynicism . . . to the assassination of President Kennedy. That's not true. People are rewriting history; President Johnson did a fine job in taking over."[77] In a speech a few months later he repeated, "Lyndon Johnson did some magnificent things for this country."[78] Then at the Democratic National Convention in August, Clinton called Johnson "a president I admired for all he did for civil rights, the elderly and the poor."[79] Shortly after the November election Clinton said he was "glad to see that there is a reassessment going on about the historic importance of President Johnson's term of office, the work he did for the Civil Rights movement, the Civil Rights Act, the Voting Rights Act. Some people are even beginning to acknowledge that his War on Poverty was not a total failure, that in fact poverty was reduced."[80]

Clinton's strong admiration for Kennedy nevertheless overshadows whatever feelings he had about Johnson. "I don't think he had a personal or psychic connection with Johnson the way he clearly did with JFK," observed Clinton biographer John Harris.[81] But several of Clinton's speechwriters and advisers argued that Clinton did feel a strong personal connection with Johnson. "Everyone knows Clinton loves JFK, but he also loves LBJ, probably equally," said Ted Widmer. "He's a huge admirer of Lyndon Johnson, and he would like Americans to have more feeling for Johnson than they do."[82] Jeff Shesol "was on a campaign to get Lyndon Johnson into" the "Third Way" and DLC speeches "because I just felt there's been this wholesale disowning of LBJ, more because of Vietnam than because of any failures of the Great Society." Clinton often told Shesol of his great respect for Johnson, Shesol noted. The president "had enormous, enormous, admiration for LBJ and what he had been able to achieve domestically."[83]

Those who worked under Clinton explained his lack of public praise for Johnson as more a reflection of the conservatism of the 1990s than of Clinton's own sentiments. "Clinton is coming after twelve years of Republican revolution," explained John Shattuck. The Reagan and George H. W. Bush years saw "a series of attacks, most of them ideological, at the very underpinnings of the Great Society, of the New Deal, and the whole concept of government delivering. In order to be elected, Clinton tacked to the center pretty sharply. He was essentially working on political territory that is very hostile to the concepts of the Great Society."[84]

The reason for Clinton's reluctance to mention Johnson was obvious to some. "Johnson [is] part of 'the bad sixties,'" said David Kusnet, a Clinton speechwriter. "Johnson was a great domestic president. But that's not how [people] remember Johnson, even though he spent his first year in office doing what John Kennedy wanted to do but couldn't do: passing the Civil Rights Bill, the civil rights law, the voting rights law, and Medicare." As Kusnet put it, "Johnson is remembered as a caricature, as an advocate of a grandiosely large government on the domestic scene." The era's New Left "are caricatured as nihilists, so both sides—Johnson and his opponents—are filed in the 'bad sixties,' while John Kennedy is filed in the 'good sixties.'" In Kusnet's view, "Clinton shrewdly tried to identify himself with the idealism of John Kennedy and with a less grandiose approach to the goals that Johnson had." But "ironically, if there's probably any figure of the sixties whom Bill Clinton may have a great and unacknowledged admiration for, it would probably be Lyndon Johnson. That would be my guess, but he knows it is impolitic . . . with either the Left or the Right in this country to say you admire Lyndon Johnson—but I bet he does."[85]

Clinton clearly had to strike a delicate balance when speaking about Lyndon Johnson. Since he could not appear to endorse any aspect of the "bad sixties," his rhetoric about LBJ could never reveal the personal admiration for Johnson that he almost certainly felt. He was far more comfortable using another liberal 1960s icon, Martin Luther King Jr., in publicly expressing his deepest sentiments about the man.

Clinton, King, and Racial Reconciliation

In 1997, commemorating the fortieth anniversary of the integration of Little Rock's Central High School, Bill Clinton said that the crisis compared in national importance to the signing of the Declaration of Independence and the Battle of Gettysburg. Clinton grew up only fifty miles from Little Rock, and "like almost all Southerners then, I never attended school with a person of another race until I went to college. But as a young boy in my grandfather's small grocery store, I learned lessons that nobody bothered to teach me in my segregated school." Clinton's grandfather had little education or money, "but in that store, in the way he treated his [African American] customers and encouraged me to play with their children, I learned America's most profound lessons: We really are all equal." Little Rock "made racial equality a driving obsession in my life."[86]

"He loved the civil rights movement," Ted Widmer said of Clinton. "He didn't talk about the 1960s too much; he talked a lot about civil rights. Civil rights were definitely front and center in his memory and in his agenda. And he did a lot to elevate the civil rights movement as a very important historical episode that all Americans have to take seriously," he added. "Think about how hard it was to get a Martin Luther King holiday and how many Republicans were against it at the time. They claimed not to have been, but they certainly were."[87]

Clinton expressed admiration for King beyond even the reverence he showed for John Kennedy. The explanation lies in their shared origins and experiences. As a fellow southerner who saw racial segregation in his own daily life, Clinton felt a more personal connection with King than with Kennedy, whose Boston upbringing, experiences, and even speech were so unlike his.

Clinton often spoke in highly personal terms of how King had inspired him. King's "I Have a Dream" speech was among the most important events of Clinton's youth. In 1998, commemorating the 1963 March on Washington, Clinton called his handshake with President Kennedy in 1963 "a great moment."

> But I think the moment we commemorate today—a moment I experi-enced all alone—had a more profound impact on my life. Most of us who are old enough remember exactly where we were on August 28, 1963. I was in my living room in Hot Springs, Arkansas. I remember the chair I was sitting in; I remember exactly where it was in the room. . . . I re-member weeping uncontrollably during Martin Luther King's speech, and I remember thinking when it was over, my country would never be the same, and neither would I.[88]

Clinton often spoke, too, of King's impact on whites. "As a son of the South, I have seen in my own lifetime how racism held all of us down and how the Civil Rights movement set all of us free," read a 1993 state-ment on the thirtieth anniversary of the March on Washington.[89] In 1995 Clinton declared that King "freed the rest of us, too, of our hatred, our bigotry."[90] On the thirty-fifth anniversary of the 1965 Selma, Alabama, march for voting rights he quoted King, who had said that the attain-ment of civil rights for African Americans would also free for the first time "those who have held them down."[91] Clinton well understood the symbolism of the King holiday. "Only three American citizens, one from each century of our history, are honored with a holiday of national scope," Clinton remarked in his Martin Luther King Day address in 1994. "Two were presidents, but the other never occupied any office except the most important in our democracy. He was a citizen. George Washington helped to create our union, Abraham Lincoln gave his life to preserve it, and Mar-tin Luther King redeemed the moral purpose of our United States."[92]

Racial reconciliation was crucial to Clinton's political persona; he saw race as central to the national divisions since the 1960s and a main cause of the Democrats' decline since 1964. Like LBJ he recognized that when the Democratic Party decided to back the civil rights movement (and es-pecially the Civil Rights Act of 1964) it risked losing at least as many white voters as it stood to gain among African Americans. He also knew that no Democratic presidential candidate since Johnson's 1964 landslide had received a majority of white votes. Healing that divide would allow progressive politics to rise again. Central to that healing process, he be-lieved, were lessons King had imparted: forgiveness, justice, and personal responsibility.

Throughout his memoir Clinton speaks of the effect on him of the civil rights movement. He described at length the anniversary celebrations marking the thirty-fifth anniversary of the march in Selma. "I loved that day in Selma," Clinton wrote. "Once again, I was swept back across the years to my boyhood longing for and belief in an America without a racial divide. Once again, I returned to the emotional core of my political life."[93] At a Congressional Black Caucus dinner in 2000 Clinton "threw away the script" and closed by noting, "Toni Morrison once said I was the first black president this country ever had." Clinton said he felt great pride in such a statement "because somewhere, in the deep and lost threads of my own memory . . . there was a deep longing to share the fate of the people who had been left out and left behind, sometimes brutalized, and too often ignored or forgotten."[94] Clinton often expressed this sense of solidarity.[95]

In addition to making numerous speeches on King holidays and on anniversaries of King's death, Clinton incorporated King into his remarks at every opportunity. He exalted King in his 1997 second inaugural address, which fell on Martin Luther King Day. "Like a prophet of old, he told of his dream that one day America would rise up and treat all its citizens as equals before the law and in the heart," Clinton said. King's dream was "the American Dream."[96] In 1998, he noted that the twenty-first century was only seven hundred days away but much could yet be accomplished. "It's about the same amount of time that, from 1961 to 1963, an active citizen named King helped James Meredith go to college, stood up to Bull Connor, wrote a letter from a jail in Birmingham, helped to organize the March on Washington, and gave a little speech," Clinton remarked playfully. "His main line was 'I Have a Dream.'"[97] Clinton used King to stress the importance of public service,[98] spoke of King's emphasis on community, and invoked him to lament the nation's loss of connectedness since the 1960s.[99] The sheer variety of ways in which Clinton thought to mention King demonstrates the deep influence the slain civil rights leader had on the president.

Yet while Martin Luther King was the formative political influence during his youth, Clinton was not above using King, as he had Kennedy, to assuage conservative sentiments among voters. He brought in King as a way to speak of the idealism of the 1960s but at the same time linked the slain civil rights leader with his own tough-on-crime measures in order to appeal to those who had drifted to the right since the 1960s. This emphasis on personal responsibility and hostility toward lawbreakers reflected the conservatism of the 1990s and marked a radical departure from the usual contexts in which Democrats spoke of King—and even, perhaps, from King's own ideas.

More often than on any other issue Clinton adduced King to demonstrate that he and King were fellow crusaders against crime. Advocating tougher gun laws, Clinton gave his most emotional speech as president in 1993 at the Mason Temple Church in Memphis, where King gave his last sermon in April 1968. Clinton said he had read "about an eleven-year-old child planning her funeral: 'These are the hymns I want sung. This is the dress I want to wear. I know I'm not going to live very long.' . . . [T]he freedom to die before you're a teenager is not what Martin Luther King lived and died for," said Clinton. The nation's problems, he declared—in words that could have been spoken by Ronald Reagan or George H. W. Bush—could not be solved "until we provide the structure, the values, the discipline, and the reward that work gives." The president talked of the need to "deal with the ravages of crime and drugs and violence," which he blamed on "the breakdown of the family and the community, and the disappearance of jobs." And he urged Americans to understand that these problems could not be solved by government alone.[100]

"That [speech] has gone down in history as Clinton's throwing away his prepared text and speaking extemporaneously," said David Kusnet. "There was no way that you were going to get Bill Clinton—who had memorized the 'I Have a Dream' speech as a high school kid—in front of several thousand Pentecostal ministers and at the pulpit where Martin Luther King gave his last speech and have [him] stick to a text, so we didn't give him a text." Instead Kusnet gave Clinton some "talking points," King's last speech, "and some general ideas. We knew that he would put it together and do a speech."[101]

Asked in 2000 to name his "best speech," Clinton answered, "The speech I gave in Mason Temple in Memphis in '93."[102] In his memoir he wrote at length about its themes, referring to it as "what many commentators later said was the best speech" of his presidency. As a sign of the importance Clinton placed on that day, he devoted more space in his 957-page memoir to excerpting this speech than to any other address, document, or text.[103] As president Clinton often returned to his 1993 Memphis speech to emphasize the need for law and order, subjects the Right had vigorously championed since the 1960s.[104] He also frequently mentioned King in connection with a plea for a decrease in violence and fewer guns and to lament the continued prevalence of crime.[105]

Clinton also used King to emphasize the need for personal responsibility. King "lived and died" for the right of every person to succeed, not "for the freedom to shoot people . . . to shoot up . . . to hate people . . .

to ignore the responsibilities of parenthood and the obligations [to] our children," he said on the King holiday in 1995.[106] On the morning of the Million Man March in 1995 Clinton noted that in the 1960s people had marched for the "dignity and opportunity" denied by discrimination. Today's march was about these things, but because of "deepening social problems that disproportionately impact black Americans, it is also about black men taking renewed responsibility for themselves, their families, and their communities. It's about saying no to crime and drugs and violence."[107]

While using King to speak against crime and violence, Clinton also enlisted him in support of an activist government. "While government could not solve all problems," he said on King's birthday in 1995, "government should not be heartless, either, and walk away. The government should be a partner" and assist people's efforts to improve their lives. "That is what Martin Luther King wanted us to do."[108] But Clinton believed that King had stressed personal change above all. While King had "asked the government to act," he recalled earlier that day, "he knew that in the end what was in the heart and the spirit and the mind . . . was even more important."[109] In these ways Clinton used King to pursue conservative ends, such as "getting tough" on crime and calling for African Americans to take personal responsibility for their situation rather than rely on an activist federal government to support them. With King as the formative political influence of his youth, Clinton knew well King's more radical message of the latter 1960s. Yet because the Right had made such effective use of the "bad sixties," he was forced to use King defensively, in connection with traditionally conservative themes. Clinton used another liberal icon of the 1960s, Robert Kennedy, in a similar way.

Clinton and RFK: Recalling the First "New Democrat"

Clinton primarily invoked Robert Kennedy, as he had King, to build support for his anticrime program. In 1994, discussing measures to reduce crime and violence, Clinton noted that recently a poor neighborhood had built a fence around itself to protect its residents from continuing gun violence. Though the community became much safer, Clinton found this ironic. "At the Berlin Wall, [President Kennedy] said . . . 'Freedom has many difficulties, and our democracy is far from perfect, but we never had to put up a wall to keep our people in.' No, we never did," Clinton said. "But now millions of us have to put up walls to keep our people out. Is that what Martin Luther King and Robert Kennedy gave their lives for? I don't think so."[110]

Like King, Robert Kennedy exerted a huge influence on Clinton. In his speeches the president constantly linked the two men together. He twice described King and Kennedy as "people I literally adored."[111] Even before his election Democrats were comparing Clinton with RFK. In nominating him at the 1992 Democratic National Convention, Mario Cuomo said that Clinton "cherishes the ideals of justice, liberty and opportunity, fairness and compassion that Robert Kennedy died for."[112] Earlier that evening Ted Kennedy had declared that like his brother Robert, Clinton "has sought to heal" divisions of race and class.[113]

Clinton drew upon a lesser-known aspect of Kennedy's career to help promote his own, invoking Robert Kennedy—as he had King—not only to call forth the inspiration and idealism of the 1960s but also to appeal to those who were repelled by the era. Clinton used Kennedy's name to justify his anticrime measures and incorporated him into his centrist governing philosophy. Most important, he identified Kennedy as the originator of his "Third Way" policies and as someone who had tried to heal the divisions of the 1960s, especially on race and Vietnam.

Clinton's first mention of Robert Kennedy occurred in June 1993, a day before the twenty-fifth anniversary of RFK's death. In the language of Clinton's centrist "Third Way" approach, he claimed that America works best when "everyone who works hard and plays by the rules" can prosper, and when opportunity is open to all. "In my lifetime, no one has addressed that challenge with greater courage or constancy than the late Senator Robert Kennedy," Clinton said. In the 1960s, when many Americans were alienated from politicians, "Kennedy had an uncommon feel for what people experienced in their daily lives. He fought to expand economic opportunity, to remind citizens that our rights are accompanied by responsibilities." Senator Kennedy strove for racial unity instead of division, he said, and always emphasized the importance of patriotism.[114]

At a Kennedy memorial the next day, Clinton recalled that just before he graduated from college in 1968, he had rejoiced in Kennedy's California primary victory and believed that Kennedy could unite the country and inspire it to solve its problems. Kennedy challenged "the grieving not to retreat into despair[,] . . . the comfortable not to be complacent[,] . . . the doubting to keep going." Clinton's Robert Kennedy was a racial unifier. "We remember him, almost captured in freeze-frame, standing on the hood of a car, grasping at out-reached hands, black and brown and white," the president said. Clinton also portrayed Kennedy as sharing the DLC's political philosophy. While Kennedy criticized poverty, "he challenged the neglected to seize their own destiny." He believed in government intervention to solve problems but "did not trust bureaucracy." He thought that "government had to do things *with* people, not for them." Kennedy "saw the world not in terms of Right and Left, but right and wrong," said Clinton, and could not be pigeonholed ideologically.[115]

While many saw Kennedy as a polarizing figure in his own time, for Clinton he was a unifying force whose leadership was desperately needed. In 1994 Clinton spoke in Indianapolis, near where Kennedy had informed an African American audience that King was dead, a speech that Clinton in 1993 had called the late senator's "finest." In his 1994 remarks Clinton said that Kennedy "beckoned Americans of all races to show compassion and wisdom in the face of violence and lawlessness." Riots had erupted that night in 1968, but not in Indianapolis. "Once again, it is time for us to heed those words," said Clinton.[116] He repeated this sentiment later at the groundbreaking for the Kennedy-King statue in Indianapolis, remarking that King's and Kennedy's message of racial, political, economic, and religious unity had inspired him to seek public office.[117]

Clinton often quoted at length from Kennedy's speeches from the 1960s, relying on the memory of Kennedy and his record as attorney general to support his own anticrime rhetoric.[118] And as he had with both John Kennedy and Martin Luther King, Clinton often alluded to Robert Kennedy's idealism.[119] The memory of Robert Kennedy always remained fresh for Clinton. In 1999 he recounted how Kennedy in 1968 had visited some of the nation's most destitute regions. At RFK's funeral, Clinton noted, "Ted Kennedy said that he and his family hoped that what their brother was to them and what he wished for others would someday come to pass for all the world. I heard it thirty-one years ago; I have never forgotten it."[120]

Clinton's references to Robert Kennedy steadily increased during his presidency. He campaigned for reelection, as he had in 1992, as a New Democrat, but Kennedy's influence on him had become stronger. In the film introduction at the 1996 Democratic National Convention he spoke of Robert Kennedy but made no mention of John Kennedy.[121] Clinton spoke most frequently about RFK, especially their similar governing philosophies, in his final two years as president. Nearing the thirtieth anniversary of Kennedy's death, Clinton said that Kennedy's efforts in the late 1960s had "great parallels to what we have been about in the last few years—trying to get people to give up the old dogmas, trying to bring people together." The current period was a perfect time to implement Kennedy's ideals, he said. "[After] that springtime in 1968," when the nation was in turmoil and divided, it was "not possible for a very long time to try to put the pieces of an American progressive movement back together." But now the chance had returned at last. The current robust economic climate "doesn't happen all that often, and we have space now, and confidence, and a sense of possibility. And we cannot squander it."[122]

Clinton credited Kennedy as the architect of his own governing philosophy. In 2000, explaining why his centrism angered conservatives, he recalled that someone he knew in the Bush White House called him in 1990, before he had decided to run for president. The two were having a serious discussion, Clinton said, when the caller abruptly interjected: "Let's just cut the crap. We've looked at this crowd [of Democrats] and we can beat them all[,] . . . but you're different. . . . [I]f you run we're going to take you out early." Clinton said that when he met with Republicans after his 1992 election, he realized that they had been in power since 1968; Carter's term they considered "purely a function of Watergate, an historical accident that they had quickly corrected." But in Clinton's view, "Carter and before him Bobby Kennedy were the precursors of the New Democrat, Third Way."[123]

Throughout his presidency Clinton frequently made this point. In his memoir Clinton observed that Kennedy won Indiana's 1968 primary by calling for dialogue between the races but also by speaking about the problems of crime and welfare, which appealed to conservatives. "In Indiana, Bobby Kennedy became the first New Democrat," Clinton wrote, preceding Carter, the DLC in 1985, and Clinton's own 1992 campaign. Kennedy "believed in civil rights for all and special privileges for none, in giving poor people a hand up rather than a handout: work was better than welfare."[124]

Two close Kennedy family confidants vigorously disputed Clinton's contention that RFK was the first New Democrat. Arthur Schlesinger called the DLC "very pro-business, the Republican wing of the Democratic Party, and I do not think Robert Kennedy would have gone to the right."[125] In 1968 Kennedy "was talking like a radical, and his proposals for the future of the Democratic Party were really quite radical," recalled Benjamin Bradlee. "Jack Kennedy was staying within the confines of the left-center wing of the Democratic Party; he was no radical, and Bobby was becoming one. If you ever saw a collection of [Robert] Kennedy's speeches at that time—not just the crowd speeches but the prepared speeches—he had obviously decided, unlike most of the Democrats who turned to the center, that he was going to turn to the left."[126]

But those who worked for Clinton strongly supported his characterization of Kennedy. The consistency and passion with which Clinton's speechwriters and advisers linked Clinton with RFK demonstrated the Democrats' desire to make effective use of the finer qualities of the 1960s while avoiding the political dangers that had, since 1980, become associated with "the sixties." To Clinton—and especially the DLC—Kennedy symbolized the best of the decade.

"I've never heard that before, but it's absolutely true" that Kennedy was the first New Democrat, said Clinton speechwriter Ted Widmer. "RFK was a different kind of Democrat, and Clinton cared about the things RFK cared about, specifically, keeping working-class people [in the party]. The big problem with liberalism in the sixties was that it alienated blue-collar families, who were the traditional core of the Democratic Party—the flag burning and the long hair. A person like Archie Bunker would have been a Democrat most of his life but would certainly be a Republican today," Widmer said. "Clinton liked those people, he came from those kinds of people, and he wanted them in the Democratic Party." Kennedy "appeals to the most liberal of liberals because he was with César Chávez, in Mississippi, and on Indian reservations," but he also appeals to "Irish Catholics and tough ethnic immigrants, and he fought against the Mafia in the fifties . . . and was tough on foreign policy—and that's how Clinton wanted to be."[127]

"The DLC identified Robert Kennedy, not John Kennedy, as the first New Democrat," observed Jeff Shesol. "Robert Kennedy was pointing in a different direction." He had not rejected the New Deal but had started "to question the effectiveness of the federal government and of centralized solutions." In the 1980s "Al From and Clinton very cautiously turned back to Robert Kennedy." Shesol emphasized that Clinton knelt at Kennedy's grave before his 1993 inauguration and "quoted Robert Kennedy like crazy, and it wasn't just because I [an RFK biographer] was there—although I had something to do with that. We always quoted Robert Kennedy in the 'Third Way' speeches," Shesol said, because Kennedy, like Clinton, "acknowledged the culture of dependency that welfare created, which was apostasy for many Democrats." Kennedy wanted to use the power of local government and "was starting to break from Democratic liberal orthodoxy" at his death. Kennedy found 1960s-style liberalism suspect, said Shesol; his rhetoric "was actually feeding some suspicion on the Left." Though in 1968 he became "more radical" on Vietnam and used some of the same "terms of denunciation as the New Left," his domestic policies "were ultimately picked up by the Republican Party and by Clinton."[128]

Al From echoed Shesol without even being asked about Kennedy's influence on Clinton. In 1947, noted From, "liberalism decided that if it was going to have a future," it must be tough on communism, and this became Truman's and John Kennedy's foreign policy. "There was a tough liberalism," but "from the sixties into the seventies a softer liberalism took hold. Bobby Kennedy hated welfare. He was tough on crime." Clinton attempted to "put opportunity and responsibility back together." When told of Shesol's analysis linking Clinton with RFK, From said, "Kennedy was an inspiration, but it was the tough liberalism that was the key." He recalled that the 1980 Democratic platform did not emphasize the word "responsibility." (Indeed, the word appears only seven times, versus nineteen times in the 2004 platform.)[129] In 1980 "the central issue became whether the search for equality began to undermine for many people their own quest for equal opportunity," said From. "I worked on the War on Poverty, and initially the Great Society was about equal opportunity," but after the 1960s it attempted "to achieve equal outcomes." In the 1960s, he added, liberals shunned quotas, but by the 1970s they were using quotas to measure a program's success.[130]

One of Robert Kennedy's closest advisers expressed even greater disenchantment with 1960s liberalism. "Most of [the Great Society] was a disaster," said Adam Walinsky, as it increased "the power of bureaucracies and of the state." The Great Society "was just the incarnation of all of the worst elements of modern life. The extension of welfare was . . . just dreadful, utterly horrid, soul destroying." RFK's goal was to empower people and to curtail the power of the bureaucracy. "Kennedy spent more energy and effort on that than any other thing that he did domestically in those years."[131]

"The Era of Big Government Is Over": Defending the "Third Way"

Clinton's extensive use of Robert Kennedy was well suited to his own main theme as president, for the DLC was Clinton's primary method for ensuring that the 1960s could not be used against him. While Clinton never directly mentioned that decade when he spoke of the DLC, he became a New Democrat precisely to insulate himself from the charge that he was a liberal from "the sixties." Clinton saw the DLC as a shield that could deflect right-wing fire.

Clinton had to be a defensive president because of a thirty-year backlash against "the sixties" and so was willing to talk about the size of government in language that no Democrat had ever spoken. "Big government does not have all the answers," he said in his 1996 State of the Union address, and "there's not a program for every problem." Clinton took credit for creating "a smaller, less bureaucratic government in Washington." In the speech's most memorable line he proclaimed that "the era of big government is over. But we cannot go back to the time when our citizens were left to fend for themselves."[132] (He repeated an even firmer qualification two days later: "The era of strong, effective government in partnership with people is not over. We're not going back to a time when people [had to] fend for themselves.")[133]

The "Third Way" formed the centerpiece of Clinton's 1996 reelection campaign, whose basic strategy was to appropriate many traditionally Republican concerns. At the 1996 Democratic National Convention he spoke at length about "crime, welfare and the deficit." These were no longer "on the rise," the president said. "The welfare system you used to complain about is not here anymore."[134] Clinton would herald similar themes throughout his second term.[135] He believed that most people would come to agree with the New Democrats' positions once they discarded "the cardboard, cut-out, superficial, negative images" Republicans "have laid on us for twenty years relentlessly, cleverly, and often effectively."[136]

In his memoir Clinton wrote that he was "amazed by some of the criticisms of the DLC from the Democratic Left" and from the press, which he attributed to the fact that "we didn't fit neatly in their ossified Democratic box." Clinton said the DLC had obvious differences with Republicans on taxes, deficits, guns, education, abortion, the environment, and on issues of race and sexual orientation. Rather than being "lacking in conviction," Clinton saw his programs as having "helped to modernize" the Democratic Party.[137]

Many Democrats argued that progressives could and should be proud of Clinton. Al From characterized the 1990s as "an era of progressive reform," not of surrender to the Right. "Clintonism was about modernizing progressivism," he said: 22.5 million jobs were created, incomes rose, poverty was reduced at a record rate, 8 million Americans moved from welfare to work, and crime diminished. "Those were all progressive ends. . . . The thing I can't understand about the Left is what they wanted from Clinton that they didn't get." If Clinton's critics who longed for the Great Society really wanted what Johnson promised, they should have embraced Clinton. "Clinton's record is clearly the best record of progressive achievement—and yet the attack on Clintonism is that he moved the party to the Right." That was false, From said. Democrats traditionally were "not the party of 'welfare, not work.' We're the party of work. The diversion from traditional Democratic and progressive ideals was not in the nineties, it was in the seventies and eighties."[138]

Harold Ickes, told that Arthur Schlesinger had lamented that Clinton abandoned liberal policies because he wanted to be liked, countered: "I don't know what policies Arthur is talking about. . . . Clinton is a genuine and total progressive, and understands the importance of government and believes in government." But Clinton thought, crucially, that Democrats could not win the presidency by "using the same language and . . . policies as in the past." To Ickes, Clinton "was an extraordinarily progressive president," and "the lower economic brackets benefited fairly considerably" during his administration. One could argue that "no president pushed as much as [he] should. That same argument was made about Franklin Roosevelt" by some in his cabinet and party. "But as Lyndon Johnson once said, and I paraphrase, 'In order to be a statesman, you have to get elected.'"[139]

Clinton's "Third Way" was an attempt to heal divisions produced by the 1960s, but his advisers emphatically denied that it repudiated the 1960s. "We would sometimes overdo the extremes: positing so-called sixties liberalism, Great Society liberalism, on one side, and then Reaganism on the other side, and then presenting the Third Way," Jeff Shesol admitted. But late in his presidency Clinton "started to resist this caricature of the 1960s." When Clinton battled Gingrich in the mid-1990s, he "had to go a certain distance in disowning the liberal emphasis on government, so he had to say very definitively, 'The era of big government was over.' It was really important for him to say that—to identify with the antigovernment surge in the country at the time," said Shesol. "And he could say it because it was consistent with—even though it was more strongly put— what he had been saying in the 1980s about the need for the Democratic Party to move away from the sixties model of liberalism. He had to stress it and maybe overstress it in response to the political climate at the time. By 1998 he had won his battle with Gingrich," Shesol continued. "And some of the antigovernment fervor had subsided a little bit, and he was sick of knocking the sixties around. I don't think he wanted to feed this notion that the Great Society was a failure. He never said it, but I don't think that he wanted even to imply it anymore—and so he would take the edge off the sixties caricature."[140]

Bill Clinton was well aware of the Right's effective use of "the sixties" as a political bludgeon between 1980 and 1992, and because he was the first baby boomer president, their strategy would only intensify with his nomination and election to the presidency after the Democrats' twelve years of exile from the White House. But since the 1960s were sacred ground to the liberal base of his party—and because the era had provided his main political inspirations—Clinton could not avoid speaking of the decade either. He therefore sought to balance the extremes of the far Left and the far Right. His New Democrat DLC positions were meant to stake out this middle terrain. Clinton referred throughout his presidency to the liberal icons of the 1960s—John Kennedy, Robert Kennedy, and Martin Luther King—but he used them to appeal to both sides of the political spectrum. He emphasized the personal inspiration he had received from each of these men, but he also enlisted them in support of quite conservative principles: reducing crime, balancing the budget, and promoting personal accountability. Clinton's rhetoric consciously harked back to the "good sixties" and carefully avoided Lyndon Johnson's "bad sixties." He adopted the same strategy when speaking of the Vietnam War and in seeking to interpret the broader legacy of the 1960s.

8

Vietnam and "the Sixties" in the Clinton Presidency

Vietnam protesting, non-inhaling, abortion-protecting, gay-rights-espousing, sexually promiscuous, Elvis-loving baby boomer.
Unnamed Republican activist, describing Bill Clinton

SOON AFTER THE 1992 election Bill Clinton received a letter from Robert McNamara, JFK and LBJ's defense secretary. "For me—and I believe the nation as well—the Vietnam War finally ended the day you were elected president," he wrote. McNamara had decided to write on hearing of Clinton's friendship at Oxford with roommate Frank Aller, a draft resister who committed suicide in 1971. "By their votes, the American people, at long last, recognized that the Allers and the Clintons, when they questioned the wisdom and the morality of their government's decisions relating to Vietnam, were no less patriotic than those who served in uniform. The anguish with which you and your friends debated our actions in 1969 was painful for you then and, I am sure, the resurrection of the issues during the campaign reopened old wounds," wrote McNamara, adding that Clinton's "dignity" in dealing with his political opponents as well as his adherence to the notion that it was important to examine fully the reasons for going to war "has strengthened the nation for all time."[1]

But McNamara's prediction proved premature, as Clinton's election only intensified the national battle over the meaning of Vietnam and the 1960s, and in doing so overshadowed his presidency. Because of the way Reagan and Bush had recast the Vietnam War as a noble military campaign undermined by "bad sixties" civilian leaders—and as the first president in nearly fifty years never to have served in the military—Clinton found himself forced to defend the war in order to pursue his goal of reconciliation.[2] Although the Right succeeded in putting Clinton on the defensive concerning Vietnam, a war he had strongly and publicly opposed in the late 1960s, he adeptly converted the controversy into an opportunity to show toughness on foreign policy.

From the day Clinton took office, the Right demonized him as a 1960s radical. Despite that burden he framed the era as a political asset, arguing that the 1960s had brought both negative and positive consequences for the nation. In moving to the political center, he skillfully merged the Right's negative version of the 1960s with the Left's nostalgia for the era's lost idealism and optimism. Clinton thus incorporated into his national narrative both the "good sixties" and the "bad sixties." For different reasons from those motivating the Right, he acknowledged the bad and expressed dismay at the loss of the hope and promise of the Kennedy years. As the 2000 election approached, however, Clinton shifted gears and began to defend the 1960s. He wanted above all to avoid squandering the peace and prosperity he had helped to create during his presidency in a repetition of late 1960s discord.

Clinton and the Damage of Vietnam

Bill Clinton tried to repair, and at times to avoid renewing, the domestic damage inflicted by Vietnam and the social upheavals of the 1960s. During his 1992 election campaign he received ten military medals as gifts from decorated Vietnam veterans who had opposed the war. "I was thinking of those veterans and their medals" during the flight to Washington four days before his inauguration, he wrote in his memoir, "hoping at last we could heal the wounds of the 1960s."[3] Like McNamara, however, he was to be disappointed on this score. Looking back just days before the 2000 election, Clinton referred to Vietnam as a key reason why critics on the Right had attacked him throughout his presidency. "I was the first baby boomer president, not a perfect person[,] . . . never claimed to be—and had opposed the Vietnam War," he said. "That made them doubly angry, because they thought I was a cultural alien and I made it [to the presidency] anyway."[4]

Forced into a defensive posture by the prevailing revisionist view of Vietnam after twelve years of Republican rule, Clinton as president rarely condemned the rationale for fighting the war in Vietnam. Any such criticism tended to come from aides rather than from Clinton himself. The most forceful statement of his views on the war's legitimacy occurred in a 1995 press briefing by Mike McCurry. Asked "for the record" about Clinton's opinion of McNamara's recent book, *In Retrospect: The Tragedy and Lessons of Vietnam*, McCurry said that Clinton "believes what the former secretary wrote is true. He believes that the war was wrong. And there were reasons to believe it was wrong even as early as the 1960s."[5]

Although in the 1960s he had been a harsh critic of the war, as president Clinton often defended America's Vietnam policy. When he was in Ho Chi Minh City in 2000, the Vietnamese Communist Party's general secretary implied that the United States had invaded Vietnam, and expressed pleasure that Clinton and many other Americans had protested against the war. "I stoutly disputed that we were an imperialist country," Clinton recalled.[6] "Mr. Chairman," Clinton told him, "we were not France. We were not colonialists."[7] Clinton often spoke about Vietnam in much the same way that Reagan and Bush had. In contrast to them, however, Clinton never once uttered the phrases "legacy of Vietnam" or "Vietnam syndrome." He presented the same idea but used different language.

The memory of Vietnam made him acutely sensitive to how he conducted foreign affairs, especially in eastern Europe and Latin America. From the start of Clinton's presidency many observers drew parallels between Vietnam and Bosnia. In a May 1993 radio interview one questioner noted that the current cover of *Time* displayed pictures of Clinton and a despondent Lyndon Johnson (the cover read "Anguish Over Bosnia: Will it be Clinton's Vietnam?"). Asked if Bosnia was potentially his Vietnam, Clinton acknowledged, "There are similarities to Vietnam," particularly "in the sense that there is a civil war and there is a national dividing line," which he explained in detail. "It's a very complicated thing," he said, as the conflict had been simmering "for a long time." But Clinton argued for two crucial differences: in Vietnam there had been no "ethnic cleansing" as in Bosnia, and "unlike [in] Vietnam," the United States was "not about to act alone. Our policy is not to do what we did in Vietnam, which was to get in and fight with one side in a civil war to assure a military victory."[8]

In that 1993 interview Clinton also referred indirectly to the Vietnam syndrome when he said that the war in Southeast Asia had made the country cautious about military intervention even when it was justified. Asked if ground troops might be sent to Bosnia, the president said again that the United States would not act "unilaterally" and fight for one side as in Vietnam. Clinton called Bosnia "the toughest foreign policy problem our country has faced in a long time. And I'm trying . . . to make sure there isn't a Vietnam problem here." But the United States would keep attempting "to save lives and to confine the conflict. . . . Just because we don't want to make the mistake we did in Vietnam doesn't mean we shouldn't be doing anything."[9]

Clinton often touched on the restrictions that the memory of Vietnam imposed on U.S. policy. One of the lessons of Vietnam, he told an interviewer, "is that even when we are extremely well motivated, heroic, and willing to die in large numbers, we cannot win a fight for someone else. . . . There are limits to what we can do." He observed, "The enormous reaction after that war happened, and after the South Vietnamese forces collapsed ten days after our final withdrawal, almost caused our country to go into a shell for a while" The lesson he drew was that "first, we overreached, and then we didn't do perhaps what we should have done to sort of stick a stake in the ground. And what I'm determined to do is learn as much as I can from history but not be imprisoned by it, and certainly not be bogged down by it."[10]

Again without naming it in so many words, Clinton invoked the Vietnam syndrome to explain his delay in sending U.S. forces into Bosnia. "We all make our mistakes and we all have our memories, but I think when a great country, because of an inaccurate reading of the facts of a situation, or being in the grip of a historical nightmare, makes an error, the consequences can be quite severe," he said in 1998, lamenting the amount of time it took the United States and its allies to intervene in Bosnia. Those outside the country who questioned the delay "didn't live through the experience that our military and our people did in Vietnam." While the conflicts differed, and while foreigners could say, "'America, why don't you understand this is not Vietnam?'" the people of America needed time to come to terms with "what we had to do, what our clear moral responsibility was, what was in our national interest. We did the right thing." Before the United States intervened, many had feared "[that] 'this is Vietnam all over again.'" While he himself was eager to act, he knew it was hard "to change the mindset [and] the psychology of a nation, when it has deeply embedded historical experiences" that influence all future decisions national leaders make.[11] In his frequent insistences that his foreign policy would not produce "another Vietnam," Clinton often echoed the rhetoric of the Right.

The memory of Vietnam reentered U.S. politics in the 1990s not only because of current crises but also because of Clinton's antiwar activities and his having avoided military service during the peak of the Vietnam conflict. Throughout his presidency the press and others kept a constant focus on Clinton's failure to serve in Vietnam. He had to field repeated questions about how his antiwar past affected his decisions as president. When Clinton lifted the embargo on trade with Vietnam in 1994, a reporter asked if his lack of service in Vietnam had affected his decision.[12] At a military hospital where he posthumously gave the Medal of Honor to a soldier killed in Somalia, the soldier's father "was furious at me and angrily told me that I wasn't fit to be commander-in-chief"—perhaps, Clinton mused, "because I had not served in Vietnam."[13]

Network interviews during the fiftieth anniversary of the D-Day invasion of Europe harped on the fact that Clinton had not served in Vietnam.
CBS's Harry Smith asked if the occasion "made you think or reconsider at
all your own lack of service during the Vietnam War."[14] Some of the questioning was quite personal, if not hostile. ABC newsman Sam Donaldson
asked Clinton what he would want to tell those at the upcoming ceremony "who resent the fact that you didn't serve, and particularly because
they believe you made a deliberate effort to avoid service."[15] NBC's Tom
Brokaw, noting "all the respect" Clinton had recently received, asked if
he regretted his "decision to avoid military service" and if he understood
why "many of the veterans who are here" resented him because he avoided serving in Vietnam and was now president.[16]

No pretext for raising this question was too contrived. In 1995 a reporter asked, with regard to his decision to allow for possible NATO air
strikes in Bosnia, "How much more difficult is it for you personally and
politically, given your failure to serve in Vietnam?"[17] In 1999, at a U.S.
airbase in Germany, Brokaw said to him, "Like so many people in your
generation, you came of age when there was an unpopular war, and you
had mixed feelings at best about the role of the military in our lives."[18] In
late 2000 Clinton visited Vietnam, the first U.S. president to do so since
1969, provoking numerous questions about his actions in the late 1960s.
"In 1969 . . . you wrote a letter saying you hated and despised the war and
had worked and demonstrated against it," one reporter said to Clinton.
"Now that you've been [president], do you still feel that way about Vietnam?"[19]

Clinton tried not to reignite controversy over the Vietnam War. When
a reporter asked about Mike McCurry's comments (quoted earlier) that
McNamara's book "vindicates your own opposition to the war," Clinton
affirmed, "I believed our policy was incorrect [and] the book supports that
conclusion," adding, "But I do not believe that the book should be used as
yet another opportunity to divide the United States over that."[20]

Healing the War Wounds

As with other issues from "the sixties," the memory of Vietnam put Clinton on the defensive. With reporters pointing to his lack of service in
Vietnam, he worked to neutralize issues the Right had used to damage
Democrats since the 1960s. Just as his "Third Way" was an attempt to
heal confrontational economic issues of the past, his Vietnam rhetoric
sought to transcend the polarization of the 1960s and leave the turmoil of
Vietnam behind.

Clinton often recalled how he had witnessed in person the divisions caused by Vietnam. At the 1995 memorial service for his mentor, Democratic senator William J. Fulbright of Arkansas, Clinton spoke of having worked for the senator during "the great struggles over the Vietnam war" in 1968, when America "was being torn apart."[21] Clinton spoke openly of trying to mend these wounds. In 1996, just after the opening ceremony of the Atlanta Olympics, he mentioned how moved he had been when "they let Muhammad Ali, purging the ghost of the Vietnam War," light the Olympic flame.[22]

Clinton gave one of his most controversial speeches at the Vietnam Veterans Memorial on Memorial Day 1993. Earlier that morning, Clinton jogged from the White House to the wall to read the names of people he knew from Hot Springs who had died in Vietnam. "I knew it would be a tough event," he wrote in his memoir, "full of people for whom the Vietnam War continued to be the defining moment in their lives and to whom the thought of someone like me as commander-in-chief was abhorrent. But I was determined to go, to face those who still held my views on Vietnam against me, and to tell all Vietnam veterans that I honored their service and that of their fallen comrades."[23]

As Clinton walked to the podium, Thomas Friedman reported, "he was greeted with a cacophony of enthusiastic applause, peppered by catcalls of 'Draft dodger!' 'Liar!' and 'Shut up, coward!'" Many veterans turned their backs when Clinton began to speak, while others tried to quiet his accusers.[24] "To all of you who are shouting," Clinton said to the protesters behind a fence, "I have heard you. I ask you now to hear me. . . . Some have suggested that it is wrong for me to be here with you today," because he had not supported the Vietnam War. "Well, so much the better. . . . Just as war is freedom's cost, disagreement is freedom's privilege. And we honor it here today. . . . Can any American be out of place?" Clinton asked, to which many "shouted back with pointed fingers: 'You! You! You!'"[25]

"These men and women fought for freedom," Clinton continued, "brought honor to their communities, loved their country, and died for it. . . . There's not a person in this crowd today who did not know someone on this wall," said the president. "Four of my high school classmates are there. . . . Let us continue to disagree, if we must, about the war. But let us not let it divide us as a people any longer."[26]

But the war's continued divisiveness was on display at the event. Some Vietnam veterans had organized a mail campaign to protest the speech and camped out before Clinton's visit with signs that read "For Shame," "Disabled and Dead Accuse You," "The Truth Convicts You," "Kinda Late Isn't It?" and "Slick Willie the Artful Draft Dodger." At the memorial several participants expressed their displeasure. "I don't want him here," said one. "A lot of the names you see on that wall were not fortunate enough . . . to do what he did." Another charged: "It is an absolute disgrace that this gutless wonder showed up here. He should be crowned King of Chutzpah." One protester argued, "He should walk along that wall and look for the name of the person who took his place. It's up there somewhere."[27]

But others expressed sympathy. "In 1968, times were in real turmoil," said one Vietnam veteran. "Whatever Clinton did he had a conscientious reason for it. I can't judge him." Others echoed Clinton's desire to move forward. "More power to him," said one supporter. "As the commander-in-chief he should be here. I'd like to think we are standing in front of something that put that war behind us."[28]

As president, Clinton attempted to heal the national divisions over Vietnam in a variety of ways. He often praised Vietnam veterans and enlisted their help to push his anticrime and antigun measures. In 1996 Clinton quoted a supporter, Mike Robbins, who had told him, "I served my country in Vietnam, in Desert Storm and by the grace of God I was never harmed," but as a police officer he had been gravely wounded by an assault weapon. Clinton had inspired him to speak out in favor of controlling guns. "Mike Robbins is the kind of person I'm fighting for," Clinton said, emphasizing Robbins's Vietnam experiences as he urged more stringent handgun control.[29]

When Clinton lifted the Vietnam trade embargo in 1994, he hoped that it would help resolve the issue of troops still listed as missing in action. "Whatever the Vietnam War may have done in dividing our country in the past," he said, "today our nation is [as] one in honoring those who served and pressing for answers about all those who did not return."[30] In Ho Chi Minh City in 2000 he declared that the MIA issue symbolized "what was possible in terms of the reconciliation of people who have been so bitterly divided."[31] Upon his return from Vietnam he expressed hope that attempts to resolve the MIA dispute could "bring us together."[32]

Clinton also tried to heal Vietnam's divisions by discussing the harm caused to veterans by the pesticide Agent Orange.[33] He often discussed this and other health effects of the war.[34] The president spoke of his Agent Orange legislation throughout the two months before the 1996 election. Touting his many work- and health-related initiatives, Clinton told supporters that he had met a disabled veteran "who served our country with honor in Vietnam, [and] who was exposed to Agent Orange," which caused birth defects in his child. "We're finally going to give some help to those people."[35]

In his attempts to heal the divisions remaining after the Vietnam War, Clinton went so far as to argue that it was just as noble as any other twentieth-century war. In his first mention of the conflict as president he defined it as an essential part of the Cold War and crucial in defeating the Soviet Union. "Recall the arenas where we played out [Cold War] conflicts," Clinton said. "Berlin. Korea. The Congo. Cuba. Vietnam. Nicaragua. Angola. Afghanistan. We competed everywhere . . . to hold freedom's line. Those efforts were worthy."[36] In contrast to his statements about the war as a young man in the 1960s, President Clinton defined Vietnam as a necessary war, on one occasion calling those about to graduate from West Point, like those buried at Arlington and those who died fighting in Vietnam, "heroes who have protected our borders, defended our interests and preserved our values."[37]

In this way Vietnam did not differ from other wars, he now argued. In an address on the military he said, "From the Revolutionary War to the Civil War, from the world wars to Korea, Vietnam, Desert Storm and the other conflicts in our history, all remind us that all of our people have given a lot in the military to protect the land we love."[38] In Korea and Vietnam "our Army shielded the free world from the forces of communism and ensured the triumph of democracy," read a 2000 proclamation commemorating the U.S. Army.[39] In this and other speeches in the final year of his presidency Clinton showed ever stronger support for the war in Vietnam in the hope of demonstrating once again Democrats' sensitivity to—and their desire to refute—the Right's charge that they did not support the military.

Clinton devoted much of his last year in office to restoring diplomatic relations with Vietnam. He had always stressed reconciliation—between the political Right and the Left, and between pro– and anti–Vietnam War factions. Now he tried to promote reconciliation between the two nations. His efforts accelerated in 2000, when he made an official visit to Vietnam. In July 2000, announcing a U.S.–Vietnamese trade agreement, Clinton noted, "From the bitter past, we plant the seeds of a better future." This pact would show the need "to let go of the past and embrace the future, to forgive and to reconcile."[40]

Later that year Clinton, the first U.S. president to visit Hanoi, spoke at Vietnam National University. In his remarks he acknowledged the suffering of the Vietnamese in the war, recalled the two-hundred-year relationship between the two countries, and commented on "the staggering sacrifice of the Vietnamese people on both sides of that conflict." Calling for greater cooperation between the two countries he said, "Let us continue to help each other heal the wounds of war, not by forgetting the bravery shown and the tragedy suffered by all sides, but by embracing the spirit of reconciliation and the courage to build better tomorrows."[41]

Attuned to the Right's success since 1980 in "blaming the 1960s," Clinton thus made a special effort to confront the issue of Vietnam directly. Whether speaking at the Vietnam Veterans Memorial, praising Vietnam veterans, working to resolve the POW/MIA issue and the problems associated with Agent Orange, or arguing for the need to move beyond the past, Clinton was acutely aware that he symbolized an era that many Americans continued to blame for the country's troubles.

Confronting "the Sixties"

In his younger days Clinton had very briefly looked the part of the "sixties" radical. In the summer of 1969, he recalled, "I'd grown long hair and a beard," and he and his friends "looked like refugees from the Woodstock festival."[42] Clinton knew how opponents would use this image against him. In 1969 Arkansas newspapers ran a photo of an antiwar protester in a tree outside the stadium at a college football game that Clinton had watched at a friend's house in London. "Shortly before my first congressional election [in 1974], my opponent's campaign workers called newspapers all over the congressional district asking if they had kept a copy of 'that picture of Bill Clinton up in the tree demonstrating.' . . . The rumor spread like wildfire and cost me a lot of votes," he recalled. Four years later a policeman "swore to several people that he was the very one who pulled me out of the tree." In 1979, ten years after the incident, a high school student asked him if he was that person in the tree. When Clinton, who was speaking at the school, asked the audience who had heard the story, "half of the students and three-quarters of the teachers raised their hands." The story continued to sprout apocryphal details: as late as 1983 a sixteen-year-old asked him, "Did you really get up in that tree without any clothes on and demonstrate against President Nixon and the war?"[43]

The perception of Clinton as a symbol of the excesses of the 1960s endured well into his presidency. The cover of an issue of *American Enterprise* in 1997, under the headline "The '60s Return," displayed a caricature of a stoned Clinton with long hair, a beard, a peace sign around his neck, and pins on his sweater reading, "HELL NO WE WON'T GO," and "FREE HUEY NEWTON." In his right hand Clinton holds a marijuana joint in a roach clip. The issue contained articles that, in the editors' words, "survey the lingering damage of the 1960s, with an eye toward reversing it." David Horowitz's contribution analyzed his former life as a 1960s radical; Glenn Loury spoke of "The Other '60s," when "not everyone became a hippie and manned the barricades"; Congressman Dana Rohrabacher of California described the rise of the Right in the 1960s; James Webb (subsequently a Democratic senator from Virginia) argued that Vietnam War protesters had wanted the North Vietnamese to win; and a variety of other articles maintained that 1960s radicals had taken over unions, public schools, and college campuses and were responsible for the recent resurgence in drug use. William Bennett closed the section with an attack on the music of the late 1960s.[44]

Congressman Newt Gingrich of Georgia did more than anyone else to link Clinton with the excesses of the 1960s. In October 1994 he referred to Clinton as "the enemy of normal Americans."[45] The day after the off-year election Gingrich denounced both Bill and Hillary Clinton as "counterculture McGovernicks" and the White House staff as a circle of "left-wing elitists."[46]

Gingrich had expressed hostility to 1960s liberalism throughout his career. In 1976 he asserted, "In my lifetime, without question, the president who lied the most and did the most damage to the United States was Lyndon Johnson." Gingrich assailed Johnson's Vietnam and economic policies and claimed that "it was Johnson's politics of irresponsible promises which led to riots on the campuses and in the cities." In 1982 he charged that "the people who built the Great Society . . . do not want to help the poor."[47]

"Until the mid-1960s," Gingrich argued, America had "an explicit, long-term commitment to creating character. It was the work ethic, it was honesty, right and wrong, it was not harming others, it was being vigilant in the defense of liberty."[48] Up through 1965, he believed, "there is a core pattern to American history. Here's how we did it until the Great Society messed everything up: don't work, don't eat; your salvation is spiritual; the government by definition can't save you." But then came the deluge. "From 1965 to 1994, we did strange and weird things as a country. Now we're done with that and we have to recover. The counterculture is a momentary aberration in American history that will be looked back upon as a quaint period of Bohemianism brought to the national elite"—by the notorious "counterculture McGoverniks"—who "taught self-indulgent, aristocratic values without realizing that if an entire society engaged in the indulgences of an elite few, you could tear the society to shreds."[49]

"Gingrich and the Republican Right had brought us back to the 1960s again," Clinton wrote in his memoir, discussing these attacks at length. "Of course, there were political and personal excesses in the 1960s, but the decade and the movements it spawned also produced advances in civil rights, women's rights, a clean environment, workplace safety, and opportunities for the poor." Clinton argued that "the right wing used the excesses of the sixties to obscure the good done in civil rights and in other areas." To Gingrich, "all sins, even those committed by conservatives, were caused by the moral relativism the Democrats had imposed on America since 1968."[50]

Gingrich's attacks provoked discussion about the decade's legacy. In response to the criticisms of the 1960s by the leader of the new Republican majority in Congress, the *New York Times* published a rare full-page opinion piece in December 1994, "In Praise of the Counterculture." Baby boomers had "profoundly altered the way Americans think about their inner lives, their fellow citizens," the environment, and when to wage war, the editors wrote. The paper expressed support for "the cultural ideals of the sixties and the decade's healthy spirit of political activism." While the era's excesses and hedonism were problematic, it was absurd "to repudiate so large a cultural event in a nation's history, or to dismiss its seminal political events as a 'McGovern-nik' aberration." Referring to the decade's many social movements, the editors argued that the counterculture had renewed the American tradition of dissent and taught the nation the need to keep a watchful eye on government. The counterculture was "a repudiation of the blind obedience and reflexive cynicism of politics as usual. It was about exposing hypocrisy, whether personal or political, and standing up to irrational authority."[51]

The amount of space the paper devoted to defending the 1960s was a measure of how much inspiration liberals received from the era as well as the extent to which conservatives' attacks on "the sixties" had put liberals on the defensive. The vigor with which many have felt the need to justify the 1960s, whether in that 1994 editorial, in Clinton's 2004 memoir, or elsewhere, testifies to the continued power of the era to define the fault lines of American politics. In many ways the Clinton years were one long national debate over the legacy of the 1960s.

The Right's attacks on Clinton as a symbol of the excesses of the decade increased after the 1994 election. R. Emmett Tyrrell Jr., in his 1996 biography of Clinton, characterized the president as a 1960s counterculture radical. Referring to Clinton's 1969 letter explaining his actions regarding the draft, Tyrrell wrote, "Clinton is a child of the late 1960s, and this particular lie is characteristic of his cohorts in protest." His letter "displayed all the 1960s student protesters' weakness for pontification, self-righteousness, and narcissism." Once he gained office, "1968's enthusiasms were dusted off and dressed up as policy." Even Clinton's health care plan "was a throwback to the self-indulgent late 1960s." Tyrrell argued that the 1960s generation "produced fewer distinguished writers and artists than almost any preceding American generation" and taken together "have done much to erase the moral order of our civilization." Both Clintons, in short, were "1960s megalomaniacs."[52]

Much of the Right's political strategy in the 1996 election consisted of similar attacks on the 1960s. At the Republican convention that summer nominee Senator Bob Dole, a World War II veteran, invoked the golden age that had preceded the 1960s: "Let me be the bridge to an America that only the unknowing call myth . . . a time of tranquility, faith and confidence in action. And to those who say it was never so, that America's not been better, I say you're wrong. And I know because I was there. And I have seen it. And I remember."[53]

Dole asserted that the nation had been in decline since the 1960s. "After decades of assault upon what made America great, upon supposedly obsolete values, what have we reaped? What have we created?" he asked. "Crime and drugs, illegitimacy, abortion, the abdication of duty, and the abandonment of children." Though government had expanded, "children are now more neglected, more abused and more mistreated than they have been in our time. This is not a coincidence." Dole declared that "permissive and destructive behavior must be opposed" and that "honor and liberty must be restored." In his most direct attack on Clinton and the baby boom generation Dole said, "It is demeaning to the nation that within the Clinton administration a corps of the elite who never grew up, never did anything real, never sacrificed, never suffered and never learned, should have the power to fund with your earnings their dubious and self-serving schemes."[54]

"Since the sixties our national life has been a running argument about, and with, the sixties," wrote George Will around the time of Clinton's reelection that year.[55] The attacks on Clinton by Gingrich, Tyrrell, and Dole illustrate how Republicans continued to blame the 1960s throughout Clinton's presidency in the belief that such criticisms would lead to electoral revenge. At the same time, Clinton, too, sought to use the 1960s to his own political advantage.

His enemies were correct up to a point in seeing him as a product of the 1960s. In 1991, after he formally announced he was running for president, Clinton and some of his oldest friends "gathered around the piano," he recalled. "We sang 'Amazing Grace' and other hymns, and a lot of songs from the sixties, including 'Abraham, Martin, and John,' a tribute to the fallen heroes of our generation. I went to bed believing we could cut through the cynicism and despair and rekindle the fire those men had lit in my heart."[56] David Maraniss ended his 1992 Clinton biography with a description of this scene. "Amazing Grace" was Clinton's "favorite hymn," Maraniss wrote, and during "Abraham, Martin, and John," Clinton "sang every verse. He knew all the words."[57]

In the late 1960s Clinton had felt a bleak sadness at what he saw occurring in the country. Upon winning his Rhodes scholarship in the spring of 1968, he felt that, at least momentarily, "there was no Vietnam, no racial turmoil, no trouble at home, no anxieties about myself or my future." Recalling that tumultuous year Clinton wrote: "Though I was sympathetic to the zeitgeist, I didn't embrace the lifestyle or the radical rhetoric. My hair was short, I didn't even drink, and some of the music was too loud and harsh for my taste. I didn't hate LBJ; I just wanted to end the war, and I was afraid the culture clashes would undermine, not advance, the cause."[58]

Others endorsed this view. Although Clinton later "had long hair at Oxford," he "was never, ever, a hippie," said former White House correspondent Todd Purdum. He of course went to college in the late 1960s, but he was "the classic good boy[,] . . . never antiestablishment, or even close to it. He might have affected hippie dress, but he always wanted to 'preserve his viability.' There was nothing at any time radical about him."[59]

Clinton was dismayed by the events of 1968. "I felt so isolated. I didn't identify with the kids raising hell or with Chicago's mayor and his rough tactics [during the Democratic National Convention], or with the people who were supporting him, which included most of the folks I had grown up among. And I was heartsick that my party and its progressive causes were disintegrating before my very eyes."[60] Clinton thus clearly belonged to the political center as far back as 1968.

For him the 1960s symbolized both the peak and the decline of Democratic power: 1968 "shattered the Democratic party." The backlash against the 1960s "would shape and distort American politics" for a generation. "The deeply embedded nightmares of 1968 formed the arena in which I and all other progressive politicians had to struggle over our entire careers. . . . [T]hose of us who believed that the good in the 1960s outweighed the bad would fight on, still fired by the heroes and dreams of our youth," wrote Clinton.[61] Since 1968, he observed in his 2004 memoir, the Right had been successful in "convincing middle America that progressive candidates, ideas, and policies are alien to their values and threatening to their security."[62]

Asked if Clinton believed that the 1960s had helped or hurt America, former Clinton press secretary Mike McCurry replied, "He is positive about the way that young people came to feel empowered to make a difference and make their voices heard" by lowering the voting age to

eighteen, helping stop the war in Vietnam, helping produce the great social movements that led to civil rights, women's rights, environmental
protections, and so on. "But he knows that some of the cultural elitism
of 1960s liberalism sent the Democratic Party in a direction that made it
lose majority support in the 1980s."[63] Erasing this caricature of the Left
drawn primarily from imagery of the 1960s became one of Clinton's central preoccupations. The challenge was how to do it.

On the one hand, Clinton frequently defended the 1960s. "I want to
thank Peter, Paul and Mary," he said in 1996, speaking of the famed 1960s
folk music trio at a fund-raising event. "They remind us that all those
terrible things that our adversaries say about the sixties are not entirely
true."[64] Yet on the other hand, while often praising the 1960s, he never
tried to present those years as universally positive. He often spoke of the
period's shortcomings and implied that there was some legitimacy to the
claims of its critics. In a 1995 speech he remarked, "Contrary to what a
lot of people say now in retrospect, the sixties were not all bad. A lot of
good things happened. A lot of people passionately believed that they had
a responsibility to help one another." Clinton enumerated "the important
advances in civil rights, and in education, and in fighting poverty." But, he
said, it was also "a time when . . . more and more people dropped out and
became more self-indulgent."[65] Interestingly, as president he never used
the words "counterculture," "hippies," or "antiwar protesters." Clinton
discussed the meaning of the 1960s for the first time as president at a
1993 Yale alumni gathering. The three years (1970 to 1973) he spent at
Yale Law School were a more troubled period for the university than the
1960s. "The most lasting image of the 1960s at Yale actually took place
two years after the graduation of the Class of 1968," wrote Carter Wiseman, a member of that class, in the *Yale Alumni Magazine.* In 1970 "the
National Guard was called out in anticipation of what was feared would
be rioting provoked by the trial in New Haven of Bobby Seale and eight
other black radicals accused of murder."[66]

In a speech at the Law School reunion Clinton offered his own decidedly mixed views of the era. He noted the gains of the 1960s but also the
decade's traumas. The speech is particularly revealing of Clinton's view
of the late 1960s because, unknown to the audience, he spoke without
a prepared text. "We gave him something," said David Kusnet, but "he
didn't like it at all. He said whoever wrote it—which might have been
me—had no idea about the seventies. And he ended up completely ex-
temporizing."[67]

Clinton described the early 1970s as the point "when the culture of
heavy rock music and drugs began to blur the sensibilities of a lot of

Americans." Janis Joplin's fatal drug overdose, coming just as he and his classmates commenced their studies together at Yale, was "symbolic of the tragedy that was those years." While acknowledging the period's great promise and the advances made for women and minorities, Clinton also recalled the limitations of 1960s liberalism, especially with regard to government programs.[68]

This was only one of several occasions when Clinton acknowledged the damage caused by the 1960s. After the Republicans succeeded in portraying him as a symbol of 1960s excesses, contributing to their takeover of Congress in 1994, Clinton tacked to the right in the run-up to the 1996 election. And part of this effort involved intensified criticism of the 1960s.

Radical elements from "the sixties" were a frequent target. "In the 1960s . . . many good things happened," Clinton said two weeks after the 1995 Oklahoma City bombing. "But the Weathermen of the radical Left who resorted to violence in the 1960s were wrong."[69] Two weeks later, in a call for gun control, Clinton demanded funding for more police officers and argued against repealing the Brady Bill and the assault weapons ban. "The people who tried to make police officers the enemy when we were having a lot of controversy in this country back in the 1960s were wrong," he said. Referring to the gun lobby, he added, "and the people who are trying to do it today are wrong."[70] A few weeks later, asked about recent inflammatory rhetoric from the Right against government agencies, Clinton similarly responded: "There were some people in the sixties and seventies who went beyond their First Amendment rights and advocated violence. And they were wrong then, and this crowd is wrong now."[71]

He criticized the 1960s in other ways as well. Like Reagan and Bush before him, in 1995 Clinton noted that "the violent crime rate tripled from the 1960s to the 1990s," but said that he had reduced it by adding police, building more prisons, and lengthening sentences.[72] Also like Reagan and Bush, Clinton blamed the 1960s for the continuing drug problem. "I have a real perspective . . . about the whole drug and crime and violence problem," Clinton told high school students in 1996. "I grew up in the sixties when most people when I was your age just got into this business. They didn't really believe drugs were dangerous until it nearly destroyed our generation. When we were younger, the United States military was nearly destroyed by it. I had a brother who nearly lost his life because of a drug problem."[73] Clinton's drug czar, General Barry McCaffrey, also blamed the 1960s for drug abuse, vowing in 1996 to "return America to a 1960's level, a pre–Vietnam era level of drug use."[74]

Like the Republicans, Clinton distinguished between the early and late 1960s regarding crime, family cohesiveness, and a sense of community, even sounding nostalgic for an earlier America. "When I was growing up, Americans could pretty much walk the streets of any city without fear of being hurt by violent crime," he said in 1996. Illegitimacy was not the problem it now is, he said, and welfare was not viewed as a permanent solution. "It was far from a perfect time, the forties and fifties and early sixties," but "people knew it when you were born, cared about you while you lived, and missed you when you died." Since then, he said, "we've seen a stunning and simultaneous breakdown of community, family and work—the heart and soul of a civilized society."[75]

Operating in a political climate in which the 1960s had been under assault for a dozen years, Clinton went out of his way repeatedly to appeal to both the Right and the Left when he spoke of the decade, co-opting many of the Right's concerns about how the 1960s had led to increases in crime and drug abuse. But he also regretted the "bad sixties" for reasons the Right could never fully appreciate: the late 1960s had cut short the promise of the early 1960s and delayed for almost a generation any impetus for progressive reform. For this reason Clinton marked the end of his presidency with a vigorous defense of the "good sixties."

Defending "the Sixties": "Don't Waste This"

Clinton's most frequent references to the 1960s occurred between July 1999 and August 2000, when he gave a similar speech wherever he went almost weekly. He maintained that the United States in the 1990s had achieved the best economic and social conditions since the early 1960s, and Americans must not waste the moment. In the words he chose Clinton displayed his evolving interpretation of the 1960s. His language and emphasis varied somewhat over time, reflecting the breadth of his feelings on issues from the era, including the Kennedys, Johnson, King, Vietnam, and the civil disturbances of those years.

According to Jeff Shesol, in the year leading up to the 2000 election Clinton attended "fund-raising dinners almost every night, because he was 'fund-raiser-in-chief.'[76] He didn't go with a text; he would just stand up and talk." Each of Clinton's addresses included a section reflecting on the 1960s. "The riff about the 1960s . . . was all Clinton," Shesol said, referring to the president's characterization of the late 1990s as a second chance for progressive reform. "He came up with that analogy himself." At the fund-raisers Clinton spoke of the "sense of possibility that there was in the 1960s, and how we had all this wealth and energy and confidence that came out of winning the Second World War and the sense of purpose and unity, and then the Kennedys and King were killed," the

Vietnam War escalated, "and the opportunities that had been there during those years of expansion collapsed," Shesol said. "And this hush would come over the audience. Clinton would say, essentially, 'We cannot let that happen again. . . . These moments in history don't come along very often.'"[77]

Clinton had spoken before of the early 1960s as a golden era. "I remember when I was a boy in the fifties and sixties," he said on one occasion in 1995. With low unemployment and inflation and strong economic growth, "we all just assumed that the American Dream would work out all right. . . . We could just almost put this country on automatic." Clinton spoke longingly of the era's sense of promise; but "then in the sixties and the seventies and the eighties, the results got a lot more mixed."[78]

He often compared the strength of the current economy to the prosperity of the early 1960s.[79] But it was in July 1999 that Clinton first articulated the notion that America was in its best shape since those golden years and that the opportunity must not be squandered. "This is the first time since the early 1960s when we had this kind of strong American economy," he told his audience, "and we have no excuse for walking away from our responsibilities."[80] One month later he expanded this analysis to distinguish between the early and late 1960s. Speaking of his plan to improve the economy he said: "We've got the best chance in my lifetime to get this done—the best chance since the early sixties. We lost control of the economy in the late sixties. . . . And we've never had a chance since then to do this."[81]

October of that year began a ten-month period when Clinton used variations of this analogy at least once a week. "Never in my life . . . has our country been in the position that we are now in," he said, referring to the chance to shape the nation's future. "The only time in my life when the times were remotely this good was in the early 1960s, and we had to deal with the civil rights challenge and the war in Vietnam and the Cold War."[82] Three days later he noted that the United States had the lowest unemployment, welfare rolls, and crime rate in nearly three decades, the "first back-to-back [budget] surpluses in forty-two years," and "the lowest poverty rate in twenty years." This was a singular opportunity, one that must not be wasted. "In the 1960s we had an economy that, for a few years, was maybe about like this. [Then] we became divided and we never got around to doing it."[83] Two days later Clinton added, "Now we have no excuse," and warned of the dangers that can occur "when you think everything is peachy-keen. Because it's easy to just relax."[84]

Clinton continued to depict the current landscape as an opportunity for America to redeem the lost opportunities of that earlier decade. In

February 2000 he observed: "Unlike [in] the 1960s, we are not as torn by internal crisis or external threat. All of us who lived through that ought to be humble enough to know that we have a chance—and for us, a second chance—to do something that comes along maybe once in a lifetime."[85] Six days later he used more personal terms, contrasting the "good sixties" with the "bad sixties" when he reflected that "in 1964 . . . America was still profoundly sad about the loss of President Kennedy, but very optimistic and very united behind President Johnson"; but this unity soon fell apart, and with it came the polarization of American politics. "You remember the election of 1968? Vote with the 'silent majority.' And it was 'us' and 'them,'" Clinton said. "If you weren't in the 'silent majority,' presumably you were in the loud minority. I know. I was one of them. And in just a few months we lost the longest economic expansion in history."[86]

Clinton soon began to include Lyndon Johnson's first year as president in the "good sixties," saying: "We united behind President Johnson. He got off to a great start. He was leading us toward passing civil rights legislation, legislation to help the poor." In 1964 the country was convinced that the current good social and economic conditions would prevail and that racial problems would be solved. But then came the 1966 race riots and the divisions over Vietnam, and by 1968, because of the events of that spring, "the country was totally divided." He stressed that he had tried to heal the divisions that still lingered so long after the 1968 election. "Those of you who are older, like me, you remember what it was like in the mid-'60s," he said, adding a remark he would repeat weekly for six months: "I have waited for thirty-five years for my country to be in a position to build the future of our dreams for our children. That's what this [election] is about."[87]

Three days later, Clinton took a more sharply partisan tone, blaming the Right for the divisions of the late 1960s. Nixon's 1968 victory "was the first election between 'us' and 'them,' a tactic that people have perfected since then"—and one that he said was also Governor George W. Bush's current strategy. But in Al Gore's candidacy the nation now had "a second chance."[88]

Clinton consistently pointed to the mid-1960s as the start of a period of national decline and argued that the nation now had the opportunity—as it had in the early 1960s—to address long-neglected problems. In this respect Clinton, like those on the Right, distinguished between a "good" and a "bad" 1960s. But while conservatives presented the late 1960s as the negative culmination of a failed liberal experiment, Clinton framed the years as a lost opportunity that had ushered in an era of intense political polarization.

The "good sixties" played a central role at the Democratic National Convention in Los Angeles in 2000. Clinton opened his speech by referring once again to President Kennedy and the early 1960s, noting, "Forty years ago, Los Angeles launched John Kennedy and the New Frontier," and it would now "launch"—perhaps a reference to Kennedy's space program—the new century's next president, Al Gore. He returned to the 1960s in his peroration. In his praise for vice presidential nominee Joseph Lieberman, Clinton said that he had known him for three decades, and "I supported him in his first race for public office in 1970, when I learned he'd been a Freedom Rider, going into danger, to register black voters in the then-segregated South." (Clinton's statement contained several errors: Lieberman was never a Freedom Rider. He went to the South in 1963 to register voters. The Freedom Riders did not register voters but tried, in 1961, to integrate public facilities. These errors were not reported at the time. Rather the important point was to establish Lieberman's 1960s idealism and the fact that he had been active in the early civil rights movement.)

Clinton's most direct reference to the 1960s came at the end of his speech, when he repeated many of the same phrases he had used during his fund-raising appearances of the previous year.[89] As Jeff Shesol, who co-wrote the speech, recalled, "That was totally his thing, and so we put it in the convention speech because it was working, and he really loved it . . . it was 90 percent his."[90]

The evening after Clinton's speech Ted Kennedy and Caroline Kennedy both appeared in prime time, symbolizing, as one commentator wrote, "the party's willingness to reach beyond the immediate memories of the eight-year Clinton administration, back to perhaps the most glowing era in its modern history."[91] Claiming that Gore represented the tradition of JFK, Senator Kennedy said, "How proud he would be of Al Gore and our party and the new barrier of bigotry we are breaking down" by nominating Lieberman, the first Jewish candidate of a major party. Kennedy linked Gore directly with his slain brothers. "There have been only three times in my life that I have supported candidates for president as early and as enthusiastically as I have supported Al Gore. Two of them were my brothers."[92]

Caroline Kennedy also connected Gore and Lieberman with Camelot. "I wouldn't be here if it weren't for the Gore family," she said, as Gore's parents had been "helpful matchmakers" during her parents' courtship. "When my brother, John, and I were growing up," she recalled, "hardly a day went by when someone didn't come up to us and say, 'Your father changed my life. I went into public service because he asked me.'" She added that she took "great pride in knowing that one of those he inspired to enter public life" was Joe Lieberman.[93]

As someone who had marched for civil rights in 1963 and could point to a strong record on defense, Lieberman represented the "good sixties." In addition, some observers surmised that Gore had chosen Lieberman because he was the first Senate Democrat to criticize Clinton's private behavior regarding the Monica Lewinsky scandal, thus insulating the party from charges that it endorsed or tolerated the sexual hedonism of the "bad sixties."

For his part Lieberman in his acceptance speech immediately invoked the Kennedy era. "In the early 1960s . . . I walked with Martin Luther King in the March on Washington. . . . I went to Mississippi, where we worked to register African Americans to vote." Gore came of age in the 1960s, he acknowledged, but not as a counterculture rebel against traditional values. Gore "believes in service to America. He volunteered for Vietnam," noted Lieberman. "Long before it became popular, Al and Tipper led a crusade to renew the moral center of this nation," he said, referring to Tipper Gore's campaign against objectionable lyrics in popular music, and they understood the concern "that our standards of decency and civility have eroded." At the end of his speech Lieberman once again recalled the early 1960s of President Kennedy.[94]

As on every other night of the convention, the 1960s were invoked during the closing night. In his acceptance speech Al Gore referred several times to the turmoil of the 1960s. After recalling that his parents had taught him the "real values" of "faith and family, duty and honor and trying to make the world a better place," he spoke of the trauma of the late 1960s. "Our nation's spirit was being depleted. We saw the assassination of our best leaders [and] appeals to racial backlash." Gore recounted at length his reasons for volunteering for service in Vietnam. In closing, he invoked the fond memory of John Kennedy, referring to "the beginning of the New Frontier."[95]

In the 2000 Democratic National Convention we see the continued power of the 1960s in American politics. All of the major addresses hailed the Kennedy years, and many made a special effort to insulate Democrats from any association with the late 1960s. As in 1992, the Democrats were again adamant about distinguishing the "good sixties" from the "bad sixties."

From the start of his presidential campaign in 1991, Bill Clinton's opponents pinned two labels on him: he was a draft dodger who had avoided service in Vietnam and he embodied the excesses of "the sixties." Though

Clinton was twice elected president, these two issues—Vietnam and the 1960s counterculture—often forced him into a defensive posture. As a consequence he made sure to speak with balance of both the good and bad aspects of the decade. As it became clear that the 2000 presidential election would be the first to pit one baby boomer against another, Clinton argued vigorously for his interpretation of the meaning of the 1960s. He appealed to the nation not to squander its current peace and prosperity, as it had strayed from the hope and promise of the early 1960s into the conflict and despair of the later 1960s. Clinton defended the decade until the end of his presidency, making a last-ditch effort to resurrect his era's reputation before he was succeeded by his fellow boomer, George W. Bush.

9

The "Un-Sixties" Candidate

GEORGE W. BUSH

Widening exasperation with Clinton in the wake of his impeachment may hasten our national rejection of the sixties values he represents. . . . George W. Bush has already begun explicitly attacking the "if it feels good, do it" culture of the sixties. . . . [H]e will run [in 2000] and govern as the anti-Clinton and the un-sixties: a committed family man devoted to traditional values and traditional beliefs, after his youthful fling with the culture of the sixties led him to reject it emphatically from firsthand knowledge of its destructiveness.

Conservative author Myron Magnet (2000)

As THE END of the Clinton presidency drew near, the political use of the 1960s only intensified. The leading Republican candidate, Texas governor George W. Bush, was openly hostile to the decade that shaped his generation. While presidents before him (Ronald Reagan and, to a lesser extent, Bill Clinton) differentiated between the "good sixties" and the "bad sixties," Bush drew no such distinctions. Consistently he characterized the 1960s as an era that destroyed all the good his father's "Greatest Generation" had achieved. Above all, he envisioned his own presidency as a personal mission to restore the nation and society he saw as having been seriously damaged by "the sixties."

In 2000 American presidential politics featured a rare trio of contrasting personalities, very close in age yet so different in outlook. Bill Clinton and George W. Bush were born forty-four days apart in the summer of 1946, graduated from high school in 1964 and from college in 1968. Al Gore, born in 1948, graduated one year behind them. Yet Bush and Gore experienced, and recalled, their encounter with the 1960s in terms of stark contrast.

As it happened, Bush and Gore each found himself responding to interview questions about the Beatles during the 2000 campaign. Gore loved

179

their late 1960s music. "Not only a new sound . . . a new sensibility . . . that incredible *gestalt* they had. *Rubber Soul* is my favorite album," he told a reporter. "I loved *Sgt. Pepper*, the *White Album. Sgt. Pepper* was a real tour de force." Bush had a different critical take. "I liked their early stuff," he said. "They did some good records. But then they got a bit weird. I didn't like all that later stuff when they got strange." The press picked up these signals. "If you think that the summit of the Beatles' output was their frat-party covers of 'Twist and Shout' and 'Money'—then George W. Bush is the man for you," declared *Time* magazine right before the election. "But if you feel that music from what Bush calls their 'weird' period—such as 'Strawberry Fields' and 'Hey Jude,' was a greater achievement in the prolific Beatles *oeuvre*—then All You Need Is Gore."[1]

The observation holds up more generally. Much of the energy of the conservative movement in the United States has come from the stubborn resistance of the Right to the events and personalities of the 1960s. Witness how much of the candidates' rhetoric in the first two presidential campaigns of the twenty-first century revolved around the contested meaning of the 1960s. To the Right, Clinton committed the ongoing sin of failing to repudiate his sins of the 1960s. By contrast, those on the Right who admitted experimenting with the counterculture claimed to have repented and returned to traditional values. As David Broder noted: "In the House of Representatives, there is a generation of young conservatives who will tell you without going into great detail, that, as President George W. Bush says, when he was 'young and foolish, he did things that were young and foolish.' Many of them [were] part of that culture before they snapped to and said, 'That ain't the way I'm supposed to be living my life.'"[2]

Asked if Bush tried to make Clinton a poster child for the excesses of the 1960s in the 2000 campaign, leading religious conservative Marvin Olasky, who advised Bush at the time, replied: "Sure. Basically you had two people, both of whom went to college in the 1960s, and one [Bush] was from the 1950s and one was from the 1970s," adding, "When we talk about the sixties we're really talking about the late sixties, the early seventies." Did Clinton succeed in moving the Democrats back toward the political center and ridding the party of the burden of the 1960s? "No," said Olasky, "because if he had been successful, then the last presidential elections would have been very different."[3]

While Bush did not refer specifically to the period, his political career had featured a running battle against the 1960s. From his first campaign for Texas governor in 1994, he engaged in a disciplined crusade to reverse what he felt were the negative political, social, and moral consequences of "the sixties." His initial debate with his opponent, incumbent governor Ann Richards, began with a questioner asking Bush what issue he considered most important for Texas and what he would do about it. "End the post–Vietnam War syndrome which blames others for society's ills," Bush replied, oddly conflating the Vietnam War and the Great Society. "All policy in Texas must say to each and every individual, 'You are accountable for your behavior.'"[4] This declaration—Bush's opening response in his very first debate—served as his central theme in that campaign and after.

As Texas governor (and later as president) Bush seldom wandered far from this theme of restoring the American virtues lost to liberalism, individualism, and hedonism. In 1998, he declared:

> Our society holds dear Judeo-Christian values that have stood the test of time: love your neighbor, give an honest day's work for an honest day's wages. Tell the truth and be honest. Don't cheat or steal. Respect others, respect their property, and respect their opinions. And always remember: You are responsible for the decisions you make. And that is the hope for my generation's legacy: that we usher in the responsibility era. We can change today's culture from, "If it feels good, do it."[5]

Yet some conservatives warned that no one could undo the 1960s. "It's a pipe dream[,] . . . hopeless and baseless cultural irredentism, to think that we can reoccupy the sixties," said conservative activist Peter Collier. "'Compassionate conservatism' [and] . . . that stuff that agglomerated in the Bush campaign of 2000 is an attempt to reverse the sixties. But of course, you never quite do it. You can do it in certain policy areas, like welfare, but you can't do it in the radical egalitarianism, which was the worst of the monsters to escape from the Pandora's box that was opened in the sixties."[6] Despite Collier's pessimism, Bush the officeholder devoted himself to salvaging a culture he viewed as having been corrupted by the 1960s.

Out of Time: George W. Bush in the 1960s

During the 1960s Yale University served as a breeding ground for future leaders of both parties. Bill Clinton graduated from its law school in 1973, and George W. Bush was in the college class of 1968. In addition, Dick Cheney, who would play a role in the presidential administrations of both George H. W. and George W. Bush, attended Yale from September 1959 until January 1961 and from January to June 1962. Three of the four candidates on the major party tickets in 2000—Bush, Cheney, and Joseph Lieberman—attended Yale in the 1960s. John Kerry graduated from Yale in 1966, Howard Dean in 1971, and Hillary Clinton from its law school in 1973.

While at Yale, George W. Bush resisted the cultural tides of the 1960s. "Bush was alive, but he wasn't noticing things" in the 1960s, said author and journalist Thomas Edsall.[7] "Bush insulated himself from the 1960s culture," agreed political scientist Darrell West. "He was very active in fraternities, and so he lived a 1950s life more than a 1960s life."[8] As David Halberstam observed: "Bush cannot be demonized as a figure of the sixties. He was not a part of the sixties. He went to college in those years, but seems completely untouched by the turmoil surrounding him and his generation then—he was oddly apolitical in tempestuous times."[9]

Bush's distaste for the 1960s stems in part from the era's stark contrast with his calm and secure childhood in the 1950s in the conservative West Texas town of Midland, population twenty-five thousand. To Joe O'Neill, a Bush childhood friend, "his homage to his parents, his respect for his elders, his respect for tradition, his belief in religion . . . that's the philosophy he grew up with here."[10] Midland had little crime, and Bush enjoyed a carefree youth, biking around town and playing Little League baseball.

"Midland was an idyllic place in which to grow up, and George W. Bush was a very typical child . . . remarkable primarily for his ordinariness," New York Times columnist Nicholas Kristof wrote in 2000. "Midland values were remarkably unshaken by the 1960s." People in Midland "stood with the establishment instead of rejecting it. Very few seem to have protested significantly against the Vietnam War, seriously used drugs, thought of police as 'pigs,' denounced their parents as oppressors, or picked up a copy of Das Kapital."[11]

Bush described the Midland of his youth as "a town of embedded values," including "a heavy dose of individualism and fairly healthy disrespect for government." The town's residents were hopeful for the future, and "in the 1950s, the moral of childhood was that the system worked." To Bush biographer Bill Minutaglio, "the lesson lasted with George W. for years. I think he truly believes that people can win the lottery if they work hard. . . . It'll all work out without government help or intrusion."[12]

For Bush "the sixties" began in 1968; all before then was calm. He described the early 1960s as a peaceful time. In recalling that era in his 1999 memoir, A Charge to Keep, Bush made no mention of John F. Kennedy, who was assassinated in Texas when Bush was seventeen years old, nor of the burgeoning civil rights protests of the "peaceful" early 1960s.

Then came 1968. "The world as we had known it changed dramatically, but not until the spring of my senior year at Yale," wrote Bush. "The sit-ins and long hair and sometimes violent protests that came to symbolize the unrest on the college campuses of the late 1960s and early 1970s were just beginning, but they had not yet arrived on our campus as my friends and I prepared to graduate. We later joked that members of the class of 1968 were the last in a long time to have short hair." To Bush, "1968 rocked our previously placid world and shocked the country, Yale, and me. In many ways that spring was the end of an era of innocence. The gravity of history was beginning to descend in a horrifying and disruptive way."[13] Bush's use of such strikingly apocalyptic language to frame the social changes of the 1960s as a national nightmare demonstrates how high the stakes are to those on the Right.

Some of that disruption hit Bush at a deeply personal level as Yale evolved dramatically during the 1960s, especially in its admission policies. Though Bush had great fun at Yale, he understood that the university was undergoing radical change. A new university president and admissions director began outreach efforts to attract the brightest minds from the nation's public schools. By 1969 Yale was a very different place than it had been when Bush was accepted only five years earlier. All three of George H. W. Bush's brothers went to Yale, but only the eldest of his four sons would attend.

Most members of George W. Bush's social stratum accepted the new meritocracy that rewarded academic skills, but Bush viewed the changes in political terms: the university was becoming too liberal. Along with coeducation, introduced in 1969, the new admissions policy profoundly changed Yale. Had Bush applied in 1968 instead of 1963, his grades and board scores might not have gained him admittance.

Bush and his peers felt especially annoyed with Yale's growing liberalism. A disgruntled graduate complained to Nicholas Lemann that after the 1965 Watts riots a teaching assistant told his class, "The solution's simple. It's income redistribution. That solves the problem," instead of, as the alumnus wanted to hear, "We have to focus on core things that will solve the problem. Skills. Education. Discipline." To the alumnus the liberal message was "'Take from the rich and give to the poor.' There was a lot of that then." Bush shared that angry response to the new Yale of the late 1960s. On the campaign trail in 2000 he said that Yale in the 1960s was full of "snobs" and "elitists." "That would make him one of the ones being looked down upon," Lemann opined. "In the venue in which his birth entitled him to noble rank, unexpected events had now made him into a populist." Lemann argued that much of Bush's hostility to the 1960s derives from his lack of success early in life compared with his father. The elder Bush, unlike his son, excelled academically and athletically in high school and college, married young, had a heroic military career, founded a successful business, and was elected to Congress—all at an early age. Individual differences between father and son aside, "they changed the rules on George W. Bush." By the mid-1960s "he was part of a displaced elite. . . . In that endless series of competitions, he kept coming up short." Bush's lack of early success, Lemann suggested, was due to the rise in the 1960s of those better qualified than he was.[14]

Bush engaged in no political activism at Yale, but he did make a choice as to whom to support in the decade's cultural and political wars: the generation of his parents. "Unlike others of his generation, like Bill Clinton or Al Gore, Mr. Bush never wore his hair long, agonized over Vietnam, wrestled with existentialism or cranked up Rolling Stones songs to annoy his parents," observed Nicholas Kristof in 2000. "Even today, Mr. Bush thunders in his stump speeches against boomer-style self-indulgence and appeals for a 'responsibility era' that in some respects sounds like the 1950s; he likes values as clean-cut as his hair." Rather than make him question his own or society's beliefs, the turmoil of the 1960s instead made Bush more rigid in outlook. "And today, much of his underlying political philosophy rests on the belief that the nation still needs to reverse the psychology of permissiveness and liberalism that began to take root in the country in the late 1960s."[15]

Although his family had extensive and long-standing ties to Yale, Bush was reluctant to send a contribution on the twenty-fifth anniversary of his graduation. His crusade against "liberal elites," according to Kristof, began at Yale in the 1960s, where "classmates began to feel guilty about their privilege, angry at their parents, distrustful of business and defiant at the system itself." To the secure Bush, such sentiments were inexplicable. As Bill Minutaglio explained to Kristof: "He was blindsided by a lack of certitude that spun him and by an ambiguity that is still spinning him today. . . . He felt that Yale and a lot of the counterculture were rejecting all the things that his family had stood for."[16]

The Yale atmosphere never felt more hostile to Bush and his family than in an encounter with the Reverend William Sloane Coffin Jr., Yale's liberal chaplain from 1958 to 1976 and an acquaintance of his father. In 1964, Bush's freshman year, his father lost his race for the Texas Senate. Reportedly, when Bush met Coffin on campus and told him who he was, Coffin responded, "Yeah, I know your father, and your father lost to a better man." (Coffin claimed to have no recollection of the incident.)[17] Bush was devastated; a friend said that he had never seen him angrier.[18] Two years later, after his father won a seat in Congress, the son was upset that fellow students criticized the congressman's conservative stances on Vietnam and civil rights.

During the 2000 campaign Coffin wrote a piece in the *New York Times* praising the activism of Yale's 1960s students and contrasting it to the passivity of students of the 1950s. In the 1960s, he noted, "a strong social consciousness was emerging," and many Yale students joined the Peace Corps. Coffin also heralded Yale's growing racial and religious diversity, coeducation, the antiwar movement, and the decline of fraternities, proudly noting that a 1967 protest at which Yale students turned in their draft cards yielded more than at any other college.[19]

Coffin claimed he was sorry not to have known Bush or Cheney at Yale, and that while some of Bush's criticisms of Yale's antiwar movement were justified, "it is also sad not to share in the action and passion of your time. Often called a decade of student unrest, the sixties would be better termed a time of ethical unrest, a time that I hope will soon come again." Coffin acknowledged, however, that most Americans did not participate in liberal politics and campus unrest.[20] Later in the campaign he was quoted in *Yale Alumni Magazine* as saying that "the social concerns of the minority were very great in the sixties," referring to Joe Lieberman's civil rights activities, clarifying that "Lieberman was in the minority. George W. Bush was in the majority."[21]

Bush's memory of the 1960s echoed Coffin's. "I don't remember any kind of heaviness ruining my time at Yale[,] . . . any protests at Yale, any big stuff," Bush said in 2000. "I had fun at Yale. I got a lot of great friends out of Yale. And I didn't pay attention. I guess there were some people who paid attention. . . . But I didn't want to be friends with these people who felt superior."[22] Nicholas Kristof asked Bush if he had ever spoken with his father "about civil rights, the Vietnam War, or other upheavals of the day." "Gosh, I can't remember . . . any long sessions sitting around," the candidate said. "There wasn't a lot of protest at Yale in '68. I don't remember that." (At Yale Bush chose not to sign a statement other seniors had signed indicating their opposition to the draft.)[23] Classmate Carter Wiseman concurred with some of these memories. "Bush had a point," he wrote. "Colorful as the reputation of 1968 is in the popular lore, much of the color has been applied retrospectively. . . . [T]he 1960s really happened in the 1970s. The year 1968 was only the turning point, and those doing the turning were relatively few in number."[24]

In the late 1960s perhaps only a third of the students were involved in Vietnam protests, said John Morton Blum, emeritus professor of history at Yale, who chaired the department in 1967. "There was a lot of antiwar sentiment, but it was not well organized, and most of what was happening in civil rights was happening off-campus," he said. "The issues that were roiling the country had not yet affected Yale." The 1968 *Yale Class*

Book, in its entry on Vietnam, noted, "The decision to state publicly a moral position on the war was not made by any large group until this fall." According to another entry, "no matter how deep the agony is over the war or the cities, the Yale student is still essentially a voyeur."[25]

To Wiseman, Bush "might be thought of as having occupied a 'parallel' Yale, a Yale more like the one of his father," who entered Yale in 1945 in the full glow of the American victory in World War II. Others corroborated Bush's memory of Yale in the 1960s. "There were really two Yales back then—one a more or less serious university, the other a cheerful, undemanding party school—and they didn't intersect very much," said Bush classmate Charles McGrath. Yale's traditional conservatism prevailed throughout much of the 1960s. In 1964 Yale alumni criticized the university for awarding Martin Luther King an honorary degree. One letter to the alumni magazine called it "disgusting," on the grounds that King had recently spent time in jail. In 1965 a collection of alumni, many faculty members, and the university's president roundly denounced history professor Staughton Lynd's trip to Hanoi, in defiance of U.S. passport regulations, with a contingent of war protesters.[26]

Protests against Vietnam increased in 1967 and 1968, but for the majority of students the conflict was rather remote until graduate school draft deferments were ended in 1968, Wiseman recalled. And though some students had been involved in the civil rights movement in the South, it too seemed distant, despite the fact that New Haven experienced race riots of its own in 1967. In Wiseman's view, although the assassinations of King and Robert Kennedy in 1968 raised awareness concerning racial issues at Yale, "powerful as the external currents of change were, they hardly engulfed [Bush's] more traditional Yale," a school better represented by Bush's fraternity than by its small chapter of SDS, the radical Students for a Democratic Society. Yale was quiet in the post–World War II years because returning veterans were eager to move forward with their lives. "And the impulse to extend that calmer time endured for many, even in the late 1960s."[27]

Another way in which Yale changed in the 1960s was in the growing hostility to fraternities. Critics believed that they were outdated and ought to be abolished. In 1964, four hundred students expressed interest in joining Bush's fraternity; a year later only two hundred did. By the early 1970s fraternities were required to give back their residence buildings to Yale, and ROTC was banned from the campus.[28] Bush was not against all of the changes taking place in the 1960s. In 1967 Glenn DeChabert, a younger Bush fraternity brother, founded the Black Student Alliance, which lobbied for courses in African American studies. Bush's friends recalled that he highly approved. But Bush's fraternity brothers "knew they were a dying breed," as one put it, referring to the class that had been accepted under less stringent admissions policies. Bush's roommate called it "the last of the happy days."[29]

With the Vietnam War raging, men of draft age faced an important decision in the late 1960s. For many, all the choices were troublesome: enlist in the army, wait to be called, volunteer for one of the other armed forces, seek a medical exemption, refuse induction, apply for conscientious objector status, or leave the country. A lucky few could hope to join their state's National Guard, which did not serve in combat overseas at that time.

"I give Clinton much credit; by the time Clinton is evading the draft, I would have," said Vietnam historian Stanley Karnow. "I applaud anybody who got out [of serving]. So I'm not even going to criticize Bush for not going. The only thing I would criticize him for is that [having] avoided getting involved, he should not stand up and be pious about criticizing other people who didn't serve and be flying the flag."[30]

Bush often expressed criticism of the way the United States had prosecuted the war. Asked in 2004 if he had been in "favor of the war in Vietnam," he replied: "I supported my government. I did. And would have gone had my unit been called up, by the way." When the interviewer noted, "But you didn't volunteer or enlist to go," Bush replied: "No, I didn't. You're right. I served. I flew fighters and enjoyed it, and provided a service to our country." Bush then amplified his views, saying: "The thing about the Vietnam War that troubles me as I look back was it was a political war. We had politicians making military decisions, and it is lessons that any president must learn, and that is to set the goal and the objective and allow the military to come up with the plans to achieve that objective." These, he argued, "are essential lessons to be learned from the Vietnam War."[31] In his memoir Bush wrote, "My inclination was to support the government and the war until proven wrong, and that only came later, as I realized we could not explain the mission, had no exit strategy, and did not seem to be fighting to win."[32]

Neither Bush nor Dick Cheney wrestled morally or intellectually with Vietnam even in the late 1960s. Cheney avoided serving in Vietnam simply because he viewed it as an impediment to his goal of earning his Ph.D. in political science at the University of Wisconsin, which he entered in 1966. Looking back on that time in an interview with David Maraniss in 2002, the vice president described himself as "a reasonably conservative Republican, generally supportive of the Johnson administration at that stage." The war and the draft were "not the most important things" on his mind, he recalled. "There's a tendency now to look back on it, those periods of the sixties, especially at a place like Wisconsin, to think of it as the centerpiece[,] . . . but it just wasn't. Not for all of us."[33]

Maraniss concluded that Cheney had "wanted nothing to do with Vietnam. He supported the war, but did not want to serve in it, and was barely interested in it one way or another." Dick Cheney and his wife, Lynne, "just wanted to do their work and move on." Maraniss noted the irony that "Cheney, like some other politicians who moved through the Vietnam era barely touched by it, would spend the rest of his career with Vietnam often in his mind. It was easier for him to ignore it while it was going on than after it was over."[34]

Five years younger than Cheney, George W. Bush was still an undergraduate in the late 1960s. For a number of liberals Bush's animosity to the period is crystallized in his dismissive attitude toward his alma mater. In 2000 *New Republic* editor Martin Peretz wrote that at Yale, Bush "learned only two things: a hostility to liberal faculty . . . and a hostility to the emerging meritocracy that threatened his social status."[35] Todd Gitlin concurred. "Bush's sixties consist of resentment against those guys who took over the institutions that he thought he was entitled to inherit, so that now Yale doesn't belong to him and his kind, but it seems to have been taken over by lefties and Jews and all kinds of unsavory people."[36]

"George W. Bush in the sixties is very touched by what he goes through," said liberal journalist and former Clinton senior adviser Sidney Blumenthal. "He's a wealthy ne'er-do-well who resents [the 1960s] and whose politics are developed as a reaction to the sixties. His experience at Yale is very telling because he was on the cusp of when Yale [changed] and he was very resentful and upset by it. He existed in a world of the past," Blumenthal explained. "The influx of the meritocracy—the end of the quota system . . . against Jews and the sudden influx of large numbers of Jews—totally transformed the place. He was left in a cultural, social backwater and didn't know how to cope with the changes."[37]

Conservatives like Bush who blame the 1960s for various cultural problems "know there is a constituency out there [who detest] the sixties," said Julian Bond. In the late 1960s Bush had "no engagement in the political movement that was whirling about him. He's not even involved in the movement of young conservatives" that was proliferating on college campuses. "The Young Americans for Freedom was growing then, and you would think—unless he had no political thoughts at all—that he'd find a home there," Bond said. Although many young people worked for Goldwater in 1964, "he's absolutely apolitical, so this decade just washes past him. But he says now that he objected to it. [Bush supporters] are people who experienced the sixties as a negative, and they carried that into their lives thereafter." Like his father and Reagan, Bush considered the 1960s "a bad time, an evil period, and [decided] that he needs to be against it."[38]

As a political candidate, then, "Bush was providing an alternative to the 1960s," said Jeff Shesol. In the 2000 campaign Bush "presented himself very much as a contrast to the sixties ideal that the Clintons supposedly embodied. . . . [He tried to] pump up his credentials as an anti-intellectual," which led him to state on the campaign trail, "'I'm not going to sit and read a 500-page book about policy.' Everything was a contrast to Clinton, an assertion of his total lack of intellectual curiosity, making it a great virtue. But it wasn't totally phony; it was true," observed Shesol. "He wasn't going to read a book. [The 1960s] barely grazed his consciousness until it presented him with a problem that he had to get out of by joining the [National] Guard. But he was not radicalized in the 1960s in the way that some of the neocon leaders of today were. . . . He didn't have much of an ideology at all."[39] Thus in many ways Bush sat out the 1960s. The same could not be said of his opponent in the 2000 election, Al Gore.

Working within "the System": Al Gore's 1960s

In 2000 longtime Gore supporter Martin Peretz, a former Harvard professor, described his student Al Gore as he knew him during his freshman seminar: "It was the 1960s, and the academic culture was much tainted by the rancor of ideological divides. Alas, the intellectual looseness that accompanied this rancor was not altogether absent from my classroom," he said. "But what I remember most about Gore was his insistent opposition—mostly by example—to that looseness and to the moral hauteur it encouraged."[40]

Though not a radical, Gore experienced "the sixties" far more deeply than Bush. The era's upheavals directly affected Gore's family. In 1970 his father, Senator Albert Gore Sr., a Tennessee Democrat, lost his bid for reelection to a fourth Senate term. As a result of that election, partly in reaction to the civil rights movement and to the Democrats' handling of the war in Vietnam, both of Tennessee's Senate seats and the governorship went to Republicans.

When Gore applied to college in the fall of 1964, he applied only to Harvard, in part because it was John Kennedy's alma mater. But Harvard in the 1960s was a far different place than it had been during the 1930s when JFK was there. Student protests rocked the campus. In Gore's sophomore year, protesters mobbed Defense Secretary Robert McNamara's car when he came to speak. When Gore was a junior, a group coordinated by SDS held a campus recruiter for Dow Chemical, the makers of napalm, captive in a classroom for five hours. In 1969, shortly before Gore graduated, demonstrators took over Harvard's main administration building, University Hall, violently clashing with police the next day. The following September students taunted the crew-cut Gore when he came back to campus in his army uniform. At Harvard Gore enjoyed the era's rock music and smoked marijuana. Though he opposed the war in Vietnam, however, he was dismayed at the behavior of the Left and did not join the 1969 takeover of University Hall or the protests at his graduation later that spring.[41]

In Gore's junior year, 1967–68, "came the rev-o-lu-tion," recalled roommate John Tyson. "The war came into our living room with the body bag count every day," and both of them followed the war closely on television. Gore and Tyson, an African American, had frequent lengthy conversations about Vietnam and race relations, discussing books by black authors. After Martin Luther King's assassination in April 1968, Gore witnessed the ensuing riots in Washington. He returned to Harvard shortly afterward, and he and Tyson tearfully talked nearly all night. "He was so upset because it had happened in Tennessee," Tyson said. "It was very, very sad, and we were sick from watching our nation burn up."[42]

That summer Gore helped write a short antiwar speech for his father to give at the Democratic National Convention in Chicago but did not join protesters when he returned to Harvard his senior year. "We weren't demonstrators," Tyson explained. "We distrusted these movements a lot because a lot of this stuff was very emotional and not well thought out. We were a pretty traditional bunch of guys, positive for civil rights and women's rights but formal[,] . . . not buying into something we considered detrimental to our country." Gore had little interest in SDS or other radical student organizations—itself a radical notion given Cambridge's far left climate.

Accounts differ as to why Gore volunteered as an enlisted man, one of only about a dozen to do so in his graduating class of 1,115, in a war he opposed. To one college friend, the actor Tommy Lee Jones, Gore explained that "if he found a fancy way of not going, someone else would have to go in his place." Gore's senior thesis adviser, Richard Neustadt, told Gore that volunteering would not curtail the chance to enter politics, the career his parents hoped for. Gore told acquaintances that his decision would aid the antiwar movement, as it might help reelect his antiwar father. Gore chose to enlist in Newark, New Jersey, to avoid publicity, passing up a chance to join the Tennessee National Guard, where a relative had secured him a spot. Al Gore was not the average private—at a ceremony in Alabama, General William Westmoreland pulled him aside for a private talk—but neither did he receive special treatment. As an army journalist he was, of course, not on the front lines. But Gore's editor in Vietnam for the *Army Flyer* newspaper said that of all his reporters and correspondents, "I didn't have one who traveled as much as he did."[43]

"Gore always was somebody that wanted to work within the system, and fundamentally respected authority even if he disagreed with it," said White House correspondent John Harris. "What he does have—Clinton does not so much have this, but a lot of sixties politicians do—is an intellectual instinct to reach for sweeping theoretical constructs and for approaching problems in a large, cosmic sense." To Harris, Gore's *Earth in the Balance* "says environmentalism should be the new 'guiding principle for civilization.' It is filled with this sweeping, cosmic language. There are a lot of sixties politicians who learned this habit."[44]

Gore applied similar language when, as vice president, he spoke of the meaning of 1969 in American history in his 1994 Harvard commencement address, his twenty-fifth reunion. Since Clinton's election in 1992 Republicans had redoubled their attacks on "the sixties." In reaction to the growing power of the Right, Gore defended the values of the 1960s generation and urged the audience to resist the impulse toward cynicism about the possibility of social change. He said that the Right, which had arisen primarily in response to the turmoil of the late 1960s, thrived on cynicism and distrust of, even contempt for, government itself.

"The world changed in important and enduring ways because of the events of 1969, a year of contradiction and contrasts, of glory and bitterness," observed Gore, recounting the year's major events: the moon landing, the Charles Manson murders, Woodstock, the My Lai massacre, and the divide over the Vietnam War. Nixon's 1969 inauguration "seemed to . . . ratify the results of a downward spiral that had begun with the assassination of President Kennedy." The second half of the 1960s was a trying time. Despite the passage of civil rights laws and the potential of the War on Poverty, the Watts riots, the escalation in Vietnam, and the assassinations of 1968 "seemed like the death of any hope." As a result, said Gore, "I left Harvard in 1969 disillusioned." These currents continued to reverberate decades later, he noted, as seen in the public's lack of faith in government. He stressed the need to renew hope, idealism, and trust, for "we are still trying to heal those wounds burned into our body politic" by the traumas of the 1960s. Gore then quoted journalist E. J. Dionne: "Just as the Civil War dominated American political life for decades after it ended, so is the cultural civil war of the 1960s, with all its tensions and contradictions, shaping our politics today. We are still trapped in the 1960s" as we grapple with issues of race and gender and "debate over the meaning of the Vietnam War."[45]

Gore used the address to define his own view of the 1960s. Six years later the 2000 presidential election would hinge in part on two starkly different assessments of the value the 1960s brought to American society. Only one year apart in college in the late 1960s, Bush and Gore carried within them radically different impressions of the time when they had joined the adult world. The 2000 election—the first between two baby boomers—was a contest over those differences.

Bush's "Compassionate Conservatism": Counteracting the 1960s

George W. Bush was not overtly "anti-sixties" during the 1960s, but an anti-"sixties" political philosophy would propel his rapid political rise. In 1993, one year before he ran for governor of Texas, Bush received a book from adviser Karl Rove, *Destructive Generation: Second Thoughts about the Sixties*, by a former Berkeley radical, David Horowitz. A founder of the New Left who had once been involved with the Black Panthers, Horowitz later became an archconservative. His book harshly attacked the 1960s. Bush later read Horowitz's autobiography, *Radical Son*. "I thought it was fascinating," he said in 2000. "There was just a lot of history I remember from my early twenties come to life. And here was somebody who blew the whistle." Horowitz, along with Myron Magnet and Marvin Olasky, advocated the tenets of "compassionate conservatism."[46] The movement had great appeal to Bush. Its ethos emphasized the power of religion to change people's actions. There was also, as Nicholas Lemann noted in 2000, "the implication, which runs through most of the faith-based social program literature, that the liberal elitists took a crack at the country's social problems in the sixties and botched the job."[47]

Bush's view of the 1960s would have profound policy repercussions. In 1993 Rove also introduced Bush to *The Dream and the Nightmare: The Sixties' Legacy to the Underclass*, by Myron Magnet.[48] According to the cover of a revised edition, the book "helped make George W. Bush president."[49] Bush claimed that the treatise influenced him more than any book besides the Bible.[50] In a promotional blurb Bush wrote that Magnet's text "crystallized for me the impact the failed culture of the sixties had on our values and society. It helped create dependency on government, undermine family, and eroded values."[51]

Indeed, Magnet blamed poverty on "sixties" culture rather than racism, economic conditions, or government policy. "American culture underwent a revolution in the 1960s, which transformed some of its most basic beliefs and values, including its beliefs about the causes of poverty," he wrote. The results for the poor were terrible, as "the new culture's beliefs downplayed the personal responsibility, self-control, and deferred gratification that it takes to succeed" and instead "celebrated an 'If it feels good, do it' self-indulgence that for the poor, whose lives have less margin for error than the prosperous, too often proved disastrous." Magnet argued that "America tried its grand experiment with the elite cultural values of the 1960s" with catastrophic results.[52]

Magnet's theories and recommendations found an eager spokesman in Bush. When he first ran for the Texas governorship in 1994, according to Hanna Rosin, "Bush aimed to replace what he saw as the 'anything goes' mentality of the 1960s with one of self-help and moral responsibility." In 1997, Rove set up a meeting for Bush with Magnet, and before long Rove and Bush "began to think about expanding the theme into a broader campaign message."[53] When the two met, Bush told Magnet that *The Dream and the Nightmare* "had changed his life," reported Bill Minutaglio.[54]

Recalling those first meetings, Magnet said that Bush "wanted to undo the cultural revolution of the sixties and lead America back to decent values and social policy based on decent values."[55] From his visits, "it was clear to me he thought an awful lot of the prevailing orthodoxy on campus in the sixties was humbug" and that the influence of "the elite culture" had hurt rather than helped the poor.[56] After Magnet spoke with Bush and his senior staff in Texas in 1998, his influence on Bush became enormous. According to Minutaglio, Magnet and Marvin Olasky were "the spiritual and intellectual godfathers of Mr. Bush's core philosophy."[57] Conservatives attested to Magnet's strong influence on Bush. "I find his argument convincing," said Lisa Schiffren. "So, by the way, does the president. The president actually listens to Myron."[58]

"Bush talks about Magnet's book more often than he does the work of other anti-sixties authors," noted Nicholas Lemann. Recalling a meeting with Bush, Magnet said that Bush told him "he'd been through the sixties. Been there, done that. It was extremely destructive. The culture was at the root of a huge proportion of America's problems, especially the underclass." This prompted Lemann to write: "So the sixties had done something much worse than push him [Bush] aside. They had ruined the lives of millions of ordinary Americans, and even, it seems, been responsible for his own wild years, even though Bush was never self-consciously a sixties person. That would lend both an aspect of personal account-settling and a large social purpose to Bush's intent in 2000 to wrest national power from the elitists and the snobs."[59]

Magnet's influence, and his argument for "compassionate conservatism" in particular, led Bush to decide that "the nation needed the same antidote to the sixties he found in his own life: religion," wrote Hanna Rosin.[60] Asked to name his favorite political philosopher at a 1999 Republican debate in Iowa, Bush promptly said, "Christ. Because he changed my heart." Asked to elaborate for his listeners, he replied: "Well, if they don't know, it's going to be hard to explain. When you turn your heart and your life over to Christ, when you accept Christ as the savior, it changes your heart. It changes your life. And that's what happened to me."[61]

In the foreword to Marvin Olasky's *Compassionate Conservatism: What It Is, What It Does, and How It Can Transform America* (2000), Bush wrote, "We started to see ourselves as a compassionate country because government was spending large sums of money and building an immense bureaucracy to help the poor." But these efforts were counterproductive, for government "cannot put hope in our hearts and a sense of purpose in our lives." Olasky understood that America could "do better than we did through programs developed in the 1960s."[62]

In conversation Olasky observed that the late 1960s saw the rise of "liberation of the individual." Once this "became the ultimate goal— trumping everything else—then all the rest of the changes followed." In Olasky's formulation, "I look back at 'the sixties' as a vast social experiment. And it just didn't work."[63]

Bush first became aware of Olasky's theories in 1993, when Rove gave Bush a copy of *The Tragedy of American Compassion*, in which Olasky attacked big government and argued that the private sector was better suited to combat poverty.[64] Olasky castigated "the key contribution of the War on Poverty: the deliberate attempt to uncouple welfare from shame." Before 1964, he claimed, welfare was only a last resort. "But in the 1960s, attitudes changed. Suddenly, it became better to accept welfare than to take in laundry." Aid to Families with Dependent Children rose dramatically "from 1965 to 1968," despite a robust economy, because the poor had been taught that welfare is "nothing to be ashamed of. The Great Society's War Against Shame was a success."[65] As governor, Bush consulted Olasky on reforming Texas's welfare policies.[66] "[Lyndon Johnson's] insistence on equal opportunity for all was bold and just," Bush wrote in his memoir. "His programs to lift people out of poverty, however, while well intentioned, proved costly and created too much dependency on government."[67]

Magnet and Olasky clarified many of Bush's long-held sentiments. Bush's animosity to the Great Society originated with his work for the oil companies in the 1970s. When Bush ran for Congress in 1978, "he basically knew about one thing: the oil business," said Jeff Shesol. "And he knew about the resentment that the oil and gas guys had for the federal government. He was educated by those guys in a way that his father wasn't." During his campaign "all he was able to do was speak angrily about how the prerogatives of these guys were being encroached upon by the government, and [how] if the government just got out of the way, then they could get back to being their entrepreneurial selves."[68]

Bush also came to believe that "we have seen an unprecedented decay in our American culture," and that this too was the fault of big government. "Our sense of personal responsibility has declined dramatically," he wrote, "just as the role and responsibility of the federal government have increased." Government programs had "accelerated and sanctioned the changes in our culture." Furthermore, he insisted, they were too expensive and could not cure society's ills.[69]

Yoshi Tsurumi, one of Bush's professors at Harvard Business School, vividly remembered Bush from his classes in 1973 because of Bush's outspoken views. Even then he was calling the New Deal socialist, the Securities and Exchange Commission an anti-business agency, and the civil rights movement "socialist/communist." Tsurumi also recalled Bush saying, "People are poor because they're lazy."[70]

Bush clearly shared Reagan's view of the Great Society as a colossal failure, but in many respects his views were even more conservative than Reagan's. Borrowing the slogan "compassionate conservatism," Bush built on Reagan's critique of the Great Society to devise his own compelling political philosophy, based primarily on a negative interpretation of 1960s social programs. But while Reagan, disgusted by "the sixties," had watched the era unfold from behind the windows of elected office, Bush experienced "the sixties" firsthand and developed a far more personal resentment toward the turmoil of those years than Reagan did. Each, though, gained the ultimate prize from the Right's consistent and successful reinterpretation of the 1960s: two terms as president.

The 1960s and the 2000 Presidential Campaign

If Bush's political identity was defined by his hostility to the 1960s, in the 2000 campaign he displayed it quite openly. He often criticized the type of person he claimed he had encountered at Yale in the 1960s. "What I disliked most were the snobs who thought that just because they had a Yale education they could tell other people how to run their lives."[71] Bush also attacked his critics, complaining: "I'm getting this rap about somehow I don't appreciate intellectuals. I do appreciate smart people. What I don't appreciate is people who think they're all of a sudden smarter than the average person because they happen to have an Ivy League degree" and then "sit down and decide for everyone else what they should do."[72]

Significantly, Bush considered Al Gore typical of the kind of person he had loathed at college. "The Yale class of '68 bred a social type George W. Bush and his friends called The Grind," wrote Hanna Rosin, "a tireless striver, more sober than his teachers, who split his time between the library and admirable social causes. Back then, King of the Grinds was Strobe Talbott, now a former deputy secretary of state, then president of the *Yale Daily News*, Rhodes scholar, and antiwar activist in a most responsible way." But Bush is also "an unmistakable product of the sixties," observed Rosin, "albeit in a different way than is normally understood by that phrase." In his gubernatorial campaign Bush defined himself politically in opposition to what he had observed at Yale in the 1960s. He and Karl Rove used this animosity as the basis of a political platform. "They began with a list of what they [saw] as sixties symptoms still infecting America: elitism, cynicism, anti-Americanism, self-absorption enforced by a penchant for psychobabble," Rosin wrote. "The stage was thus set to replay those old college turf wars as Campaign 2000, Bush vs. Al Gore, Harvard '69."[73]

Both southern baby boomers who attended elite prep schools, both Ivy Leaguers, both sons of prominent officeholders, as individuals Bush and Gore couldn't have been less alike, a point not lost on Bush senior, who often had reason to be disappointed in his eldest son. In the 2000 campaign candidate Bush playfully told audiences, "Can you imagine how much it hurt to know that Dad's idea of the perfect son was Al Gore?"[74] Gore—like Clinton—assiduously campaigned for student government; when he entered Harvard, he immediately ran for the freshman council. Throughout his political life Bush openly mocked such earnestness. "People who know him say he's itching to take on Al Gore in the general election," wrote Nicholas Lemann in 2000. "When Bush talks about Gore, he does so in a way that makes it clear that he has him pegged as a member of the liberal-intellectual coterie that rose to power in the sixties." Bush believed that the election "is going to be a regular guy versus an archetypal member of the new elite—no contest."[75]

Despite Bush's eagerness to confront Gore, his candidacy faced several major challenges. President Clinton's approval rating in his second term never dipped below 55 percent; when he left office it stood at 68 percent.[76] In part because the peace and prosperity of the 1990s gave him little room to attack the Democrats on substance, Bush decided to campaign on the issue of "values," hoping to draw sharp personal contrasts between him-

self and Gore. "I was raised in Midland, Texas [where] people are independent thinkers and when they think of government, they think of it
in terms of patriotism and that's about it," Bush said in an interview.
"There's kind of a healthy disrespect for faraway government, and there is
[*sic*] no class distinctions in Midland; it's just pretty much who you are is
who you are. To the extent I understand the man's [Gore's] biography, he
was raised in Washington, D.C. And I think inherent in that statement is
a difference of philosophy."[77]

Asked why Americans would want to change leadership when a solid
majority believed that they were better off and more prosperous than before the Clinton-Gore years, Bush replied that while people had become
wealthier, "there's a larger issue and [that is] the issue of values. People
are concerned about an era, really—and the way I like to summarize it
is, 'If it feels good, do it, and if you've got a problem, blame somebody.'"
Americans were "concerned about a culture that seems to have undermined family and respect." Government could enact legislation, but it
could not "get people to love one another."[78]

Accepting his party's nomination at the 2000 Republican National Convention, Bush proclaimed that the nation had lost its way under President
Clinton after twelve years of successful leadership from the generation
that came of age during World War II. "My father was the last president of
a great generation, a generation of Americans who stormed beaches, liberated concentration camps, and delivered us from evil," Bush said.[79]

By contrast, he charged, Clinton the baby boomer had wasted his time
in office and damaged the military. "Our current president embodied the
potential of a generation—so many talents, so much charm, such great
skill. But in the end, to what end?" Echoing Reagan's critique of Carter in
1980, Bush said, "If called on by the commander-in-chief today, two entire divisions of the Army would have to report, 'Not ready for duty, sir.'"
Bush invoked the caricature of Clinton as a 1960s radical hostile to the
military. With his own election, he pledged, "we will give our military . . .
a commander-in-chief who respects our men and women in uniform and a
commander-in-chief who earns their respect." And in a remark insinuat-
ing that Clinton had misunderstood the Vietnam War—and to remind his
audience that Clinton had avoided military service in the 1960s—Bush
declared, "A generation shaped by Vietnam must remember the lessons of
Vietnam: When America uses force in the world, the cause must be just,
the goal must be clear, and the victory must be overwhelming."[80]

Bush claimed that the two baby boomers currently serving as president and vice president had refused to mature. Subtly echoing song lyrics
from two popular 1960s rock groups—The Who and Crosby, Stills, Nash

and Young—Bush said: "Our generation has a chance to reclaim some essential values, to show we have grown up before we grow old. But when the moment for leadership came, this administration did not teach our children, it disillusioned them." He promised to correct the errors of others who had come of age in the 1960s. Bush spoke of how his upbringing had shaped his values and his attitudes toward government, then focused on what he had learned from the 1960s. "We must usher in an era of responsibility. My generation tested limits, and our country in some ways is better for it," he said, mentioning increased rights for women and minorities and concern for the environment. Nevertheless, "at times we lost our way, but we're coming home."[81]

References to the 1960s both implicit and explicit continued throughout the fall campaign, as both parties tried to use the era to their advantage. When asked in one debate to describe his approach to military and foreign policy issues, Gore spoke of having volunteered for military service in Vietnam. In return, Bush labeled Gore a 1960s-era Democrat. When Gore criticized Bush's tax cuts for the wealthy and his lack of proposals for spending on social programs, Bush countered that Gore's plan "would grow the federal government in the largest increase since Lyndon Baines Johnson in 1965." While Gore emphasized his Vietnam service, Bush claimed that Gore personified the excesses of baby boomers, trying to link Gore with Clinton's personal behavior. Asked why he had raised charges against Gore of possible fund-raising abuses, Bush said: "People need to be held responsible for the actions they take in life. I think that's part of the need for a cultural change."[82] Although it was Bush who had lived much of his young adulthood by the credo of self-indulgence, he succeeded in claiming the mature, responsible "good sixties" for himself and burdening his opponent with all the negative connotations of the "bad sixties."

As president Bush continued to think in terms of transforming the culture and reversing trends that had begun in the 1960s. In 2002, interpreting the events of September 11, 2001, in his State of the Union address, he said: "Our enemies believed America was weak and materialistic, that we would splinter in fear and selfishness. They were as wrong as they are evil." Praising the nation's response to the attacks, Bush said, "It was as if our entire country looked into a mirror and saw our better selves." He then uttered a phrase he had used repeatedly since his first race for Texas governor in 1994: "For too long our culture has said, 'If it feels good, do it.'" Now, he said, "America is embracing a new ethic and a new creed: 'Let's roll.' In the sacrifice of soldiers, the fierce brotherhood of firefighters, and the bravery and generosity of ordinary citizens, we have glimpsed what a new culture of responsibility could look like." The present "time of adversity," he said, "offers a unique moment of opportunity—a moment we must seize to change our culture."[83]

From 1994 to 2004—as governor, presidential candidate, and commander in chief—George W. Bush successfully used his anti-"sixties"—and, by extension, anti-Clinton and anti-Gore—identity and message as his partisan weapon of choice. It enabled Bush to carry the 2000 election—the nation's first election between two baby boomers and, in many ways, a battle over two competing versions of the 1960s. It also offered American voters an unusually polarized set of choices.

Bush's political rise from Texas to the White House taught him the potency of his anti-1960s message and his call to restore lost American virtues and certainties. But of all the U.S. presidential elections since 1960, none pitted competing visions of the 1960s against each other more starkly than his drive for reelection in 2004. As in 2000, the election matched two baby boomers against each other, but this time with even sharper focus and intensity as the election turned on the single most divisive issue of "the sixties": the Vietnam War.

10

Framing John Kerry

THE 2004 PRESIDENTIAL CAMPAIGN AND "THE SIXTIES"

The Bush campaign was relentless in portraying Kerry as an exemplar of everything that's wrong with the sixties. . . . We seesawed between each side trying to use the sixties for their purposes, both overtly and in a subterranean way.

Journalist Todd Purdum (2004)

THE 2004 ELECTION CAMPAIGN reignited the simmering fight over discordant memories of the 1960s by focusing on the most painful issue of that time: the war in Vietnam. The Democrats tried to take advantage of nominee Senator John Kerry's distinguished service record in the war: Kerry, a navy lieutenant, was awarded a Silver Star, a Bronze Star with Combat V for valor, and three Purple Hearts. As a decorated hero, to the Democrats he seemed emblematic of the "good sixties": a selfless volunteer who answered John Kennedy's challenge to "ask what you can do for your country" by joining the military in time of war. Kerry, however, had also vigorously protested against the war when he got back from Vietnam. This enabled Bush to use the 1960s against Kerry and to brand him as one more northeastern liberal example of the "bad sixties"—one of the longhaired elitist protesters who had caused America to lose the war in Vietnam. The wounds of the 1960s continued to bleed in 2004.

"Gallant Warrior, Principled Dissident": John Kerry's 1960s

Like George Bush, John Kerry spent a good portion of the 1960s at Yale (class of 1966), though his undergraduate experience was more like Al Gore's at Harvard than Bush's: interested in politics and public issues, he became president of the Yale Political Union, was elected by his classmates to give the senior oration, volunteered for officer candidate training in the U.S. Navy in his senior year, and was sent to Vietnam shortly after graduating. Upon his return from the war, Kerry became a prominent spokesman for the protest group Vietnam Veterans Against the War in 1970–71. "Unlike Mr. Bush, Mr. Gore or Mr. McCain," observed columnist Frank Rich during the 2004 campaign, Kerry "is the first in either party to have been both a leader in combat in Vietnam and a leader in the antiwar movement; he represents both the establishment that fueled our misadventure in Southeast Asia and the counterculture that changed America, for better and for worse, in revolt against it."[1] Kerry's campaign focused on his Vietnam service. He was frequently flanked by Vietnam veterans at rallies and in his ads. In fact his campaign may have been saved by a fellow veteran, propelling Kerry to victory in the Democratic primaries: only days before the Iowa caucuses, Jim Rassmann, a former Green Beret who served with Kerry in Vietnam but had not seen him since, flew to Iowa to tell an emotional story of how a wounded Kerry had saved his life when he was thrown overboard by an explosion.

Although by 2004 he had served Massachusetts in the Senate for nearly twenty years, Kerry's distinguished service in Vietnam remained his chief appeal for many Democratic primary voters. The main obstacle for any Democrat challenging Bush in the wake of 9/11 and ongoing conflicts in Iraq and Afghanistan was to prove that he could wage war effectively. Democrats chose Kerry partly because they believed that Republicans would not be able to tag him as weak on defense issues—as they had so many other Democrats since the 1960s—and that he was thus the most "electable" Democrat. In February 2004 party chairman Terry McAuliffe argued that one of Kerry's main assets was his "chest full of medals."[2] To his supporters, Kerry's candidacy was especially attractive because he appealed to a core segment of Democrats: those who had come to believe by the late 1960s that the Vietnam War was wrong. Furthermore, he had volunteered for the war, an act they took as symbolic of early 1960s idealism. As Todd Purdum reported, Kerry's service and protest history gave him "the cachet of gallant warrior and principled dissident," an attractive combination to Democrats.[3] "The biggest doubt about Democrats coming into this election was on the military: Do they respect the military and will they support spending for the military?" said Democratic pollster Stan Greenberg in the summer of 2004. "Kerry is making considerable progress on that."[4]

The Kerry campaign imagery focused primarily on events from the second half of the 1960s, but the early 1960s were there to be used as well. Many saw striking similarities between John F. Kerry and John F. Kennedy: Massachusetts Catholics elected to the Senate, decorated war veterans who had attended elite New England boarding schools and Ivy League colleges. Kennedy—as he had been for Clinton—was Kerry's political role model in his formative years. Kerry gave his first political speech as a student at St. Paul's School in November 1960, just before the presidential election, in support of Kennedy. Kerry was a passionate Kennedy supporter among a predominantly conservative Republican student body. He had been in the crowd when JFK gave his last campaign speech before the election at Boston Garden. Looking back on that event, Kerry recalled: "Suddenly I felt as if I were part of his campaign. It was exhilarating."[5]

In 1962 Kerry volunteered for Ted Kennedy's Senate campaign. At the time he was dating Jacqueline Kennedy's half-sister Janet Jennings Auchincloss. Kerry even met President Kennedy that summer in Rhode Island. Upon arriving to spend the weekend with Janet, Kerry, who was late, happened to stumble upon the president alone in the Auchincloss mansion, looking out over the Atlantic from a window. When the president walked over to greet Kerry, the soon-to-be college freshman said awkwardly, "Hi, I'm John Kerry." Later that day Kerry joined a group to sail with Kennedy. The two met again several weeks later at the America's Cup race, after which Kerry even had a quick discussion alone with Kennedy. "Nothing incredible," Kerry remembered. "But boy, it was memorable."[6]

Yet despite the many similarities with Kennedy, Kerry—unlike Clinton—shied away from comparisons with him, in part because he thought his Vietnam record would speak for itself. Clinton talked openly of his handshake with Kennedy, but Kerry never drew attention to the fact that he had actually met and spoken with Kennedy several times. Even though Kerry and Kennedy shared the same initials, "you don't see him picking up on the Kennedy stuff," noted Rick Perlstein in the summer of 2004.[7] Kerry hardly mentioned Kennedy, though he told biographer Douglas Brinkley of his admiration for him.

Donna Shalala, asked at the time if the election was "going to revisit the 1960s," answered: "I doubt it. Most of the people that are going to vote weren't here in the 1960s."[8] Indeed, anyone younger than forty-five had no direct connection to Vietnam—as combatants, potential draftees, or protesters. Forty percent of Americans had not even been born in 1975, when the last U.S. troops left Vietnam. But the 2004 election showed just how powerfully the memory of Vietnam and the 1960s in fact lived on.

1960s Nostalgia in the Democratic Primaries

During the 2004 Democratic primaries, commentators spoke often of the "good" and "bad" 1960s. Republican pundit David Brooks imagined the typical Iowa Democratic voter as a teacher in her fifties, "a moderate,

optimistic, progressive educator who wants to believe in politics again."
To Brooks, such a voter longed for the spirit of the "good sixties": "Conservatives sometimes say that Democrats want to go back to the 1960s of Woodstock and the peace movement. That's not quite right. The quintessential Democrat here doesn't want to return to the angry, disruptive, long-hair style of the late 1960s. She wants to return to the confident, short-hair, pre-counterculture mood of the early 1960s."[9]

The memory of the 1960s, regardless of which part of the era was being recalled, still struck a powerful emotional chord for many Democrats, no matter how accurate or inaccurate the recollection might be. Eight days after a disappointing third-place finish in Iowa, Howard Dean, the antiwar candidate who a few weeks earlier had been widely favored to win the nomination, came in second in the New Hampshire primary. Attempting to rekindle his flagging campaign, in a speech to supporters Dean invoked nostalgia for the 1960s. "When I was twenty-one years old, it was the end of the Civil Rights movement, and America had suffered greatly. The Rev. Dr. Martin Luther King, Jr. was killed that year," Dean recalled inaccurately, and Robert F. Kennedy soon after. (Dean in fact turned twenty-one on November 7, 1969, a year and a half after the assassinations of King and Kennedy.) He then proceeded to blur other events from the 1960s into a single year in which he supposedly turned twenty-one: the deaths of four girls in the bombing of a Birmingham, Alabama, church (actually in 1963); the Civil Rights Act (passed in 1964); the Voting Rights Act (passed in 1965); Thurgood Marshall's confirmation to the Supreme Court (actually in 1967); and the introduction of Medicare (passed in 1965). In the 1960s, Dean declared, "We felt like we were all in this together, that if one person was left behind, then America wasn't as strong as it should be or as good as it could be."[10] His passionate delivery and the audience's enthusiastic reaction showed that historical accuracy mattered less than the emotional responses "the sixties" still called forth.

"By now the 1960s have come to resemble a *Rashomon* scene in which two actors crouch on a rainy veranda revisiting versions of an imaginary narrative to a third," observed a reporter. "On one side is the man who remembers the schisms of the sixties splitting a generation asunder. . . . On the other is a man who recalls a decade that cleared the cultural stage for dialogue involving women, blacks and gays." In light of the latter, "sentimentality about 1968 may have a certain predictable appeal." As historian Bruce Schulman argued, "Dean's attempts to rehabilitate his candidacy turn on 1960s authenticity, portrayed as the antithesis of public relations and spin." Others defended Dean's address despite its inaccuracy. One conservative called it "uplifting and genuine." Roger Wilkins offered the opinion that "every person has a right to interpret 1968 in his own way." It was a pivotal year, Wilkins said, and referring to Dean's critics added: "People are too harsh. . . . It's important to keep the ideals alive, to let people know it can all be had again."[11]

Emphasis on the 1960s intensified with the growing sentiment that Iraq was becoming another Vietnam. As early as the fall of 2003, only six months after the start of the Iraq War, critics began making the comparison. "Americans remain haunted by the specter of a defeat in some distant realm," Stanley Karnow wrote. While the war in Iraq began well, it was now "apparent that Iraq, if not exactly 'another Vietnam,' could degenerate into an equally calamitous debacle." Karnow accused Bush of repeating his predecessors' errors. Just as each president since World War II had asserted that Vietnam was central to the Soviets' desire for power, "similarly, Bush . . . has portrayed himself as a crusader and Saddam Hussein as the evil genius behind international terrorism." Karnow noted other similarities as well. In neither case did leaders produce credible evidence for the war's justification, and in both conflicts the United States was unable to defeat a popular insurgency. Most important, in both instances the United States claimed it was making great progress while the evidence of the fighting contradicted the claim. Bush's optimistic prognoses "remind me of the bulletins from Vietnam that reassured us that 'victory is just around the corner,'" Karnow wrote.[12]

Explaining why Vietnam continued to linger in the national imagination, Frank Rich observed, "We want to believe that the wounds of Vietnam have long since been anesthetized by the panacea we call closure" and that the tensions of the Cold War were in the past. "And yet: Even as the actual war fades in memory, Vietnam still looms as a festering culture war, a permanent fixture of the national collective unconscious, always on tap for fresh hostilities," said Rich. "How do you ask a man to be the last man to die for a mistake?" he wrote, quoting Kerry's 1971 testimony before the Senate Foreign Relations Committee, concluding, "The question [still] hangs in the air . . . in 2004."[13]

That year's election also renewed debate over how much military experience a president needed. Since the Cold War's end in 1991 the candidate with the most military experience had lost every general election. Clearly military service was not viewed as essential. Decorated Vietnam veteran and Medal of Honor winner Bob Kerrey, Democratic senator from Nebraska, failed to capture the 1992 Democratic nomination. George H. W. Bush, twice awarded the Distinguished Flying Cross as a navy pilot in World War II, and Bob Dole, awarded two Purple Hearts and a Bronze Star, both lost presidential elections to Bill Clinton, a candidate with no military experience. In 2000 George W. Bush, the delinquent National Guardsman, won the Republican nomination over John McCain, who spent more than five years as a prisoner of war in Vietnam, and then in the general election defeated Al Gore, who had served in Vietnam as an army journalist. But after 9/11 "the president-as-warrior seems painfully relevant," wrote one reporter. "And the old question—what did you do in your generation's war?—is back, with a vengeance." As a consequence, what Bush and Kerry did in the late 1960s and early 1970s came under renewed scrutiny.[14]

"Next year is the thirty-year anniversary of the fall of Saigon," observed political scientist Darrell West in early 2004, looking ahead to the upcoming presidential campaign, "so we will see a lot of Vietnam imagery." He noted, "Reagan ran against Vietnam. Bush the father ran against Vietnam. Vietnam is almost as controversial today as it was forty years ago," adding, "the fact that Kerry was in the middle of the antiwar movement gives Republicans a big target to say, 'People were dying in Vietnam and this guy was sitting next to Jane Fonda.'"[15] Sure enough, soon after his New Hampshire primary victory Kerry's critics began to portray him as a radical 1960s figure. In early February an anti-Kerry group circulated on the Internet a blurred image of Kerry sitting several feet behind Fonda at a 1970 antiwar rally in Valley Forge, Pennsylvania. Within days a doctored photograph was posted in which Kerry appeared to be sitting right next to Fonda at a 1971 antiwar rally in Mineola, New York; the photo of Kerry had been merged with another of Fonda addressing a 1972 antiwar rally in Miami. The doctored photo even had a fake Associated Press logo superimposed on it to make it appear genuine.[16]

Democrats earnestly believed that Kerry's Vietnam service would prevent the Right from using the 1960s against him, but they were mistaken. "It's hard to do this kind of scurrilous thing with the Jane Fonda pictures against someone who took three bullets in Vietnam," one Kerry adviser responded confidently to the hoax. "It's hard to say that someone who's served in combat, been decorated for bravery, is soft on defense."[17]

But others would come to view the incident as symbolic of a strategy that deftly manipulated memories of the 1960s. "The attempt to portray [Kerry] as some kind of Jane Fonda–like figure [was] a continuation of the sixties-demonization process that has gone on for some forty years," wrote David Halberstam. "Though two citizen movements of the sixties—the Civil Rights movement and the antiwar movement—represented, I believe, citizen politics at its best, they were vilified in the tidal change of American politics." As Halberstam saw it, "both movements might have taken place at the very center of American life, but the poster boy for the sixties was a stoned hippie at Woodstock. A vacuum had been created, and the new Republican Party rushed in."[18]

"Jane Fonda has been roped into a comeback," observed Frank Rich, "drafted into a political attack on Mr. Kerry." The anti-Kerry group that published the photo "portrays him as a radical, a traitor and, worst of all, 'hippielike.' The *Weekly Standard* characterizes the antiwar Vietnam veterans of that time as 'hairy men, many with *Easy Rider* mustaches.'" To Rich, such rhetoric was "meant to complement the ubiquitous Vietnam-era photo of a decidedly clean-shaven, unhippielike Mr. Bush at the moment he is joining the Texas Air National Guard," with his father about to pin bars to his uniform. Simultaneously, an Internet group "rushed to brand Mr. Kerry with another trait associated with sixties antiwar counterculture: sexual hedonism," spreading a fabricated story that Kerry, like Bill Clinton, was romantically involved with an intern. "Maybe that other 'hippielike' activity, drug use, will be the next up to bat," Rich wrote.[19]

The Right focused intently on Kerry's antiwar past. Republican congressman Steve Buyer said, "[Kerry] can't run on a war record when his true record is an antiwar record."[20] Conservatives charged that the senator still longed for the activism and counterculture of the late 1960s. "Kerry seems to be living in another time, playing a movie of Vietnam over and over in his mind," wrote Byron York of the *National Review*. He criticized Kerry's 1969 decision to buy a movie camera to reenact the incident in Vietnam for which he earned a Purple Heart and a Silver Star, and for playing the film in an interview during his 1996 Senate campaign. In that interview, York said, Kerry fast-forwarded, froze, and rewound the footage, played portions in slow motion, and provided commentary. "In John Kerry's home-entertainment center, it's always 1969. It's sometimes that way in his campaign, too," York wrote. Jimi Hendrix music played at Kerry rallies, and Peter Yarrow of Peter, Paul, and Mary accompanied the candidate on his tour bus. When Yarrow sang "Puff, the Magic Dragon" at a campaign stop in Iowa, "Kerry lifted his fingers to his mouth for a quick toke on an imaginary joint. You can almost see his thick mane of silver hair returning to the shaggy brown 'do' of those days."[21]

York's reference to Kerry's hair to characterize him as a dangerous 1960s radical was a deliberate choice, for "the sixties" immediately evoke physical imagery in people's consciousness. "When you see those [old] photographs of John Kerry with the long hair, it looks so bizarre," said former political reporter Don Baker. Conservatives "are capitalizing on this exotic appearance from our perspective forty years later. . . . I haven't seen any photographs of [Bush] from the seventies that look very much different than the way he looks today," Baker observed. "But John Kerry—boy, he went all the way in terms of the seventies look, and now he's paying a price for that."[22]

Republicans were arguing that Kerry "was a longhair, he was a protester, he hated his country and his government," said Jeff Shesol in the summer of 2004. "They're trying to take the Kerry of the early 1970s and make him into a 'sixties radical.' When George Bush was drinking beer, Kerry volunteered to go to Vietnam. But they'll rewrite the narrative if [Democrats] let them."[23]

Throughout the spring of 2004, Kerry's conservative critics insisted that he was the one who had raised the subject. "This whole debate about John Kerry in the war, nobody cares, except him. . . . [H]e's so obsessed with the sixties," argued conservative activist David Keene. To his detriment, Kerry's focus on his Vietnam experience brought up "the whole question of the credibility of the Democratic Party on defense questions." When Kerry won the Hawaii primary, said Keene, "he released a statement saying how great it was to win the primary of this last place he stopped before he went to Vietnam. It's not exactly how most people think of Hawaii."[24]

Pierre du Pont acknowledged "a lot of echoes from 1968" in the 2004 campaign. "The 1960s have started to come back," he declared. In the 1980s "Democrats said, 'We don't want to be called a liberal because this conservative guy [Reagan] is doing so much better than we liberals did before. We ought to get rid of the L-word.' But, it's back in the Democratic Party, too. Kerry, he's a sixties liberal," du Pont said.[25]

Others on the right were also quick to link Kerry to the excesses of the 1960s. "The sixties were a cultural clash," emphasized Brent Bozell. Whereas political battles get resolved by elections, "cultural wars take place over a generation. And what was launched in the sixties hasn't been resolved." To Bozell, the rise of the Right was attributable to "the aftershocks of the cultural war that began in the sixties." The era's protesters and drug users "didn't go away. They grew up, but they went into other fields: the media, education, the arts, Congress. And one of them is running for president."[26]

Kerry was doubtless influenced by the 1960s, but was he in fact a radical when he joined the antiwar movement in the early 1970s, as the Right contended? Those who worked alongside Kerry in Vietnam Veterans Against the War recalled that he "often took steps to moderate the group's actions, believing it was better—for it, and him—to work within the political system that he ultimately sought to join," wrote Todd Purdum. "When he organized the mass march on Washington that resulted in his Senate testimony, Ms. Fonda was nowhere to be seen." Kerry had adamantly argued that the organization's April 1971 Washington protest must not be marked by violence. At the time he was criticized by the group's increasingly radical members. He disagreed with the idea of suing Nixon to end the war and soon left the group over, in his words, "differences in political philosophy." He was not involved in later, more radical stunts, such as the 1972 takeover of the Statue of Liberty and protests at the Republican National Convention.[27]

Other accounts also described a less-than-radical Kerry. In the eighteen months he worked with the group, "the clean-shaven, shorter-haired, neatly dressed Mr. Kerry, dozens of veterans recalled in interviews, had little patience for any [radical or violent behavior]," wrote one reporter. "He was almost always the most conservative man in the room." As Al Hubbard, one of the organization's leaders in the early 1970s, saw it, "he was working in the system, and he wanted to stay in the system. He had his own personal agenda. I think he was just kind of doing dress rehearsals for public office."[28] Even a once-confidential F.B.I. memorandum of April 29, 1971, part of twenty thousand pages of previously secret F.B.I. files released during the 2004 presidential campaign, described Kerry as a "popular and eloquent figure" who was "glib, cool, and displayed best what the moderate elements wanted to reflect."[29]

To some 2004 observers it was Bush, not Kerry, who better represented "the sixties." "Bush doesn't take responsibility for his actions. To me, that's the 1960s," said political scientist Alan Wolfe. "Bush is a far more sixties figure than John Kerry, because in the sixties you tried to get out of the war, which is exactly what Bush did. You didn't volunteer; nobody I knew volunteered," Wolfe said, describing Kerry as "a countercultural figure resisting the 1960s, whereas Bush is much more part of that 'me-first' generation." Narcissism dominated the decade, Wolfe stated, and "Bush is the most narcissistic man in public life I've ever seen," whereas Kerry "embodies an old or almost aristocratic idea of service, and he made a certain amount of sacrifice." So even though Kerry's politics, not Bush's, reflected the decade, "culturally, it looks the other way around."[30]

Although he reacted against the era, "Bush, more than is immediately apparent, is himself a sixties President," wrote Nicholas Lemann. "Bush's sixties side shows itself in the form of an unperturbed confidence that the world can now be remade entirely." Lemann called Bush's effort to democratize the Middle East "right out of 'The Times They Are A-Changin'.'" Asking if Middle Easterners were "somehow beyond the reach of liberty . . . condemned by history or culture to live in despotism . . . never to know freedom," Bush had declared that everyone "has the ability and the right to be free." To Lemann such rhetoric recalled another 1960s Bob Dylan song, "Blowin' in the Wind."[31]

The campaign became in due course a battle over competing definitions of the 1960s. "The piece of the sixties that Kerry is reviving is his
military service in Vietnam. And of course his opponents will want to revive the other part of the Kerry sixties, which is his opposition to the war
when he came back, and try to tar him with that," explained historian
Alan Brinkley in March 2004.[32] Within weeks Kerry's opponents would
begin to do exactly what Brinkley predicted.

In 1971, testifying before the Senate Foreign Relations Committee,
Kerry spoke of a Detroit antiwar conference where veterans had described
how "they had personally raped, cut off ears, cut off heads, taped wires
from portable telephones to human genitals and turned up the power,
cut off limbs, blown up bodies, randomly shot at civilians, razed villages
in a fashion reminiscent of Genghis Khan, shot cattle and dogs for fun,
poisoned food stocks and generally ravaged the countryside of South Vietnam." Kerry had been told by the veterans that these were "not isolated
incidents but crimes committed on a day-to-day basis with the full awareness of officers at all levels of command." Now, Todd Purdum wrote in
2004, Kerry's "words have come back to haunt his presidential campaign,"
as Bush supporters "question whether Mr. Kerry is 'a proud war hero or
angry antiwar protester.'"[33]

Republicans launched an attack on Kerry for his 1971 statements
soon after the thirty-third anniversary of his testimony. Representative
Joe Wilson, a South Carolina Republican, remarked that "in a sad act of
political theater, John Kerry accused American soldiers of rape, torture,
murder, and even offered up comparisons to Genghis Khan." Texas Republican Sam Johnson asked: "Is it any wonder my comrades from Vietnam and I have a nickname for him similar to Hanoi Jane? He is called
Hanoi John."[34]

Two days later, on April 24, Bush released a $10 million ad campaign
criticizing Kerry's voting record on military issues. At the same time a
Bush adviser said she was disturbed that in 1971 Kerry had "participated
in the ceremony where veterans threw their medals away, and he only
pretended to throw his." A day later Vice President Dick Cheney joined
the discussion in remarks at Westminster College in Missouri, where
Winston Churchill made his 1946 "Iron Curtain" speech, questioning
Kerry's Senate record "on vital issues of national security." Cheney's remarks outraged Democrats. Senator Richard Durbin expressed outrage
that Cheney, who had "used his deferments to avoid military service,"
was now attacking "a man who volunteered, risked his life, and received
awards from this country for his heroism." Kerry told an Ohio paper that
"veterans are going to be very angry at a president who can't account for

his own service in the National Guard, and a vice president who got every deferment in the world and decided he had better things to do, criticizing somebody who fought for their country and served."[35]

Commentators differed sharply as to why the memory of Vietnam continued to linger. "I thought the Vietnam War was over," said conservative political commentator William Kristol in a PBS *NewsHour* discussion with liberal journalist Tom Oliphant. "Thirty-five years ago is thirty-five years ago. Let's have a debate about Iraq, not about Vietnam." Oliphant noted that both candidates were using Vietnam for political gain. For Kerry, "it's central to his biography," while for Bush, it was important "to poke holes in that biography and cause people to doubt it. It's politics more than it's Vietnam history."[36]

Others were not so sure. "We live under the shadow of [the 1960s]. And that's never been clearer than in the last months," remarked Maurice Isserman in May 2004. The divisions over Iraq resembled those over Vietnam, he said, and predicted that "if it turns out the war in Iraq is World War II—liberation of Paris—Bush wins. If it turns out that it's Vietnam— endless stalemate, endless bloodletting, murky goals, atrocities—then Bush loses." Kerry's campaign "is counting heavily that their version of John Kerry's role in the 1960s will prevail" over Bush's effort to brand him as unpatriotic. In Isserman's view, "the manipulation of the images left over from the sixties continues to define the basic fault lines of American politics."[37]

Some thought that Kerry's rapid rise to the nomination in 2004 revealed the party's internal tensions brought on by the 1960s. "The sixties won't go away because there was such a huge division over the war," commented Josh Gilder, a speechwriter for Reagan and George H. W. Bush. Kerry's campaign showed "how confused [Democrats] are about it. They're pretending that they think of all Vietnam vets as heroes," but in the 1960s "that is not how they treated any of them coming back. They called them war criminals, they held up offensive signs to them, they greeted them with contempt . . . born largely out of a sense of shame on their part because they didn't go to war themselves. . . . They took the easy way out."[38]

This continued anger toward "the sixties" provided fuel to the Right. Columnist Maureen Dowd remarked: "It's amazing . . . how obsessed conservatives still are with pulverizing that decade. Their disgust with the sixties spurs oxymoronic—and moronic—behavior." Dowd believed that Bush officials viewed the Iraq War as "banishing post-Vietnam ambivalence about using force and toughening up what they saw as the Clintonesque sixties mentality—a weak, pinprick-bombing, if-it-feels-good-do-it attitude. Their new motto was: If it makes someone else feel bad, do it," she quipped. "W., who had tuned out during the sixties, preferring frat parties to war moratoriums and civil rights marches . . . was on board with his regents' retro concerns" and invaded Iraq in part "to expunge the ghosts of Vietnam." On a personal note Dowd remarked that although she herself did not "appreciate the sixties" at the time, "I've become nostalgic for the idealistic passion of the sixties" and regretted "how far we've come from the spirit" of the decade.[39]

Kerry himself spoke of the Right's efforts to invoke the specter of the late 1960s. "I find it kind of sad and almost pathetic that thirty-five years later these same arguments are made," he said. His critics "haven't gotten over the war. . . . [T]hey blame me for something that was much bigger." Indeed, for the Right, Kerry was even more a symbol of 1960s anarchy than Clinton ever was. "Mr. Clinton was a minor player in the culture wars of those days," wrote Purdum, "while Mr. Kerry was a major one, a lightning rod whom some contemporaries can neither forget nor forgive."[40]

"The Sixties" and the National Conventions

On the opening night of the 2004 Democratic National Convention, Bill Clinton emphasized Kerry's biography in a way that recalled the idealism and emphasis on selfless service of the early 1960s. "During the Vietnam War, many young men, including the current president, the vice president and me, could have gone to Vietnam and didn't," said the former president. "John Kerry came from a privileged background. He could have avoided going too, but instead, he said: Send me." Clinton then proceeded to speak of Kerry's Vietnam service and of his support for various public policy measures, each time repeating the refrain, "John Kerry said: Send me." Clinton closed his remarks with a plea that recalled Kerry's Vietnam service in the navy. "Since we're all in the same boat, we should choose a captain of our ship who is a brave, good man, who knows how to steer a vessel through troubled waters, to the calm seas and the clear skies of our more perfect union. . . . Send John Kerry."[41]

In his acceptance speech three days later Kerry immediately addressed a charge that had haunted Democrats since the 1960s: that they were unpatriotic. He began, "I'm John Kerry, and I'm reporting for duty," adding, "We are here tonight because we love our country." Kerry spoke of his father's service in World War II. As Clinton had, Kerry recalled the promise and idealism of the early 1960s, declaring that during his high school years, "John Kennedy called my generation to service. It was the beginning of a great journey, a time to march for civil rights, for voting rights, for the environment, for women, for peace. We believed we could change the world. And you know what? We did. But we're not finished."[42]

The first mention of Vietnam in Kerry's speech was an acknowledgment of the fellow Vietnam veterans who had welcomed him to the stage that evening. He and they had "fought for this nation because we loved it," and "we still know how to fight for our country." Recalling his combat experience in Vietnam, and not coincidentally drawing a parallel with the war to Iraq, he said: "I know what kids go through when they're carrying an M-16 in a dangerous place, and they can't tell friend from foe. . . . I know what it's like to write letters home telling your family that everything's all right, when you're not sure that that's true. As president, I will wage this war [in Iraq] with the lessons I learned in war."[43]

Kerry never mentioned his antiwar past but referred instead to those who did not believe that Democrats were patriotic. "Before wrapping themselves in the flag," such people must realize that when some "say America can do better, that is not a challenge to patriotism; it is the heart and soul of patriotism. You see that flag up there?" he asked, pointing to the rafters. "I fought under that flag. . . . That flag flew from the gun turret right behind my head and it was shot through and through and tattered, but it never ceased to wave in the wind. It draped the caskets of men that I served with and friends I grew up with. . . . [It] doesn't belong to any president . . . to any ideology . . . to any party. It belongs to all the American people."[44]

One veteran liberal activist was pleased that Kerry mentioned the inspiration he received from the 1960s. "There was a line in Kerry's acceptance speech[,] . . . 'We marched for civil rights and peace and now we've got more things to march for,'" recalled Staughton Lynd. "To me, that line meant more than anything else in his talk, because Clinton obviously had a left-handed relationship to the sixties; that is, he went to Oxford to dodge the draft." Because Lynd taught at Yale when Kerry was there, "I understand where John Kerry was coming from—that is, critical of the war, but at the same time plugged into this whole mindset of 'For God, For Country, and For Yale,' and volunteering for officer candidate school, and then appalled by the death of some of his friends needlessly, as he perceived it." Though Lynd differed from Kerry ideologically, "I can understand his trajectory, and it means something to me that a guy who threw his ribbons, if not his medals, over the White House fence is running for president."[45]

In the weeks following Kerry's speech, some believed that he had successfully taken the political dialogue past issues relating to old divisions. "This election in some ways is the first that is maybe moving beyond fighting over the sixties," Bruce Schulman hoped after the Democratic convention. The obsession "doesn't seem to be so dominant the way it was during the politics of the 1990s."[46]

But in the month after the convention, the anti-Kerry group Swift Boat Veterans for Truth unleashed a large national ad campaign attacking Kerry's war record. Calling itself "a non-partisan group representing more than 250 Swift Boat veterans who served with Senator John Kerry in Vietnam," the group said it was "an independent organization dedicated to correcting the false statements made by Senator Kerry about his service record in Vietnam and the service records of the men who served with him." Denying that it was "affiliated with any political party . . . or any candidate,"[47] the group would nonetheless spend $22.4 million opposing John Kerry's presidential bid.[48]

In fact none of the veterans who appeared in the ads were crew members on the boat Kerry commanded. Although they claimed that they had "served with John Kerry," the best they could say was that they had been on other swift boats—hardly the same thing. Notably, all of Kerry's crewmates endorsed the senator for president. Nevertheless, the ads succeeded in attracting enormous media attention. In one television ad, "Any Questions?" Vietnam veterans spoke directly to the camera. After two of them declared, "I served with John Kerry," a montage of recorded voices was heard against a background of ominous music and pictures of a longhaired Kerry and other war protesters:

John Kerry has not been honest about what happened in Vietnam.

He is lying about his record.

I know John Kerry is lying about his first Purple Heart, because I treated him for that injury.

John Kerry lied to get his Bronze Star. I know, I was there, I saw what happened.

His account of what happened and what actually happened are the difference between night and day.

John Kerry has not been honest.

And he lacks the capacity to lead.

When the chips were down, you could not count on John Kerry. John Kerry is no war hero.

He betrayed all his shipmates. He lied before the Senate.

John Kerry betrayed the men and women he served with in Vietnam.

He dishonored his country, he most certainly did.

I served with John Kerry.

John Kerry cannot be trusted.[49]

In 1996 Adrian L. Lonsdale, a member of the group, had made a statement at a news conference in support of Kerry, who was seeking reelection to the Senate, mentioning the "bravado and courage of the young
officers that ran the Swift Boats." But in an interview shortly after the
2004 ad aired Lonsdale expressed a very different sentiment. "We won
the battle. Kerry went home and lost the war for us. He called us rapers
and killers and that's not true. If he expects our loyalty, we should expect
loyalty from him."[50]

Three more television ads appeared in August, followed by three in
September and two in October. In response to the group's initial attacks,
former Georgia Democratic senator Max Cleland, who lost three limbs
fighting in Vietnam, attempted to deliver personally to Bush, vacation-
ing at his Texas ranch, a letter, signed by eight Democratic senators who
were veterans, demanding that Bush renounce the group's ads. Cleland
was stopped by a Secret Service agent and a state trooper. "For those of us
in the Vietnam era, we're having to go through Vietnam again," Cleland
told reporters.[51]

That evening PBS aired a roundtable discussion on why Vietnam
continued to play such a large role in American politics. "The elder
George Bush said in his inaugural in 1989 the Vietnam War cleaves us
still," noted presidential historian Michael Beschloss. "That was only
fourteen years after the end of the war. Here we are almost thirty years
later, and it still does." To Beschloss, "Vietnam is a Rorschach test" of
one's sentiments toward the 1960s, particularly since Kerry had sought
to use his war record to exhibit strength on military matters. The PBS
commentators expressed surprise that Vietnam remained an issue. Historian Richard Norton Smith had thought that "the historical significance"
of the recent Democratic convention "was that the Democrats had finally managed to lay the ghost of Vietnam to rest. I think I was probably
premature."[52]

At the very height of late August's anti-Kerry ads veteran Democratic
figures offered suggestions. "The lesson of the 1988 campaign is that negative campaigning must be dealt with head-on," said Michael Dukakis.
"I didn't do that," he recalled, and hoped that Kerry would not repeat
his mistake.[53] Others believed that Bush's attack strategy would eventually backfire. "I was surprised that the Republicans forced the issue of
the sixties, because this would call attention to Bush's lack of a military
record and that Kerry has a military record of some honor," said Arthur
Schlesinger. "But I guess they wanted to destroy Kerry. . . . They used the
longhaired testimony and so on. But I think it will eventually boomer-
ang," he predicted.[54]

"The presidential campaign is doing the time warp. Again," wrote Todd Purdum three days later. More than three decades after Kerry's Senate testimony, "the still-living cast of characters has revived the debate that has roiled the nation since the 1960s." Bush and Kerry supporters "were squaring off in the ideological, cultural and class divide that began with Vietnam," continued with Nixon's "appeal to the 'silent majority,' and remains as current as George W. Bush's election-year appeal to the 'heart and soul of America' in the theater of a new war." As Michael Kazin told Purdum, "the 60's was a domestic civil war, and a lot of the issues have never been resolved about whether the war was right or not. The veterans are dividing on that issue, as much as on the issue of what Kerry did or didn't do, said or didn't say 30 years ago," but "culture wars tend to go on and on and on, especially when the people involved in starting them are still alive."[55]

In the days before their September convention Republicans vehemently attacked Kerry's Vietnam record. Bob Dole went so far as to charge that "with three Purple Hearts, he never bled that I know of. And they're all superficial wounds." He later apologized after Kerry telephoned him to protest the smear. At the convention Morton Blackwell mocked Kerry by handing delegates adhesive bandages decorated with small purple hearts, which many wore on their face and hands.[56] George H. W. Bush was asked if the use of Vietnam in the campaign was "legitimate." Noting that in the 1960s he supported LBJ's Vietnam policy, Bush claimed that the issue was whether Kerry's 1971 testimony "impugning the . . . integrity and the honor of those who were still serving" was justified; therefore questions about Kerry's charges were "legitimate." Kerry's testimony, he said, "brutalized people that were still serving or who had served." Bush then praised the U.S. troops' reception on their return after the Gulf War. "Vietnam veterans [were] marching with the Desert Storm veterans. . . . I was emotional when I saw it, saying, 'They're getting their just due at last.'" When asked, "But that's different than John Kerry's service overseas, right?" Bush said it was not, because Kerry "came back and said people were gouging eyes out."[57] The former president's remarks gave an unmistakable signal that Republicans would continue to make an issue of Kerry's anti-Vietnam protests.

Running against "the Sixties": The Fall 2004 Campaign

"Who would have thought that almost thirty years after the last Americans left Saigon we would still be arguing in a presidential campaign about who went to Vietnam and how well they served?" wrote David Halberstam in September 2004. "But that's the nature of Vietnam—it never really leaves us. It was the second American Civil War, us against ourselves, the blue America against the red America—indeed, one America blue and the other red these days in no small part because of that war."[58]

Liberals stoked the same fires as conservatives by presenting Iraq as another Vietnam. "You won't see us militarily intervening in foreign countries for a long time after this war," predicted Michael Dukakis the week before the Republican convention.[59] As Frank Rich put it, "Vietnam keeps popping out of America's darkest closet." Beyond the fact that Kerry served in Vietnam while Bush did not, this recurrent reference to Vietnam was due to "a televised war in Iraq that resembles its Southeast Asian predecessor in its unpopularity, its fictional provocation and its unknown exit strategy." Neither the Iraq War nor "its Vietnam undertow" would disappear soon, Rich went on to suggest. "But while Vietnam cannot be escaped, that hasn't stopped both [candidates] from working overtime in their fruitless efforts to escape it. Their motives could not be more different," he argued, as Bush feared comparisons between Iraq and Vietnam, while Kerry feared talk of his Vietnam protests.[60]

Kerry tried vigorously to obscure his antiwar past. The autumn of 2004 saw the release of a Kerry film biography, *Going Upriver: The Long War of John Kerry*, produced by George Butler, a friend of Kerry's since the 1960s. The first third of the film focused on Kerry's Vietnam service while the rest documented his 1971 involvement with the antiwar movement. But on the campaign trail Kerry completely avoided the subject of his antiwar past. His supporters urged him to speak to the issue. "The person who might benefit most from seeing *Going Upriver* is Mr. Kerry himself," wrote Rich, noting that a CIA officer from "the Kerry-Bush generation" had recently written, "It takes a special courage to speak out against a cause for which you were once prepared to die." To Rich, "the courageous hero of George Butler's film [is] all but invisible in the cautious candidate running for president." Noting that Kerry's views against the Vietnam War at the time were widely shared, Rich urged him to draw the comparison between Iraq and Vietnam.[61]

One week before the election Bush turned to a 1960s icon to argue his case. Throughout 2004 Kerry was reluctant to compare himself to JFK. In the campaign's closing days it was Bush—like Reagan before him—who invoked Kennedy. On October 26 Bush said that Kerry's "record not only stands in opposition to me, but in opposition to the great tradition of the Democrat [*sic*] Party of America. The party of Franklin Roosevelt and Harry Truman and John Kennedy is rightly remembered for confidence and resolve in times of crisis." But, Bush maintained, "Senator Kerry has turned his back on 'pay any price' and 'bear any burden,' and he has replaced those commitments with 'wait and see' and 'cut and run.'"[62]

Bush's comments—again as Reagan's had—angered Democrats. "It's hard for me to listen to President Bush invoking my father's memory to attack John Kerry," read a statement from Caroline Kennedy, who praised Kerry's courage and strength. "President Kennedy inspired and united the country and so will John Kerry," she added. "President Bush is doing just the opposite. All of us who revere the strength and resolve of President Kennedy will be supporting John Kerry on Election Day."[63] Kennedy special counsel Theodore C. Sorensen wrote the next day that Bush's use of Kennedy "proves once again that he has no shame."[64]

With Bush's victory over Kerry in the November election—nearly thirty-five years after the 1960s came to an end—the media reached for various political and cultural issues related to that decade to explain his reelection. Bush won, a reporter wrote, because in Ohio an anti–gay marriage ballot measure significantly boosted Republican turnout.[65] In Iraq, U.S. soldiers referred to Republican attacks on Kerry's antiwar past to explain their vote for Bush. One soldier who said he "believes the attacks on Mr. Kerry's military record have substance" thought that "Kerry looks like he folds under pressure. To me he seems too jittery. They say his medals are false." Another army private criticized Kerry's past protests against the Vietnam War.[66]

"The first thing Democrats must try to grasp as they cast their eyes over the smoking ruins of the election is the continuing power of the culture wars," wrote Thomas Frank three days after the election. "Thirty-six years ago, President Richard Nixon championed a noble 'silent majority' while his vice president, Spiro Agnew, accused liberals of twisting the news. In nearly every election since," Frank argued, "liberalism has been vilified as a flag-burning, treason-coddling, upper-class affectation."[67]

Maureen Dowd also saw the results as one more attack on the 1960s. Karl Rove "is happy to crush the liberal elites inspired by Kennedy's New Frontier," she wrote a few days after Bush's victory. "Like the president, vice president and defense secretary, General Karl wanted to wipe out the gray, if-it-feels-good-do-it, blame-America-first, doused-in-Vietnam-guilt sixties and turn the clock back to the black-and-white Manichaean values of the 50s."[68]

Republican strategists referred as well to the 1960s to explain Bush's victory. "We have come to an ending point in a long transition that began in 1968," asserted former national Republican Party chairman Donald L. Fowler a week after Kerry's defeat. Since 1968 "the old Roosevelt majority coalition has cracked and creaked away under various kinds of racial, religious, social and international forces, and this election was the end point in that transition."[69]

Many others were eager to point to the candidates' own experiences in the 1960s to explain the election results. At Yale, Kerry and Bush "had disliked each other before they knew each other," wrote Evan Thomas after Bush's win. "Bush did not remember Kerry but he knew the type: sanctimonious suck-ups who looked down on fun-loving fellows like George W. Bush." To Bush, "guys like Kerry were not out just to ruin Yale. They wanted to take over the whole country, to impose the smug, know-it-all liberal ideology on regular, God-fearing, hardworking Americans." The hostility between Bush and Kerry, Thomas wrote, "went beyond party or ideology or styles of leadership. Each saw the other as a symbol of the wrong side of the great post-1960s divide."[70]

Bush's reelection "shows that the political strategy that conservative Republicans developed in the late 1970s is still viable," wrote the *New Republic*'s John B. Judis. Bush won victories in formerly Democratic states by stressing military and cultural issues. In the 1970s, Judis later wrote, the Right "appealed to white, working-class voters enraged by Democrats' support for civil rights, feminism, and peaceful co-existence with the Soviet Union."[71] To Andrei Cherny, a Kerry campaign worker, many voters viewed Democrats as belonging to "the culturally different 'other' that Republicans have had so much fun and success castigating since the late sixties."[72]

"John Kerry thought that he could be a healing figure to close the loop with the sixties," commented Todd Purdum. "He had the whole package: he had been a valorous sailor in that war; he had protested the war vigorously; and then he had worked to heal the rift in accounting for the missing." During the campaign, Purdum thought, "'Gee, it might just work.' Kerry seemed to have it all sealed up." Yet Bush's election victory demonstrated "that the politicians who emerged from their youth in the sixties comparatively unscathed are the ones who did not go to Vietnam. Bush skipped the sixties," Purdum observed. "Clinton, while he was part and parcel of the sixties, also had an element of having skipped it because he skipped the war." In any case, Clinton in the 1960s was "on the fringes of the antiwar movement, [whereas] Kerry was a leader of it."[73]

When Mark Shields and David Brooks were asked who they thought were the year's "political losers," Shields replied, "The biggest loser is the Vietnam credential." For three candidates—Kerrey in 1992, McCain in 2000, and Kerry in 2004—"the Vietnam experience has been used against them by their opponents, and effectively." Despite the fact that Kerry volunteered twice, his "Vietnam experience was held against him," while

Cheney and Bush—who "didn't want to go, chose not to go and signed a document to that effect"—benefited from their lack of service. "I wonder if anybody who's served in Vietnam, however honorably, will be elected president," Shields mused. Brooks also spoke of the 1960s when summarizing the year in politics. When Democrats were asked "what they longed for, it was not the late sixties, it was the early sixties," Brooks said. "It was John Kennedy. I think people hate the violence of the late sixties but long for the early sixties."[74]

Many on the right vehemently believed that Kerry lost precisely because he was a countercultural figure. "I come back to the sixties," said Thomas Reed. "The idiocy was to start staging rock concerts [toward the end] of the campaign," Reed went on to say, referring to the "Vote For Change" tour, more than fifty concerts in swing states headlined by Bruce Springsteen. "That's a big reminder to all those middle-class folks in Ohio that 'oops, remember who this guy is. This is the longhaired preacher of Woodstock that's running for president.'" To Reed, "it energized a whole bunch of my generation and others, saying: 'By golly I'm going to bust my butt and get down there and vote. We do not want one of those Woodstock characters in the White House.'"[75]

There was a broad consensus that the use of the 1960s lay at the heart of the 2004 election. "The sixties has been useful to the Right," said Roger Wilkins, LBJ's assistant attorney general. "The Right feels badly about Vietnam because they believe that there was treason—all the kids peeing on the flag." As a result "the Democratic Party is hopelessly unable to deal with military issues, which made John Kerry vote for the [Iraq] war." To Wilkins, it was logical that the 1960s lingered, and the Right had an incentive to keep memories of the era alive. "They paint a picture of Democrats behaving badly."[76] According to Harold Ickes, "Republicans have used Vietnam to reinforce their contention coming out of the sixties that the Democrats were soft on communism, that you couldn't trust them with national security, that they would jeopardize the safety of the nation."[77]

Kerry's tortured syntax regarding Iraq throughout the 2004 campaign—for example, his inability to call his vote in favor of the war a mistake—exemplified how the 1960s continued to haunt Democrats. "Obviously he did some heroic things in the war itself, but John Kerry's great moment was to play a significant role in the antiwar movement, and he felt [that in the campaign] he had to recast it and suppress that," Frank Rich said. "It made him look completely disingenuous. The Democrats . . . just don't know what to do with the 1960s."[78]

Asked why Democrats did not speak of the antiwar movement as part of "the sixties," Bob Woodward suggested: "In the middle of the Iraq War [and] a wave of semi-patriotism, it is very difficult to talk [politically against] war . . . to separate the war from those who are fighting the war. All of the [Democratic] politicians are looking for the way to [say,] 'I support the troops, but I don't support the war.'" He went on, "Look at all of American history: Has an antiwar candidate ever won the presidency?" While in the navy in the 1960s, Woodward himself had thought Vietnam "was wrong . . . a mistake," and that those who fled to Canada to escape the draft were "courageous. [But] I don't think those people could run for president and get elected." Noting Kerry's complicated relationship with the era, Woodward summed up: "What Kerry was trying to do was to find that space, that 'viability within the system,' of having been a war hero, but somebody who protested the war, and in part the electorate said, 'No, that is too ambiguous.' There is not that space." He continued: "It's too nuanced, kind of, 'Which side are you on? Who are you?'. . . One of the legacies, the shadows, of Vietnam and of the sixties is that the space—the safe ground—that Kerry tried to find as both war hero and antiwar protester was unavailable in American politics."[79] Proving Woodward's point, John Kerry would speak with pride of his antiwar record in his remarks at the 2008 Democratic National Convention, something he had never felt quite free to do when he was running for president. "Sometimes loving your country demands you must tell the truth to power," a fired-up Kerry told the assembled delegates.[80]

Indeed, leading Democrats emphasized how successfully the Right had used the 1960s to discredit Kerry. As Bill Bradley put it, "Kerry's central identity was as the Vietnam War veteran and prosecutor. He won the primaries because he convinced people that he had a better chance to win. Why? . . . Because he was not vulnerable on the two issues that Republicans attack Democrats on." Bradley summed these up as "One: 'You're soft on defense.' How could that be? He's a decorated Vietnam War veteran. Two: 'He's soft on crime.' How could that be? In Vietnam he killed people, and as a prosecutor he sent people to jail. So he's safe. Well, guess what, he wasn't safe. By choosing to make that his central identity, he allowed the Republicans to undermine him in a tried-and-true way: all they had to do was resurrect the wars of the sixties."[81]

Conclusion

THE PERSISTENT POWER
OF THE 1960s

*You can tell if you were a liberal or a conservative if you thought
the sixties were a good or a bad decade.*

Former Republican senator Rick Santorum (2007)

LIBERAL DEMOCRATS RECALL the 1960s as a high point of American
idealism. They long for the sense of promise of John Kennedy's presidency, exemplified by the Peace Corps, the New Frontier, and the feeling of
optimism Kennedy inspired. Liberals also admire the Great Society's efforts—and accomplishments—in fighting poverty, improving health care,
and providing educational opportunities to all Americans. The nobility of
the civil rights movement and the revolutionary civil rights legislation of
the mid-1960s remain for many Democrats the peak of America's quest
for social justice in the twentieth century. Today's liberals also admire
the spirited attempt by many in the 1960s—especially the young—to stop
what they viewed as an immoral invasion of a third world nation. The
Left also praises the women's and environmental movements that arose
in the 1960s and the era's loosening of traditional restraints in general.

Conservatives, by contrast, see the 1960s as the beginning of the decline of beloved American values: self-reliance, self-discipline, personal
responsibility, strong local communities, and love of country. Though
they fiercely opposed him at the time, those on the Right claim to admire
Kennedy today. In their narrative, everything fell apart after Kennedy's
death: the government needlessly intervened into state prerogatives on
racial issues and waged a futile, costly, and ineffective War on Poverty,
while the rebellious antics of a group of spoiled children cost the nation
victory in Vietnam. According to this view the malevolent forces unleashed by the 1960s continue to reverberate throughout American life,
causing drug abuse, crime, and other social ills.

221

In the ongoing struggle over how to remember the period, the Right dominated presidential politics from 1968 through 2004 with its distinction between the "good sixties" of John Kennedy and the "bad sixties" of Lyndon Johnson and Richard Nixon. Democrats were never able to refute or combat these characterizations effectively. The question remains: Why?

Beginning with Ronald Reagan in 1980, the Right successfully used the "bad sixties" as a political weapon against liberalism, the Great Society, and activist government. Reagan rose to the presidency, after eight years of vigorous hostility to "the sixties" as governor of California, on a platform that vowed to return the nation to a fondly remembered more peaceful time—an idealized version of 1950s America. Reagan's rise was assisted by the twin issues of Vietnam and Watergate, as both served to discredit government in general. It was Reagan who pioneered the rhetorical concept of "the sixties" and who understood that the turmoil of the decade could provide an opening for the conservative movement, which after Johnson's 1964 landslide victory had seemed doomed to political extinction. Reagan may have publicly and privately despised the 1960s, but that period of intense argument and turmoil is precisely what made his political career.

As a candidate during the 1970s and as president during the 1980s, Reagan put the Left on the defensive by repeating, mantra-like, that the Great Society was a costly failure that corrupted the nation's moral, social, cultural, political, and economic life. His charge that the Great Society differed substantially from the New Deal enabled him to sidestep critics who claimed that he sought to overthrow FDR's legislative triumphs. Nor was Reagan politically damaged by the perception that his animosity to Johnson's domestic agenda was driven by hostility to African Americans.

At the same time, Reagan skillfully co-opted the glowing memory of John Kennedy to justify tax cuts and a vigorously anticommunist foreign policy. Reagan boldly claimed that he was Kennedy's heir and that the post-1960s Democrats had departed dramatically from JFK's agenda. This willingness to wrap himself in Kennedy's mantle of legitimacy was especially pronounced during his 1984 reelection campaign. Reagan may not have supported Kennedy in the early 1960s, but he eagerly used the memory of JFK for political gain, referring to Kennedy in his public statements more than to any other president of either party.

Just as Reagan knew that the Vietnam debacle had shattered America's self-confidence, however, he understood that the continued public longing for a restored Camelot might damage the Right. Fearing that an excessively grandiose foreign policy could pose a threat to conservatives, Reagan aimed to restore national morale by talking tough on defense without committing large-scale forces overseas in order to avoid overreaching and thereby provoking cries of leading the United States into "another Vietnam." As he did with Kennedy, Johnson, and the social disturbances of the era, Reagan used Vietnam in a way that ensured maximum political success for the Right. He claimed to have banished the ghosts of "the sixties" with Central American policies that overcame the "Vietnam syndrome." Yet his reliance on covert action, as revealed by the exposure of the Iran-contra affair, demonstrated that the syndrome had persisted into the 1980s, belying Reagan's bold claims to the contrary. Most of all, Reagan harked back rhetorically to an earlier time in America's past, before the upheavals of the 1960s, most vividly in his farewell address, when he emotionally recalled the nation's values before "the sixties" changed them. Reagan's extensive appeal to nostalgia formed an essential part of his efforts to blame the 1960s.

George H. W. Bush continued Reagan's anti-"sixties" drumbeat. Bush owed his victory in the 1988 election to a host of divisive social issues carried over from the 1960s—the American flag, patriotism, and a heated debate over what constituted a "real American"—and his success in that campaign emboldened him to continue blaming the 1960s throughout his term as president. Bush charged that the Great Society had squandered resources and done more harm than good. He even suggested that liberal antipoverty programs caused the 1992 Los Angeles riots. Bush pledged to replace ineffective government policies to fight poverty and social breakdown with his "Thousand Points of Light" program, relying on volunteerism to combat the nation's problems. Vice President Dan Quayle, the first baby boomer to run on a national ticket, and his wife, Marilyn, spoke out sharply against the 1960s counterculture and in favor of traditional "family values." In foreign affairs, Bush claimed that he had reversed the damage of the 1960s, especially through the victorious 1991 Gulf War, which he frequently said "kicked the Vietnam syndrome."

The Right saw Bill Clinton's rise to the presidency in 1992 as the tragic victory of a poster child for all that was wrong about the 1960s. Clinton understood how the Right had made the "bad sixties" work to its advantage and astutely took a defensive posture toward those times. He spoke often of the personal inspiration he drew from his heroes, John and Robert Kennedy and Martin Luther King Jr. Contrary to expectations and to their images in popular memory, Clinton invoked these beloved liberal icons in support of a centrist-to-conservative agenda, tacking with the prevailing political winds of his era. He called for a smaller federal government, balanced budgets, tougher crime control, and a reduced role for govern-ment in solving problems. Navigating between Right and Left, Clinton's centrist positions—the "New Democrat" policy prescriptions of the Democratic Leadership Council—merged the "good sixties" and the bad.

Clinton's efforts reconciled his admiration for the Kennedy brothers and King with the stubborn fact that by 1992 the nation had undergone a relentless twelve-year attack on "the sixties" by Reagan and Bush. Clin-ton had to speak of his personal heroes in a manner that would fit the conservative tenor of the times, a challenge that only became more urgent once Republicans took control of Congress in 1994. A fundamentally de-fensive president, Clinton owed his political success in no small measure to the way he appealed to those who remembered fondly the hope, prom-ise, and idealism of the 1960s but were at the same time repelled by the new norms and standards of behavior the era had ushered in. Clinton's dif-ficult balancing act was evident when he was forced to speak of the most divisive issue of the 1960s, the Vietnam War, a conflict he had opposed. In the final year of his presidency he resorted to using "the sixties" as a political weapon of his own, urging the nation to seize the opportunity provided by the sound economic footing created during his tenure—an opportunity painfully missed once before as a result of the nightmares of the late 1960s.

Rather than waning with the passage of time, memories of the 1960s only intensified in the elections of 2000 and 2004. (The 2000 race was the first since 1948 in which no candidate on either party's ticket had served in World War II. In 2000 and again in 2004, all the major party candi-dates except John Edwards had graduated from college in the 1960s.) Baby boomers Al Gore and George W. Bush, so close in age and background, drew widely divergent lessons from the 1960s. George W. Bush, class of '68, defeated both Al Gore, class of '69, and John Kerry, class of '66, by running against the "bad sixties." In 2000 Bush pledged to obliterate the "If it feels good, do it" attitude which he said had tainted the 1960s and the Clinton presidency and to restore dignity to the Oval Office. In 2004 he used another trope from the 1960s to defeat John Kerry, depicting him as a longhaired antiwar protester disloyal to the uniform he had worn in Vietnam. Kerry's and Gore's vain attempts to link themselves in voters' minds with the "good sixties" vividly proved the Right's enduring abil-ity, first demonstrated by Ronald Reagan, to put the Democrats on the defensive.

In politics, one cannot occupy two spaces. That Gore was far from a wild-eyed radical and Kerry was a highly decorated Vietnam War veteran did not ultimately matter. Since Kerry had protested the Vietnam War, he could not also have been a war hero, the Right's narrative argued—regardless of the fact that many veterans had been protesters. Likewise, despite the fact that Gore was a happily married father and grandfather, he could not represent "family values," for Gore was vice president to another child of the late 1960s whose marital difficulties and sexual indiscretions had been fully exposed. He, too, could not be both.

For the Republicans, the phenomenon worked in a positive direction. The fact that Bush had a history of substance abuse and had avoided active military service in the 1960s did not resonate in the face of campaign slogans describing him as a God-fearing, born-again, family-oriented war president. Bush convinced voters that he belonged to the "good sixties" and that Clinton, Gore, and Kerry represented the "bad sixties." In 2004—just as it had for the prior twenty-four years—the political use of the 1960s once again helped decide the direction of American politics. Ever since 1970 the nation had argued over the 1960s, and the discussion showed no signs of running out of energy. How much longer it would continue to demarcate the fault lines of American politics remained to be seen.

The more than 120 sources I interviewed for this book in 2004 and early 2005 strenuously debated the meaning of the 1960s. Yet for all their differences, both liberals and conservatives saw the 1960s in strikingly similar ways. Since the decade ended, Democrats and Republicans have vigorously debated whether "the sixties" benefited or harmed the nation, and each has used the era to draw sharp contrasts with the political opposition. Yet the interviews revealed three crucial similarities.

First, both Republican and Democratic speechwriters understood and harnessed the power of the 1960s to shape the national narrative in the elections from 1980 to 2004. "The Democrats remember Kennedy and the antiwar protests, especially the Clinton people," said C. Landon Parvin. "They see it fondly. But . . . we forget that there were people being killed by bombs back then" by campus radicals. "That is what Reagan saw, and the Democrats saw it as a romantic period." To Parvin, one's view of the 1960s defines one's political allegiance. "You have this one older group that sees it as an era of rage and violence, and this other group that sees it as a romantic period when they blossomed. And so there's a split there in terms of how they see the sixties."[1]

Liberal Democrats offered a strikingly similar analysis. "The 1960s were the crucible in which our worldview was formed," said Jeff Shesol. "Those who came of age politically in subsequent decades inherited one worldview or the other. This is true not only of liberals, who look back to the activism of the Kennedys and of LBJ, of the civil rights movement,"

Shesol said. "The same ferment was going on among conservatives, a natural evolution accelerated by the events of the sixties." To Shesol, "the 1960s were the period in which both sides figured out who they were and what they believed. And we haven't departed dramatically from that understanding of ourselves. . . . The 1960s are the litmus test for one's ideology."[2]

Indeed both liberals and conservatives agreed that the 1960s gave rise to the two factions that now compete politically. "Many Americans [separated] from one another in the 1960s and have never reunited," said Curt Smith. "That more than anything accounts for the polarization and division in the country today."[3] To Maurice Isserman, the 1960s decade "is just one of those fault lines in American history that seems to define everything afterwards for a generation or two. Just as the Civil War was a fault line of the nineteenth century, so the 1960s proved to be in our own time."[4]

Second, it is clear that liberals and conservatives both have reason to be angry at the 1960s. "If you look back on the sixties, [whether] you're Right or Left, you see things that you don't like from the Johnson administration," said Craig Shirley. "If you're on the Left, you don't like the Vietnam War. And if you're from the Right, you might not like the Vietnam War either, because you lost it, or set it up to be lost, but you also don't like the Great Society."[5]

And third, since many of these frustrations remain, the argument over the 1960s is not only about the past but also about current conditions. I found that figures from both the Right and the Left were profoundly unhappy with the present, and each believed that America had declined since the 1960s. Liberals argued that something significant had been lost. "A lot of the sixties were focused on the poor, the disenfranchised, the inner cities, economic development, and that is almost gone from the political dialogue now," said Harold Ickes.[6] To Roger Wilkins, "the coarsening of the culture" following the 1960s "was distressing."[7] Helen Thomas lamented the lack of 1960s-caliber leadership. Reflecting in 2004 on the slain Kennedy brothers and King she said: "You don't find people like that anymore. We have no statesmen today."[8] Archibald Cox regretted that "politics seems to be so lacking in ideals and principles."[9]

In 2004 and 2005 the Right shared the Left's intense dissatisfaction. "There are the two nations from the 1960s, and my part of the nation right now does not have a voice," said Curt Smith.[10] To Robert Bork, "the student radicals and others of the sixties . . . gradually grew and moved into positions of responsibility." The negative values of the 1960s "are still with us."[11] Brent Bozell observed that "just because Republicans are running the shop doesn't mean that conservatism is succeeding."[12] Craig Shirley argued that since the 1960s the media had moved leftward, and "the public school system has become a laboratory for anticonservative thinking."[13] Phyllis Schlafly complained, "What the courts have done [since the 1960s] is to stymie every legislative effort to maintain decency."[14] As far as Eugene Meyer was concerned, "the sixties generation won the sexual revolution."[15] In Ed Meese's view, "conservatives are losing."[16] Richard Viguerie believed that cultural conservatives "lost the battle during the 1960s, and we've never regained our footing. For many of us it's the most important thing; nothing else matters."[17] Paul Weyrich declared: "We have [lost], because we never fought. We just simply retreated."[18]

Thus despite their many electoral triumphs since 1968 and another under way in the reelection bid of George W. Bush, the men and women of the Right felt a sense of defeat. This explains why conservatives continued to blame "the sixties" and kept the argument about the decade alive. Although many liberals believed that such claims merely served as a rallying call for the Right—"If you're perceived to be behind, you can actually organize better, even though you may actually be ahead," said John Shattuck—in many areas the Right does in fact have reason to be frustrated.[19]

Conservatives have been in power much of the time since 1968 but have failed to implement their policies in several key areas. The size of the government has only increased since the 1960s; films and other forms of popular entertainment continue to be drenched in violence and sex; environmentalism and diversity movements march steadily forward; illegal immigration continues; abortion remains legal; and women's and gay rights have expanded. While the Right has seen victories in the economic and political spheres, the movement in the 1960s for increased liberalization of personal and work life has steadily proceeded. Acceptance of alternative lifestyles shows no sign of abating. Though the move toward privatization has had some success, the public sector continues to expand. And Republicans were unable to remove Bill Clinton from office during his impeachment trial, a particularly strong blow to social conservatives. Their losses mounted as the Democrats regained control of both houses of Congress in 2006 and the White House in 2008.

Finally, the Right has been forced to accept the civil rights movement's triumphs of the 1960s. Whereas Congressman George H. W. Bush voted against the 1964 Civil Rights Act, his son hosted a ceremony at the White House on the fortieth anniversary of the legislation. In his remarks the president gave extensive praise not just to King but to John Kennedy and, most especially, to Lyndon Johnson.[20] When Rosa Parks died in October 2005, Bush delivered a gracious tribute.[21] And Bush honored King at length at the November 2006 groundbreaking for the King Memorial on the Mall in Washington in a moving speech that Bill Clinton could have delivered.[22] The progress toward racial justice is far from finished. But the gains of the 1960s have been all but universally accepted. Though conservatives have actively campaigned against "the sixties" since at least 1964, they have been forced—albeit reluctantly, in some cases—to accept many of the victories of the era.

The memory of the 1960s and its contested political use continued after Bush's 2004 reelection. Like her husband, Hillary Clinton was widely seen as a product of the 1960s. Her strong early polling in the 2008 race for the Democratic presidential nomination caused some to dread that the wounds of the 1960s would continue to fester. "If Clinton is elected, American politics over the next years will be as brutal and stagnant as now," wrote conservative commentator David Brooks in 2006. "The 1960's Bush-Clinton psychodrama would go on and on."[23]

A desire to move beyond the battles of the 1960s played a key role in another candidate's view of the political terrain. "In the back-and-forth between Clinton and Gingrich, and in the elections of 2000 and 2004, I sometimes felt as if I were watching the psychodrama of the Baby Boom generation—a tale rooted in old grudges and revenge plots hatched on a handful of college campuses long ago—played out on the national stage," wrote Barack Obama in 2006. "The victories that the sixties generation brought about—the admission of minorities and women into full citizenship, the strengthening of individual liberties and the healthy willingness to question authority," had improved America. "But what has been lost in the process, and has yet to be replaced, are those shared assumptions—that quality of trust and fellow feeling—that bring us together."[24] David Brooks, after his interview with Obama, argued that he understands "it's time to move beyond the political style of the baby boom generation," since that style "is highly moralistic and personal, dividing people between who is good and who is bad. Obama himself has a mentality formed by globalization, not the S.D.S."[25]

At the same time, the 2006 midterm elections demonstrated the continued pull of the 1960s. Observers used "the sixties" as shorthand for failed Democratic policies. "[Democratic National Committee chairman Howard] Dean has come to embody a species of Democrat that a lot of Americans of both parties find off-putting: the sixties antiwar liberal, reborn with a laptop and a Prius," wrote one journalist in an October profile.[26] "Democrats are torn between two visions of their history," said another: one that stressed withdrawal from the "Vietnam" of Iraq and one that was still reacting to George McGovern's 1972 loss by trying to show that Democrats were as tough on national defense as Republicans. A sketch accompanying the article featured two donkeys, the symbol of the Democratic Party, facing each other. One wore boxing gloves, the other hippie attire: sandals, a 1960s-style vest, a flower in its hand, and a peace symbol around its neck.[27]

Following the Democrats' capture of Congress in the 2006 midterm elections, the argument over Iraq intensified, and along with it a vigorous debate over the meaning of the Vietnam War. The lesson of the conflict, George W. Bush proclaimed during his brief November 2006 visit to Hanoi, was that "we'll succeed unless we quit."[28] In April 2007 Ted Kennedy called the Iraq War "George Bush's Vietnam," while Republican representative John Boehner, the minority leader of the House, declared: "Our enemies understand what happened in Vietnam. When this Congress voted to cut off funding, we left Vietnam. We left chaos and genocide in the streets of Vietnam because we pulled the troops out and didn't have the will to win."[29] Later that month the army denied permission for Joan Baez to join John Mellencamp at a performance for wounded veterans at the Walter Reed Army Medical Center. The *New York Times* opined, "What is astounding is that somebody apparently could not get past the image of willowy Joan singing 'Blowin' in the Wind' nearly 40 years ago."[30] As another commentator wrote, "the hullabaloo over Joan Baez reminds us we're still living in the shadow of the sixties."[31]

On his website in January 2007 Barack Obama made clear that he would soon announce his presidential run. In his remarks he emphasized that although the struggles of the 1960s were far from finished, as an African American he had benefited from the era. But he wanted America's leaders to move beyond the preoccupations of the baby boomers. This was a new challenge, John Broder wrote, as "for 20 years or longer the cultural and political divides of the '60s served as presumed signposts to a candidate's character." The enormous sketch accompanying Broder's article showed a smiling Obama leaping over five figures dressed in a variety of stereotypical hippie clothing.[32]

While Obama claimed to want to transcend the 1960s, it remains striking how that era continues to shadow him, for better or worse. His popularity can be attributed in considerable measure to the persistent longing for that icon of the 1960s, John Kennedy. In Chicago, Obama worked at a law firm with veteran Democratic Party insider Newton Minow. Minow initially was against Obama's decision to run for president but changed his mind when he saw Obama on television working the crowd after a speech in late 2006. "I adored Jack Kennedy, and I saw the 21st century version of Jack Kennedy in my mind," Minow said.[33] To liberal columnist Bob Herbert, Obama "has the cadences that remind you of King but the cool that reminds you of Kennedy—John, not Robert."[34] One voter wrote the phrase "The Kennedy Package" when asked by a photographer to write on a chalkboard her reasons for supporting the first-term senator.[35] Public endorsements from Ted Kennedy and Caroline Kennedy helped propel Obama to victory in the primaries, and he soon named the latter to the group of advisers assigned to pick his vice presidential running mate. When Al Gore endorsed Obama after the end of the primaries, the former vice president drew extensive comparisons between Obama and JFK.[36]

Earlier in 2008, Obama had consciously distanced himself from the "bad sixties." "Ronald Reagan changed the trajectory of America, in a way that Richard Nixon did not, and in a way that Bill Clinton did not," Obama said in January. "The country was ready for it," the senator explained, after "all the excesses of the 1960s and 1970s. . . . He just tapped into what people were already feeling."[37]

Yet Obama's quest to finally get past the battles over "the sixties" appeared to run aground in April 2008. In a debate with Hillary Clinton he was asked about a variety of issues that all had their origins in the late 1960s—the "bad sixties." He was pressed about inflammatory comments by his pastor, the Reverend Jeremiah Wright, himself a product of the Black Power movement. Wright thus "dragged Obama into the '60s maelstrom that he had pledged to be an antidote to," Maureen Dowd wrote.[38] Obama was asked about accusations of being personally close to a former member of the 1960s radical group Weather Underground. Even Obama's going without a flag pin in his lapel was a topic of extended discussion, one that brought to mind the charges in the late 1960s that the Democrats lacked patriotism, as well as George H. W. Bush's ostentatious embrace of the flag in his 1988 campaign against Michael Dukakis.

Clearly the debate over the 1960s had not lost its power to define American politics. Hillary Clinton's unwillingness to quit the Democratic race in May 2008 reminded many Democrats of an earlier election year. One headline blared, "Dems Make Us Wonder: Is it 1968 or 2008?" next to a picture of Robert Kennedy, who had carried on the fight against Hubert Humphrey until his assassination in June 1968.[39] Clinton's reference to Kennedy's assassination in the context of justifying her staying in the race until June 2008 immediately caused an uproar. On the fortieth anniversary of RFK's death an ABC news profile of the late senator compared Obama to Robert Kennedy. When Clinton finally conceded, Tom Hayden argued that in her campaign she took "race-baiting and red-baiting positions she never would have adopted in the late sixties." Hayden lamented, "The Democratic Party consultant class has been counseling retreat from the sixties ever since . . . the sixties."[40]

Most important, despite his professed desire to move the country beyond the 1960s, Obama soon eagerly adopted the Democratic playbook from elections past by looking to the early 1960s while shunning the late 1960s. At a May 2008 commencement address, standing in for the ailing Ted Kennedy, he said that John F. Kennedy's 1961 inaugural address had inspired him to become a community organizer.[41] Obama's July 2008 speech before an enormous crowd in Berlin evoked Kennedy's 1963 "Ich bin ein Berliner" speech. And Obama drew approving references to JFK when he too chose an older, more experienced Senate insider as his running mate.

At the Democratic convention in August 2008 Ted Kennedy gave a stirring speech in support of Obama, mentioning that his brother had also given the American people hope.[42] In introducing her uncle, Caroline Kennedy said—in words that were strikingly similar to her previous endorsements—"I have never had someone inspire me the way people tell me my father inspired them, but I do now: Barack Obama."[43] A few days later, on the forty-fifth anniversary of Martin Luther King's "I Have a Dream" address, Obama gave his acceptance speech outdoors before a huge crowd at a stadium—the first candidate to do so since John Kennedy in 1960. One presidential historian noted that "the Obama campaign has been purposely modeling its acceptance speech after JFK."[44] In his remarks Obama mentioned FDR once and JFK twice, the second time to argue that Democrats were the party of military strength. The speech climaxed with a stirring reference to the words spoken forty-five years before by "a young preacher from Georgia."[45] Following the speech, musical selections blasted the audience, one of them Bruce Springsteen's "Born in the U.S.A." People danced gleefully in the aisles.

No attention, however, was given to another milestone. Obama's speech came a day after the one hundredth anniversary of the birth of Lyndon Johnson, who passed the most sweeping civil rights legislation since Lincoln. LBJ's Civil Rights Act of 1964 and Voting Rights Act of 1965 helped make Obama's speech possible. But the millions of Americans watching never once heard Johnson's name. Obama's evocation of the 1960s was all about the "good sixties." The more things had changed in American politics since the 1960s, it seemed, the more they had remained the same.

Never before had two presidents from different parties served complete back-to-back eight-year terms or been so very close in age. When George W. Bush left office in 2009, the presidency had been occupied since 1993—a sixteen-year period—by two political adversaries who graduated from college in 1968, the peak of the division and turmoil of "the sixties." The memory of the 1960s has dominated American politics far longer than the decade itself lasted and has not yet run its course. The much-discussed national divide between Republican "red states" and Democratic "blue states" stems primarily from the fight over "the sixties." In the 2008 presidential election Republican John McCain, a decorated Vietnam-era prisoner of war, relied on the tried-and-true strategy of "blaming the sixties" that had propelled Ronald Reagan and two presidents named George Bush into the White House, though this time, against a backdrop of urgent national crises and an opponent who hadn't been born when the 1960s began, the strategy failed.

Nevertheless, as the campaign showed, "the sixties" are long dead but still not buried. So long as politicians who came of age in the 1960s seek high office—and perhaps longer—the tensions of the era will retain their power.

Appendix
ALPHABETICAL LIST AND IDENTIFICATIONS OF INDIVIDUALS INTERVIEWED

Askew, Ken   Senior speechwriter for President George H. W. Bush.

Atkinson, Frank   Worked in the Reagan Justice Department and was counselor to the attorney general during Reagan's second term.

Baker, Don   Retired *Washington Post* political reporter; covered Virginia and national politics from 1970 to 2000.

Baker, James A., III   One of only a handful of Americans to have held three cabinet-level positions, Baker was President Reagan's chief of staff in his first administration, secretary of the treasury in his second, and President George H. W. Bush's secretary of state. He also headed five successive presidential campaigns.

Bakshian, Aram   Nixon and Ford speechwriter who was also President Reagan's director of speechwriting.

Barash, David   Professor of psychology at the University of Washington and author of *The L Word: An Unapologetic, Thoroughly Biased, Long-Overdue Explication and Celebration of Liberalism.*

Bauer, Gary   Reagan's undersecretary of education and domestic policy adviser from 1985 to 1989; ran for the 2000 Republican nomination for president.

Berman, William   Professor of history at the University of Toronto.

Blackwell, Morton   Longtime conservative activist; attended the 1968 Republican convention as a Reagan alternate delegate from Louisiana, served from 1981 to 1983 in Reagan's White House, and became president of the Leadership Institute, a training ground for conservatives.

Bloom, Alex   Professor of history at Wheaton College in Norton, Mass.

Blumenthal, Sidney   Liberal journalist; assistant and senior adviser to President Clinton from 1997 to 2001.

Bok, Derek   Professor at Harvard University and Harvard's president from 1971 to 1991.

Bond, Julian   Civil rights activist; in 1960 co-founded the Student Nonviolent Coordinating Committee (SNCC). Became chairman of the board of the NAACP in 1998.

Bork, Robert H. Conservative legal scholar. A former judge, Bork was unsuccessfully nominated for the U.S. Supreme Court by Ronald Reagan in 1987.

Boyer, Paul Professor emeritus of history at the University of Wisconsin.

Bozell, Brent, III Founder of the conservative Media Research Center, the nation's largest media watchdog organization. Bozell's father, whose brother-in-law was conservative icon William F. Buckley, ghostwrote Barry Goldwater's seminal 1960 text, *Conscience of a Conservative*, considered the bible of the Right

Bradlee, Benjamin C. Vice president at large and former executive editor of the *Washington Post*.

Bradley, Bill Former three-term New Jersey Democratic senator; ran for president in 2000.

Brands, H. W. Professor of history at the University of Texas.

Brazile, Donna A longtime Democratic Party activist and election strategist, Brazile worked for Democratic candidates in every presidential election between 1976 and 2000, when she served as Al Gore's campaign manager.

Brinkley, Alan Professor of history at Columbia University.

Broder, David Longtime *Washington Post* political columnist.

Butler, M. Caldwell Virginia Republican congressman from 1970 to 1982.

Cannon, Lou Author of six books on Reagan.

Carlucci, Frank Nixon's undersecretary of health, education, and welfare, and Reagan's deputy defense secretary, national security adviser, and secretary of defense.

Chomsky, Noam Professor emeritus of linguistics at Massachusetts Institute of Technology; prominent political activist and critic of U.S. foreign and domestic policy.

Collier, Peter Former co-editor with David Horowitz of *Ramparts*, flagship magazine of the New Left in the 1960s; subsequently switched to the Right.

Cox, Archibald Solicitor general under Kennedy; appointed the first special prosecutor for the Watergate investigation. He died on May 29, 2004.

Dallek, Robert Professor of history at Boston University.

Deaver, Michael One of Reagan's closest advisers and his assistant and deputy chief of staff from 1981 to 1985. He died on August 18, 2007.

Delli Carpini, Michael Dean of the Annenberg School for Communication at the University of Pennsylvania.

Devine, Don Vice chairman of the American Conservative Union; ran the Office of Personnel Management in Reagan's first term.

Dolan, Anthony R. President Reagan's chief speechwriter for eight years. Dolan also served on Reagan's senior staff for the duration of his presidency and was the principal author of Reagan's 1983 "Evil Empire" speech.

Donnelly, Elaine Conservative activist and president of the Michigan Center for Military Readiness; worked on Reagan's 1980 campaign.

Dukakis, Michael Former governor of Massachusetts and Democratic presidential nominee in 1988; professor of political science at Northeastern University.

du Pont, Pierre S., IV   Republican governor of Delaware from 1977 to 1985; ran for president in 1988.

Edelman, Peter   Professor of law at Georgetown University Law Center; was Clinton's assistant secretary of health and human services before resigning in protest over Clinton's decision to sign the 1996 Welfare Reform Bill.

Edsall, Thomas   Covered national politics for the *Washington Post* from 1981 to 2006 and wrote several books on American politics before going on to teach journalism at Columbia University.

Ellsberg, Daniel   Longtime political activist and former military analyst who in 1971 released the Pentagon Papers to the *New York Times*.

Fahrenkopf, Frank J., Jr.   Chairman of the Republican National Committee from 1983 to 1989.

Feulner, Edwin   President of the Heritage Foundation, the nation's leading conservative think tank.

FitzGerald, Frances   Journalist and author of *Fire in the Lake: The Vietnamese and the Americans in Vietnam* (1972).

Frank, Thomas   Liberal journalist and bestselling author of *What's the Matter with Kansas? How Conservatives Won the Heart of America*.

Franz, Wanda   President of the National Right to Life Committee.

Freeman, Jo   Longtime liberal activist and the author of *At Berkeley in the Sixties: The Education of an Activist, 1961–1965*.

From, Al   Founder and CEO of the Democratic Leadership Council, a group of centrist Democrats founded in 1985.

Gilder, Josh   Speechwriter for President Reagan in his second term; also wrote for candidate George H. W. Bush in 1988.

Gitlin, Todd   Co-founded Students for a Democratic Society (SDS) in 1962 before becoming a professor of journalism and sociology at Columbia University.

Glastris, Paul   Editor in chief of *Washington Monthly*, senior fellow at the Western Policy Center, and speechwriter for President Clinton from 1998 through 2001.

Glazer, Nathan   Neoconservative commentator.

Halberstam, David   Pulitzer Prize–winning journalist and historian. He died on April 23, 2007.

Harris, John   *Washington Post* journalist and author of a political biography of Bill Clinton; covered the White House beginning in 1995.

Hart, Gary   Colorado Democratic senator from 1974 to 1986; ran twice for the presidency in the 1980s.

Hayden, Tom   Key participant in the antiwar and civil rights movements of the 1960s and co-founder of the student activist group Students for a Democratic Society (SDS) in 1962.

Hodgson, Godfrey   British historian and associate fellow at the Rothermere American Institute at Oxford; has written widely on recent American history.

Horowitz, David   Former co-editor with Peter Collier of *Ramparts*, flagship magazine of the New Left, in the 1960s; later became a prominent conservative activist and head of the Center for the Study of Popular Culture.

Ickes, Harold   President Clinton's deputy chief of staff between 1992 and 1996.

Irvine, Don   Chairman of Accuracy in Media, the nation's oldest conservative media watchdog organization, founded by his father, Reed Irvine.

Isserman, Maurice   Professor of history at Hamilton College and co-author of *America Divided: The Civil War of the 1960s.*

Jacobson, Gary   Professor of political science at the University of California at San Diego whose research examines public attitudes toward the military.

Judge, Clark   Speechwriter and special assistant to both President Reagan and Vice President Bush.

Judis, John   Senior editor for the *New Republic* who was an active member of Students for a Democratic Society in the 1960s and the founding editor of *Socialist Revolution* in 1969.

Karnow, Stanley   A leading historian of the Vietnam War.

Katzenbach, Nicholas   Deputy attorney general in the Kennedy administration; also served as attorney general and undersecretary of state in the Johnson administration.

Kazin, Michael   Professor of history at Georgetown University and co-author of *America Divided: The Civil War of the 1960s.*

Keene, David   President of the American Conservative Union, the nation's oldest conservative lobbying organization, founded months after Lyndon Johnson's 1964 landslide victory over Barry Goldwater.

Kirk, Paul   Chairman of the Democratic National Committee from 1985 to 1989.

Kline, Mal   Executive director of Accuracy in Academia, the largest and oldest conservative watchdog group for higher education.

Knight, Kathleen   Professor of political science, Barnard College.

Kusnet, David   Speechwriter for Democratic presidential candidates Walter Mondale, Michael Dukakis, and Bill Clinton.

LaRouche, Lyndon   Political activist and perennial Democratic presidential candidate.

Lynd, Staughton   Veteran radical labor activist; was professor of history at Yale in the 1960s.

Maraniss, David   As a staff reporter for the *Washington Post*, won the 1993 Pulitzer Prize for his coverage of Bill Clinton's life and career.

May, Clifford   From 1997 to 2001 was the Republican National Committee's director of communications; went on to run the Foundation for the Defense of Democracies.

McCurry, Mike   President Clinton's press secretary between 1995 and 1998.

Meese, Edwin, III   One of Reagan's most trusted advisers, served as Governor Reagan's chief of staff from 1969 through 1974 and as President

Reagan's counselor and attorney general; became a fellow at the Heritage Foundation.

Meyer, Eugene B. Director of the Federalist Society, the nation's leading conservative think tank for legal issues.

Middleton, Harry J. Speechwriter for President Johnson; went on to become director of the LBJ Library and Museum and executive director of the LBJ Foundation.

Miroff, Bruce Political science professor at the State University of New York at Albany who did his undergraduate and graduate work at the University of California at Berkeley between 1962 and 1974.

Moore, Stephen A leading conservative activist and founder and former president of the conservative economic lobbying organization the Club for Growth.

Murphy, John Speech communication professor at the University of Georgia.

Olasky, Marvin University of Texas professor of journalism and editor of the biblical weekly news magazine *World*. Considered the father of George W. Bush's slogan "compassionate conservatism"; was an informal adviser to Bush in 2000.

Parmet, Herbert Historian and biographer of John F. Kennedy and George H. W. Bush.

Parvin, C. Landon A speechwriter for the Reagans at the White House and later a consultant to the former president.

Perlstein, Rick Journalist and historian of the 1960s; author of books on Barry Goldwater and Richard Nixon.

Purdum, Todd White House correspondent for the *New York Times* from 1994 to 1996; covered the 2004 presidential campaign for the paper.

Rae, Nicol Professor of political science at Florida International University.

Reed, Thomas C. Longtime Reagan confidant and special assistant for national security policy.

Rich, Frank Op-ed columnist for the *New York Times*.

Ritter, Kurt Professor of speech communication at Texas A&M University.

Robinson, Peter Chief speechwriter to Vice President Bush from 1982 to 1983 and special assistant and speechwriter to President Reagan from 1983 to 1988.

Robinson, Ron President of Young America's Foundation, the nation's largest conservative college outreach program.

Rohde, David University Distinguished Professor of American Politics at Michigan State University; subsequently a member of the Duke University faculty.

Rossinow, Doug Professor of history at Metropolitan State University in Minnesota and author of *The Politics of Authenticity: Liberalism, Christianity, and the New Left in America*.

Rusher, William Former publisher of *National Review* and an early mentor of the conservative youth group Young Americans for Freedom; participated in Goldwater's and Reagan's campaigns in the 1960s.

Sabato, Larry   Professor of political science at the University of Virginia.

Schiffren, Lisa   Vice President Quayle's speechwriter in 1991 and 1992.

Schlafly, Phyllis   Conservative antifeminist founder of the Eagle Forum; best known for her successful campaign against the Equal Rights Amendment. Schlafly has attended every Republican convention since 1952.

Schlesinger, Arthur M., Jr.   Democratic activist and historian of American liberalism who wrote speeches for the presidential campaigns of Adlai Stevenson, John F. Kennedy, Robert Kennedy, and Ted Kennedy; served as special assistant to the president in the Kennedy administration and was Albert Schweitzer Professor Emeritus of Humanities at the City University of New York Graduate Center. He died on February 28, 2007.

Schulman, Bruce   Boston University history professor.

Shalala, Donna   President Clinton's secretary of health and human services; subsequently president of the University of Miami.

Shattuck, John   Chief executive officer of the John F. Kennedy Library Foundation; President Clinton's undersecretary of state for democracy, human rights, and labor, and Clinton's ambassador to the Czech Republic.

Shesol, Jeff   A member of President Clinton's senior staff between 1998 and 2001; served as deputy assistant to the president and a deputy director for presidential speechwriting.

Shields, Mark   Liberal pundit who worked on the presidential campaigns of Robert Kennedy, Sargent Shriver, and Edmund Muskie.

Shirley, Craig   A paid consultant for the Reagan White House from 1985 to 1988; was also a consultant to Vice President Bush and an informal consultant to him during his presidency.

Smith, Curt   President George H. W. Bush's speechwriter from 1989 to 1993; wrote more speeches for him than any other writer.

Spencer, Stuart K.   Longtime Republican strategist and Reagan confidant; managed Reagan's 1966 run for governor of California and worked with him throughout his career.

Stimson, James   Political science professor at the University of North Carolina.

Thernstrom, Stephan   Winthrop Professor of History at Harvard University and a leading neoconservative scholar.

Thomas, Helen   Has covered every president since Kennedy and for fifty-seven years was White House correspondent for United Press International.

Viguerie, Richard   Political and campaign strategist, activist, writer, and conservative spokesman; in 1961 became executive secretary of Young Americans for Freedom, the conservative youth group. From 1965 owned conservative direct marketing and advertising companies.

Walinsky, Adam   In 1964 became Robert Kennedy's legislative assistant, advising Kennedy in his work on foreign and domestic issues.

Weinberger, Caspar   Reagan's secretary of defense from 1981 to 1987. He died on March 28, 2006.

West, Darrell   Professor of political science at Brown University.

Weyrich, Paul Legendary founding father of the modern conservative movement and co-founder of the Heritage Foundation and the Moral Majority. He died on December 18, 2008.

Whitehurst, G. William Former Republican member of Congress; represented Virginia's Second Congressional District from 1969 to 1987. **Widmer, Ted** Speechwriter for President Clinton from 1997 to 2000.

Wilkins, Roger Noted civil rights leader and journalist; professor of history and American culture at George Mason University. Was an assistant attorney general during the Johnson administration.

Wirth, Timothy Democratic senator from Colorado from 1986 to 1992; was a deputy assistant secretary of education in the first Nixon administration and Clinton's undersecretary of state for global affairs.

Wolfe, Alan Political science professor and director of the Boisi Center for Religion and American Public Life at Boston College.

Woodward, Bob Assistant managing editor at the *Washington Post* and well-known chronicler of presidential politics.

Zinn, Howard Veteran radical activist and professor emeritus of political science at Boston University; author of *A People's History of the United States*.

Notes

Introduction

Epigraph: Bill Clinton, BookExpo America, Chicago, June 3, 2004.

1. Philip Elliott, "McCain Mocks Clinton Woodstock Project," *USA Today*, October 24, 2007.

2. Jim Rutenberg, "The Ad Campaign: A Focus on the '60s, When McCain Was a P.O.W.," *New York Times*, July 9, 2008.

3. Jim Rutenberg, "Group Plans Ad Criticizing Obama's Ties to Ex-Radical," *New York Times*, August 22, 2008.

4. Jim Rutenberg, "Obama Campaign Wages Fight against Conservative Group's Ads," www.nytimes.com, August 27, 2008.

5. For this book, a liberal is defined as "one who believes in more government action to meet individual needs." This use of the term can be traced back to 1932, when Franklin Roosevelt defined it while campaigning for president: "Say that civilization is a tree which, as it grows, continually produces rot and dead wood. The radical says: 'Cut it down.' The conservative says: 'Don't touch it.' The liberal compromises: 'Let's prune, so that we lose neither the old trunk nor the new branches.'" William Safire, *Safire's New Political Dictionary: The Definitive Guide to the New Language of Politics* (New York: Random House, 1993), 407. Although conservatives since 1980 have used "liberal" and "the Left" interchangeably, in the 1960s the New Left, as it was called then, grew out of a hatred for liberals, who the New Left believed were too willing to engage in Vietnam and too cautious about making needed reforms at home. At the same time, liberals in the 1960s had nothing but contempt for the New Left. Nevertheless, here "liberal" and "the Left" mean the same thing, as that is how the terms have been used with growing frequency since 1970. Likewise for our purposes a conservative is "a defender of the status quo who, when change becomes necessary in tested institutions or practices, prefers that it come slowly, and in moderation." Modern conservatism is against "government regulation of the economy" and intrusive federal power. As with "liberal" and "Left," I use "conservative" and "the Right" interchangeably to signify a hostility to programs such as affirmative action, school busing for racial balance, increased spending for health and education, the expansion of the welfare state, and the principle of greater tolerance for racial and sexual differences. In the period under study the Right also argued for a more aggressive stance toward communism, for so-called traditional family values, and for supply-side economics and a preference for the free market over active government. Ibid., 144.

6. Curt Smith, interview with the author, May 7, 2004. Smith worked for President Bush from 1989 to 1993, drafting more speeches for him than any other writer. Unless otherwise noted, all interviews quoted in this book were conducted by telephone; the first time each interviewee is mentioned, a brief biographical description will appear in the note.

7. Craig Shirley, interview with the author, July 1, 2004. Shirley was a paid consultant for the Reagan White House from 1985 to 1988, as well as a consultant to Vice President Bush and an informal consultant once he became president.

8. Ken Askew, senior speechwriter for President George H. W. Bush, interview with the author, May 5, 2004.

9. Bill Bradley, interview with the author, December 14, 2004. A former three-term New Jersey Democratic senator, Bradley ran for president in 2000.

10. Caspar Weinberger, interview with the author, June 23, 2004. Weinberger was secretary of defense from 1981 to 1987. He died on March 28, 2006.

11. Robert H. Bork, interview with the author, February 8, 2005. A former judge, Bork was unsuccessfully nominated for the U.S. Supreme Court by Ronald Reagan in 1987.

12. Alessandra Stanley, "Marilyn Quayle Says the 1960's Had a Flip Side," *New York Times*, August 20, 1992.

13. Phyllis Schlafly, interview with the author, April 7, 2004. The conservative antifeminist founder of the Eagle Forum, Schlafly has attended every Republican convention since 1952 and is best known for her successful campaign against the Equal Rights Amendment.

14. Lisa Schiffren, Vice President Quayle's speechwriter in 1991 and 1992, interview with the author, February 4, 2005.

15. Gary Bauer, e-mail interview with the author, June 16, 2004. President Reagan's undersecretary of education and domestic policy adviser from 1985 to 1989, Bauer ran for the 2000 Republican nomination for president.

16. Hanna Rosin, "The Seeds of a Philosophy: Horowitz Cited as Key Influence on Bush," *Washington Post*, July 23, 2000.

17. George W. Bush, Acceptance Speech at the Republican National Convention, Philadelphia, August 3, 2000, www.pbs.org/newshour/election2000/gopconvention/george_w_bush.html.

18. Frank Rich, op-ed columnist for the *New York Times*, interview with the author, January 12, 2005.

19. Jeff Shesol, interview with the author, June 29, 2004. A member of President Clinton's senior staff between 1998 and 2001, Shesol served as deputy assistant to the president and as a deputy director of presidential speechwriting.

20. For a study of how history is shaped by competing generations, see William Strauss and Neil Howe, *Generations: The History of America's Future, 1584 to 2069* (New York: William Morrow, 1991).

21. See Nicholas Kristof, "George W. Bush's Journey: Confronting the Counterculture," *New York Times*, June 19, 2000.

22. Bob Woodward, investigative reporter, author, and assistant managing editor of the *Washington Post*, interview with the author, Washington, D.C., December 15, 2004.

23. Tom Hayden, e-mail correspondence with the author, May 17, 2004. Hayden was a key participant in the antiwar and civil rights movements of the 1960s and co-founder of the activist group Students for a Democratic Society (SDS) in 1962.

1. "The Sixties"

Epigraph: Barack Obama, *The Audacity of Hope: Thoughts on Reclaiming the American Dream* (New York: Three Rivers Press, 2006), 32.

1. David Kusnet, speechwriter for Democratic presidential candidates Walter Mondale, Michael Dukakis, and Bill Clinton, interview with the author, June 30, 2004.

2. Ibid.

3. Paul Kirk, Democratic National Committee chairman from 1985 to 1989, interview with the author, April 1, 2004.

4. Edwin Feulner, interview with the author, Washington, D.C., December 15, 2004. The Heritage Foundation is the nation's leading conservative think tank.

5. Schlafly interview, April 7, 2004.

6. Peter Collier, interview with the author, May 5, 2004. Former editor, along with David Horowitz, of *Ramparts*, the flagship magazine of the New Left in the 1960s; Collier switched to the Right after the 1960s.

7. C. Landon Parvin, interview with the author, April 16, 2004. Parvin was a speechwriter for the Reagans at the White House and later a consultant to the former president.

8. Peter Robinson, interview with the author, May 25, 2004. Robinson was chief speechwriter to Vice President Bush from 1982 to 1983 and special assistant and speechwriter to President Reagan from 1983 to 1988.

9. *Washington Post* political columnist David Broder, interview with the author, April 27, 2004.

10. Bork interview, February 8, 2005.

11. Daniel Ellsberg, interview with the author, December 28, 2004. Ellsberg is the longtime political activist and former military analyst who in 1971 released the Pentagon Papers to the *New York Times*.

12. Thomas C. Reed, Reagan confidant and special assistant for national security policy, interview with the author, January 5, 2005.

13. Benjamin C. Bradlee, interview with the author, Washington, D.C., December 15, 2004. Vice president at large of the *Washington Post*, Bradlee served as executive editor of the paper from 1968 to 1991.

14. David Maraniss, interview with the author, March 9, 2004. A staff reporter for the *Washington Post*, Maraniss won the 1993 Pulitzer Prize for national reporting for his coverage of Bill Clinton's life and career.

15. Godfrey Hodgson, interview with the author, October 11, 2004. Hodgson, a British historian and associate fellow at the Rothermere American Institute at Oxford, has written widely on recent American history. The historians Alan Brinkley (interview with the author, New York City, March 23, 2004) and Herbert Parmet (interview with the author, May 7, 2004) expressed similar views.

16. Rick Perlstein, journalist and historian of the 1960s, interview with the author, July 7, 2004.

17. Thomas Frank, interview with the author, September 21, 2004. Frank is the bestselling author of *What's the Matter with Kansas? How Conservatives Won the Heart of America*.

18. Alan Brinkley, professor of history at Columbia University, interview with the author, New York City, March 23, 2004.

19. Pierre S. du Pont IV, interview with the author, May 5, 2004. Du Pont was Republican governor of Delaware from 1977 to 1985 and ran in the 1988 presidential primaries.

20. Smith interview, May 7, 2004.

21. Broder interview, April 27, 2004.

22. Kusnet interview, June 30, 2004.

23. Brinkley interview, New York City, March 23, 2004.

24. Smith interview, May 7, 2004.

25. Feulner interview, Washington, D.C., December 15, 2004.

26. Morton Blackwell, interview with the author, July 6, 2004. Blackwell attended the 1968 Republican convention as a Reagan alternate delegate from Louisiana, served from 1981 to 1983 in Reagan's White House, and became president of the Leadership Institute, a training ground for conservatives.

27. Schiffren interview, February 4, 2005.

28. Bork interview, February 8, 2005.

29. Stuart K. Spencer, interview with the author, August 5, 2004. A longtime Republican strategist and Reagan confidant, Spencer managed Reagan's 1966 run for California governor and worked with him throughout his career.

30. L. Brent Bozell III, founder of the conservative Media Research Center, the nation's largest media watchdog organization, interview with the author, June 3, 2004. Bozell's

father, whose brother-in-law was conservative icon William F. Buckley, ghostwrote Barry Goldwater's seminal 1960 text *Conscience of a Conservative,* considered the bible of the Right.

31. David Keene, interview with the author, May 4, 2004. The American Conservative Union, the nation's oldest conservative lobbying organization, was founded months after Lyndon Johnson's 1964 landslide victory over Goldwater.

32. Paul Weyrich, interview with the author, April 23, 2004. Weyrich co-founded the Heritage Foundation and the Moral Majority. He died on December 18, 2008.

33. Stephen Moore, interview with the author, July 2, 2004. A leading conservative activist, Moore founded and served as president of the conservative economic lobbying organization the Club for Growth.

34. Michael Dukakis, professor of political science at Northeastern University, interview with the author, Boston, August 25, 2004. Dukakis was the 1988 Democratic presidential nominee.

35. Timothy Wirth, interview with the author, May 26, 2005. Democratic senator from Colorado from 1986 to 1992, Wirth was a deputy assistant secretary of education in the first Nixon administration and President Clinton's undersecretary of state for global affairs.

36. Gary Hart, interview with the author, March 2, 2004. Democratic senator from Colorado from 1974 to 1986, Hart ran for the presidency in 1984 and 1988.

37. Noam Chomsky, interview with the author, April 30, 2004. Chomsky, a prominent political activist and critic of U.S. foreign and domestic policy, is professor emeritus of linguistics at Massachusetts Institute of Technology.

38. Arthur M. Schlesinger Jr., interview with the author, August 30, 2004. Democratic activist and historian of American liberalism, Schlesinger wrote speeches for the presidential campaigns of Adlai Stevenson, John F. Kennedy, Robert Kennedy, and Edward Kennedy; served as special assistant to the president in John F. Kennedy's administration; and was Albert Schweitzer professor emeritus of humanities at the City University of New York Graduate Center. He died on February 28, 2007.

39. Liberal pundit Mark Shields, interview with the author, June 30, 2004. Shields worked on the presidential campaigns of Robert Kennedy, Sargent Shriver, and Edmund Muskie.

40. Helen Thomas, interview with the author, October 4, 2004. Thomas has covered every president since Kennedy and for fifty-seven years was White House correspondent for United Press International.

41. Bruce Schulman, Boston University history professor, interview with the author, August 10, 2004; Derek Bok, Harvard University professor and president of Harvard from 1971 to 1991, interview with the author, October 5, 2004.

42. Michael Deaver, interview with the author, July 14, 2004. Deaver was one of Reagan's closest advisers and his assistant and deputy chief of staff from 1981 to 1985. He died on August 18, 2007.

43. Weyrich interview, April 23, 2004.

44. Bork interview, February 8, 2005.

45. Smith interview, May 7, 2004.

46. Doug Rossinow, interview with the author, September 21, 2004. A professor of history at Metropolitan State University in Minnesota, Rossinow is the author of *The Politics of Authenticity: Liberalism, Christianity, and the New Left in America.*

47. Journalist and author Frances FitzGerald, interview with the author, New York City, March 25, 2004.

48. Rich interview, January 12, 2005.

49. Jo Freeman, interview with the author, June 20, 2004. Freeman is the author of *At Berkeley in the Sixties: The Education of an Activist, 1961–1965.*

50. Maurice Isserman, professor of history at Hamilton College and co-author of *America Divided: The Civil War of the 1960s*, interview with the author, May 6, 2004.

51. Bok interview, October 5, 2004.

52. Chomsky interview, April 30, 2004.

53. Bradley interview, December 14, 2004.

54. Dukakis interview, Boston, August 25, 2004.

55. Roger Wilkins, interview with the author, December 21, 2004. The noted civil rights leader and journalist, a professor of history and American culture at George Mason University, was an assistant attorney general during the Johnson administration.

56. Ibid.

57. Anthony R. Dolan, interview with the author, May 11, 2004. Dolan was President Reagan's chief speechwriter for eight years.

58. Bruce Miroff, interview with the author, November 24, 2004. A political science professor at the State University of New York at Albany, Miroff did his undergraduate and graduate work at the University of California at Berkeley between 1962 and 1974.

59. David Halberstam, Pulitzer Prize–winning journalist and historian, interview with the author, November 13, 2004. He died on April 23, 2007.

60. Schlesinger interview, New York City, August 26, 2004.

61. Shesol interview, June 29, 2004.

62. Hodgson interview, October 11, 2004.

63. Donald J. Devine, interview with the author, July 19, 2004. Vice chairman of the American Conservative Union, Devine ran the Office of Personnel Management in President Reagan's first term.

64. Ron Robinson, president of the Young America's Foundation, interview with the author, July 12, 2004. The foundation is the nation's largest conservative campus outreach program.

65. Richard Viguerie, interview with the author, June 1, 2004. Political and campaign strategist, activist, writer, and conservative spokesman, in 1961 Viguerie became executive secretary of Young Americans for Freedom, the conservative youth group. Since 1965 he has owned conservative direct marketing and advertising companies.

66. Keene interview, May 4, 2004.

67. William Rusher, interview with the author, March 30, 2004. Former publisher of the *National Review* and an early mentor of Young Americans for Freedom, Rusher participated in Goldwater's and Reagan's campaigns in the 1960s.

68. Frank Atkinson, interview with the author, July 12, 2004. Atkinson worked in the Reagan Justice Department and was counselor to the attorney general during Reagan's second term.

69. Frank J. Fahrenkopf Jr., interview with the author, March 22, 2004. Fahrenkopf chaired the Republican National Committee from 1983 to 1989.

70. Edwin Meese III, interview with the author, Washington, D.C., December 15, 2004. A fellow at the Heritage Foundation and one of Reagan's most trusted advisers, Meese served as Governor Reagan's chief of staff from 1969 through 1974 and as President Reagan's counselor and attorney general.

71. Spencer interview, August 5, 2004.

72. Viguerie interview, June 1, 2004.

73. Don Irvine, interview with the author, December 22, 2004. Irvine is chairman of Accuracy in Media, the nation's oldest conservative media watchdog organization.

74. Ibid.

75. Hart interview, March 2, 2004.

76. Kusnet interview, June 30, 2004.

77. Paul Glastris, interview with the author, June 22, 2004. Editor in chief of the *Washington Monthly* and senior fellow at the Western Policy Center, Glastris was a speechwriter for President Clinton from 1998 through 2001.

78. John Shattuck, interview with the author, May 6, 2004. President Clinton's undersecretary of state for democracy, human rights, and labor and Clinton's ambassador to the Czech Republic, Shattuck is chief executive officer of the John F. Kennedy Library Foundation.

79. Peter Edelman, interview with the author, May 19, 2004. A professor of law at Georgetown University Law Center, Edelman was assistant secretary of health and human services before resigning in protest over President Clinton's decision to sign the 1996 Welfare Reform Bill.

80. Lewis Powell Jr. to Eugene B. Sydnor Jr., Chairman, Education Committee, "Attack on American Free Enterprise System: The Powell Memorandum," U.S. Chamber of Commerce, August 23, 1971.

81. Ibid.

82. Ronald Reagan, First Inaugural Address, January 20, 1981, www.reagan.utexas.edu/ archives/speeches/publicpapers.html. Unless otherwise noted, all of Ronald Reagan's speeches and other statements cited in this chapter are available at this site and can be accessed by date.

83. The Watergate burglary was partly aimed at finding information to discredit Nixon's enemies, especially those in the rapidly growing antiwar movement. As Nixon's former chief of staff Robert Haldeman said, "Without the Vietnam War there would have been no Watergate." Fred Emery, *Watergate: The Corruption of American Politics and the Fall of Richard Nixon* (New York: Touchstone, 1994), 8.

84. H. W. Brands, professor of history at the University of Texas, interview with the author, March 4, 2004. See also Brands, *The Strange Death of American Liberalism* (New Haven: Yale University Press, 2001).

85. Lou Cannon, author of six books on Reagan, interview with the author, April 27, 2004.

86. James A. Baker III, interview with the author, Houston, June 14, 2004. One of only a handful of Americans to have held three cabinet-level positions, Baker was President Reagan's chief of staff in his first administration, secretary of the treasury in his second, and President George H. W. Bush's secretary of state. He also headed five successive presidential campaigns.

87. G. William Whitehurst, interview with the author, June 11, 2004. Whitehurst represented Virginia's Second Congressional District from 1969 to 1987.

88. Bok interview, October 5, 2004.

89. Shattuck interview, May 11, 2004.

90. Hodgson interview, October 11, 2004.

91. Aram Bakshian, interview with the author, May 19, 2004. A speechwriter for Nixon and Ford, Bakshian was also President Reagan's director of speechwriting.

2. Blaming "the Sixties"

Epigraph: James A. Baker III, interview with the author, Houston, June 14, 2004.

1. Deaver interview, July 14, 2004.

2. Ibid.

3. Remarks to Chapter Presidents of the Catholic Golden Age Association, August 31, 1984, www.reagan.utexas.edu/archives/speeches/publicpapers.html. Unless otherwise noted, all of Ronald Reagan's speeches and other statements cited in this chapter are available at this site and can be accessed by date.

4. Ronald Reagan, *An American Life* (New York: Pocket Books, 1990), 139. In fact, during the Johnson-Goldwater presidential contest of 1964, the Great Society had not yet been enacted. Johnson announced the program in May, but the legislation was not passed until the following year. But looking back, Reagan depicted Barry Goldwater's 1964 candidacy as an antidote to those programs.

5. For approval rating, see www.gallup.com/poll/116677/Presidential-Approval-Ratings-Gallup-Historical-Statistics-Trends.aspx#2.

6. Even the Heritage Foundation would never make such a claim. See www.heritage.org/Research/Welfare/Test030701b.cfm.

7. "A Time for Choosing," Los Angeles, October 27, 1964.

8. Parvin interview, April 16, 2004.

9. Spencer interview, August 5, 2004.

10. Civil rights activist Julian Bond, interview with the author, November 16, 2004. In 1960 Bond co-founded the Student Nonviolent Coordinating Committee (SNCC) and in 1998 became chairman of the board of the NAACP.

11. Blackwell interview, July 6, 2004.

12. Adam Clymer, "Michael Deaver, Shaper of Reagan's Image, Dies at 69," *New York Times*, August 29, 2007; Deaver interview, July 14, 2004.

13. Eugene B. Meyer, interview with the author, July 16, 2004. Meyer is president of the Federalist Society, the nation's leading conservative think tank for legal issues.

14. Fahrenkopf interview, March 22, 2004.

15. Reagan, *An American Life*, 153–54.

16. "The Creative Society," University of Southern California, April 19, 1966, www.reaganlibrary.com/reagan/speeches/speech.asp?spid=2. As president, Reagan would use the term "Creative Society" on three occasions. See Remarks at the Conservative Political Action Conference Dinner, March 20, 1981; Address before a Joint Session of the Congress on the State of the Union, January 25, 1983; Remarks at a Senate Campaign Fundraiser for Representative Ed Zschau, Los Angeles, September 7, 1986.

17. Gubernatorial Inaugural Address, January 5, 1967; see also Address to California Republican Assembly, Long Beach, Calif., April 1, 1967; Address to United Republicans of California Convention, Long Beach, Calif., May 6, 1967, www.reagan.utexas.edu/archives/speeches/govspeech/govspeech.htm.

18. Reagan, *An American Life*, 170.

19. "Town Meeting of the World: The Image of America and the Youth of the World—with Sen. Robert F. Kennedy and Gov. Ronald Reagan," CBS, May 15, 1967. Reagan was in Sacramento, Kennedy in New York, and each answered questions from students in London, reagan2020.us/speeches/.

20. Reagan, *An American Life*, 176, 178.

21. Second Gubernatorial Inaugural Address, January 4, 1971, www.reagan.utexas.edu/archives/speeches/govspeech/govspeech.htm.

22. Reagan, *An American Life*, 188, 197.

23. "We Will Be as a City upon a Hill" (Speech Announcing His Presidential Intentions for the 1976 Election), Conservative Political Action Conference, Washington, D.C., January 25, 1974, reagan2020.us/speeches/.

24. "To Restore America," March 31, 1976, reagan2020.us/speeches/.

25. "The New Republican Party," Fourth Annual CPAC Convention, February 6, 1977, reagan2020.us/speeches/.

26. Ibid.

27. Reagan, *An American Life*, 198–99.

28. Acceptance Speech before the Republican National Convention, Detroit, July 17, 1980, reagan2020.us/speeches/.

29. First Inaugural Address, January 20, 1981, reagan2020.us/speeches/.

30. Broder interview, April 27, 2004.

31. Elaine Donnelly, correspondence with the author, June 28, 2004. Donnelly is president of the Michigan Center for Military Readiness; she worked on Reagan's 1980 campaign.

32. John Meyers, "A Letter from the Publisher," *Time*, February 23, 1981, 3.

33. Otto Friedrich, "To Reform the System," ibid., 36.

34. Strobe Talbott, "To Rebuild the Image," ibid., 68.

35. Lance Morrow, "To Revive Responsibility," ibid., 73–74.

36. George H. W. Bush, *All the Best, George Bush: My Life in Letters and Other Writings* (New York: Scribner, 1999), 311.

37. James A. Baker III, "The First Hundred Days: Ronald Reagan and the Return of Confidence," speech before the Houston Chamber of Commerce, April 27, 1981, Anthony Dolan Files, ser. 1: Speech Drafts, box 2, folder 14, Baker Remarks: Houston Chamber of Commerce–04/27/1981 (2), Ronald Reagan Presidential Library, Simi Valley, Calif.

38. Proclamation 4843: Older Americans Month, 1981, April 29, 1981.

39. White House Office of Speechwriting: Speech Drafts: Records, 1981–89, box 24, State of the Union 1/26/82 (4), Reagan Library.

40. See Remarks at a White House Luncheon Honoring the Astronauts of the Space Shuttle *Columbia*, May 19, 1981; Remarks at the Dedication of the James Madison Memorial Building of the Library of Congress, November 20, 1981; Remarks to Department of Transportation Employees in the Senior Executive Service, January 12, 1982; Remarks at the Swearing-In Ceremony for New United States Citizens in White House Station, New Jersey, September 17, 1982; Remarks at a White House Luncheon for Members of the President's Task Force on Private Sector Initiatives, December 8, 1982; Radio Address to the Nation on the Observance of Mother's Day, May 7, 1983. In January 1984 James Baker declared that Reagan had "inherited a wasteland." But thanks to Reagan, now "all of us are walking tall and standing proud again." Anthony Dolan Files, ser. 1: Speech Drafts, box 24, folder 25, Jim Baker: Executive Forum Speech–01/20/1984, Reagan Library.

41. Reagan, *An American Life*, 330.

42. Outline for State of the Union Address (Elliott) (State of the Union 1/25/84), Anthony Dolan Files, ser. 1: Speech Drafts, box 25, folder 1, State of the Union–01/25/1984 (13), Reagan Library.

43. Address before a Joint Session of the Congress on the State of the Union, January 25, 1984.

44. "Ours Is Not a Sick Society," September 4, 1970. Quoted in Amos Kiewe and Davis W. Houck, *A Shining City on a Hill: Ronald Reagan's Economic Rhetoric, 1951–1989* (Westport, Conn.: Praeger, 1991), 68. See also nolefttturns.ashbrook.org/comment.asp?blogID=8317.

45. Second Gubernatorial Inaugural Address, January 4, 1971, www.reagan.utexas.edu/archives/speeches/govspeech/govspeech.htm.

46. "We Will Be as a City upon a Hill."

47. Address before a Joint Session of the Congress on the Program for Economic Recovery, April 28, 1981.

48. See Remarks at the Annual Convention of the National Association of Secondary School Principals, Las Vegas, February 7, 1984; Remarks at the Annual Conference of the National League of Cities, March 5, 1984; Radio Address to the Nation on Education, May 12, 1984; Radio Address to the Nation on the Summer Olympic Games, July 28, 1984; Message to the Annual Conference of the National Urban League, Cleveland, July 30, 1984; Paul Laxalt, speech at Republican Convention nominating President Reagan, Dallas, August 22, 1984; all in Anthony Dolan Files, ser. 5: Subject Files, box 79, folder 6, Convention, 1984 (6), Reagan Library; Remarks at a Reagan-Bush Rally in Charlotte, N.C., October 8, 1984; Remarks at a Reagan-Bush Rally in Dayton, Ohio, October 12,

1984; Remarks to Members of the Congregation of Temple Hillel and Jewish Community Leaders in Valley Stream, N.Y., October 26, 1984; Radio Address to the Nation on the Presidential Campaign, October 27, 1984.

49. "Prouder, Stronger, Better," television ad, 1984 presidential campaign, www.livingroomcandidate.org/commercials/1984.

50. Remarks Accepting the Presidential Nomination at the Republican National Convention, Dallas, August 23, 1984.

51. Walter Mondale and Ronald Reagan, Presidential Debate, October 7, 1984, Louisville, Ky., www.debates.org/pages/debtrans.html.

52. Memorandum from Bruce Chapman, Anthony Blankley, and John Roberts II to Edwin Meese III, January 4, 1985, White House Office of Records Management (hereafter WHORM), Subject File, 1981–1989, SP100 286398–289883, Reagan Library.

53. Second Inaugural Address, January 21, 1985.

54. Remarks on Receiving the Final Report of the National Commission on Excellence in Education, April 26, 1983.

55. Remarks at a Ceremony Honoring the 1983–1984 Winners in the Secondary School Recognition Program, August 27, 1984.

56. Radio Address to the Nation on Education, September 8, 1984.

57. Remarks at a Senate Campaign Fundraiser for Representative James T. Broyhill, in Greensboro, N.C., June 4, 1986.

58. Remarks at a White House Ceremony Honoring the National Teacher of the Year, April 9, 1984.

59. Remarks to the National Governors' Association: Department of Education Conference, Columbia, Mo., March 26, 1987.

60. Remarks at the Commencement Ceremony for Area High School Seniors in Chattanooga, Tenn., May 19, 1987.

61. Remarks at the Annual Convention of the National Association of Evangelicals, Columbus, Ohio, March 6, 1984. See also Remarks on Signing the Just Say No to Drugs Week Proclamation, May 20, 1986.

62. Remarks at a White House Briefing for Service Organization Representatives on Drug Abuse, July 30, 1986.

63. Parvin interview, April 16, 2004.

64. Remarks to Media Executives at a White House Briefing on Drug Abuse, March 7, 1988.

65. Remarks at a White House Ceremony Honoring Law Enforcement Officers Slain in the War on Drugs, April 19, 1988. See also Remarks at the United States Coast Guard Academy Commencement Ceremony in New London, Conn., May 18, 1988; Remarks at the National Conference on Corporate Initiatives for a Drug Free Workplace, June 9, 1988.

66. Remarks to the Students and Faculty of Archbishop Carroll and All Saints High Schools, Washington, D.C., October 17, 1988.

67. Meese interview, Washington, D.C., December 15, 2004.

68. Remarks at the Mid-Winter Congressional City Conference of the National League of Cities, March 2, 1981.

69. Address before a Joint Session of the Congress Reporting on the State of the Union, January 26, 1982. See also Message to the Congress Transmitting the Annual Economic Report of the President, February 10, 1982; Remarks at a Ceremony Honoring Youth Volunteers, April 25, 1985.

70. Anthony Dolan Files, ser. 2: Speech Drafts by Other Writers, box 70, folder 25, Private Meeting with Black Reagan-Bush Supporters (Parvin)—07/09/1981, Reagan Library.

71. Message to the Congress Transmitting Proposed Employment Legislation, March 11, 1983.

72. Remarks on Signing an Executive Order on Minority Business Enterprise Development, July 14, 1983.

73. Remarks at a Fundraising Dinner for Howard University, May 20, 1982; Remarks at a White House Briefing for Minority Business Owners, July 15, 1987.

74. Remarks at the Annual Meeting of the United States Chamber of Commerce, April 26, 1982.

75. See Remarks at the Annual Meeting of the American Bar Association, Atlanta, August 1, 1983; Remarks to Employees at the Ivorydale Soap Manufacturing Plant, St. Bernard, Ohio, October 3, 1985; Remarks to Representatives of Ethnic and Fraternal Benefit Organizations during a White House Briefing on Tax Reform, October 17, 1985. For the economy since the 1960s, see Radio Address to the Nation on the First Session of the Ninety-eighth Congress, November 19, 1983; President's Remarks during a Meeting with Cuban American Leaders, March 19, 1984.

76. Radio Address to the Nation on the Economy, June 23, 1984; Radio Address to the Nation on the Agricultural and Steel Industries, September 22, 1984; Remarks at a White House Meeting with Members of the Business Council, February 19, 1986.

77. See, e.g., Radio Address to the Nation on the Federal Budget, April 12, 1986.

78. Remarks at the Annual Meeting of the International Association of Chiefs of Police, New Orleans, September 28, 1981.

79. Remarks at the Annual Convention of the Lions Club International, Dallas, June 21, 1985. See also Remarks at the Annual Conference of the National Sheriffs' Association, Hartford, Conn., June 20, 1984; Remarks on Signing the Victims of Crime Week Proclamation, April 19, 1985.

80. Meese interview, Washington, D.C., December 15, 2004.

81. Robert Bork, interview with Brian Lamb on *Booknotes*, C-Span, December 4, 1996, discussing *Slouching Towards Gomorrah: Modern Liberalism and American Decline* (New York: ReganBooks, 1996).

82. Bork interview, February 8, 2005.

83. Remarks at a White House Briefing for Members of the National Law Enforcement Council, July 29, 1987.

84. Remarks at a White House Briefing on the Nomination of Robert H. Bork to Be an Associate Justice of the Supreme Court of the United States, September 30, 1987. See also Remarks on Signing the German-American Day Proclamation, October 2, 1987.

85. Radio Address to the Nation on Volunteerism and the Supreme Court Nomination of Robert H. Bork, October 3, 1987. See also Statement on the Supreme Court Nomination of Robert H. Bork, October 9, 1987; Address to the Nation on the Supreme Court Nomination of Robert H. Bork, October 14, 1987; Remarks at a White House Briefing on Proposed Criminal Justice Reform Legislation, October 16, 1987.

86. Newt Gingrich to President Reagan, October 13, 1987, WHORM, Subject File, 1981–1989, SP1188, 492893, Bork, Robert, Confirmation, D.C., 10/14/87 (140 pages), Reagan Library. Gingrich also attached a lengthy outline, a circulated memorandum titled "Bork: A Proposed Battle for the Common Good." Gingrich was not the only conservative to use such apocalyptic language. In a hand-delivered letter to Reagan of October 13, 1987, Maiselle Dolan Shortley, chair of the National Conservative Action Committee, labeled opponents of Judge Bork a "lynch mob" (ibid.).

87. Address to Conservative Political Action Conference Dinner, February 11, 1988.

88. Shields interview, June 30, 2004.

89. Blackwell interview, July 6, 2004.

90. Meyer interview, July 16, 2004.

91. Viguerie interview, June 1, 2004.

92. Bauer e-mail interview, June 16, 2004.

93. Collier interview, May 5, 2004.

94. Shirley interview, July 1, 2004.

95. Bakshian interview, May 19, 2004.

96. Du Pont interview, May 5, 2004.

97. Irvine interview, December 22, 2004.

98. Rusher interview, March 30, 2004.

99. David Horowitz, interview with the author, May 10, 2004. The former editor, along with Peter Collier, of *Ramparts*, the flagship magazine of the New Left in the 1960s, Horowitz later became a prominent conservative activist and head of the Center for the Study of Popular Culture.

100. Remarks at a White House Reception for Delegates to the National Leadership Conference of Teen-Age Republicans, June 23, 1981.

101. See, e.g., Remarks at a Presentation Ceremony for the 1983 Young American Medals for Bravery, August 28, 1984.

102. Remarks at the 1981 White House Conference on Aging, December 1, 1981.

103. Reagan, *An American Life*, 155.

104. Remarks at an Ecumenical Prayer Breakfast, Dallas, August 23, 1984.

105. Remarks at the Annual Convention of the National Religious Broadcasters Association, February 1, 1988.

106. Smith interview, May 7, 2004.

107. Bork interview, February 8, 2005.

108. Remarks at the Annual Meeting of the National Association of Towns and Townships, September 12, 1983.

109. Peggy Noonan, *What I Saw at the Revolution: A Political Life in the Reagan Era* (New York: Ivy Books, 1990), 11–14.

3. A Tale of Two Sixties

Epigraph: Peggy Noonan, note to Ronald Reagan accompanying her first draft of his farewell address, 1989. WHORM, Subject File, 1981–1989, Address to the Nation (Farewell), 1/11/89 (800 pages), SP1314, 589277 (8), Reagan Library.

1. Address to the Nation on the Federal Budget and Deficit Reduction, April 24, 1985, www.reagan.utexas.edu/archives/speeches/publicpapers.html. Unless otherwise noted, all of Ronald Reagan's speeches and other statements cited in this chapter are available at this site and can be accessed by date.

2. Peggy Noonan, *What I Saw at the Revolution: A Political Life in the Reagan Era* (New York: Ivy Books, 1990), 238.

3. Remarks at a Fundraising Reception for the John F. Kennedy Library Foundation, June 24, 1985.

4. Ibid.

5. Noonan, *What I Saw at the Revolution*, 4–9.

6. Remarks at Reception for Kennedy Library Foundation.

7. Noonan, *What I Saw at the Revolution*, 240.

8. Robinson interview, May 25, 2004.

9. *The Cumulated Indexes to the Public Papers of the Presidents of the United States: Ronald Reagan, 1981–1989* (Lanham, Md.: Bernan Press, 1995), 60; Paul R. Henggeler, *The Kennedy Persuasion: The Politics of Style since JFK* (Chicago: Ivan R. Dee, 1995), 180.

10. Shields interview, June 30, 2004.

11. Bozell interview, June 3, 2004.

12. Smith interview, May 7, 2004.

13. Feulner interview, Washington, D.C., December 15, 2004.

14. Fahrenkopf interview, March 22, 2004.

15. Deaver interview, July 14, 2004.

16. Adam Walinsky, interview with the author, June 10, 2004. In 1964 Walinsky became Robert Kennedy's legislative assistant with responsibility for much of Senator Kennedy's work on foreign and domestic issues until his assassination.

17. Schlesinger interview, August 30, 2004.

18. Shields interview, June 30, 2004.

19. Archibald Cox, interview with the author, April 15, 2004. Cox was appointed the first special prosecutor for the Watergate investigation. He died on May 29, 2004.

20. Kusnet interview, June 30, 2004.

21. Henggeler, *The Kennedy Persuasion*, 174.

22. Jeffrey M. Jones, "Bush's Approval Rating in Perspective: Most Other Presidents Had Worse Low Points," Gallup Poll, March 30, 2005, www.gallup.com/poll/15463/Bushs-Approval-Rating-Perspective.aspx.

23. Joseph Carroll and Frank Newport, "A Gallup Poll Review of the Clinton Presidency: Bill Clinton's Job Approval Rating Went Up, Not Down, during the Impeachment Years," June 21, 2004, www.gallup.com/poll/12058/Gallup-Poll-Review-Clinton-Presidency.aspx.

24. Lydia Saad, "Americans: Kennedy Assassination a Conspiracy; No Consensus about Who Was Involved," Gallup News Services, November 21, 2003, www.gallup.com/poll/9751/Americans-Kennedy-Assassination-Conspiracy.aspx.

25. Herbert Parmet, interview with the author, May 7, 2004. Parmet has also written a biography of George H. W. Bush.

26. Schulman interview, August 10, 2004.

27. Fahrenkopf interview, March 22, 2004.

28. Perlstein interview, July 7, 2004.

29. Schulman interview, August 10, 2004.

30. David Greenberg, "History Lesson: Tax Cuts in Camelot? JFK Lowered Taxes, but Supply-Siders Wrongly Claim He's Their Patron Saint," *Slate*, January 16, 2004, www.slate.com; David Shreve, "President Kennedy and the 1964 Tax Cut," Miller Center at the University of Virginia Presidential Recordings Project, Spring 2001; Robert Shrum, "Varnish Remover: JFK as Forrest Gump," *Slate*, August 15, 1997, www.slate.com.

31. Blackwell interview, July 6, 2004.

32. Moore interview, July 2, 2004.

33. Meese interview, Washington, D.C., December 15, 2004.

34. Weyrich interview, April 23, 2004.

35. Remarks at the Illinois Forum Reception, Chicago, September 2, 1981.

36. Remarks at an Ohio State Republican Fundraising Reception, Cincinnati, November 30, 1981.

37. Oval Office interview with the President, December 23, 1981.

38. Remarks to Business and Trade Representatives during a White House Briefing on the Fiscal Year 1986 Budget, February 4, 1985.

39. Remarks at the "Prelude to Independence" Celebration, Williamsburg, Va., May 30, 1985.

40. Dolan interview, May 11, 2004.

41. See Remarks at the National Conference of the National Federation of Independent Business, June 22, 1983; Radio Address to the Nation on Federal Income Taxes, April 9, 1983; Address before a Joint Session of the Congress on the State of the Union, January 25, 1984; Remarks at the Annual Senate-House Fundraising Dinner, May 10, 1984; Radio Address to the Nation on Administration Policies, August 18, 1984; Remarks at a Reagan-Bush Rally, Cupertino, Calif., September 3, 1984.

42. Remarks at the Annual Convention of the National Association for the Advancement of Colored People, Denver, June 29, 1981. See also Remarks at a Reagan-Bush Rally,

Brownsville, Texas, October 2, 1984. Many questioned his claim. "'A rising tide lifts all boats' is a classic conservative illusion. . . . It's not true," said Godfrey Hodgson. Hodgson's research demonstrated that between 1980 and 1992 middle-class incomes fell, while income of the top 5 percent grew by 30 percent and of the top 1 percent by 78 percent. Hodgson interview, October 11, 2004; Godfrey Hodgson, *More Equal Than Others: America from Nixon to the New Century* (Princeton: Princeton University Press, 2004), 291.

43. Moore interview, July 2, 2004.

44. Collier interview, May 5, 2004.

45. Reed interview, January 5, 2005.

46. Weyrich interview, April 23, 2004.

47. Horowitz interview, May 10, 2004.

48. Remarks on Presenting the Presidential Citizens Medal to Raymond Weeks at a Veterans Day Ceremony, November 11, 1982.

49. Address to the Nation on Strategic Arms Reduction and Nuclear Deterrence, November 22, 1982.

50. Ronald Reagan, *An American Life* (New York: Pocket Books, 1990), 295. See also Address to the Nation on National Security Adviser, February 26, 1986.

51. Remarks at the National Leadership Forum of the Center for International and Strategic Studies of Georgetown University, April 6, 1984.

52. Address before a Joint Session of the Tennessee State Legislature, Nashville, March 15, 1982. See also Address to the Nation on Defense and National Security, March 23, 1983; Remarks at a Mississippi Republican Party Fundraising Dinner, Jackson, June 20, 1983; Address at the United States Naval Academy Commencement Exercises, Annapolis, May 22, 1985; Statement on Signing the International Security and Development Cooperation Act of 1985, August 8, 1985; Remarks at a White House Meeting with 1984 Reagan-Bush Campaign Supporters, November 6, 1985.

53. Address to the Nation on United States Policy in Central America, May 9, 1984. Reagan extensively invoked Kennedy to build support for his Central American policy. See Address to the Nation on the Situation in Nicaragua, March 16, 1986; Address to the Permanent Council of the Organization of American States, October 7, 1987.

54. *Cumulated Indexes: Ronald Reagan*, 60.

55. Paul Laxalt, speech at Republican Convention nominating President Reagan, Dallas, August 22, 1984, Dallas, Anthony Dolan Files, ser. 5: Subject Files, box 79, folder 6, Convention, 1984 (6), Ronald Reagan Presidential Library, Simi Valley, Calif.

56. Reagan's only references as president to McGovern came in the election years 1984 and 1988. *Cumulated Indexes: Ronald Reagan*, 74.

57. Remarks Accepting the Presidential Nomination at the Republican National Convention, Dallas, August 23, 1984.

58. Remarks at a Polish Festival, Doylestown, Pa., September 9, 1984.

59. Remarks at a Reagan-Bush Rally, Endicott, N.Y., September 12, 1984; Remarks at Dedication Ceremonies for Santa Maria Towers, Buffalo, N.Y., September 12, 1984; Remarks at a Reagan-Bush Rally, Hammonton, N.J., September 19, 1984.

60. Remarks at a Reagan-Bush Rally, Waterbury, Conn., September 19, 1984.

61. Remarks at a Reagan-Bush Rally, Cedar Rapids, Iowa, September 20, 1984.

62. Remarks at the Annual Family Oktoberfest, Milwaukee, September 26, 1984.

63. Remarks and a Question-and-Answer Session at Bowling Green State University, Bowling Green, Ohio, September 26, 1984; Remarks to Employees at a Rockwell International Facility, Palmdale, Calif., October 22, 1984.

64. Remarks at a Reagan-Bush Rally, Louisville, Ky., October 7, 1984.

65. Remarks at a Reagan-Bush Rally, Warren, Mich., October 10, 1984.

66. Walter Mondale and Ronald Reagan Presidential Debate, Louisville, Ky., October 7, 1984, www.debates.org/pages/debtrans.html.

67. President's Remarks at a Reagan-Bush Rally, Fairfield, Conn., October 26, 1984.

68. Anthony Dolan Files, ser. 1: Speech Drafts, box 31, folder 6, Reagan-Bush Rally, Fairfield, Conn., 10/26/84, Reagan Library.

69. Remarks at a Reagan-Bush Rally, Boston, November 1, 1984.

70. "101 Academics Buy Ad to Back Mondale," *New York Times*, October 31, 1984.

71. Kirk interview, April 1, 2004.

72. Clifford May, interview with the author, April 22, 2004. Head of the Foundation for the Defense of Democracies, from 1997 to 2001 May was the Republican National Committee's director of communications.

73. Elaine Donnelly, correspondence with the author, June 28, 2004.

74. Presidential Debate, October 7, 1984, Louisville, Ky., www.debates.org/pages/debt-rans.html.

75. Meese interview, Washington, D.C., December 15, 2004.

76. Meyer interview, July 16, 2004.

77. Blackwell interview, July 6, 2004.

78. Viguerie interview, June 1, 2004.

79. Reagan, *An American Life*, 316.

80. Radio Address to the Nation on the American Family, December 3, 1983. See also Radio Address to the Nation on Welfare Reform, February 15, 1986; Address before a Joint Session of Congress on the State of the Union, January 25, 1988.

81. Presidential Remarks, DropBy Briefing on Welfare Reform, February 9, 1987.

82. Remarks at the Annual Meeting of the National Alliance of Business, September 14, 1987.

83. Deaver interview, July 14, 2004. In his criticism of welfare in his 1967 gubernatorial inaugural address, wrote Lou Cannon, Reagan used "words that foreshadowed President Bill Clinton by three decades." Lou Cannon, *Governor Reagan: His Rise to Power* (New York: Public Affairs, 2003), 174. In Cannon's account—the most comprehensive analysis to date of Reagan's governorship—welfare reform dominated Reagan's second term as governor, which began in 1971 (348–62).

84. W. Elliot Brownlee and Hugh Davis Graham, eds., *The Reagan Presidency: Pragmatic Conservatism and Its Legacies* (Lawrence: University of Kansas Press, 2003), 363.

85. Interview with Representatives of the *Washington Times*, November 27, 1984. He repeated these assertions frequently in the months to come, often word for word. See Interview with Ann Devroy and Johanna Neuman of *USA Today*, January 17, 1985; Interview with the *Wall Street Journal*, February 7, 1985; Interview with Representatives of College Radio Stations, September 9, 1985. Reagan often blamed the Great Society for the deficit. See Remarks at the Annual Meeting of the Chamber of Commerce of the United States, April 29, 1985; Remarks at a White House Meeting with Reagan-Bush Campaign Leadership Groups, October 7, 1985; Interview with Lou Cannon and David Hoffman of the *Washington Post*, February 10, 1986; Remarks at the 1987 Reagan Administration Executive Forum, March 30, 1987.

86. Remarks at a Republican Party Fundraising Reception, October 11, 1988.

87. Reagan, *An American Life*, 198.

88. Shesol interview, June 29, 2004.

89. Meese interview, Washington, D.C., December 15, 2004.

90. Bork interview, February 8, 2005.

91. Bozell interview, June 3, 2004.

92. Remarks at the Young Leadership Conference of the United Jewish Appeal, March 13, 1984.

93. Schlafly interview, April 7, 2004.

94. Remarks at the Annual Dinner of the Knights of Malta, New York, January 13, 1989.

95. Bakshian interview, May 19, 2004.

96. Robinson interview, May 25, 2004.

97. Remarks and a Question-and-Answer Session with Regional Editors and Broadcasters, February 10, 1986.

98. Remarks at a Kansas Republican Party Fundraising Luncheon, Topeka, September 9, 1982.

99. Remarks to Religious Leaders at a White House Meeting on Tax Reform, October 29, 1985.

100. Remarks at a Fundraising Dinner Honoring Former Representative John M. Ashbrook, Ashland, Ohio, May 9, 1983.

101. Michael Kazin, professor of history at Georgetown University and co-author of *America Divided: The Civil War of the 1960s*, interview with the author, June 1, 2004.

102. Interview with Midwest Regional Reporters on Foreign and Domestic Issues, March 20, 1984. See also Remarks to the House Republican Caucus on the Budget Deficit, March 21, 1984; Radio Address to the Nation on Welfare Reform, February 15, 1986.

103. Interview with Tom Winter and Joseph Baldacchino Jr. of *Human Events*, December 6, 1984.

104. Remarks to the Students and Faculty at North Carolina State University, Raleigh, September 5, 1985. See also Remarks at a Senior Citizens Forum on Tax Reform, Tampa, September 12, 1985.

105. Remarks at a White House Briefing for Members of the American Legislative Exchange Council, May 1, 1987; Remarks to State and Local Republican Officials on Federalism and Aid to the Nicaraguan Democratic Resistance, March 22, 1988.

106. White House Office of Speechwriting, Speech Drafts: Records, 1981–89, box 349, Radio Talk: Welfare Reform, Presidential Radio Talk: Welfare, Saturday, February 7, 1987, Reagan Library.

107. "Table B-29—Number and Median Income (in 1985 Dollars) of Families and Persons, and Poverty Status, by Race, Selected Years, 1960–85," White House Office of Speechwriting, Speech Drafts: Records, 1981–89, box 349, DropBy Briefing on Welfare Reform, 2/9/87 (3), Reagan Library. These same figures are used in Mark Green, *Reagan's Reign of Error* (New York: Pantheon, 1987), 159.

108. In separate interviews Thomas Edsall, Mark Shields, Robert Dallek, and Michael Kazin also referred to these statistics when asked about Reagan's contention that poverty increased during the Great Society. Edsall interview, November 19, 2004; Shields interview, June 30, 2004; Dallek interview, March 6, 2004; Kazin interview, June 1, 2004. Sidney Blumenthal called Reagan's charge that the Great Society increased poverty and broke up the family "utterly false. The Great Society led to the greatest decrease in poverty since the New Deal. . . . Conservatives make up [their evidence]." Sidney Blumenthal, interview with the author, July 10, 2004. A liberal journalist, Blumenthal was an assistant and also a senior adviser to President Clinton from 1997 to 2001.

109. Schlesinger interview, New York City, August 26, 2004.

110. Nicholas Katzenbach, interview with the author, June 28, 2004. Katzenbach was Kennedy's deputy attorney general; he also served as attorney general and undersecretary of state in the Johnson administration.

111. "As a guy who had pulled himself up by his bootstraps, Johnson was enamored with that notion of American progress," Shesol said. "He was not a big fan of welfare." Johnson was approached "with some ideas about welfare reform in about '64–'65, and he just didn't want to talk about it—not because he didn't think the welfare system needed to be reformed, [but] just because he didn't want to talk about the welfare system. He just wasn't comfortable with it. He disliked the culture of dependency (although he probably never would have called it that) and food stamps." Shesol interview, June 29, 2004.

112. Ibid.

113. Bozell interview, June 3, 2004; Clark Judge, speechwriter and special assistant to President Reagan and Vice President Bush, interview with the author, June 2, 2004; Moore interview, July 2, 2004.

114. David Leonhardt, "U.S. Poverty Rate Was Up Last Year," *New York Times* August 31, 2005.

115. Remarks at the Annual Convention of the National Association for the Advancement of Colored People, Denver, June 29, 1981.

116. Memorandum to Ron Franklin from McClaughry regarding NAACP Speech, June 5, 1981, Anthony Dolan Files, ser. 2: Speech Drafts by Other Writers, box 70, folder 19, NAACP Speech (Parvin)–06/29/1981 (3), Reagan Library.

117. Memorandum to Ed Gray and Landon Parvin from McClaughry regarding NAACP Speech, June 16, 1981, ibid.

118. Memorandum to Tony Dolan and C. Landon Parvin from Mike Horowitz regarding NAACP Speech, June 26, 1981, ibid. Mike Horowitz was general counsel for the Office of Management and Budget from 1981 to 1985.

119. Remarks at a Rally in Richmond, Va., for Gubernatorial Candidate Marshall Coleman, October 27, 1981. Reagan repeated this anecdote a few weeks later; see Remarks at a "Salute to a Stronger America" Republican Fundraising Dinner, Houston, November 13, 1981.

120. Remarks at a National Black Republican Council Dinner, September 15, 1982. See also Remarks at a Fundraising Dinner Honoring Former Representative John M. Ashbrook.

121. Remarks at a Fundraising Dinner for Howard University, May 20, 1982; Remarks and a Question-and-Answer Session with the Student Body of Providence–St. Mel High School, Chicago, May 10, 1982; Remarks at a National Black Republican Council Dinner, September 15, 1982.

122. Schlafly interview, April 7, 2004.

123. Meese interview, Washington, D.C., December 15, 2004.

124. Blackwell interview, July 6, 2004.

125. Remarks to Members of the National Association of Minority Contractors, June 27, 1984.

126. Remarks at the Tuskegee University Commencement Ceremony, Tuskegee, Ala., May 10, 1987.

127. Reagan, *An American Life*, 150.

128. Ibid., 638.

129. Lena Williams, "Most of U.S. Will Honor Dr. King, but Some Still Dispute the Holiday," *New York Times*, January 18, 1987.

130. Steven V. Roberts, "Senate Votes Holiday to Honor Dr. King," *New York Times*, October 20, 1983.

131. Steven V. Roberts, "Senators Are Firm on King Holiday," *New York Times*, October 19, 1983.

132. William Safire, "Happy King's Birthday," *New York Times*, October 20, 1983.

133. Roberts, "Senators Are Firm on King Holiday."

134. Roberts, "Senate Votes Holiday to Honor Dr. King."

135. Steven V. Roberts, "King Holiday: Balky Minority in G.O.P.," *New York Times*, October 21, 1983.

136. Roberts, "Senate Votes Holiday to Honor Dr. King."

137. Roberts, "King Holiday: Balky Minority in G.O.P."

138. President's News Conference, October 19, 1983.

139. Bernard Weinraub, "Mondale Seeks to Allay Southern Fears on Image," *New York Times*, October 21, 1983.

140. Roberts, "King Holiday: Balky Minority in G.O.P."

141. "Editorial Desk: Not a 35-Year Question," *New York Times*, October 21, 1983.

142. Anthony Lewis, "The Real Reagan," *New York Times*, October 24, 1983.

143. Francis X. Clines, "Reagan's Doubts on Dr. King Disclosed," *New York Times*, October 22, 1983.

144. Ibid. See also Caroline Rand Herron and Michael Wright, "A National Day for Dr. King," *New York Times*, October 23, 1983.

145. Robinson interview, May 25, 2004.

146. Ibid.

147. Kiron Skinner, "The Odd Couple," *New York Times*, January 19, 2004.

148. Cannon interview, April 27, 2004.

149. Ibid.

150. Katzenbach interview, June 28, 2004.

151. Bradley interview, December 14, 2004.

152. Isserman interview, May 8, 2004.

153. Kazin interview, June 1, 2004.

154. Al From, interview with the author, December 22, 2004. From was the founder and CEO of the Democratic Leadership Council, a group of centrist Democrats organized in 1985.

155. Broder interview, April 27, 2004.

156. Harold Ickes, President Clinton's deputy chief of staff from 1992 to 1996, interview with the author, January 20, 2005.

157. Harry J. Middleton, e-mail interview with the author, May 7, 2004. Middleton went on to serve as the director of the LBJ Library and Museum and executive director of the LBJ Foundation.

158. Kirk interview, April 1, 2004.

159. Katzenbach interview, June 28, 2004. See also Nicol Rae, *The Decline and Fall of the Liberal Republicans: From 1952 to the Present* (New York: Oxford University Press, 1989); Rae, *Southern Democrats* (New York: Oxford University Press, 1994); Dan T. Carter, *The Politics of Rage: George Wallace, the Origins of the New Conservatism, and the Transformation of American Politics* (Baton Rouge: Louisiana State University Press, 2000).

160. Maraniss interview, March 9, 2004.

161. Ted Widmer, speechwriter for President Clinton from 1997 to 2000, interview with the author, December 1, 2004.

162. Katzenbach interview, June 28, 2004.

163. Wilkins interview, December 21, 2004.

164. Ibid.

4. Reagan and the Memory of the Vietnam War

Epigraph: Remarks at Memorial Day Ceremonies Honoring an Unknown Serviceman of the Vietnam Conflict, May 28, 1984. www.reagan.utexas.edu/archives/speeches/public-papers.html. Unless otherwise noted, all of Ronald Reagan's speeches and other statements cited in this chapter are available at this site and can be accessed by date.

1. Radio Address to the Nation on POW's and MIA's in Southeast Asia, July 19, 1986.

2. Deaver interview, July 14, 2004.

3. Reed interview, January 5, 2005.

4. Thomas interview, October 4, 2004.

5. Weinberger interview, June 23, 2004. See also Caspar Weinberger, *In the Arena: A Memoir of the 20th Century* (Washington, D.C.: Regnery, 2003); Weinberger, *Fighting for Peace: Seven Critical Years in the Pentagon* (New York: Warner Books, 1991).

6. Cannon interview, April 27, 2004.

7. Lou Cannon, *President Reagan: The Role of a Lifetime* (New York: PublicAffairs, 1991), 289–90.

8. FitzGerald interview, New York City, March 25, 2004.

9. Cannon, *President Reagan*, 290.

10. Weinberger interview, June 23, 2004.

11. Speech by Secretary of Defense Caspar Weinberger at National Press Club, November 28, 1984, www.airforce-magazine.com/MagazineArchive/Documents/2004/January%202004/0104keeperfull.pdf.

12. Cannon, *President Reagan*, 300–302.

13. George Shultz, *Turmoil and Triumph: My Years as Secretary of State* (New York: Scribner, 1993), 650.

14. Ronald Reagan, *An American Life* (New York: Pocket Books, 1990), 466.

15. Shultz, *Turmoil and Triumph*, 106.

16. Ibid., 625.

17. Ibid., 646.

18. Ibid., 285–86.

19. Reagan, *An American Life*, 478–80.

20. Shultz, *Turmoil and Triumph*, 294.

21. Address before a Joint Session of the Congress on Central America, April 27, 1983.

22. WHORM, Subject File, 1981–1989, Central America Speech 4/27/83 [Address before a Joint Session of Congress], SP283-22, 133556 (1), Ronald Reagan Presidential Library, Simi Valley, Calif. According to Thomas Reed, the Vietnam syndrome taught Americans "that great nations cannot withstand decade-long bleeding for no purpose." Reed interview, January 5, 2005.

23. Reagan, *An American Life*, 475.

24. Al Keller to President Reagan, April 28, 1983, WHORM, Subject File, 1981–1989, Central America Speech 4/27/83.

25. Hart interview, March 2, 2004.

26. Meese interview, Washington, D.C., December 15, 2004.

27. Reagan, *An American Life*, 451.

28. Whitehurst interview, June 11, 2004.

29. Baker interview, Houston, June 14, 2004.

30. Weinberger interview, June 23, 2004.

31. Reagan, *An American Life*, 456.

32. Ronald Reagan, *The Reagan Diaries*, ed. Douglas Brinkley (New York: HarperCollins, 2007), 192.

33. Reagan, *An American Life*, 456–57.

34. Stephen Zunes, "The U.S. Invasion of Grenada: A Twenty-Year Retrospective," *Global Policy Forum*, "Foreign Policy in Focus," October 2003, www.globalpolicy.org/empire/history/2003/10grenada.htm#author.

35. Shultz, *Turmoil and Triumph*, 552–53.

36. Peggy Noonan, *What I Saw at the Revolution: A Political Life in the Reagan Era* (New York: Ivy Books, 1990), 14–15.

37. Bernard Gwertzman, "Shultz Likens Latin Left to Indochina Communists," *New York Times*, April 26, 1985.

38. Steven Roberts, "Reagan Still Pushing Rebel Aid, Backed by Disgruntled Democrats," *New York Times*, April 26, 1985.

39. Remarks on Presenting the Medal of Honor to Master Sergeant Roy P. Benavidez, February 24, 1981.

40. Anthony Dolan Files, ser. 1: Speech Drafts, box 1, folder 18, Medal of Honor Ceremony–02/23/1981 (1), Reagan Library.

41. Remarks on Presenting the Medal of Honor to Master Sergeant Roy P. Benavidez.

42. Remarks at Memorial Day Ceremonies Honoring an Unknown Serviceman of the Vietnam Conflict, May 28, 1984. See also Remarks at a Ceremony Honoring an Unknown Serviceman of the Vietnam Conflict, May 25, 1984.

43. President Reagan to Mr. and Mrs. George Brooks, July 17, 1984; President Reagan to Mr. B. T. Collins, July 3, 1984, WHORM, Subject File, 1981–1989, Vietnam Unknown Soldiers Entombment, Arlington National Cemetery, 5/28/84, SP885, 228757 (8), Reagan Library.

44. Robert L. Eastburn to President Reagan, May 31, 1984, ibid.

45. "Convention, 1984," Anthony Dolan Files, ser. 5: Subject Files, box 79, folder 1, Convention, 1984 (5), Reagan Library.

46. Remarks at a Reagan-Bush Rally, Hammonton, N.J., September 19, 1984.

47. In a 1985 live performance of the song, Springsteen emphasized the soldier's death by repeating the word "gone" four times at the end of this line, and near the song's end, after a desperate long scream, Springsteen sang in anguish: "He's all gone!" Bruce Springsteen, *Live/1975–85*, Sony Records, 1986.

48. "Born in the U.S.A.," by Bruce Springsteen, Columbia Records, 1984; quoted by permission.

49. All this occurred despite Springsteen's open opposition to its use. "People have a need to feel good about the country they live in," Springsteen said. "But what's happening, I think, is that that need—which is a good thing—is getting manipulated and exploited." Todd Leopold, "The Age of Reagan: President Loomed Over the '80s, an Era at Odds with Itself," June 16, 2004, www.cnn.com. Springsteen said elsewhere that the song describes someone seeking "to strip away that mythic America which was Reagan's image of America. He wants to find something real, and connecting." Eric Alterman, *It Ain't No Sin to Be Glad You're Alive* (Boston: Little Brown, 1999), 157.

50. Jim Cullen, *Born in the U.S.A.: Bruce Springsteen and the American Tradition* (Middletown, Conn.: Wesleyan University Press, 1997), 6–8.

51. Remarks at Dedication Ceremonies for the Vietnam Veterans Memorial Statue, November 11, 1984.

52. Reagan, *The Reagan Diaries*, 277.

53. Remarks at a Memorial Day Ceremony at Arlington National Cemetery, May 26, 1986.

54. Remarks at the Veterans Day Ceremony at the Vietnam Veterans Memorial, November 11, 1988.

55. Rusher interview, March 30, 2004.

56. Weinberger interview, June 23, 2004.

57. Perlstein interview, July 7, 2004.

58. Jerry Lembcke, *The Spitting Image: Myth, Memory, and the Legacy of the Vietnam War* (New York: New York University Press, 1998), 184, 188.

59. Ellsberg interview, December 28, 2004. See also Daniel Ellsberg, *Secrets: A Memoir of Vietnam and the Pentagon Papers* (New York: Viking, 2002).

60. FitzGerald interview, New York City, March 25, 2004.

61. Stanley Karnow, leading historian of the Vietnam War, interview with the author, April 19, 2004. See also Stanley Karnow, *Vietnam: A History* (New York: Penguin, 1997).

62. Halberstam interview, November 13, 2004.

63. Ellsberg interview, December 28, 2004.

64. E-mail to author from Jimmy Carter Presidential Library, Atlanta, October 1, 2006.

65. Ralph Blumenthal, "Syndrome Found in Returned G.I.'s," *New York Times*, June 7, 1971.

66. Boyce Rensberger, "Delayed Trauma in Veterans Cited: Psychiatrists Find Vietnam Produces Guilt and Shame," *New York Times*, May 3, 1972. This medical and psychological use of the term continued throughout the 1970s. See Tom Wicker, "The Vietnam Disease," *New York Times*, May 27, 1975.

67. "Veteran Acquitted in Drug Case," *New York Times*, September 20, 1980.

68. Richard Reinhold, "Mentally Wounded Are Rare, but Not Nearly Rare Enough," *New York Times*, April 15, 1979.

69. Richard Severo, "U.S., Despite Claims of Veterans, Says None Are Herbicide Victims," *New York Times*, May 28, 1979.

70. "Veteran Acquitted in Drug Case."

71. "Bill Allows Call-Up of 50,000 Reserves for 90 Days' Duty," *New York Times*, December 14, 1975.

72. Martin Tolchin, "Political Advisers Gain Foreign Role," *New York Times*, July 18, 1978.

73. Karnow interview, April 19, 2004.

74. Hedrick Smith, "Crisis Alters Attitude in U.S.," *New York Times*, December 2, 1979.

75. Arthur Schlesinger Jr., "No, Let's Debate Our Iran Policy," *New York Times*, December 13, 1979.

76. Peter Navarro, "If Thailand Is Periled," *New York Times*, July 9, 1980.

77. Howell Raines, "Reagan Calls Arms Race Essential to Avoid a 'Surrender' or 'Defeat,'" *New York Times*, August 19, 1980.

78. Ellsberg interview, December 28, 2004.

79. Karnow interview, April 19, 2004.

80. Meese interview, Washington, D.C., December 15, 2004.

81. Remarks during a White House Briefing on the Program for Economic Recovery, February 24, 1981.

82. William Safire, "The Savings of Salvador," *New York Times*, February 26, 1981.

83. Address at Commencement Exercises at the United States Military Academy, West Point, May 27, 1981. See also Remarks in Los Angeles at a California Republican Party Fundraising Dinner, May 25, 1982.

84. Anthony Dolan Files, ser. 2: Speech Drafts by Other Writers, box 70, folder 2, West Point Commencement (Rohrabacher)–05/20/1981, Reagan Library.

85. Remarks at a Fundraising Dinner for the Republican Majority Fund, September 27, 1983.

86. Interview with Guillermo Descalzi of the Spanish International Network, September 13, 1985.

87. Remarks at a White House Briefing for Supporters of United States Assistance for the Nicaraguan Democratic Resistance, March 10, 1986.

88. Remarks at the Heritage Foundation Anniversary Dinner, April 22, 1986.

89. Remarks at a White House Briefing for Supporters of United States Assistance for the Nicaraguan Democratic Resistance, June 16, 1986.

90. Rusher interview, March 30, 2004.

91. Deaver interview, July 14, 2004.

92. Bakshian interview, May 19, 2004.

93. Reed interview, January 5, 2005.

94. Halberstam interview, November 13, 2004.

95. Bradlee interview, Washington, D.C., December 15, 2004.

96. William Berman, professor of history at the University of Toronto, interview with the author, February 26, 2004.

97. Todd Gitlin, professor of journalism and sociology at Columbia University, interview with the author, February 23, 2004.

98. Meyer interview, July 16, 2004.

99. Ellsberg interview, December 28, 2004.

100. Dukakis interview, Boston, August 25, 2004.

101. Wirth interview, May 26, 2005.

102. Walter Isaacson, "The Reagan Evolution," *New York Times Book Review*, October 31, 2004, 9.

103. Howard Zinn, interview with the author, April 15, 2004. Zinn, professor emeritus of political science at Boston University, is the author of *A People's History of the United States*.

104. Karnow interview, April 19, 2004.

105. "Falwell Blazed Trail in American Politics, Religious Right," *NewsHour with Jim Lehrer*, PBS, May 15, 2007, www.pbs.org/newshour/bb/remember/jan-june07/falwell_05-15.html.

106. Remarks and a Question-and-Answer Session with Reporters on the Second Anniversary of the Inauguration of the President, January 20, 1983.

107. Remarks at a Fundraising Luncheon for Carroll A. Campbell and Thomas F. Hartnett, Columbia, S.C., July 24, 1986. This message formed the core of his speeches in support of Republican candidates in the 1986 midterm elections. See also Remarks at a Campaign Rally for Senator Jeremiah A. Denton, Montgomery, Ala., September 18, 1986; Remarks at a Campaign Rally for Senator Mack Mattingly, Atlanta, October 8, 1986.

108. Letter Accepting the Resignation of Richard G. Darman as Assistant to the President and Deputy to the Chief of Staff, February 1, 1985.

109. Reagan, *The Reagan Diaries*, 685–86.

110. Farewell Address to the Nation, January 11, 1989.

111. Ibid.

112. Ibid.

5. Remembering Vietnam and the Civil Rights Movement

Epigraph: George H. W. Bush, *All the Best, George Bush: My Life in Letters and Other Writings* (New York: Scribner, 1999), 106.

1. David Hoffman Collection, series: 1988 Campaign Files, box 10, folder 7, George Bush, Presidential Library, College Station, Texas.

2. *All the Best*, 389–90.

3. Maureen Dowd, "Bush Boasts of Turnaround from 'Easy Rider' Society," *New York Times*, October 7, 1988.

4. Dan Quayle, Acceptance Speech at the Republican National Convention, New Orleans, August 17, 1988, *Congressional Quarterly*, August 20, 1988, 2357.

5. Maureen Dowd, "Quayle Makes Case in 'Show Me' State," *New York Times*, August 26, 1988.

6. Vice Presidential Debate, Omaha, October 17, 1988, www.debates.org/pages/debtrans.html.

7. Dowd, "Bush Boasts of Turnaround from 'Easy Rider' Society."

8. Dukakis interview, Boston, August 25, 2004.

9. Kusnet interview, June 30, 2004.

10. Darrell West, professor of political science at Brown University, interview with the author, February 23, 2004.

11. Berman interview, February 26, 2004.

12. Senator John F. Kennedy, "Acceptance Speech of the New York Liberal Party Nomination," September 16, 1960, www.pbs.org/wgbh/amex/presidents/35_kennedy/psources/ps_nyliberal.html.

13. David Barash, interview with the author, March 18, 2004. A professor of psychology at the University of Washington, Barash is the author of *The L Word: An Unapologetic, Thoroughly Biased, Long-Overdue Explication and Celebration of Liberalism* (New York: William Morrow, 1992). See also Ronald D. Rotunda, *The Politics of Language: Liberalism as Word and Symbol* (Iowa City: University of Iowa Press, 1986).

14. Kusnet interview, June 30, 2004.

15. Maureen Dowd, "Bush Ridicules Dukakis for Belatedly Saying That He Is a Liberal," *New York Times*, November 1, 1988.

16. Nicol Rae, professor of political science at Florida International University, interview with the author, March 3, 2004.

17. Donna Brazile, e-mail interview with the author, February 28, 2004. Brazile worked for Democratic candidates in every presidential election between 1976 and 2000, when she served as Al Gore's campaign manager.

18. Bauer e-mail interview, June 16, 2004.

19. Maureen Dowd, "Bush, in Scalding Address, Says Rival Would Make World Riskier," *New York Times*, August 5, 1988.

20. Dowd, "Bush Ridicules Dukakis for Belatedly Saying That He Is a Liberal."

21. Maureen Dowd, "Bush, Sensing Landslide, Ridicules Rival," *New York Times*, November 3, 1988.

22. *The Cumulated Indexes to the Public Papers of the Presidents of the United States: Ronald Reagan, 1981–1989* (Lanham, Md.: Bernan Press, 1995), 230.

23. Welcome Rally, New Orleans Convention Center, August 14, 1988, www.reagan.utexas.edu/archives/speeches/publicpapers.html. Unless otherwise noted, all of Ronald Reagan's speeches and other statements cited in this chapter are available at this site and can be accessed by date.

24. Anthony Dolan Files, ser. 1: Speech Drafts, box 66, folder 13, Address: Welcome Rally, New Orleans Convention Center–08/14/1988 (2), Ronald Reagan Presidential Library, Simi Valley, Calif. See also Remarks at the National Convention of the American Legion, Louisville, Ky., September 6, 1988; Remarks at a Republican Campaign Rally in Voorhees, N.J., November 4, 1988; Remarks at a Republican Campaign Rally in San Bernardino, Calif., November 1, 1988.

25. Josh Gilder, interview with the author, June 30, 2004. Gilder was a speechwriter for President Reagan in his second term who also wrote for Bush in the 1988 campaign.

26. Rossinow interview, September 21, 2004.

27. Michael Rogin, "'Make My Day!' Spectacle as Amnesia in Imperial Politics," in *Cultures of United States Imperialism* (Durham: Duke University Press, 1993), 524; Sean Wilentz, "Condi Rice, (Bad) Historian," April 13, 2004, www.salon.com.

28. Parmet interview, May 7, 2004.

29. President's News Conference, June 27, 1989, bushlibrary.tamu.edu/research/public_papers.php. Unless otherwise noted, all of George H. W. Bush's speeches and other statements cited in this chapter are available at this site and can be accessed by date.

30. Remarks Announcing the Proposed Constitutional Amendment on Desecration of the Flag, June 30, 1989.

31. George H. W. Bush, Inaugural Address, January 20, 1989.

32. George H. W. Bush, with Victor Gold, *Looking Forward* (New York: Doubleday, 1987), 90, 98–99.

33. Bush, *All the Best, George Bush,* 111–13, 148.

34. Halberstam interview, November 13, 2004.

35. Remarks at the Dedication Ceremony for the Vietnam Veterans Memorial, Dallas, November 11, 1989.

36. The first version was eliminated by Chriss Winston. Office of Speechwriting, 1, series: Speech Files, Drafts, 1989–1993, box 37, folder 4, Vietnam Memorial—Dallas 11/10/89 [OA 3537] [1], Bush Library.

37. Remarks and a Question-and-Answer Session at a Luncheon for Regional Editors and Broadcasters, September 15, 1989.

38. Question-and-Answer Session with the Youth Collaborative Mentor Group, Cincinnati, January 12, 1990.

39. Bush, *All the Best, George Bush,* 319–20, 609.

40. Remarks and a Question-and-Answer Session with the Magazine Publishers of America, July 17, 1990.

41. Jerry Lembcke, *The Spitting Image: Myth, Memory, and the Legacy of the Vietnam War* (New York: New York University Press, 1998), quotes on 25, 186, 11, 129, 186.

42. Bush, *All the Best, George Bush*, 511.

43. Exchange with Reporters in Kennebunkport, Maine, February 17, 1991.

44. Remarks to the American Legislative Exchange Council, March 1, 1991.

45. Smith interview, May 7, 2004.

46. Office of Speechwriting, 1, series: Speech Files, Drafts, 1989–1993, box 85, folder 1, Veterans Briefing 3/4/91 [OA 6030], Bush Library.

47. Remarks to Veterans Service Organizations, March 4, 1991. These off-the-cuff remarks were incorrectly transcribed as part of the prepared speech.

48. Office of Speechwriting, 1, series: Speech Files, Drafts, 1989–1993, box 8, folder 1, Veterans Briefing 3/4/91 [OA 6030], Bush Library.

49. Remarks at University of Michigan Commencement Ceremony, Ann Arbor, May 4, 1991.

50. Office of Speechwriting, 2, series: Speech Files, Backup, Chron File, 1989–1993, box 100, folder 2, Michigan Commencement 5/4/91 [OA 8322] [2], Bush Library.

51. Office of Speechwriting, 2, series: Speech Files, Backup, Chron File, 1989–1993, box 100, folder 1, Michigan Commencement 5/4/91 [OA 8322] [1], Bush Library.

52. Remarks to Liberty Mutual Insurance Employees in Dover, N.H., January 15, 1992.

53. Remarks and a Question-and-Answer Session at a Rotary Club Dinner, Portsmouth, N.H., January 15, 1992. See also Remarks to the Veterans of Foreign Wars National Convention, Indianapolis, August 17, 1992; Remarks to the American Legion National Convention, Chicago, August 25, 1992.

54. Bush, *All the Best, George Bush*, 574–75.

55. Baker interview, Houston, June 14, 2004.

56. Bush, *All the Best, George Bush*, 11.

57. Baker interview, Houston, June 14, 2004.

58. Ibid.

59. James A. Baker III, with Thomas M. DeFrank, *The Politics of Diplomacy: Revolution, War and Peace, 1989–1992* (New York: G. P. Putnam's Sons, 1995), 333.

60. Frank Carlucci, interview with the author, July 28, 2004. Carlucci served as Nixon's undersecretary for health, education, and welfare and as President Reagan's deputy defense secretary, national security adviser, and secretary of defense.

61. Shirley interview, July 1, 2004.

62. Baker, *The Politics of Diplomacy*, 331.

63. Gary Jacobson, professor of political science at the University of California at San Diego, interview with the author, July 1, 2004. Jacobson's research examines public attitudes toward the military.

64. FitzGerald interview, New York City, March 25, 2004.

65. Weinberger interview, June 23, 2004.

66. Smith interview, May 7, 2004.

67. Karnow interview, April 19, 2004.

68. Bond interview, November 16, 2004.

69. Woodward interview, Washington, D.C., December 15, 2004.

70. Colin Powell, with Joseph E. Persico, *My American Journey* (New York: Random House, 1995), 148, 207–8.

71. Ellsberg interview, December 28, 2004.

72. Dukakis interview, Boston, August 25, 2004.

73. Shattuck interview, May 11, 2004.

74. Schulman interview, August 10, 2004.

75. Bush, *All the Best, George Bush*, 88.

76. Ibid.

77. Herbert Parmet, *George Bush: The Life of a Lone Star Yankee* (New York: Scribner, 1997), 108.

78. Bush, *All the Best, George Bush*, 89–90.

79. Ibid., 85–86.

80. George H. W. Bush, with Victor Gold, *Looking Forward* (New York: Doubleday, 1987), 91–92. Bush later repeated the perception that the Democrats took African American voters for granted (*Looking Forward*, 253).

81. Ibid., 253.

82. Richard W. Stevenson, "Bush Says Political Problems Won't Change His Agenda," *New York Times*, October 5, 2005.

83. "We made some very, very significant efforts" to reach African American voters, Baker insisted, "both in the '76 Ford campaign and in the '78 and '79 Bush campaigns—and we were not able to make much of a dent." One reason, he thought, may have been the move away from the Republican Party among African Americans during the Nixon years. Baker added, "The black voter was also more susceptible, I think, to being influenced by the leadership of some of the black organizations which purported to be interested in their welfare but who were really more interested in welfare-run organizations." Those leaders told their constituencies that "it was always the Democrats who provided for the low-income folks, and they represented a large portion of the low-income electorate." Baker interview, Houston, June 14, 2004.

84. Bush, *Looking Forward*, 92–93. Bush also discussed this incident at length in *All the Best, George Bush*, 107.

85. Remarks at the United Negro College Fund Dinner, New York City, March 9, 1989.

86. Office of Speechwriting, 1, series: Speech Files, Drafts, 1989–1993, box 5, folder 13, United Negro College Fund 3/9/89 [OA 2772] [2], Bush Library.

87. Remarks at the United Negro College Fund Dinner.

88. Remarks at a White House Ceremony Commemorating the Twenty-fifth Anniversary of the Civil Rights Act, June 30, 1989.

89. Office of Speechwriting, 1, series: Speech Files, Drafts, 1989–1993, box 20, folder 9, 1964 Civil Rights Act—25th Anniversary 6/30/89 [OA 2786], Bush Library. See also two memoranda of June 28, 1989: Nelson Lund, associate counsel to the president, to Chriss Winston; and Jim Pinkerton to Chriss Winston; both in ibid. To this day, southern congressional Republicans are insistent about not singling out their region on issues regarding race. For example, as the *New York Times* reported on June 22, 2005 (Carol Hulse, "Rebellion Stalls Extension of Voting Act"), "House Republican leaders abruptly canceled a planned vote to renew the Voting Rights Act on Wednesday after a rebellion by lawmakers who said the civil rights measure unfairly singled out Southern states." Southern Republicans also argued that tremendous progress had already been made, and that such a bill was unnecessary.

90. Speech Files, Drafts, 1989–1993, box 20, folder 9, 1964 Civil Rights Act—25th Anniversary 6/30/89 [OA 2786].

91. Remarks on the Observance of National Afro-American (Black) History Month, February 25, 1991.

92. Office of Speechwriting, 1, series: Speech Files, Drafts, 1989–1993, box 84, folder 4, Black History Month 2/25/91 [OA 6029], Bush Library.

93. Remarks on Signing the Martin Luther King Jr. Federal Holiday Proclamation, January 9, 1990.

94. Remarks on Signing the Martin Luther King, Jr., Federal Holiday Commission Extension Act, May 17, 1989.

95. Office of Speechwriting, 1, series: Speech Files, Drafts, 1989–1993, box 20, folder 9, 1964 Civil Rights Act—25th Anniversary 6/30/89 [OA 2786], Bush Library.

96. George H. W. Bush, "Color or Character: How Will Our Children Be Judged?" *Washington Times*, January 12, 1990.

97. Memorandum from Mary Kate Grant to Chriss Winston, December 14, 1989, Office of Speechwriting, 1, series: Speech Files, Drafts, 1989–1993, box 43, folder 4, Martin Luther King Essay for *Washington Times* 1/15/90 [OA 4390], Bush Library.

98. Remarks on Signing the Martin Luther King Jr. Federal Holiday Proclamation, Atlanta, January 17, 1992.

99. Office of Speechwriting, 1, series: Speech Files, Drafts, 1989–1993, box 126, folder 8, Martin Luther King Birthday 1/17/92 [OA 6096] [2], Bush Library.

100. Office of Speechwriting, 1, series: Speech Files, Drafts, 1989–1993, box 41, folder 9, NAACP Fundraising 12/15/89 [OA 3540] [2], Bush Library.

6. George H. W. Bush and the Great Society

Epigraph: Curt Smith, interview with the author, May 7, 2004.

1. George H. W. Bush, *All the Best, George Bush: My Life in Letters and Other Writings* (New York: Scribner, 1999), 77.

2. Ibid., 87, 90.

3. George H. W. Bush, with Victor Gold, *Looking Forward* (New York: Doubleday, 1987), 90.

4. Office of Speechwriting, 2, series: Speech Files, Backup, Chron File, 1989–1993, box 100, folder 4, Michigan Commencement 5/4/91 [OA 8322] [4], George Bush Presidential Library, College Station, Texas.

5. Clipping, "Persian Gulf Teach-in Draws Large Crowds on Campus," *Michigan Alumnus*, Office of Speechwriting, 2, series: Speech Files, Backup, Chron File, 1989–1993, box 100, folder 8, Michigan Commencement 5/4/91 [OA 8322] [8], Bush Library.

6. Memorandum to Tony Snow, Office of Speechwriting, 2, series: Speech Files, Backup, Chron File, 1989–1993, box 100, folder 6, Michigan Commencement 5/4/91 [OA 8322] [6], Bush Library.

7. Memorandum from Peggy Dooley to Tony Snow, "University of Michigan Pre-Advance," April 29, 1991, Office of Speechwriting, 2, series: Speech Files, Backup, Chron File, 1989–1993, box 100, folder 2, Michigan Commencement 5/4/91 [OA 8322] [2], Bush Library.

8. Remarks at the University of Michigan Commencement Ceremony, Ann Arbor, May 4, 1991, bushlibrary.tamu.edu/research/public_papers.php. Unless otherwise noted, all of George H. W. Bush's speeches and other statements cited in this chapter are available at this site and can be accessed by date.

9. Speech Files, Backup, Chron File, 1989–1993, box 100, folder 6, Michigan Commencement 5/4/91 [OA 8322] [6].

10. Remarks at the University of Michigan Commencement Ceremony.

11. Office of Speechwriting, 2, Series: Speech Files, Backup, Chron File, 1989–1993, box 100, folder 6, Michigan Commencement 5/4/91 [OA 8322] [6].

12. Office of Speechwriting, 2, Series: Speech Files, Backup, Chron File, 1989–1993, box 100, folder 2, Michigan Commencement 5/4/91 [OA 8322] [2].

13. Remarks at the University of Michigan Commencement Ceremony.

14. Robert Pear, "Focusing on Welfare: Bush Plays Private Acts of Decency against the Government as a Helper," *New York Times*, May 11, 1991. Found in Office of Speechwriting, 7, series: Dan McGroarty, Subject File, 1988–1993, box 1, folder 1, [Domestic Policy] n.d. [OA 8677], Bush Library.

15. Ibid.

16. Smith interview, May 7, 2004.

17. Gilder interview, June 30, 2004.

18. George H. W. Bush, Acceptance Speech at the Republican National Convention, New Orleans, August 18, 1988, www.americanrhetoric.com/speeches/georgehbush-1988rnc.htm.

19. George H. W. Bush, Inaugural Address, January 20, 1989.

20. Remarks at a White House Ceremony Commemorating the Twenty-fifth Anniversary of VISTA, January 31, 1990.

21. Remarks at a White House Ceremony Celebrating the Twenty-fifth Anniversary of Head Start, May 24, 1990.

22. Remarks on Signing the National Volunteer Week Proclamation, April 10, 1989; Remarks at the Presentation Ceremony for the President's Volunteer Action Awards, April 11, 1989; Remarks at the Daily Points of Light Celebration, Orlando, Fla., September 30, 1991; Remarks on Signing the Martin Luther King, Jr., Federal Holiday Proclamation, Atlanta, January 17, 1992.

23. Remarks at a Celebration of the Points of Light, January 14, 1993.

24. "Points of Light," 1, Office of Speechwriting, 9, series: Tony Snow, Subject File, 1988–1993, box 2, folder 11, [Daily Points of Light 6/22/89] [OA 8679], Bush Library.

25. Baker interview, Houston, June 14, 2004.

26. Moore interview, July 2, 2004.

27. Broder interview, April 27, 2004.

28. Address to the Nation on the Civil Disturbances, Los Angeles, May 1, 1992.

29. Fitzwater mentioned specifically Deputy Secretary of Health and Human Services Connie Horner and Vice President Quayle's chief of staff, William Kristol. Marlin Fitzwater, *Call the Briefing! A Memoir of Ten Years in the White House with Presidents Reagan and Bush* (Xlibris, 2000), 424.

30. James Gerstenzang, "White House Blames 'Liberal Programs' for Riots," *Los Angeles Times*, May 5, 1992.

31. Fitzwater, *Call The Briefing!* 427–28.

32. Teleconference Remarks to the American Newspaper Publishers Association, May 6, 1992.

33. John Miller, "Ronald Reagan's Legacy: His Destructive Economic Policies Do Not Deserve the Press's Praise,"*Dollars & Sense*, July–August 2004, www.dollarsandsense.org/archives/2004/0704miller.html.

34. "Outline of Remarks on Violence in Los Angeles," Office of Speechwriting, 2, series: Speech Files, Backup, Chron File, 1989–1993, box 157, folder 6, National Address on Los Angeles Riots 5/1/92 [OA 7573] [1], Bush Library.

35. Remarks on Arrival in Los Angeles, May 6, 1992.

36. Office of Speechwriting, 2, series: Speech Files, Backup, Chron File, 1989–1993, box 159, folder 2, Los Angeles Arrival Statement 5/6/92 [OA 7573], Bush Library.

37. "Anecdotal Information," Office of Speechwriting, 2, series: Speech Files, Backup, Chron File, 1989–1993, box 159, folder 3, Military and Law Enforcement—Los Angeles 5/6/92 [OA 7573], Bush Library.

38. Remarks at Mount Zion Missionary Baptist Church, Los Angeles, May 7, 1992; Remarks to Community Leaders, Los Angeles, May 8, 1992; Remarks at a Bush-Quayle Fundraising Dinner, Philadelphia, May 11, 1992; Remarks to Town Hall of California, Los Angeles, May 29, 1992.

39. "Strategies for Welfare Reform," Domestic Task Force of the Select Committee on Hunger, U.S. House of Representatives, April 9, 1992, 2–11 passim, Office of Speechwriting, 2, series: Speech Files, Backup, Chron File, 1989–1993, box 162, folder 7, California Town Hall 5/29/92 [OA 7574], Bush Library.

40. Office of Speechwriting, 9, series: Tony Snow, Subject File, 1988–1993, box 2, folder 19, [Domestic Political 1989–1991] [OA 8680], Bush Library.

41. Dan Quayle, "Restoring Basic Values: Strengthening the Family," San Francisco Commonwealth Club, May 19, 1992.

42. Ibid.

43. Ibid.

44. Ibid.

45. Schiffren interview, February 4, 2005.

46. Andrew Rosenthal, "After the Riots: Quayle Says Riots Sprang from Lack of Family Values," *New York Times*, May 20, 1992.

47. Russell Baker, "To Cloud Men's Minds," *New York Times*, May 23, 1992.

48. Rosenthal, "After the Riots."

49. Gwen Ifill, "Clinton Sees Bush Engaging in Empty Talk on Families," *New York Times*, May 22, 1992.

50. "Dan Quayle's Fictitious World," editorial, *New York Times*, May 22, 1992.

51. Michael Wines, "Views on Single Motherhood Are Multiple at White House," *New York Times*, May 21, 1992.

52. Anthony Lewis, "The Frozen President," *New York Times*, May 24, 1992.

53. Wines, "Views on Single Motherhood Are Multiple at White House."

54. The President's News Conference with Prime Minister Brian Mulroney of Canada, May 20, 1992.

55. Wines, "Views on Single Motherhood Are Multiple at White House."

56. Andrew Rosenthal, "The Politics of Morality: Speech by Quayle on Family Values Raises Questions about Thrust of Bush Campaign," *New York Times*, May 22, 1992.

57. Moore interview, July 2, 2004.

58. Perlstein interview, July 7, 2004.

59. Wirth interview, May 26, 2005.

60. Katzenbach interview, June 28, 2004.

61. Perlstein interview, July 7, 2004.

62. Chomsky interview, April 30, 2004.

63. Bradlee interview, Washington, D.C., December 15, 2004.

64. Cox interview, April 15, 2004.

65. Donna Shalala, interview with the author, June 7, 2004. In 2001 Shalala became president of the University of Miami.

66. Hayden, e-mail correspondence with the author, May 17, 2004.

67. Halberstam interview, November 13, 2004.

68. Isserman interview, May 8, 2004. Other critics of the Right's view of the Great Society also noted that the Vietnam War drained crucial resources, in particular Godfrey Hodgson (interview, October 11, 2004).

69. Perlstein interview, July 7, 2004.

70. Bush enlisted in the military after graduating from Phillips Andover Academy in the spring of 1942, not in December 1941.

71. Patrick Buchanan, Speech at Republican National Convention, Houston, August 17, 1992, www.americanrhetoric.com/speeches/patrickbuchanan1992rnc.htm.

72. Lance Morrow, "1992 *Time* Magazine Man of the Year: William Jefferson Clinton," *Time*, January 2, 1992.

73. Bay Buchanan, "And the Party Blinked," *New York Times*, September 3, 2008.

74. Smith interview, May 7, 2004.

75. Alessandra Stanley, "Marilyn Quayle Says the 1960's Had a Flip Side," *New York Times*, August 20, 1992; Michael Kelly, "A Contest of 2 Generations, Molded by 2 Different Wars," *New York Times*, August 30, 1992.

76. Broder interview, April 27, 2004.

77. Schiffren interview, February 4, 2005.

78. Ibid. President Bush also alluded to the sins of the 1960s in his convention address. After describing changes around the world over the previous four years, he said, "If I had stood before you four years ago and described this as the world we would help to build, you would have said, 'George Bush, you must have been smoking something, and you

must have inhaled,'" a slap at Bill Clinton's admission that he had tried marijuana in the 1960s but "didn't inhale." Acceptance Speech at the Republican National Convention, Houston, August 20, 1992.

79. Kelly, "A Contest of 2 Generations, Molded by 2 Different Wars."

80. Hayden e-mail correspondence with author, May 17, 2004.

81. Remarks to the Community in St. Louis, September 28, 1992. He repeated this a month later in Remarks to the International Association of Chiefs of Police, Detroit, October 25, 1992.

82. Andrew Rosenthal, "Bush, in Florida, Steps Up Personal Attack on Clinton," *New York Times*, October 4, 1992.

83. Remarks at a Victory '92 Dinner, Houston, October 8, 1992. Bush leveled a similar attack later that month, even making a rare mention of his own military service. Remarks and a Question-and-Answer Session in Billings, Mont., October 25, 1992. In the closing days of the race Bush again branded Clinton as unpatriotic. Michael Wines, "As Presidential Race Nears End, the Attacks Continue," *New York Times*, November 1, 1992.

7. Bill Clinton and the Heroes of the 1960s

Epigraphs: Bill Clinton, BookExpo America, Chicago, June 3, 2004; President William J. Clinton, Message to Congress, "The Unfinished Work of Building One America," January 15, 2001, clinton6.nara.gov/. Unless otherwise noted, all of Bill Clinton's speeches and other statements cited in this chapter are available at this site and can be accessed by date.

1. Speech by President in History Class, Selma, Calif., September 5, 1995.

2. "President Clinton Remarks re: Kennedy Legacy in Rose Garden," John Fitzgerald Kennedy Library, Boston.

3. Robin Toner, "Democrats Give Clinton Their Blessing: Cuomo Hails 'New Voice for America,'" *New York Times*, July 16, 1992.

4. William J. Clinton, *My Life* (New York: Alfred A. Knopf, 2004), 418.

5. "Bill Clinton: The Man from Hope," July 16, 1992, www.clintonfoundation.org/video.htm?title=Bill%20Clinton:%20The%20Man%20from%20Hope.

6. Bill Clinton, Acceptance Speech to the Democratic National Convention, New York City, July 16, 1992, www.4president.org/speeches/billclinton1992acceptance.htm.

7. Ickes interview, January 20, 2005.

8. Clinton, *My Life*, 331–32, 365, 395.

9. Lance Morrow, "1992 *Time* Magazine Person of the Year: William Jefferson Clinton," *Time*, January 2, 1992.

10. Clinton, *My Life*, 469.

11. Meese interview, Washington, D.C., December 15, 2004.

12. Rusher interview, March 30, 2004.

13. Hodgson interview, October 11, 2004.

14. Horowitz interview, May 10, 2004.

15. Moore interview, July 2, 2004.

16. Widmer interview, December 1, 2004.

17. Gitlin interview, February 23, 2004.

18. Glastris interview, June 22, 2004.

19. John Harris, interview with the author, July 12, 2004; Benjamin C. Bradlee, interview with the author, Washington, D.C., December 15, 2004; Todd Purdum, interview with the author, December 8, 2004.

20. Bork interview, February 8, 2005.

21. Meese interview, Washington, D.C., December 15, 2004.

22. Hart interview, March 2, 2004.

23. Schlesinger interview, New York City, August 26, 2004.

24. Wilkins interview, December 21, 2004.

25. Bradley interview, December 14, 2004.

26. Dukakis interview, Boston, August 25, 2004.

27. Hart interview, March 2, 2004.

28. Kirk interview, April 1, 2004.

29. Cox interview, April 15, 2004.

30. Shattuck interview, May 11, 2004.

31. Shields interview, June 30, 2004.

32. Robert Dallek, professor of history at Boston University, interview with the author, March 6, 2004.

33. Brands interview, March 4, 2004.

34. Clinton, *My Life*, 473.

35. Ibid., 480.

36. "Picturing the Presidents," *New York Times*, November 20, 1993.

37. Speech by President to the Cooper Union Community, New York, May 12, 1993.

38. Speech by President to House Democrats, July 20, 1993.

39. Speech by President to Boys Nation, July 24, 1993.

40. Speech by President on Defense Conversion, San Bernardino, Calif., May 20, 1994.

41. Speech by President to UCLA Seventy-fifth Anniversary Convocation, May 20, 1994.

42. See Remarks by President at Bush Library Dedication, November 6, 1997; Speech by President at Girls Nation Event, July 17, 1998; "Clinton: Kennedy's Death Hard for Nation," *USA Today*, July 21, 1999.

43. Speech by President at JFK Library Dinner, March 2, 1998.

44. Speech by President at Kennedy Library, October 29, 1993.

45. Speech by President on Peace Corps Twenty-fifth Anniversary, June 19, 1996.

46. Clinton, *My Life*, 547.

47. See, e.g., Speech by President to the U.S. Chamber of Commerce, February 23, 1993; Speech by President in National Service Address, March 1, 1993.

48. State of the Union Address, February 17, 1993.

49. Speech by President at JFK Library Dinner, March 2, 1998.

50. Shattuck interview, May 11, 2004.

51. Speech by President to American Society of Newspaper Editors, April 13, 1994.

52. Speech by President to Boys Nation, July 29, 1994.

53. Remarks by President to U.S. and Pacific Jakarta Business People, Jakarta, Indonesia, November 16, 1994.

54. Remarks by President and Vice President, Economic Conference Opening, Portland, Ore., June 27, 1995.

55. Speech by President at Home Ownership Summit, June 6, 1996.

56. Bill Clinton, Acceptance Speech at the Democratic National Convention, Chicago, August 29, 1996.

57. See Remarks by President and Vice President, Knoxville, Tenn., October 10, 1996; Speech by President, Bangor, Maine, November 4, 1996. Clinton continued throughout his second term to refer to Kennedy in this fashion. See Speech by President to North Carolina Legislature, March 13, 1997; Speech by President at Democratic Governors Association Dinner, February 23, 1998; and Speech by President to National School Board Association, February 1, 1999.

58. John Zogby and Chris Conroy, "Presidential Greatness," November 30, 2004, www.zogby.com/news/readnews.cfm?ID=939.

59. www.gallup.com/poll/26608/Lincoln-Resumes-Position-Americans-TopRated-President.aspx.

60. voices.washingtonpost.com/behind-the-numbers/2007/07/approval_highs_and lows.html.

61. Clinton, *My Life*, 71.

62. Ibid., 196.

63. Schlesinger interview, New York City, August 26, 2004.

64. Clinton, *My Life*, xxv–xxvi.

65. Speech by President on Rosa Parks, June 15, 1999.

66. See Speech by President on Medicare Fortieth Anniversary, July 25, 1995; Speech by President at Blue Ribbon Schools Event, October 28, 1999; Presidential Radio Address, July 8, 2000; Presidential Statement on Medicare Program, July 12, 2000.

67. Presidential Radio Address on Health Care Reform, July 23, 1994.

68. Presidential Statement on Voting Rights Act, June 17, 1993.

69. Speech by President to Boys Nation, July 24, 1993.

70. Speech by President at University of Texas at Austin, October 16, 1995. See also Speech by President at Luncheon Gala, Dallas, October 16, 1995.

71. Interview with Associated Press, November 16, 2000. He twice acknowledged in writing in 1998 that portions of the War on Poverty were effective. See Presidential Statement on Community Opportunities Act, October 27, 1998; Presidential Statement on Economic Development, November 13, 1998. At times Clinton very vaguely, and very briefly, expressed sympathy with the goals of Johnson's domestic programs. See Speech by President upon Arrival in Texas, May 7, 1999.

72. Speech by President at Dinner Honoring Governor Evan Bayh, December 1, 1997.

73. Press Briefing on the Budget, February 2, 1998.

74. Press Briefing by Leon Panetta and Alice Rivlin on Budget and Deficit, July 12, 1994.

75. *BusinessWeek*, June 29, 1999. Clinton again defended Johnson's programs in an interview three days later but also immediately mentioned the flaws of Johnson's legislation. *USA Today*, July 2, 1999.

76. *New York Times*, July 11, 1999.

77. Speech by President at Reception for Jane Harman, February 3, 2000.

78. Speech by President at Friends of Patrick Kennedy Lunch, July 28, 2000.

79. Bill Clinton, Speech at Democratic Convention, Los Angeles, August 14, 2000. He repeated this statement a few months later. See Speech by President at New York Senate Dinner, October 4, 2000.

80. Interview with Associated Press, November 16, 2000.

81. John Harris, interview with the author, July 12, 2004. A *Washington Post* reporter who covered the White House beginning in 1995, Harris is the author of *The Survivor: Bill Clinton in the White House.*

82. Widmer interview, December 1, 2004.

83. Shesol interview, June 29, 2004.

84. Shattuck interview, May 11, 2004.

85. Kusnet interview, June 30, 2004.

86. Speech by President at Central High School, Little Rock, Ark., September 25, 1997.

87. Widmer interview, December 1, 2004. Others who worked under Clinton had similar memories, including Paul Glastris (interview with the author, June 22, 2004).

88. Speech by President in Commemoration of Martin Luther King March, Oak Bluffs, Mass., August 28, 1998. Clinton at other times spoke of the significance of the summer of 1963 and how he wept as he watched the television broadcast of King's speech at the March on Washington. See, e.g., Speech by President on Affirmative Action, July 19, 1995.

89. Statement on the Thirtieth Anniversary of the March on Washington for Jobs and Freedom, August 28, 1993.

90. Remarks by President at Denver Martin Luther King Commemoration, January 16, 1995.

91. Clinton, *My Life*, 897.

92. Speech by President at Howard University, January 17, 1994. Clinton repeated this last phrase on the King holiday in 1996. See Speech by President at King Commemorative Service, Atlanta, January 15, 1996.

93. Clinton, *My Life*, 896–97.

94. Ibid., 923.

95. "Black people all over America knew that the drive to impeach me was being led by right-wing, white Southerners who had never lifted a finger for civil rights." Ibid., 840.

96. Second Inaugural Address of William J. Clinton, January 20, 1997.

97. Speech by President at Medals of Freedom Event, January 15, 1998.

98. Speech by President at Howard University, January 17, 1994; Speech by President to AmeriCorps on Martin Luther King Day, January 18, 1999.

99. Speech by President at Martin Luther King Day Event, January 17, 2000.

100. Speech by President, Memphis, November 13, 1993.

101. Kusnet interview, June 30, 2004.

102. Interview, *New York Times*, December 28, 2000.

103. Clinton, *My Life*, 559–60.

104. See Speech by President at Howard University, January 17, 1994; Speech by President on Crime Initiative, Boston, January 18, 2000.

105. See Remarks by President at Groundbreaking for King-Kennedy Statue, Indianapolis, May 14, 1994; Speech by President at Jefferson-Jackson Day Luncheon, Indianapolis, May 14, 1994; Speech by President at Beverly Hills Fundraiser, May 20, 1994; Remarks by President at South Central Martin Luther King Birthday Celebration, Los Angeles, January 16, 1995.

106. Remarks by President at Denver Martin Luther King Commemoration, January 16, 1995.

107. Speech by President at University of Texas at Austin, October 16, 1995.

108. Remarks by President at South Central King Birthday Celebration, Los Angeles, January 16, 1995.

109. Remarks by President at Denver Martin Luther King Commemoration, January 16, 1995.

110. Speech by President at Jefferson-Jackson Day Luncheon, Indianapolis, May 14, 1994.

111. Speech by President at Dinner for Kathleen Kennedy Townsend, Hyannis Port, Mass., August 5, 2000; Bill Clinton, Speech at Democratic National Convention, Los Angeles, August 14, 2000.

112. Address Delivered by Mario Cuomo Nominating William J. Clinton for the Presidency, New York City, July 15, 1992.

113. Robin Toner, "Democrats Give Clinton Their Blessing: Cuomo Hails 'New Voice for America,'" *New York Times*, July 16, 1992.

114. Presidential Radio Address, June 5, 1993.

115. Speech by President at RFK Memorial Mass, June 6, 1993.

116. Presidential Radio Address on Renewing Social Values, May 14, 1994.

117. Remarks by President at Groundbreaking for King-Kennedy Statue, Indianapolis, May 14, 1994.

118. Speech by President on Safe Schools and Communities, Worcester, Mass., August 27, 1998.

119. Speech by President at AmeriCorps Event, College Park, Md., February 10, 1999. Clinton was fond of using this quotation when he spoke to AmeriCorps volunteers. See Speech by President to AmeriCorps, Philadelphia, October 11, 2000.

120. Speech by President at DNC Dinner, Cincinnati, July 26, 1999.

121. "Bill Clinton: 1996 Convention Video," August 26, 1996.

122. Speech by President at DLC Conversation, June 4, 1998. Later that day Clinton again argued that his own successes marked a return to the Democratic triumphs of the 1960s. Speech by President at South Dakota Victory Fund Dinner, June 4, 1998. See also Presidential Radio Address on Robert Kennedy, June 6, 1998.

123. President Interviewed by Joe Klein of the *New Yorker*, July 5, 2000.

124. Clinton, *My Life*, 122.

125. Schlesinger interview, August 30, 2004.

126. Bradlee interview, Washington, D.C., December 15, 2004.

127. Widmer interview, December 1, 2004.

128. Shesol interview, July 2, 2004.

129. For the 1980 Democratic Platform, see www.presidency.ucsb.edu/showplatforms. php?platindex=D1980; for the 2004 Democratic Platform, see www.democrats.org/pdfs/ 2004platform.pdf.

130. From interview, December 22, 2004.

131. Walinsky interview, June 10, 2004.

132. State of the Union Address, January 23, 1996.

133. Speech by President at Conference of Mayors Reception, January 25, 1996. Clinton would continue to emphasize his "Third Way" throughout 1996. See Speech by President to the People of Taylor, Mich., March 4, 1996; Speech by President to National Association of Counties, March 5, 1996; Presidential Statement on Sustainable Development Report, March 7, 1996; Speech by President to Democratic Leadership Council, December 11, 1996.

134. Bill Clinton, Acceptance Speech at the Democratic National Convention, Chicago, August 29, 1996.

135. State of the Union Address, January 27, 1998; Speech by President to Conference of Mayors, January 30, 1998; Speech by President at Kennedy-King Dinner, Alexandria, Va., October 22, 1999; interview with John Harris of the *Washington Post* aboard *Air Force One* en route to Washington, D.C., August 8, 2000; interview, *New York Times*, December 28, 2000.

136. Speech by President at New Democrat Network Dinner, July 13, 1998.

137. Clinton, *My Life*, 381–82.

138. From interview, December 22, 2004.

139. Ickes interview, January 20, 2005.

140. Shesol interview, June 29, 2004.

8. Vietnam and "the Sixties" in the Clinton Presidency

Epigraph: Quoted in Guy Trebay, "1968: That Was the Year That Was," *New York Times*, February 1, 2004.

1. William J. Clinton, *My Life* (New York, Alfred A. Knopf), 469.

2. Before Clinton, Franklin D. Roosevelt was the last president never to have worn a military uniform. Born in 1882, FDR was too young to serve in the Spanish American War; during the First World War he was assistant secretary of the navy (1913–1920).

3. Clinton, *My Life*, 469–70.

4. Interview with *Rolling Stone Magazine* II aboard *Air Force One* en route Los Angeles, November 2, 2000. See also interview with Mark Knoller, CBS Radio, Dover, N.H., January 15, 2001, clinton6.nara.gov/. Unless otherwise noted, all of Bill Clinton's speeches and other statements cited in this chapter are available at this site and can be accessed by date.

5. Press Briefing by Mike McCurry, April 14, 1995.

6. Interview with CNN, Ho Chi Minh City, Vietnam, November 19, 2000.

7. Interview with *New York Times*, December 28, 2000.

8. Remarks by President on WFAN Radio, May 12, 1993. He had also stressed this point in remarks the previous day. See Speech by President at Fenton High School, Bensonville, Ill., May 11, 1993.

9. Remarks by President on WFAN Radio, May 12, 1993.

10. Interview with CBS aboard USS *George Washington*, June 5, 1994.

11. Interview with Radio Free Asia, June 24, 1998.

12. Remarks by President on Lifting Vietnam Trade Embargo, February 3, 1994.

13. Clinton, *My Life*, 554.

14. Interview with CBS aboard USS *George Washington*, June 5, 1994.

15. Interview with ABC aboard USS *George Washington*, June 5, 1994.

16. Interview with NBC aboard USS *George Washington*, June 5, 1994.

17. Remarks by President in Photo Op with Congressional Leaders, July 11, 1995.

18. Interview with Tom Brokaw, NBC News, Spangdahlem Air Base, Germany, May 5, 1999.

19. Interview with Associated Press aboard Air Force One en route to Bandar Seri Begawan, Brunei Darussalam, November 16, 2000. See also Interview with CNN, Ho Chi Minh City, Vietnam, November 19, 2000.

20. Presidential Press Conference on Welfare Reform, April 18, 1995.

21. Speech at Fulbright Memorial Service, February 17, 1995.

22. Speech by President at DNC Fundraiser, San Francisco, July 23, 1996.

23. Clinton, *My Life*, 522.

24. Thomas Friedman, "Clinton, Saluting Vietnam Dead, Finds Old Wound Is Slow to Heal," *New York Times*, June 1, 1993.

25. Remarks at a Memorial Day Ceremony at the Vietnam Veterans Memorial, May 31, 1993; Friedman, "Clinton, Saluting Vietnam Dead, Finds Old Wound Is Slow to Heal."

26. Remarks at a Memorial Day Ceremony at the Vietnam Veterans Memorial, May 31, 1993. See also a speech Clinton delivered earlier that day, Remarks by the President at Memorial Day Ceremony at Arlington National Cemetery, May 31, 1993.

27. Friedman, "Clinton, Saluting Vietnam Dead, Finds Old Wound Is Slow to Heal."

28. Ibid.

29. Speech by President at Royal Oak, Mich., August 27, 1996.

30. Remarks by President on Lifting Vietnam Trade Embargo, February 3, 1994. See also Speech by President at VFW Mid-Winter Conference, March 6, 1995.

31. Interview with CNN, Ho Chi Minh City, Vietnam, November 19, 2000. See also Interview with Associated Press, November 16, 2000.

32. Interview with *New York Times*, December 28, 2000.

33. Speech by President at VFW Mid-Winter Conference, March 6, 1995.

34. Speech by President at Agent Orange Announcement, May 28, 1996.

35. Speech by President to People of Providence, R.I., September 28, 1996. He also discussed Agent Orange in his post-election victory speech. See Speech by President at Supporters Reception, November 6, 1996.

36. Speech on Russia, April 1, 1993.

37. Presidential Radio Address, May 29, 1993.

38. Presidential Radio Address on U.S. Armed Forces, May 25, 1996. He repeated this point often. See Speech by President at Arlington National Cemetery, May 30, 1994; Proclamation on Memorial Day, May 22, 1998; Proclamation on Veterans Day, November 9, 1998.

39. Proclamation on Anniversary of the U.S. Army, June 13, 2000. See also Proclamation on Veterans Day, November 10, 2000.

40. Remarks by President on Vietnam Bilateral Trade Agreement, July 13, 2000.

41. Speech by President to Vietnam National University, November 17, 2000. Clinton stressed this healing message throughout his trip. See Speech by President to the Viet-

namese Business Community, November 19, 2000; Interview with CNN, Ho Chi Minh City, Vietnam, November 19, 2000.

42. Clinton, *My Life*, 157.

43. Ibid., 163–65.

44. *American Enterprise* 8, no. 3 (May–June 1997).

45. Ann Devroy and Charles R. Babcock, "Gingrich Speech Gives Lobbyists a Strategy for Midterm Elections," *Washington Post*, October 14, 1994.

46. Associated Press, November 10, 1994.

47. Amy Bernstein and Peter Bernstein, eds., *Quotations from Speaker Newt: The Little Red, White, and Blue Book of the Republican Revolution* (New York: Workman Publishing, 1995), 82–83, 119.

48. Eric Alterman, "Newt vs. the '60s," *Rolling Stone*, December 29, 1994–January 12, 1995, 86.

49. Todd Gitlin, "Straight from the Sixties," *American Prospect* 7, no. 26 (May 1, 1996–June 1, 1996), www.prospect.org/cs/articles?article=straight_from_the_sixties; *New York Times*, November 10, 1994, and January 21, 1995.

50. Clinton, *My Life*, 634–35.

51. "In Praise of the Counterculture," *New York Times*, December 11, 1994.

52. R. Emmett Tyrrell, *Boy Clinton: The Political Biography* (Washington, D.C.: Regnery, 1996), 36, 37, 56, 94, 213, 214, 285. Tyrrell was editor in chief of *American Spectator*, a magazine he founded in 1967 to combat what he saw as creeping campus radicalism.

53. Bob Dole, Acceptance Speech to the Republican National Convention, San Diego, August 15, 1996, www.4president.org/speeches/dolekemp1996convention.htm.

54. Ibid.

55. George Will, introduction to Steven Macedo, ed., *Reassessing the Sixties: Debating the Political and Cultural Legacy* (New York: W. W. Norton, 1997), 3.

56. Clinton, *My Life*, 375–76.

57. David Maraniss, *First in His Class: A Biography of Bill Clinton* (New York: Simon and Schuster, 1995), 464.

58. Clinton, *My Life*, 116–17.

59. Todd Purdum, interview with the author, December 8, 2004. Purdum was the *New York Times* White House correspondent from 1994 to the end of 1996 and covered the 2004 presidential campaign for the paper.

60. Clinton, *My Life*, 131.

61. Ibid., 144–45.

62. Ibid., 200.

63. Mike McCurry, President Clinton's press secretary between 1995 and 1998, interview with the author, April 23, 2004.

64. Speech by President at DNC Fundraiser, San Francisco, July 23, 1996.

65. Speech by President at Georgetown University, July 6, 1995.

66. Carter Wiseman, "In the Days of DKE and S.D.S.," *Yale Alumni Magazine*, February 2001, www.yalealumnimagazine.com/issues/01_02/bush.html.

67. Kusnet interview, June 30, 2004.

68. Speech by President at Yale Alumni Luncheon, October 9, 1993.

69. Speech by President at Michigan State University, May 5, 1995.

70. Remarks by President in Photo Op with Law Enforcement Steering Committee, May 19, 1995.

71. Speech by President at Billings, Mont., Town Hall Meeting, June 1, 1995.

72. Remarks by President at Community Center, Jacksonville, Fla., September 1995.

73. Remarks by President to Students at Eleanor Roosevelt High School, Greenbelt, Md., March 7, 1996.

74. Press Briefing by General McCaffrey on Drug Strategy, April 29, 1996.

75. Speech by President at Pennsylvania State University Commencement, May 10, 1996.

76. Clinton attended 203 fundraisers in a thirteen-month span; see Mike Allen, "Tax Reform: A Balk?" *Time*, December 12, 2005, 23.

77. Shesol interview, June 29, 2004.

78. Speech by President at Georgetown University, July 6, 1995.

79. Speech by President to U.S. Conference of Mayors, June 23, 1997; Remarks by President on Income and Poverty Report, September 29, 1997.

80. Speech by President at Pine Ridge Reservation, S.D., July 7, 1999.

81. Interview with PBS *Nightly Business Report*, August 11, 1999.

82. Speech by President at Fundraiser for Hillary Clinton, October 22, 1999.

83. Speech by President at Broadway for Hillary Clinton Event, New York, October 25, 1999.

84. Speech by President at Reception for Senator David Bonior, October 27, 1999.

85. Speech by President at Reception for Congresswoman Maxine Waters, February 22, 2000.

86. Speech at Democratic Governors Association Annual Dinner, February 28, 2000.

87. Speech by President at DNC Luncheon, February 29, 2000.

88. Speech by President at Democratic Senatorial Campaign Committee Dinner in California, Private Residence, San Francisco, March 3, 2000.

89. Speech by President at Democratic Convention, Los Angeles, August 14, 2000.

90. Shesol interview, June 29, 2004.

91. Ian Christopher McCaleb, "Lieberman to Accept Vice Presidential Nomination," August 16, 2000, www.cnn.com.

92. Ted Kennedy, Speech at Democratic National Convention, Los Angeles, August 15, 2000, www.pbs.org/newshour/election2000/demconvention/kennedy.html.

93. Caroline Kennedy, Speech at Democratic National Convention, Los Angeles, August 15, 2000, www.npr.org/news/national/election2000/demconvention/speech.ckennedy.html.

94. Joseph Lieberman, Acceptance Speech at Democratic National Convention, Los Angeles, August 16, 2000, www.pbs.org/newshour/election2000/demconvention/lieberman.html.

95. Al Gore, Acceptance Speech at the Democratic Convention, Los Angeles, August 17, 2000, www.pbs.org/newshour/election2000/demconvention/gore.html.

9. The "Un-Sixties" Candidate

Epigraph: Myron Magnet, *The Dream and the Nightmare: The Sixties' Legacy to the Underclass* (San Francisco: Encounter Books, 1993), 8–9.

1. Martin Lewis, "John, Paul, George and . . . Al?!" *Time*, November 6, 2000.

2. Broder interview, April 27, 2004.

3. Marvin Olasky, interview with the author, March 15, 2005. A University of Texas professor of journalism and the editor of the biblical weekly news magazine *World*, Olasky is considered the father of George W. Bush's slogan "compassionate conservatism" and was an informal adviser to the Bush campaign in 2000.

4. James Fallows, "When George Meets John," *Atlantic*, July–August 2004, 70.

5. Remarks by Governor George W. Bush, Powell Lecture Series, Texas A&M University, April 6, 1998.

6. Collier interview, May 5, 2004.

7. Thomas Edsall, interview with the author, November 19, 2004. Edsall covered national politics for the *Washington Post* from 1981 to 2006 and wrote several books on American politics. He went on to teach journalism at Columbia University.

8. West interview, February 23, 2004.

9. David Halberstam, "Of War and Presidents," *Vanity Fair*, September 2004, 263.

10. Nicholas Kristof, "A Philosophy with Roots in Conservative Texas Soil," *New York Times*, July 11, 2000.

11. Ibid.

12. Ibid.

13. George W. Bush, with Karen Hughes, *A Charge to Keep* (New York: William Morrow, 1999), 46, 48.

14. Nicholas Lemann, *Sons: George W. Bush and Al Gore*, 3rd ed. (Redmond, Wash.: Slate eBooks, 2000), slate.msn.com/ebooks.

15. Nicholas Kristof, "George W. Bush's Journey: Confronting the Counterculture," *New York Times*, June 19, 2000.

16. Ibid.

17. Ibid.

18. Hanna Rosin, "The Seeds of a Philosophy: Horowitz Cited as Key Influence on Bush," *Washington Post*, July 23, 2000.

19. William Sloane Coffin, "Formative Years at Yale," *New York Times*, August 10, 2000.

20. Ibid.

21. Carter Wiseman, "In the Days of DKE and S.D.S.," *Yale Alumni Magazine*, February 2001, www.yalealumnimagazine.com/issues/01_02/bush.html.

22. Rosin, "The Seeds of a Philosophy: Horowitz Cited as Key Influence on Bush."

23. Kristof, "George W. Bush's Journey: Confronting the Counterculture."

24. Wiseman, "In the Days of DKE and S.D.S."

25. Ibid.

26. Ibid.

27. Ibid.

28. Ibid.

29. Rosin, "The Seeds of a Philosophy: Horowitz Cited as Key Influence on Bush."

30. Stanley Karnow, interview with the author, April 19, 2004.

31. Interview with Tim Russert, *Meet the Press*, NBC, February 8, 2004.

32. Bush, *A Charge to Keep*, 50. A few pages later Bush claims that he "learned the lesson of Vietnam. Our nation should be slow to engage troops. We must not go into a conflict unless we go in committed to win. We can never again ask the military to fight a political war" (55).

33. David Maraniss, *They Marched into Sunlight: War and Peace, Vietnam and America, October 1967* (New York: Simon & Schuster, 2003), 112–13.

34. Ibid., 514–15.

35. Martin Peretz, "Do We Want an Intellectual President?" *New Republic Online*, August 10, 2000, www.tnr.com.

36. Gitlin interview, February 23, 2004.

37. Sidney Blumenthal, interview with the author, July 10, 2004. Blumenthal served as an assistant and senior adviser to President Clinton from 1997 to 2001.

38. Bond interview, November 16, 2004.

39. Shesol interview, July 2, 2004.

40. Peretz, "Do We Want an Intellectual President?"

41. Melinda Henneberger, "Al Gore's Journey: A Character Test at Harvard," *New York Times*, June 21, 2000.

42. Ibid.

43. Ibid.

44. Harris interview, July 12, 2004.

45. Remarks delivered by Vice President Al Gore, Harvard University Commencement, June 9, 1994, clinton2.nara.gov/WH/EOP/OVP/speeches/harvard.html. The quo-

tation is from E. J. Dionne, *Why Americans Hate Politics* (New York: Simon and Schuster, 1992), 11.

46. Rosin, "The Seeds of a Philosophy: Horowitz Cited as Key Influence on Bush."

47. Lemann, *Sons: George W. Bush and Al Gore.*

48. Ibid.

49. Magnet, *The Dream and the Nightmare*, front cover.

50. Rosin, "The Seeds of a Philosophy: Horowitz Cited as Key Influence on Bush."

51. Magnet, *The Dream and the Nightmare*, back cover.

52. Ibid., 1–6 passim.

53. Rosin, "The Seeds of a Philosophy: Horowitz Cited as Key Influence on Bush."

54. Bill Minutaglio, "The Godfathers of 'Compassionate Conservatism,'" *Dallas Morning News*, April 16, 2000.

55. Ibid.

56. Rosin, "The Seeds of a Philosophy: Horowitz Cited as Key Influence on Bush."

57. Minutaglio, "The Godfathers of 'Compassionate Conservatism.'"

58. Schiffren interview, February 4, 2005.

59. Lemann, *Sons: George W. Bush and Al Gore.*

60. Rosin, "The Seeds of a Philosophy: Horowitz Cited as Key Influence on Bush."

61. Frank Bruni, "Bush Tangles with McCain over Campaign Financing," *New York Times*, December 14, 1999.

62. Marvin Olasky, *Compassionate Conservatism: What It Is, What It Does, and How It Can Transform America* (New York: Free Press, 2000), xi–xiii passim.

63. Olasky interview, March 15, 2005.

64. Rosin, "The Seeds of a Philosophy: Horowitz Cited as Key Influence on Bush."

65. Marvin Olasky, *The Tragedy of American Compassion* (Wheaton, Ill.: Crossway Books, 1992), 174, 168, 182–83.

66. Minutaglio, "The Godfathers of 'Compassionate Conservatism.'"

67. Bush, *A Charge to Keep*, 169.

68. Shesol interview, July 2, 2004.

69. Bush, *A Charge to Keep*, 172, 229–32.

70. Nicholas Kristof, "Mr. Bush's Glass House," *New York Times*, September 15, 2004; Mary Jacoby, "The Dunce," September 16, 2004, www.salon.com. Bush aide Dan Bartlett denied that Bush ever made these statements (Kristof, "Mr. Bush's Glass House").

71. Wiseman, "In the Days of DKE and S.D.S."

72. Rosin, "The Seeds of a Philosophy: Horowitz Cited as Key Influence on Bush."

73. Ibid.

74. Kristof, "George W. Bush's Journey."

75. Lemann, *Sons: George W. Bush and Al Gore.*

76. David E. Rosenbaum, "The Latest in Second Term Scandals," *New York Times*, October 31, 2005.

77. Interview on *NewsHour with Jim Lehrer*, PBS, April 27, 2000, www.pbs.org/newshour/election2000/candidates/bush_4-27d.html.

78. Ibid.

79. George W. Bush, Acceptance Speech at the Republican National Convention, Philadelphia, August 3, 2000, www.pbs.org/newshour/election2000/gopconvention/george_w_bush.html.

80. Ibid.

81. Ibid.

82. Al Gore and George W. Bush Presidential Debate, Boston, October 3, 2000, www.debates.org/pages/debtrans.html. Two weeks before the election Bush repeated, "For too long, our culture has sent the message, 'If it feels good, do it. If you've got a problem, blame somebody else.'" Remarks by Governor George W. Bush, Pittsburgh, October 26, 2000.

83. State of the Union Address, January 29, 2002, archives.cnn.com/2002/allpolitics/ 01/29/bush.speech.txt/. He repeated these sentiments two days later, as well as several times during his first term. See Remarks by the President at Georgia Welcome, Atlanta, January 31, 2002, fdsys.gpo.gov/fdsys/pkg/WCPD-2002-02-04/pdf/WCPD-2002-02-04-Pg154.pdf; Remarks by the President at Bush-Cheney 2004 Reception, Washington, D.C., June 17, 2003, fdsys.gpo.gov/fdsys/pkg/WCPD-2003-06-23/html/WCPD-2003-06-23-Pg776.htm; George W. Bush: President's Radio Address, July 17, 2004, fdsys.gpo.gov/ fdsys/pkg/WCPD-2004-07-26/pdf/WCPD-2004-07-26-Pg1324.pdf.

10. Framing John Kerry

Epigraph: Todd Purdum, interview with the author, December 8, 2004.

1. Frank Rich, "You Can't Skip Vietnam Twice," *New York Times*, February 22, 2004.

2. Jake Tripper, "The Medals Don't Matter," *New York Times*, February 16, 2004.

3. Todd Purdum, "In '71 Antiwar Words, a Complex View of Kerry," *New York Times*, February 28, 2004.

4. Robin Toner, "Kerry Presents Himself as a Patriot with a Different View," *New York Times*, June 4, 2004.

5. Douglas Brinkley, *Tour of Duty: John Kerry and the Vietnam War* (New York: William Morrow, 2004), 35.

6. Ibid., 36, 37.

7. Perlstein interview, July 7, 2004.

8. Shalala interview, June 7, 2004.

9. David Brooks, "Iowa Democrats Are Keeping the Faith," *New York Times*, January 21, 2004.

10. CNN television broadcast, January 29, 2004.

11. Guy Trebay, "1968: That Was the Year That Was," *New York Times*, February 1, 2004.

12. Stanley Karnow, "Vietnam's Shadow Lies across Iraq," *Los Angeles Times*, September 26, 2003.

13. Rich, "You Can't Skip Vietnam Twice."

14. Robin Toner, "Still the Question: What Did You Do in the War?" *New York Times*, February 15, 2004.

15. West interview, February 23, 2004.

16. Carla Marinucci, "Doctored Kerry Photo Brings Anger, Threat of Suit," *San Francisco Chronicle*, February 20, 2004.

17. Toner, "Still the Question: What Did You Do in the War?"

18. David Halberstam, "Of War and Presidents," *Vanity Fair*, September 2004, 256.

19. Rich, "You Can't Skip Vietnam Twice."

20. Ibid.

21. Byron York, "John Kerry's Time Warp: For the Democratic Candidate, It's Always 1969," February 27, 2004, www.nationalreview.com. Fortunately for the Kerry campaign, network news decided against running video of the Iowa incident.

22. Don Baker, interview with the author, June 29, 2004. Baker was a *Washington Post* political reporter who covered Virginia and national politics from 1970 to 2000.

23. Shesol interview, July 2, 2004.

24. Keene interview, May 4, 2004.

25. Du Pont interview, May 5, 2004.

26. Bozell interview, June 3, 2004.

27. Purdum, "In '71 Antiwar Words, a Complex View of Kerry."

28. David Halbfinger, "Kerry's Antiwar Past Is a Delicate Issue in His Campaign," *New York Times*, April 24, 2004.

29. Todd Purdum, "F.B.I. Papers Describe Role of Young Kerry against War," *New York Times*, May 6, 2004.

30. Alan Wolfe, political science professor and director of the Boisi Center for Religion and American Public Life at Boston College, interview with the author, July 8, 2004.

31. Nicholas Lemann, "Comment: Democracy Hypocrisy," *New Yorker*, December 8, 2003, www.newyorker.com.

32. Brinkley interview, New York City, March 23, 2004.

33. Purdum, "In '71 Antiwar Words, a Complex View of Kerry."

34. "Vietnam Echoes," *NewsHour with Jim Lehrer*, PBS, April 27, 2004, www.pbs. org/newshour/bb/politics/jan-june04/vietnam_04-27.html.

35. Ibid.

36. Ibid.

37. Isserman interview, May 6, 2004.

38. Gilder interview, June 30, 2004.

39. Maureen Dowd, "Not Feeling Groovy," *New York Times*, July 4, 2004.

40. Todd Purdum, "What They're Really Fighting About," *New York Times*, August 29, 2004. Purdum was quoting Kerry from earlier in the summer.

41. Bill Clinton, Speech at the Democratic National Convention, Boston, July 26, 2004, www.pbs.org/newshour/vote2004/demconvention/speeches/clinton_bill.html.

42. John Kerry, Acceptance Speech at the Democratic National Convention, Boston, July 29, 2004, www.pbs.org/newshour/vote2004/demconvention/speeches/kerry.html.

43. Ibid.

44. Ibid.

45. Staughton Lynd, longtime radical labor activist and professor of history at Yale in the 1960s, interview with the author, August 5, 2004.

46. Schulman interview, August 10, 2004.

47. SBVT Press Release, "Swift Boat Veterans for Truth Disavow Florida Political Flyer," August 21, 2004, horse.he.net/~swiftpow/index.php?topic=Releases.

48. David M. Herszenhorn, "Billionaires Start $60 Million Schools Effort," *New York Times*, April 25, 2007.

49. See www.swiftvets.com/index.php?topic=Ads.

50. Kate Zernike and Jim Rutenberg, "Friendly Fire: The Birth of an Anti-Kerry Ad," *New York Times*, August 20, 2004.

51. *NewsHour with Jim Lehrer*, PBS, August 25, 2004.

52. Ibid.

53. Dukakis interview, Boston, August 25, 2004.

54. Schlesinger interview, New York City, August 26, 2004.

55. Purdum, "What They're Really Fighting About."

56. "Delegates Mock Kerry with 'Purple Heart' Bandages," September 1, 2004, www. cnn.com.

57. Interview on *NewsHour with Jim Lehrer*, PBS, September 2, 2004.

58. David Halberstam, "Of War and Presidents," *Vanity Fair*, September 2004, 252.

59. Dukakis interview, Boston, August 25, 2004.

60. Frank Rich, "Coming Soon: Kerry's 'Apocalypse Now,'" *New York Times*, September 12, 2004.

61. Ibid.

62. Campaign Remarks in Onalaska, Wis., October 26, 2004, www.presidentialrhetoric.com/campaign/speeches/bush_oct26.html. Republicans would repeat throughout Bush's second term this charge that Democrats had become weak on defense since the early 1960s and again invoked Kennedy to argue that the Democrats could not fight the war on terror. Days before Senator Joseph Lieberman was defeated in the August 8, 2006, Connecticut Democratic primary by antiwar candidate Ned Lamont, reporter Jim

Rutenberg ("In Wake of News, a Plan," *New York Times,* August 13, 2006) revealed that "Republican talking points, reviewed by Mr. Rove and Sara Taylor, the White House political director," had already gone "out to state committees across the country, with statements like 'Ned Lamont's victory over a distinguished public servant like Joe Lieberman represents the end of a tradition of proud Democrat leaders in the mold of FDR, Harry Truman, Scoop Jackson and JFK.'"

63. "Caroline Kennedy Tells Bush to Stop Invoking JFK," Agence France-Presse, October 27, 2004.

64. Theodore C. Sorensen, Letter to the Editor, *New York Times,* October 28, 2004.

65. James Dao, "Same-Sex Marriage Issue Key to Some G.O.P. Races," *New York Times,* November 4, 2004.

66. Robert F. Worth, "Most of the Troops in Iraq Have Other Things Than the Election on Their Minds, Like War," *New York Times,* November 4, 2004.

67. Thomas Frank, "Why They Won," *New York Times,* November 5, 2004. See also Thomas Frank, *What's the Matter with Kansas? How Conservatives Won the Heart of America* (New York: Metropolitan, 2004).

68. Maureen Dowd, "Rove's Revenge," *New York Times,* November 7, 2004. In 2005 she wrote that Bush, Cheney, and Gingrich "wanted to wipe out the psychedelic 'if it feels good do it' post-Vietnam sixties and go back to the black-and-white 50s [and] yank us back in a time machine to a place before Vietnam was lost, free love was found, Roe v. Wade was enacted." Maureen Dowd, "Inherit the Windbags," *New York Times,* February 3, 2005. Other columnists also framed Bush's presidency as a challenge to the ethos of the 1960s. To David Brooks, "[Bush] thinks in long durations. 'I got into politics initially because I wanted to help change a culture,' he says, referring to his campaign against the instant gratifications of the 1960's counterculture. And he sees his efforts today as a series of long, gradual cultural transformations." David Brooks, "Ends Without Means," *New York Times,* September 14, 2006.

69. Adam Nagourney, "Kerry Advisors Point Fingers at Iraq and Social Issues," *New York Times,* November 9, 2004.

70. Evan Thomas, "How Bush Did It," *Newsweek,* November 15, 2004.

71. John B. Judis with Ruy Teixeira and Marisa Katz, "30 Years' War: How Bush Went Back to the 1970s," *New Republic,* November 15, 2004, 15.

72. Andrei Cherny, "Renewed Deal: How FDR Spoke about Values," *New Republic,* November 22, 2004, www.andreicherny.com/my_weblog/2007/10/renewed-deal-ho.html.

73. Purdum interview, December 8, 2004.

74. *NewsHour with Jim Lehrer,* PBS, December 31, 2004.

75. Reed interview, January 5, 2005.

76. Wilkins interview, December 21, 2004.

77. Ickes interview, January 20, 2005.

78. Rich interview, January 12, 2005.

79. Woodward interview, Washington, D.C., December 15, 2004.

80. "How insulting to suggest that those who question the mission, question the troops. How pathetic to suggest that those who question a failed policy, doubt America itself. . . . Patriotism is not love of power, or some cheap trick to win votes—patriotism is love of country. Years ago when we protested a war, people would weigh in against us saying, 'My country right or wrong.' Our answer? Absolutely, my country right or wrong. When right, keep it right. And when wrong, make it right. Sometimes loving your country demands you must tell the truth to power." John Kerry, Speech at Democratic National Convention, Denver, August 27, 2008, www.demconvention.com/john-kerry/.

81. Bradley interview, December 14, 2004.

Conclusion

Epigraphs: Former Republican Senator Rick Santorum, Brown University, April 5, 2007; quoted in Iren Chen, "Forget the War on Terror," *Brown Alumni Monthly*, May/June 2007.

1. Parvin interview, April 16, 2004.
2. Shesol interview, June 29, 2004.
3. Smith interview, May 7, 2004.
4. Isserman interview, May 6, 2004.
5. Shirley interview, July 1, 2004.
6. Ickes interview, January 20, 2005.
7. Wilkins interview, December 21, 2004.
8. Thomas interview, October 4, 2004.
9. Cox interview, April 15, 2004.
10. Smith interview, May 7, 2004.
11. Bork interview, February 8, 2005.
12. Bozell interview, June 3, 2004.
13. Shirley interview, July 1, 2004.
14. Schlafly interview, April 7, 2004.
15. Meyer interview, July 16, 2004.
16. Meese interview, Washington, D.C., December 15, 2004.
17. Viguerie interview, June 1, 2004.
18. Weyrich interview, April 23, 2004.
19. Shattuck interview, May 11, 2004.
20. Richard Stevenson, "Bush Marks Anniversary of the Civil Rights Act," *New York Times*, July 2, 2004.
21. Monica Davey, "Two Sets of Parks Memories, from before the Boycott and After," *New York Times*, October 26, 2005.
22. President George W. Bush, Remarks at Ceremonial Groundbreaking of the Martin Luther King Jr. National Memorial, November 13, 2006, http://transcripts.cnn.com/TRANSCRIPTS/0611/13/cnr.01.html.
23. David Brooks, "Hillary and the Ports," *New York Times*, March 12, 2006.
24. Obama, *Audacity of Hope*, 36–37.
25. David Brooks, "Run, Barack, Run," *New York Times*, October 19, 2006.
26. Matt Bai, "The Inside Agitator," *New York Times Sunday Magazine*, October 1, 2006, 92.
27. David D. Kirkpatrick, "'Antiwar' and Other Fighting Words," *New York Times*, October 29, 2006.
28. David E. Sanger and Helen Cooper, "Bush Praises Vietnam's Rise," *New York Times*, November 18, 2006.
29. Scott Shane, "The Complicated Power of the Vote to Nowhere," *New York Times*, April 1, 2007.
30. "Unwanted Folk," *New York Times*, May 3, 2007.
31. Joshua Zeitz, "Reliving the Sixties," May 4, 2007, www.americanheritage.com.
32. John Broder, "Shushing the Baby Boomers," *New York Times*, January 21, 2008.
33. Todd Purdum, "Raising Obama," *Vanity Fair*, March 2008, 318.
34. Bob Herbert, "The Obama Phenomenon," *New York Times*, January 5, 2008.
35. See www.scouttufankjian.com/main.php.
36. Barack Obama, interview with the editorial board of the *Reno Gazette-Journal*, January 14, 2008, www.youtube.com/watch?v=HFLuOBsNMZA; for a transcript see www.nytimes.com/ref/us/politics/21seelye-text.html. See also "Obama and the Gipper," *Wall Street Journal*, January 19, 2008, A12.

37. Al Gore speech endorsing Barack Obama, Detroit, Michigan, June 16, 2008, http://transcripts.cnn.com/TRANSCRIPTS/0806/16/bn.01.html.

38. Maureen Dowd, "Praying and Preying," *New York Times*, April 30, 2008.

39. *San Francisco Examiner*, May 8, 2008.

40. Tom Hayden, "Hillary Clinton, a Winning Speech," June 7, 2008, Huffington Post, www.huffingtonpost.com/tom-hayden/hillary-clinton-a-winning_b_105851.html.

41. Katie Zezima, "Standing In for Kennedy, Obama Embraces Legacy," *New York Times*, May 26, 2008.

42. Ted Kennedy, Speech at Democratic National Convention, Denver, August 25, 2008, www.americanrhetoric.com/speeches/convention2008/tedkennedy2008dnc.htm.

43. Caroline Kennedy, Speech at Democratic National Convention, Denver, August 25, 2008, www.demconvention.com/caroline-kennedy-schlossberg/.

44. Patrick Healy, "Decades Later, John Kennedy's 'New Frontier' Speech Echoes," *New York Times*, August 28, 2008.

45. Barack Obama, Acceptance Speech at Democratic National Convention, Denver, August 28, 2008, www.demconvention.com/barack-obama/.

Index

Brown, Pat, 32
Brown, Willie, 119
Brzezinski, Zbigniew, 85
Buchanan, Bay, 128
Buchanan, Patrick, 46, 123, 127–28
Buckley, James, 23
Buckley, William F., Jr., 23
Bush, George H. W., 8, 15, 36, 93, 204
    and George W. Bush, 196
    on Great Society, 112, 113–18, 119, 121,
        223
    and Gulf War, 8, 223
    on John Kennedy, 97, 109
    in 1988 campaign, 93, 94–98, 223
    in 1992 campaign, 127–30
    patriotism as theme of, 94, 96, 98–101,
        130
    and racial issues, 93–94, 98, 107–12,
        115
    and Vietnam syndrome, 8, 102, 223
    on Vietnam War, 99–101, 215
Bush, George W., 141, 194–95
    battle of, against "the sixties," 9, 179,
        180–81, 184, 189, 192–98
    and "compassionate conservatism,"
        192, 194, 195
    experiences of, in 1960s, 9, 181–87,
        188–89, 208, 218
    and George H. W. Bush, 196
    on Great Society, 194–95
    on John Kennedy, 216–17
    praise by, for some 1960s gains, 7,
        227–28
    and racial issues, 28, 108, 187, 227,
        228
    resentment felt by, 9, 183–84, 195
    in 2000 campaign, 175, 195–98, 205,
        224
    in 2004 campaign, 210, 214, 216–18,
        224
    on Vietnam War, 187–88, 197, 229,
        276n32
Bush, Prescott, 114
Business Week, 143
Butler, George, 216
Buyer, Steve, 206

Califano, Joseph A., Jr., 116–17
campus unrest, 31
Cannon, Lou, 25–26, 72–73, 234
    on Ronald Reagan, 31, 65, 71
Carlucci, Frank, 104–5, 234
Carter, Jimmy, 3, 26, 84, 86, 142, 152

Central America, 52, 74–76, 78–79, 92.
        See also El Salvador; Nicaragua
Cheney, Dick, 106, 181, 187–88, 209–10
Cherny, Andrei, 218
Chomsky, Noam, 17, 19, 125, 234
Civil Rights Act of 1964, 107, 109, 227
civil rights legislation, 33. *See also* Civil
        Rights Act of 1964; Voting Rights Act
        of 1965
civil rights movement, 67–68, 176, 203,
        227–28
    Bill Clinton on, 133, 145–49
    George H. W. Bush and, 106–12
    Ronald Reagan on, 62, 63–65
    see also King, Martin Luther, Jr.
Cleland, Max, 214
Clinton, Bill, 11, 17, 131–37, 169–70,
        204–5
    attacks on, for 1960s role, 129, 131,
        135, 159, 161–69, 177–78
    avoidance of term "liberal" by, 135–36
    as baby boomer, 8, 113, 134–35
    and crime, 147–49, 172–73
    and Democratic Leadership Council,
        134, 150, 153, 154, 155, 224
    effort by, to bridge 1960s divisions, 132,
        150, 156, 159, 162–66, 175
    failed impeachment of, 227
    on "good" and "bad" 1960s, 131–32,
        133, 141, 145, 159, 172–73, 175–76
    and Great Society, 143, 144, 270n71
    and John Kennedy, 129, 132, 133, 136,
        137–41, 144, 151, 230, 231
    and Lyndon Johnson, 142, 145, 156,
        175, 270nn71,75
    in 1960s, 10, 133, 135, 142, 166, 170
    praise by, for 1960s gains, 167–68,
        170–71, 175
    in presidential campaigns:
        1992, 12, 113, 129, 131–33, 150, 159
        1996, 3, 141, 151, 155, 169, 172
        2000, 173, 176–77
        2004, 211
    and racial issues, 136, 145–49, 151, 176
    recasting of liberal 1960s icons by, 8–9,
        131–32, 137–41, 145–54, 156–57,
        223–24
    on role of government, 133–34, 136,
        140–41, 143, 149, 150–51, 154–56,
        223–24
    "Third Way" espoused by, 9, 132, 144,
        150, 155, 156, 272n133
    on Vietnam War, 158–66

BERNARD VON BOTHMER was born and raised in New York City and received a B.A. with honors from Brown University, an M.A. from Stanford University, and a Ph.D. in American history from Indiana University. He teaches American history at the University of San Francisco and at Dominican University of California. He lives in San Francisco with his wife, Jane, and his two daughters, Athena and Tatiana.

LaVergne, TN USA
13 February 2011
216391LV00001B/6/P